The Small Regiment

Volume 1

Origins of the Clan MacKinnon 100 BCE-1621CE

Gerald McKinnon FSA Scot
E. Edwards McKinnon FSA Scot

Edited by
Valeria Greenwood

Clan MacKinnon
2017

First published in 2017 by
Clan MacKinnon Publishing
Canada
ISBN 978-0-9958655-0-1

Photo Credits
© Martin Lawrence, martinlawrncephotography.com   287
© E. Edwards McKinnon   34,44,105,106,127,153,156,159,264,306
© Royal Commission on the Ancient and Historical Monuments of Scotland
                                                    86, 107,134,138,157
© Wyrdlight.com   90
© John Allan   184
© Kim Traynor   175
© David Iliff   187
© Stewart   204
W Edward Wigfull   251
© Julian Douse   275
© Martin McCarthy Tumulus   284
© Jon Haylett   313

type setting, cover and interior design
Gerald A. McKinnon, Prince George

Dedication

To

Madam Anne MacKinnon of MacKinnon
Chief of the Clan MacKinnon

this
history is respectfully dedicated

The arms of William Alexander MacKinnon of MacKinnon as depicted circa 1884

Quarterly; 1st; Vert, a boars head couped with a shank bone in its mouth Argent; 2nd; Azure, a triple towered castle Argent; 3rd; Or, a galley Sable pennants flying Gules; 4th; Argent, a hand couped proper holding a cross crosslett Sable; all within a bordure Or.
Crests; above a gentleman's helmet mantled Gules doubled Argent; dexter; a boars head couped with a shank bone in its mouth proper; sinister; a mans head with a beard affronte couped at the neck wearing an antique crown gutte de sange all proper
Supporters; dexter; a male lion proper; sinister; a leopard proper
Mottos; on an escrol beneath the supporters this motto: AUDENTES FORTUNA JUVAT, Fortune Favours the Brave; on a second escrol beneath the first this motto: CUIMHNICH BAS ALPAN, Remember the death of Alpin

Introduction

The Name MacKinnon

Was
Blessed by Charles Stuart, Prince Regent,
Honoured by Napoleon Buonapart, Emperor of France,
Remembered affectionately by Samuel Johnson,
If you bear it, carry it through life like an ensign, for it is ancient and respected.
Let not its honour be diminished while it is in your keeping
C.R. MacKinnon

As this volume goes to print, there has been no other effort at a full history of the Clan MacKinnon. We do have the two editions of the *Memoirs of Clan Fingon* by the Rev. D. MacKinnon. The first edition in 1884 and the second in 1899. The most notable of the shorter articles that have been published is *The Clan MacKinnon* by Donald MacKinnon, which appears in a 1939 edition of *SMT Magazine and Scottish Country Life*. Both *Memoirs* and *The Clan MacKinnon* were intended only as synopsis and not intended to be comprehensive histories. As a result, most MacKinnons know only what is presented in the "potted histories" which are all too common among the available clan and tartan books and on the internet. Over the years there has been no other serious attempts to tell our story.

The intention of this volume is to provide a solid introduction to MacKinnon history. We briefly discuss where we come from and how we came to have settled in the Hebrides. Then, in considerably more detail, we discuss what we know of the policies that enabled the clan to survive until the early 1600s. While we have some indication of early clan structure, but lack specifics, we know that clans were continually changing and adapting. The early 17th century is the period during which the clan system in the Scottish Highlands was forever changed. By then the clans had by then become the familiar clans of the mid 1700s. This volume ends during 1621, the date generally believed to be a period of pivotal change in our knowledge of clan society. The other planned volumes of this series will take up the telling of our story from here.

During years of painstaking research, we strove to place MacKinnon history firmly within the context of its Hebridean environment. We tell the story of the MacKinnon's place within the society of the Isles and how the people of the Hebrides helped shape the overall history of Scotland as a nation. We endeavour to explain how the Islanders struggled with the Scottish kings as they attempted to incorporate the Hebrides into the growing Kingdom of Scotland. We have made every effort to make this story meaningful to MacKinnons all over the world by maintaining a Hebridean focus.

Because this book tells the whole story of the events that MacKinnons participated in, the reader will be better able to understand why the chiefs may have done what they did. We can better understand their motivations, alliances, and something of the culture they lived in. Because we have told our story from the beginning, the reader does not have to be an expert in Scottish or British history to enjoy and understand this work.

For the most part, this work is well referenced. The sources given in the end notes, however, are not exhaustive and are there to encourage other descendants of MacKinnon to take the investigation of our history further. The appendix is added as the documents originally appeared with little or no translation. It was thought that in this way they convey a little of the manner of the times in which they were prepared. With a little effort, they may be comfortably read and understood.

Modern techniques and the ease of DNA testing is challenging the traditional history of many clans. It was long believed that the MacNeils of Barra were descended from the Irish prince, Nail of the Nine Hostages. But DNA clearly shows the owners of Kismul castle have a Norse heritage.

There are currently too few participants in a MacKinnon DNA project to enable us to adequately map our descent. However, the results so far support the traditional view that a clan was composed of people of various linages--not all of them related to the clan's chiefs.

The structure of a clan may be understood to be that of a triangle, with the chief at the apex. Just below the chief are the *Duine Usail,* his immediate blood relatives. The *Duthaich Dane* or "common folk" of the clan was a group made up of two smaller parts. The *Duthaich Fine* or "true people" were the clan's folk who believed themselves related by blood to the chief. The *Sencliath* were the "people of the soil" meaning those who inhabited the lands before the coming of the chiefs. This structure of a clan appears to be supported by MacKinnon DNA.

While researching this volume, we attempted to substantiate the story of the Iona Chalice. This is the ancient silver chalice which was reported to have belonged to John MacKinnon, the Abbot of Iona. After being lost for several centuries, it was purported to have been owned by a prominent MacKinnon family as late as the 1890s. We have made every effort to determine the fate of the chalice. Was it still in private hands or possibly in a museum collection? Many years and much postage was expended in the unsuccessful search. We must leave this to be taken up by other historians.

It is important for readers to note that it is customary to refer to men and women of stature by their territorial designations. We have attempted to introduce figures by their full names as well as their territorial and traditional titles. Some of the more common ones are:

Argyll	-refers to the chiefs of the Clan Campbell
Mac Cailein Mor	-refers to the chief of the Clan Campbell
MacIain	-refers to the MacDonald of Ardnamurchan
Clan Iain Mor	-refers to the MacDonald of Islay
Keppoch	-refers to the MacDonald of Keppoch
Clanranald	-refers to the MacDonald of Clanranald
Glengarry	-refers to the MacDonald of Glengary
Sleat	-refers to the MacDonald of Sleat
Huntly	- refers to the chief of the clan Gordon
Dunvegan	-refers to the chief of the MacLeods of Skye
Coll	-refers to the MacLean of Coll
Duart	-refers to the MacLean of Duart

Contents

Maps

Illustrations

Family Charts

Appendix

Chapter 1
THE DISTANT ORIGINS

T he Celtic peoples originated somewhere near the head
waters of the Danube River. Over the next several
centuries, they spread from the Baltic, through middle
Europe, to the Atlantic Coast. By 500 BCE (Before Common Era), they
had settled in Cisalpine Gaul and had driven the Illyrians from Hungary.
Two hundred years later, about 300 BCE, the Celtic tribes began to drift
apart as they travelled vast distances, occupied and then settled ever
larger areas of land. The loss of cohesion and the eventual disappearance
of the early Celtic confederation may have been caused by the increasing
distances between the various tribes as they spread out over Western
Europe. One of the scattered Celtic tribes founded Galatia in Spain, while
another sacked Delphi in Greece and others proceeded further eastward.

The Celtic colonisation of the British Isles began about 400 BCE
with the arrival of small bands of settlers from the European mainland.[1]
These early pioneers were the descendants of the Celtic tribes known as
the Belgae.[2] They eventually spread from the south, of what is now
modern England and Wales, into Ireland but did not get as far north as
Scotland. Those who settled in Ireland had their capital at Ermania and
became the heroes of the ancient Red Branch of the Ultonian story cycle.[3]
The Picts, who were first noticed in Scotland by the Romans in 279 CE
(Common Era), are thought to have been descended from a pre-Celtic
aboriginal people.[4]

The distant ancestors of the Clan MacKinnon were among the
last wave of Celtic immigrants to reach Britain. They are thought to have
arrived in the British Isles in about 100 BCE, some three hundred years
after the first migration. These Celts, descended from those who settled
Galatia in Spain, called themselves Goidels, Melesian or Scotti. Settling
mainly in modern England and Ireland, these later pioneers also did not
push as far north as modern Scotland.

2

The
Celtic Migration
500-100 BCE

Modern national borders are shown in white outline to indicate the scale of the migration

Ermania

Tara

400 BCE

Goidel
Scotti
Melesian
100 BCE

Galata

200 BCE

Cisalpine
Gaul

Belgae
500-200 BCE

Celtic Origins
800 BCE

500-200 BCE

Delphi

Chapter 1

LOCATON
OF
DALRIADA

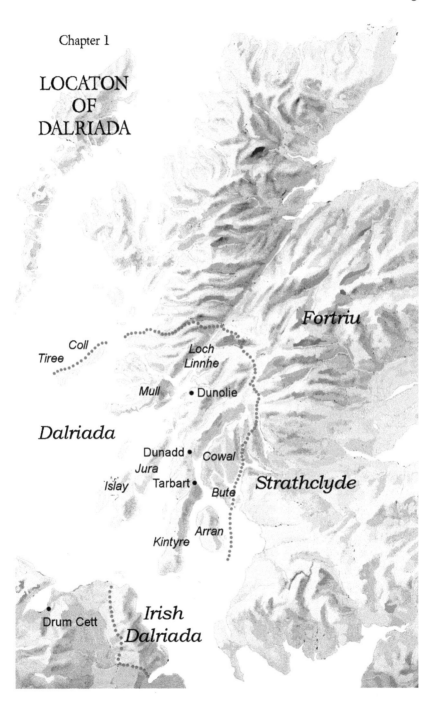

Fortriu

Coll

Tiree

Loch
Linnhe

Mull   • Dunolie

Dalriada

Dunadd •   Cowal

Jura

Islay   Tarbart •   Bute

Strathclyde

Arran

Kintyre

• Drum Cett   Irish
Dalriada

4

Initially, the Scotti would have been a very small minority in the British Isles. Eventually, however, the descendants of the second wave of settlers would become the dominant group in Ireland, pushing the earlier occupants northward into the small area of Ulster.[5]

In the last half of the first century CE, a Scotti chief called Tuathal founded a kingdom in the Irish province of Meath with a stronghold on the sacred hills of Tara.[6] This kingdom, which was also known by the name of Tara, grew to challenge the neighbouring states of Munster and Leinster and then threatened the old Ultonian clans to the north. At the end of the forth or the beginning of the fifth century CE, Tara, under the leadership of Niall of the Nine Hostages, was paramount in Ireland.

During these times, travel across the Irish Sea was not difficult and the Irish Scotti had developed extensive contacts by raiding, commerce and settlement with mainland Britain.[7] The familiarity of the Irish Celts with the affairs on the island of Britain may be illustrated by their easy and peaceful colonisation of the area to the southwest of modern Scotland, which would later be known as Dalriada. Modern archeology indicates there were two separate migrations into this area.[8] The first migration was led by Cairbre Riada of the Liffey.[9] Fleeing from a famine in his native Munster, Cairbre Riada founded Irish *Dal-Riada* (Riada's share) around Dunseverick between the Antrim mountains and the sea in about 330 CE.

The marriage of Cairbre Riada's heir, Eoch Dubhlein (c.337), to the daughter of the Pictish King, Ubdaire of Alba, indicates that Scottish Dalriada was also peacefully settled during this period.[10] Cairbre Riada's followers included folk who would later be known as the *Cinel* (people of) Lorn and Angus.[11]

The Cinel Lorn, from whom the MacKinnons are descended, settled lands which stretched from Loch Lomond in the east to the isles of Coll and Tiree in the west, from across Loch Linnhe in the north, to northern Cowal and Kintyre in the south. The Cinel Angus settled Islay and Jura.

A second migration, led by Fergus Mor MacErc, occurred at least 125 years later and was made up of the Cinel nGabrain who settled the districts of Kintyre, Cowal, Bute and the Isle of Arran. It was the Cinel nGabrain who established the well-known strongholds at Dunadd and Tarbert. There is evidence of a third migration to Dalriada in the late

400s by Fergus Mor, who led yet another group of Scotti settlers from Ireland. Fergus Mor was succeeded by his son who is historically known to have died in 507.

End Notes
Chapter 1

1. Williams, R., *Lords of the Isles*, Hogarth Press, London, 1984.

2. Modern scholars refer to them as P-Celts. The Brythonic *British* languages are Welsh, Cornish and Breton. These languages make use of the sound "p".

3. The Ultonian Clans settled ancient Ulster in the North of Ireland.

4. Encyclopedia Britannica, University of Chicago, Chicago, 1988.

5. The Romanized Britons would later call the inhabitants of Ireland, Scotti, and those of Scotland, Cale-daoine, (spearmen).

6. Tauthal was the grandfather of the warrior king, Conn of the Hundred Battles.

7. By circa 400-500 CE, Roman-British agricultural and craft-working tools, as well as watermill technology, had been imported into Ireland. See: Dark, K. "Changing Places? 5th and 6th Century Culture in Britain and Ireland," *Minerva, Vol.13 #6, Nov/Dec 2002*, 38-9.

8. Laing, L. & J., *The Picts and the Scots*, Sutton, Wrens, Mid-Glamorgan, 1993, 39.

9. Williams, R., *Lords of the Isles*, Hogarth Press, London, 1984, 6.
Laing, L. & J. *The Picts and the Scots,* Sutton, Wrens, Mid-Glamorgan, 1993.

10. The sons of Eoch Dubhlein, The Three Collas, are thought to have lived on Colonsay, which is in the district occupied by the Cinel Lorn. They are said to have returned to Ireland, where they won swordland among the Ulaigh which they called Oriel *(Airgialla)*. The men from Oriel would later return to Scottish Dalriada with Fergus and settle among the Cinel Lorn.

11. Lorn, Angus & Fergus, the legendary founders of Dalriada, are the sons of the Irish king Erc and grandsons of Conn of the Hundred Battles.

Chapter 2
DALRIADA

L *ornd moir* (Lorn Mor), the founder of the Cinel Lorn, had at least six sons: Eochaid, Cathbad, Muredach, Fuindenam, Fergus Salach and Maine.[1] The sons and grandsons of Lorn Mor, in turn, founded the separate kindred groups of which the Cinel Lorn was made up. Eochaid, the eldest son, founded the Cinel nEochaid from whom the Clan MacKinnon is ultimately descended.

The Cinel Lorn occupied the largest land area held by the three kindreds who made up Dalriada. Their holdings were the islands of Tiree, Coll, Iona, Mull, Colonsay, with Ardnamurchan, as well as Morven and modern Lorn on the Scottish mainland. The main stronghold of the Cinel Lorn was at Dunollie.

We don't know as much as we would like regarding the internal organization of the Cinel Lorn nor of the relationships between the various families or tribes of which it was composed. Some of the names of the main groupings and the areas which they inhabited have, however, survived through the ages. The Cinel Fergus Salach occupied Nether Lorn; the Cinel Cathbad held Mid-Lorn and Cinel nEochaid lived in Upper Lorn.[2] Although it is thought that the occupation of these lands by the Cinel Lorn was peaceful and not the result of martial conquest, there may have been some displacement of the original population.[3]

The earliest written record which we have concerning the settlement in Western Scotland dates from about the tenth century.[4] This document is thought, by many of the scholars who have studied it, to be a copy of an earlier seventh century census of the peoples of Dalriada. Importantly, this record gives the numbers of each tribe's contribution to the high king's hosting or gathering of warriors in times of danger. It states that every grouping of 20 houses was expected to furnish two boats and 28 oarsmen. From this roll, the Cinel Lorn numbered some 420

Dalriada
Showing the lands
and tribes of the
Cinel Lorn

houses, the Cinel Angus 430, and the Cinel nGabrain 560.[5] It has been estimated that this muster of 2,000 men would indicate a total population of Dalriada to be some 7,000 to 8,000 persons.[6] The Cinel Lorn, which would eventually rise to greatness, began as the smallest of the three major kindreds of Dalriada.

We know this early society was determined and ordered by kinship.[7] The basic unit was the *durbfine*, a family grouping of four generations which included the common ancestor. Groups of interrelated families, or durbfine, would form a *Tauth*. Each Tauth was headed by a *Righ* or king. Several righ would have been subordinate to the *Ur-Righ* (over king), and several of these larger groups, in turn, would have followed an *Ard Righ* (high king). The positions of both chiefs and kings were hereditary only within their respective durbfines.

It was the durbfine who inherited the position or title and chose the individual on whom it would be placed. The titles, therefore, were not necessarily handed on from father to son, but rather given to the most capable candidate who could have been a brother, nephew or other relation to the office holder. The successor was chosen by the king while he was still alive and, during that time, was called the *Tanaire-Righ* (second to the king). The Gaelic word *Righ,* which is often translated into English as king, does not have the same sovereign implications as its English counterpart. While it is now understood that an English king could rule by divine right or intimidation, a righ, on the other hand, would rule by the consent of his council and of the people being governed.

An event in the year of 561 would forever alter the fortunes of one of the smaller islands in the district of the Cinel Lorn. In that year, Conall, the Ard Righ of Dalriada, invited Saint Columba to visit his kingdom.[8] Columba was a prince of the northern Ui Neill in Ireland and so was related by blood to the royal durbfine of Lorn. His advanced education and majestic mien very much suited Columba to his established role of respected statesman.

By 561, Columba was an extremely well-respected and important political figure throughout the whole of the area surrounding the Irish Sea. In his youth, Columba had been a warrior and he carried the scars of his early battles all of his life. As a poet, he authored verse marked by imagery and grace. His stature in the poetic community was enhanced by his spirited defence of the Irish bardic class when it was threatened with extinction by an offended Irish king. These qualities, and the kindness he displayed to the sick, hungry and distressed, secured the homage of the Gael to Saint Columba for hundreds of years after his death.

After making a landfall in Kintyre, and no doubt visiting his host at Dunadd, Dalriada's capital, Columba made his way to Iona. It was on that small island that Columba established the community of Celtic monks which would soon do so much to keep the fires of civilisation alive in Western Europe. The monastery which Columba founded was not the first Christian holy site on the island. Columba had been preceded by Saint Oran, who had arrived several years before and established various churches in the district of the Cinel Lorn before dying of the plague in 549.

Before Columba's arrival, there were Christian holy sites on the islands of Iona, Mull and Colonsay. Being an astute statesman, Columba may have selected Iona for his monastery because of its well-established importance as a holy site to both the Scots and the Picts.[9] The high regard for Iona's sanctity felt by the Picts is indicated by its use as a burial place for their western kings.

During the time that Columba was involved in establishing his community on Iona in 562, another Irish missionary, Saint Moluag, founded a settlement (562) on the northern end of the island of Lismore. While Saint Columba became widely venerated by the Highland Gael, Saint Moluag seems to have been specially important to the Cinel Lorn.[10] After his death in 592, the *MacDhunshleive* (MacLeay) of Lismore became the hereditary keepers of the *Bachuil Mor* (sacred staff) of Saint Moluag. Tradition claims that this crozier was carried before the armies of Lorn and used at the installation ceremonies of its chiefs and kings.[11]

In 574, *Duncanthe* (Duncan), Ard Righ of Dalriada, was killed while successfully defending his kingdom from an invasion by the Irish King, Boetan of Ulster.[12] Irish Dalriada had been paying Boetan tribute, but it appears he may now have also wanted the over-kingship of Scottish Dalriada as well. The fleet of Scottish Dalriada, which numbered some 150 vessels, would have been a powerful addition to Boetan's force. With Duncan's death, Dalriada had lost its Ard Righ and his sons, Eoghan and Aedan, had an equal claim within the durbfine. To avoid a divisive conflict within the royal kindred, Columba claimed the ancient Druidic prerogative of naming the one destined to be king. Columba's choice of Aedan served to strengthen Dalriada's political position and security with its neighbours.[13] At the ceremony marking Aedan's inauguration as Ard Righ, Columba warned that Dalriada would continue to prosper only if it did not war against Columba's kinsmen, the Irish Ui Neill.

Boetan, upset by his defeat at the hands of Duncan and the subsequent naming of Aedan as Ard Righ, formally submitted his claim to Scottish Dalriada before the Olave Brieve in Ireland.[14] The claim was heard at the convention of Drum Ceatt in the territory of Columba's kin, the Ui Neill, during the year 575. Aed, the Irish Ard Righ in whose presence the claim was heard, was a cousin to Columba. It may have been Boetan's belief that, under these circumstances, the suit was lost so he stayed away from the convention, while both Aedan and Columba attended.

The convention's judgment recognised and affirmed Scottish Dalriada's autonomy. Dalriada's traditional responsibilities were acknowledged by assigning its *"slogad"* and *"fecht"* to the men of Ireland, while the taxes due a superior, known as *"cain"*, *"cobach"* and the use of its fleet, were to remain in *Alba* (Scotland).[15] Thus, Dalriada would continue in its obligation to contribute to the defence of Northern Ireland and to participate in military expeditions if requested by the Ard Righ of the Ui Neil. But the symbolic tax of seven shields, seven horses, seven hounds, seven slaves and the military service due to a superior chief or king was abolished.[16] This ruling, made by the high court of Ireland and witnessed by its High King, effectively made Scottish Dalriada an independent country.

Columba's choice of Aedan for the office of Ard Righ proved to be a fortunate one for Dalriada. Aedan worked hard to secure the independence of the new country. In 580 he defeated the pirates who had been raiding the coast and isles of Dalriada when he destroyed their base on Orkney. A few years later, he drove King Boetan and his men from the Isle of Man, stopped an Angle invasion and joined with the Britons of Strathclyde in a mutual defence against the Southern Picts.

On Aedan's death in 605, there was chaos as civil war divided the country. Eventually, Aedan's grandson, Domnal Brec, emerged as the strongest of the contending leaders and so succeeded to the throne in 637.

Unlike the period of his grandfather's rule, Domnal Brec's reign was to prove disastrous for the kingdom. After a series of indecisive battles against the Picts, Domnal Brec led the Scots in an attack on Ireland. With the support of a distant kinsman named Comgal Claen, Domnal Brec ravaged the lands of Domnal, the then Ard Righ of Ireland and leader of the Ui Neil.[17] In 637 the hurriedly gathered Ui Neill decisively defeated the Scots and their allies at the battle of *Mag Rath* (Moyra).

In his initiation of this military campaign, Domnal Brec had violated a 62 year-old tradition by attacking Dalriada's Irish kin, the Ui Neill. He disregarded the convention of Drum Ceatt and the warning which Columba had given during Aedan's inauguration. The convention of Drum Ceatt had given Dalriada's *"fecht"* and *"slogad"* to the men of Ireland the *Ui Neill.* Columba's warning stated that Dalriada would prosper only as long as it did not war against his kinsmen, the *Ui Neill,* would be fulfilled with tragic consequences. From this time forward, things began to go badly for Dalriada.

There are no records extant which explain why, in 642, Domnal Brec attacked Dalriada's other traditional allies, the Britons of Strathclyde. The outcome of this ill-omened adventure cost Domnal Brec his life and a defeated Dalriada was placed firmly under British rule. The Angles of Northumbria were quick to take advantage of this discord and subjugated all three of their neighbours: the Scots, the Britons and the Picts. Northumbrian rule, however, does not seem to have included military occupation of these nations and was likely limited to the payment of tribute. But a weakened and divided Dalriada was not able to resist the military occupation by the Britons of Strathclyde and so found itself in the position of having two masters.[18]

It was not until 35 years later, in 677, that things were to change. *Ferchar Fada* (Fergus the Tall) of the Cinel Lorn was now the recognised and undisputed war leader of Dalriada.[19] Fergus the Tall, being a descendent of Baotan, the son of Eochaid, the grandson of Lorn, was from the territory of the Cinel nEochaid on the north side of the Loch Linnhe.[20] Fergus the Tall, while leading the Cinel Lorn, was able to negotiate some measure of cooperation with the leaders of the Cinel nGabrain, the Canall Crandamna, led by Domnal Brec's brother and his sons Mailduin and Domnal Doon, in the struggle to win Dalriada's independence.

The union of the two major kindreds of Dalriada was not, however, to prove an harmonious nor a solid one. The two kindreds did not always work together and, indeed, often opposed each other as their dynastic struggles continued. Neither kindred was powerful enough to have one of its leaders acknowledged as Ard Righ of Dalriada, so during this period there was no recognised Ard Righ of the whole country.

There were, however, three major battles fought between the Scots of a militarily united Dalriada and the Britons of Strathclyde in 678. These battles were: Dunlocho, Liacemaelain and Doirad Eilinn, but none of them proved decisive. During 683 Fergus the Tall, of the Cinel Lorn: and Brude, King of the Picts, were able to form an alliance against both the Cinel nGabrain and Brude's Pictish enemies. In that year, the united forces of the Cinel Lorn and the Picts besieged and captured Dunadd, the principal stronghold of Dalriada, and Dunduirn, the main stronghold in the Pictish province of *Fortriu* (Fortrenn).

The success of Fergus the Tall and his allies, the Picts, worried Ecgfrid the King of Northumbria, who resolved to gain the complete military subjugation of both kingdoms. In preparation for the attack on Dalriada, Ecgfrid dispatched his general, Berct, to invade Ireland in 684. The attack on Ireland was designed to eliminate any possibility of Fergus the Tall receiving aid from his Irish cousins. The Northumbrian army devastated the whole of the area along the Irish seaboard from Dublin to Drogheda.

The following year, Ecgfrid, himself, lead the Northumbrians in the main assault on the West. They crossed the Firth of Forth at Stirling and burned Tula Aman, while a large detachment invaded Dalriada and burned Dunollie, the capital of the Cinel Lorn.[21] King Brude and the Pictish army retreated northward before the advancing Northumbrians. Elated with their success, the numerically superior Northumbrians hurried forward, eager to catch their weakened enemies. They followed King Brude closely into the Sidlaw Hills of Angus. At *Dun Nechtain* (Lingaran), the united forces of the Scots and Picts together were able to ambush and destroy their pursuers. This decisive victory over the Northumbrians removed their suzerainty from all three peoples: the Scots, Britons and Picts. The Angles of Northumbria were never again able to force the payment of tribute from their neighbours.[22]

When their father died in 697, the sons of Fergus the Tall, Ainfellach and Selbec, turned on each other in a violent struggle for the throne of Dalriada.[23] Ainfellach, who initially succeeded his father, was captured by his brother Selbec when the latter attacked and burned the stronghold of Dunollie.[24] Selbec then sent his brother to Ireland in chains, where he disappeared. With his brother out of the way, Selbec assumed the dual titles of Ur-Righ of the Cinel Lorn and Ard Righ of Dalriada. His supremacy was, however, challenged by the leaders of several other families or tribes of the Cinel Lorn. It would take Selbec three years to either defeat his rivals or sway them to his side. Finally, in 701, he secured his position in the Cinel Lorn by destroying the leaders the Cinel Cathbode, the strongest and most persistent of the rival tribes-- thus ending the war for the leadership of the Cinel Lorn, but the struggle for Dalriada continued.

The Britons of Strathclyde, attempting to take advantage of the lack of unity between the three tribes of Dalriada, struck and, in 704, defeated the Scots at Glenlemnae. The British force was not strong enough to follow up their victory and Dalriada remained independent. Several years later, Selbec blocked yet another British invasion at Loch Arklet on the east side of Loch Lomond.

Selbec spent the years following this victory unifying the country. In 712 he besieged Dun Averty, the stronghold of the Cinel nGabrain in Kintyre, and rebuilt Dunollie in 714. The Britons of Strathclyde and Scots of Dalriada were to fight once again during what appears to have been a border dispute. For various reasons, now long forgotten, this disagreement became quite heated and a war erupted.

The last battle between the Scots and the Britons took place at the head of Loch Lomond in 717.[25] Dalriada, finally winning a decisive victory, put an end to hostilities and the threat of further war. After holding the office of Ard Righ of Dalriada for 26 years, Selbec left secular life in 723, retiring to a monastery and handing the leadership of the country back to the Cinel nGabrain.

The Synod of Whitby met in 664 to discuss the merits of the competing Columbian and Roman church practice. Though the discussions emphasised a proper method of selecting the date for Easter and the shape of the tonsure worn by monks, the convention was really weighing the relative overall merits of each church. At the end of the Synod, it was decided the Church of Rome would be the official church of both the Picts and the Angles. Saint Columba was no longer recognised as the patron saint east of Drum Alban. He was replaced by Saint Peter who, himself, would be replaced several hundred years later by Saint Andrew.

Some 54 years later, during 718, the Columbian clergy were officially expelled from all of the lands east of the Drum Alban. Thus, in the eighth century, the western Scots and Britons were separated from their old allies, the Picts, by religious concepts as well as geography.[26] Iona was to remain a major centre of learning and many of the ancient records (annals) describing the events in Scotland and Ireland, which have survived to the present time, were written there.[27]

In the early eighth century, the political relationships between the nations of the North began to change. The Picts aligned themselves more with the Angles of Northumbria, while the Scots and Britons once again grew closer to each other. The new differences between the Picts and the Scots flared into open warfare when Alpin, the brother of Dalriada's Ard Righ, Eochach, disposed Drust, the King of the Picts.[28] This act started a civil war among the Picts in which there were four equally strong claimants for the Pictish crown. The ultimate winner of the throne was a brutal tyrant named Angus mac Fergus whose victory was to have a profound effect on the history of Dalriada.

The Cinel nGabrain, however, was not destined to hold the office of Ard Righ of Dalriada for very long. On the death of Eochach, the Ard Righ, in 733, the Cinel Lorn again asserted its powerful influence.[29] Dugal, the son of Selbec, took the title of Ard Righ, while Murdoch the Good, the son of Ainbceallach, became Ur-Righ of the Cinel Lorn.[30] Almost immediately following Dugal's inauguration, word arrived that Dalriada's fleet was required to aid Flaithbert, the Ard Righ of Ireland. While on his way across the Irish sea to provide the assistance requested, Dugal, the Ard Righ of Dalriada, was involved in an incident which was to upset the fragile alliance between the Scots and the Picts and precipitate a new round of wars.

There are two versions of what transpired. In the first, Dugal, who made a stop at Tory Island while on his way to Ireland, found Brude, the son of Angus mac Fergus, King of the Picts, in the church of Troagh.[31] Dugal is said to have violated the sanctuary of the church by forcibly dragging the unfortunate Brude outside of the building and making him a prisoner. In the second version of the story, Dugal is said to have carried off Forai, the daughter of Brude and niece of Angus mac Fergus. There is no way for us to know which event, if either, actually occurred. Either event, however, would prove a bad omen for the start to an already ill-fated expedition. Flaithbert and his allies from Dalriada were soundly defeated by his foe, Aeda Eoghan, on the River Bann.

Angus mac Fergus, taking advantage of the Scot's loss and subsequent weakness, invaded Dalriada in revenge for the foul treatment received by his kinsmen. In 734, he destroyed the fort of Dun Leithfinn and dispersed the leadership of the Cinel Lorn. Dugal, the Ard Righ, was wounded in battle by Angus, but was able to escape to Ireland. The other leaders of the Cinel Lorn did not survive unscathed from this invasion: Tilarg, the son of Congus, was betrayed by his brother and drowned. The son of Droston was captured in the vicinity of Dunollie. Only the Ur-Righ, Murdoch the Good, was able to escape the wrath of Angus mac Fergus.

Two years later, Angus mac Fergus returned and completed the conquest of Dalriada. This time he captured Dunadd, burned Creic and caught two of Selbec's sons: Dugal, who had returned from Ireland, and Feradach. Angus mac Fergus was now firmly in control of most of Dalriada.

Desperate to regain their lost territories, the Cinel nGabrain under the Ur-Righ, Alpin, whose rash actions began the chain of events that put Angus mac Fergus on the Pictish throne, attacked the Picts in Cowal.[32] About this same time, the Cinel Lorn, under the command of Murdoch the Good, burst from northern Dalriada attacking the Picts who lived on the plain of Mamann.[33] The warriors of the Cinel Lorn were intercepted, however, by a large body of men led by Talorgan mac Fergus, the Pictish King's brother, at Cnuce in Calatros.[34] The ensuing battle saw the Cinel Lorn soundly defeated by the Picts and the Ur-Righ, Murdoch the Good, and most of his leading men were slain. Due to the sudden loss of so many of its leaders, the Cinel Lorn was forced to relinquish the leadership of Dalriada to the Cinel nGabrain. However, while Angus mac Fergus lived, Dalriada remained a Pictish province and was not united under its own Ard Righ. Dalriada would not regain its strength and independence until Angus mac Fergus died a natural death many years later.

It was not until 38 years had passed, in 772, that Selbec II, son of Eoghan of Lorn, was named Ard Righ of Dalriada. The civil wars between the kindreds of Dalriada and the wars with the Picts were at long last over. Dalriada enjoyed 22 years of peace, security and independence. This tranquil period would end with the appearance of a new and more awesome threat than had ever appeared before. In the year 794, the annals first mention the appearance of Vikings in the Hebrides. Isolated raids had probably occurred in the islands during the previous couple of years, but, as the annalists were mainly concerned with church affairs, it is possible that the earlier raids may not have been thought worthy of mention. During the large raid of 794, however, the whole of the Western Isles were quickly and utterly laid waste and Columbian monastery on Iona, which unfortunately lies on the sea route to Ireland, was plundered for the first time by the Norsemen.

The threat from the north was aggravated by the outbreak of a new civil war which erupted on the death of Selbec II. The Cinel nGabrain took the throne of Dalriada and Eocha'annuine was given the title of Ard Righ. The annalists report that the new Ard Righ took no measures to end the violence. Instead, he appears to have waited for his rivals to spend their energy and resources in fighting each other. The relationships between the three tribes of Dalriada must have been bitter indeed if they could not unite in the face of their deadliest common enemy. Incredibly, Eocha'annuine was able to hold on to his title and survive the initial Viking onslaught. Once his position as Ard Righ was secured, he was able to mend the relations between the Scots and the Picts. He even cemented the peace by marrying a Pictish Princess named Urguis, the daughter of the King of Fortriu.

End Notes
Chapter 2

1. Bannerman, "Senchus Fer N-Alban", *Celteca, Vol. 4, Dublin Institute for Advanced Studies, 1966.*

2. Skene, W. F., *Celtic Scotland*, Edinburgh, David Douglas, 1886, Vol. 1, 230.

3. Dun Cul Bhuirg, on the west coast of Iona, as well as the village site at Laraichean, may have been occupied by an earlier people up until the arrival of the Cinel Lorn. (RCAHMS).

4. *The Senchus fer nAlban* (Tradition of the men of Alba). This is a record which is concerned with the lineages of the three *cinel* (people) of Dalriada and records the holdings of each group in Argyll.

5. Williams, R., *Lords of the Isles*, Hogarth Press, London, 1984, 12.

6. The expeditionary force of the Cinel Lorn totaled some 700 men. Of these, 100 were from Argyll.

7. Launay, O., *The Civilization of the Celts*, Ferne, Geneva, 1978.

8. Williams, R., *Lords of the Isles*, Hogarth Press, London, 1984, 39, Saint Columba, or as he is called in Gaelic, Columcille (Colum of the church).

9. The border between Alba and Dalriada seemingly ran through Colonsay, Iona and Mull. There is a cairn on Iona known as Cul Ri Arin (back to Ireland) and on Mull there is a corresponding cairn known as Cul Ri Alba. Cul Ri Alba is on the slopes of Ben Mor.

10. The churches dependent on Saint Moluag's community of Lismore were: Cill Moluag in Raasay, Cill Moluag on Skye, Cill Moluag on Tiree, Cill Moluag on Mull, Teampul Mor on Lewis, Teampul Mholuig in Ness, Kilmalu in Morven, Kilmalu of Invarery and Cill Moluag of Inverfarigaig.

11. MacDugall, W., *Journeying in MacDougall Country*, Milo Printing, Maine, 1984, 133.

12. Both Duncan and his successor Aedan belonged to the royal durbfine of the Cinel nGabhrain.

13. Aedan's mother was the daughter of a Christian king of Strathclyde and, through her, he was a nephew of the Christian, King Urien of Cumbria and

Manau in Gododdin. Aedan's wife may have been a granddaughter of King Brude MacMaelcheon of Alba.

14. The chief judge in the highest court in Ireland.

15. Cain   -a yearly tax of 7 shields, 7 horses, 7 hounds and 7 slave
    Fech   - participation in military expeditions
    Slogad -hosting, a full scale war muster.
    Cobach - military service

16. Williams, R., *Lords of the Isles*, Hogarth Press, London,1984, 43.

17. Comgal Claen was King of the Ulaigh, who were the Cruithnigh of Irish Dalriada. There appears to have been a long relationship between the Ulaigh and the Cinel Lorn--not all of it was peaceful. Domnal, the Irish Ard Righ, was the son of Aed who heard the convention of Drum Ceatt.

18. MacKenzie, W. C., *The Highlands and Islands of Scotland*, Moray Press, Edinburgh, 1949, 56.

19. The nine clans listed in the MS of 1467, as descended from Fearchar Fada, are: Clan Duff (the Kings of Moray), Mac Nachtan, MacIntoshe, Clan Cameron, MacGregor, MacKinnon, MacQuarrie, MacMillan and the MacLennans. Of these, the genealogies of the MacKinnon, MacQuarrie, MacMillan and the MacLennans show a descent from Cormac, Bishop of Dunkeld and father of Fhionghuin. The traditional genealogy of the Cinel Lorn is given in the *"Genelaig Albanensium"* (Genealogy of the Kings of Scotland). The descent of Fearchar Fada of the Cinel nEchdach is traced backwards through eleven generations (over a period of about 330 years) to an ancestor of Lorn Mor, Echach Munremair in Ireland. *"Anbcellach, mc fherchair fhotal, mc fhergusa, mc cholman, mc bottain, mc muredaig, mc loairnd mair, mc eirc, mc echach munremair"*.

20. Skene, *Celtic Scotland*, David Douglas, Edinburgh, 1886, Vol 1, 264-267.

21. Tula Aman is River Almont Hillock, we no longer know where this is.

22. This was likely the single most important battle in the whole history of Britain. If the Angles had won the day, it is probable that Scotland, as we know it, would never have existed. See: MacKenzie W.C., *The Highlands and Islands of Scotland,* Moray Press, Edinburgh, 1949, 57.

23. Williams W.C., *Lords of the Isles*, Hogarth Press, London, 1984, 56.

24. Skene, *Celtic Scotland*, Edinburgh, David Douglas, 1886, Vol 1, 272-4.

25. This occurred at the north end of Loch Lomand at a stone called Miniree (Clach na Breatan).

26. MacKenzie, W. C., *The Highlands and Islands of Scotland*, Moray Press, Edinburgh, 1949, 59.

27. Laing, L. & J., *The Picts and the Scots*, Sutton, Wrens, Mid-Glamorgan, 1993, 49.

28. A member of the Cinel nGabhrain Alpin may have had a Pictish mother, but is not the Name Father of the clan Alpin.

29. Skene, *Celtic Scotland*, David Douglas, Edinburgh, 1886, Vol 1, 290-1.

30. Called Muredhaugh Maith (Murdoch the Good) by the ancient bards. Brown, *History of the Highlands*, Fullarton, Edinburgh,1885, Vol. 1, 72, & MacKenzie W. C., *The Highlands and Islands of Scotland*, Moray Press, Edinburgh, 63

31. A church founded by Saint Columba.

32. This is the Alpin who started the Pictish civil war by leading a coup against King Drust.

33. Between the Carron and the Avon Rivers.

34. Now called Calatria.

Chapter 3
VIKINGS

T he Vikings were always ready and able to quickly exploit any weakness they found in their opponents. In 798, just two years after Eocha'annuine assumed the throne, the Vikings once more plundered the Western Isles.

They found Iona a particularly rich target. At this time, it was the head of all of the Columban Churches of both Scotland and Ireland and contained a great deal of treasure. Iona was attacked and burned in 802, and yet again, four years later, in 806. During the later raid, 68 members of the community were slain by the brutal raiders. With the raids now becoming more frequent, it was decided that the increasing danger to the monks on Iona justified removing them from their vulnerable situation and the bulk of the community was moved to Ireland for safety.

A new monastery, named Kells, was built at Cennanus in the Irish province of Meath. Kells was completed in 814 and became the focus for the Columban Church in Ireland. The *Book of Kells*, as well as the *Book of Durrow*, which are two of the most important surviving books produced by the early Gael, may actually have been created on Iona in the eighth century and carried across to Ireland during the move to safety.[1] No other books from Iona's well-stocked library are known to have survived. The monastery of Dunkeld took Iona's place in Scotland when it was recognised as the centre of the Columban Church to the east of the Irish Sea.[2]

The Norse had evidently heard of the relics of Saint Columba, which were supposedly still on Iona and, in 823, came for them.[3] By this time, all of the monastery's other treasures had been taken to Kells when the bulk of the monastic community had moved, so there was little left at Iona to be taken by the raiders. During this particular raid, the Vikings captured and interrogated the Abbot, Saint Blamhoc, whom they murdered because he would not tell them where the sacred relics were hidden.[4]

We can assume that the Vikings did not know the real nature of the relics of Saint Columba. Had they found them, they may have been sorely disappointed to find that the famed treasure was just a collection of old bones. Once the Viking fleet left the island, the relics were recovered by the surviving monks and kept safe for many hundreds of years afterwards.[5]

The Cinel Lorn once again succeeded to the throne of Dalriada when Dugal became Ard Righ in 826.[6] The annals claim Dugal had a short but peaceful reign. This may only mean, however, that there was no civil war on his assumption of power.

The Viking raids were increasing in strength and numbers and, indeed, may have been the reason why Dugal's reign was so short. Dugal was to be the last of the Cinel Lorn to hold the title of Ard Righ of Dalriada. On his death in 833, the title passed to Alpin, the son of Eocha'annuine and the Pictish Princess Urgusa. Alpin was a member of the Cinel nGabrain and was the last of the Scoto-Irish kings of Dalriada. He was also an aggressive leader who did not live very long. During his short reign, he led his men in battles against both the Picts and the Britons of Strathclyde. Exactly how Alpin died is not really known, as there are two quite different stories which have him killed at differing times and places.[7] In one version, he is killed and decapitated while fighting King Brude of the Picts for the Pictish throne in 834. The other tells of his leading an invasion into the British territories of Strathclyde. In this version, he is killed near Laicht Castle, which is on the ridge that divides Galloway from Kyle.

Although Alpin was not of the Cinel Lorn, and indeed only reigned for one or two years, he was commemorated in the ancient motto of the Clan MacKinnon *"Cuimhnich bas Alpin"* (Remember the Death of Alpin) and the old MacKinnon crest which was a couped crowned head. A Clan Alpin confederation would be formed in the early 1500s, soon after the fall of the Lordship of the Isles, in which the member clans would each claim descent from him.

In the years following the 830s, the Viking raids would have been increasingly launched from bases established in the Hebrides. After Dublin was captured by the Viking Chief Turgeis in 836, raids were also launched from Ireland.[8] That same year, Kenneth mac Alpin, the son of Alpin, the Ard Righ of Dalriada, called on Gofraidh mac Fearghus, the *Toisseach Oirgiall* (Chief of Oriel), to settle with a number of his men and their families in Dalriada to strengthen it against the Norsemen. Gofraidh must have led a successful

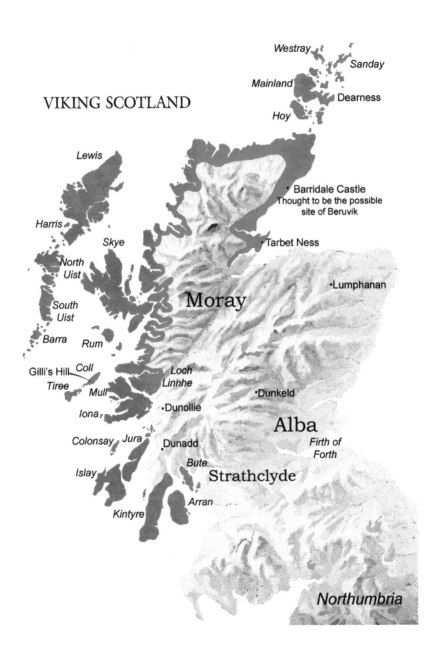

campaign against the raiders because, on his death in 853, he was recorded as having been *Toisseach Innis Gall* (Chief of the Islands of the Gael-the Hebrides).

Until 837, the Viking raids were carried out by a relatively small numbers of ships, but thereafter there were raids by fleets of some 60 or even more ships. The severity of the raids and increasing numbers of raiders forced the abandonment, in 843, of the two main strongholds of the Dalriada; Dunadd, which was the capital of the Cinel nGabhrain, and Dunolie, the capital of the Cinel Lorn.[9]

The abandonment of these ancient strongholds may indicate that a large-scale exodus eastward across the Drum Alban, by the population of Dalriada, was underway. The *Orkneying Saga* states *"the Hebrideans were so scared of them [the Vikings], they hid whatever they could carry either in among the rocks or underground."*

The Cinel nEochaid, a branch of the Cinel Lorn who lived on the north side of the Loch Linnhe, may have migrated northeastward into Moray, where they founded the royal line from which Macbeth was descended.[10] The Cinel nGabrain migrated into the area north of the Firth of Forth and united with the Picts under Kenneth mac Alpin. However, not all of the Scots of Dalriada fled the Norse. Remnants of the population appear to have remained in their native districts, but life for them would become increasingly difficult.

The tempo of the raids and the numbers of Viking ships in the Irish sea steadily increased until the year 850, when the Norse King of Dublin was challenged by a large fleet of Danes.[11] The Norse prevailed, but the severe losses they suffered led to a diminished number of raids for 64 years.[12]

By the late 800s and early 900s, the Hebrides were not just occupied, but were actually settled by the Norse.[13] The Western Isles had became an integral part of the Norse-dominated North Atlantic community--a maritime world heavily dependent upon ships for communication and trade.

In the region once held by the Cinel Lorn, the Norse settled on the islands of Coll, Tiree, Colonsay and possibly areas of Mull.[14] On Mull, the Norse stayed close to the coastlines and do not seem to have ventured far inland.[15] The Gaelic culture of the Hebrides was very similar to that of the Norse--a patriarchal society headed by petty kings and chiefs, the bottom rung of which was held by slaves.

The Norse did not attempt to eliminate the Scottish culture nor its social structures, but rather sought to dominate them. They simply took over the Scottish pattern of land ownership and administration, putting themselves into the key positions of the kings and chiefs. In almost all of their settlements, the Norse built their rectangular longhouses directly above the sites of the earlier Scottish buildings.[16] These longhouses would, in time, evolve into the familiar black houses in which the Islanders lived for so long. Generally, the two cultures blended by intermarriage as Norse farmers took local wives. However, there were instances where the local population was forcibly subdued and, in consequence, reduced to a very inferior status.[17]

Along with settlement, came inclusion in the Norse trading network. The trade route through the Hebrides led from Dublin to Norway and then along the coasts of France and Spain to the Mediterranean. The Norse imported several products which were made in the Hebrides; among them was wool, leather jewellery and a coarse, tufted cloth, which was made to resemble fur.[18] Ominously, because of its proximity to the Hebrides, Dublin was the major centre of the Norse slave trade.[19] Slaves were regularly bought, sold and sent to anywhere in the Viking world where they were needed.

The demands of trade required broad, deep-draught vessels to transport bulky freight and livestock. These cargo ships required proper quays as they could not easily be loaded or unloaded on a beach. Dun Ara, which is located in the district of Mishnish at the north end of Mull, may have been one of the stopping places for Norse traders. Dun Ara, itself, was built on the summit of a prominent rock outcropping and is thought to have been a hall house fortified by a surrounding curtain wall.[20] There was a small settlement at the base of the outcropping and an artificial harbour. This harbour, which incorporates a small jetty, a quay, a boat landing and two small boat houses, all within close proximity of each other, may be unique in the Hebrides.

The native cohesion in the islands dissolved with increased, but transitory, Norse settlement. Although the Hebrides were technically under the rule of the King of Norway, his direct influence was slight. Viking warlords set themselves up as petty kings and lords over either individual or groups of islands, depending on the inclination and abilities of the individual warrior.

The Norseman, Ketil Flatnef, attempted to bring some order to the chaos when, in 890, he declared himself King of the Isles. The kingdom did not outlast Ketil's lifetime and, when Ketil died in the Hebrides, his family emigrated to Iceland.

In 954 the island of Mull is known to have been a kingdom itself, which was called "Rioghachd na Drealluin".[21] The name is Gaelic, which may indicate that remnants of the Cinel Lorn still held sway on the island during this time. However, some measure of order eventually developed in the Isles when they were incorporated into the Earldom of Orkney.[22] In the tenth century, this powerful earldom encompassed all of Viking Scotland and maintained a firm grip on the whole of the Hebrides.

The Earls of Orkney appointed their own administrators and representatives to the islands. One of the more famous of these was the Earl Gilli, who resided on the island of Coll between 980 and 1014, and was the *scat* (tax) collector for the Earl Sigurd. Earl Gilli's residence, known as Du clach, was built on the hill of *Cnoc Ghillibreidhe* (Gilli's hill) on Coll, where its ruins are still visible today.[23]

For a long period, the old Norse rituals, various pagan Celtic beliefs and a primitive Christianity were equally accepted throughout the islands and all were practised simultaneously. Perhaps it was a result of intermarriage which enabled the Norse to adopt Christianity so easily during the 900s. As the acceptance of Christianity grew, so did the Norse and Danes' respect for Christian Saints and holy places. The Norse would eventually even come to share the Scottish and Irish veneration for Saint Columba and Iona.[24]

Following the move of the Columban monastery to Kells, a small Christian community had remained on Iona to maintain the sacred sites. Records of the doings of this small group of dedicated monks are fragmentary, so there is little known of their lives. The records we have, however, indicate there was a Bishop Finghin of Iona who died in 966.[25] Finghin may have held the office of Abbot from 959 when his predecessor Duibduin died, but we cannot be sure of this.

Some Norsemen are also recorded as seeking out the church for various reasons other than plunder. In 970 Auly, son of the Dane Setric, took refuge on Iona after the battle of Temora. Following an active career as warrior, pirate and petty king, Olaf Krovan withdrew to Iona, where he became a monk in 980.[26]

On Iona, there are several gravestones and cross slabs dating from the 10th century which display Scandinavian patronage. One cross slab has a runic inscription along one side which was translated as "Kali son of Aulus laid this stone over brother Fugl."

The instability and violence of the Norse rule continued through the 11th and 12th centuries and the surviving records are often confused and incomplete. The Irish annalist Tigernac reports that Cellach mac Finganne (MacKinnon) was one of the Comites *(Maormors)* of Alba during 976.[27] But there is seemingly no other existent mention of him.

The Danes swept through the Hebrides in 986 and again in 987, murdering Gaels and Norse alike, leaving only slaughter and destruction in the wakes of their longships. In the north, Finlay mac Ruaire mhic Domnal, the *Righ Mureb* (King of Moray), and head of the Cinel Lorn, was locked in a struggle for control of Caithness and Sutherland with Sigurd the Stout, Norse Jarl of Orkney.[28] This must have been a long, contentious war, as neither side was able to remove the other. Loyalties were tested, and sometimes failed, in these contests for land and power. Finlay may have had the support of his two brothers, Donald and Maol-Brigte. The sons of Maol-Brigte; Maol-Coluim and Gilli-Comgain, however, still held lands in Lorn and fought with Sigurd against their uncle in Moray.[29]

Maol-Coluim may have been with Sigurd at Dublin in 1014 when the Norse assembled the largest Viking army ever gathered. The reason for this awesome gathering was a much-anticipated conquest of Ireland. The Earl of Orkney, the King of Man and all the other notable Viking chiefs were there with their hosts of longships and well-armed warriors. Sigurd, the Earl of Orkney, even led a large Gaelic Hebridean contingent from Harris, Skye and many of the smaller islands. The Battle of Clontarf pit Norse and Hebridean warriors against the Celtic Irish army of the Ard Righ, Brian Boru. Although Brian Boru was killed, the Irish victory broke the power of the Norse kings of Man in Ireland and severely weakened that of the Earls of Orkney in the Hebrides. That Maol-Coluim was one of the few who fought for the Norse and survived the battle, is indicated by a record that he and his brother, Gilli-Comgain, assassinated their Uncle Finlay in 1020. Maol-Coluim held the titles of King of Moray and head of the Cinel Lorn for the nine years preceding his death in 1029.

Macbeth MacFinlay succeeded his cousin, Maol-Coluim, to the leadership of the Cinel Lorn.[30] Macbeth continued to maintain

28

the traditionally strong relationships between Ireland and Lorn, while the latter remained the central part of his power base. When the Jarl Thorfinn of Orkney refused to recognise Macbeth's claim to the lands of Caithness and Sutherland, war erupted between the two.[31] Gilli-Comgain, Macbeth's cousin and the brother of the late Maol-Coluim, contested the kingship of Moray and sided with the Viking Chief Thorfinn in the struggle against his cousin.

MacBeth appointed his nephew Moddan to the position of *Moramer* (chief or governor) of Caithness and ordered him to collect the tribute from Thorfinn.[32] Thorfinn, of course, refused to pay. In the ensuing battle, Moddan was defeated and sent back to MacBeth's capital at Beruvik empty-handed.

In an attempt to enforce his claim over the Northern territories, MacBeth and Moddan organised what was to become a prolonged campaign against Thorfinn. This time, MacBeth led an expedition by sea to Caithness, while Moddan led his troops overland. Unfortunately for the Cinel Lorn, they both suffered defeat--MacBeth in a naval fight with Thorfinn just east of Dearness, and Moddan in Caithness where he was beaten by Thorkell Fosterer. The defeat of this two-pronged attack must have been a major setback for MacBeth. In order to continue the campaign, he had to call on reinforcements from southern Scotland, Kintyre and Ireland.[33]

The newly-raised force was also defeated in a naval fight at Tarbet Ness off the coast of Cromarty in Easter Ross. The only recorded success in MacBeth's campaign was the defeat of his cousin, Gille-Comgain, and 50 of his men in 1032. However, in spite of his several defeats by Thorfinn, MacBeth survived and was now the undisputed leader of the Cinel Lorn and *Righ Mureb* (King of Moray). With the death of Gille-Comgain, MacBeth was free to marry his widow, Gruoch nic Boedhe. Gruoch was a princess of the Cinel nGabhrain and, as a large land owner in Fife, she was wealthy and influential in her own right.

The old King of Scotland, Malcolm II, *Ard Righ Alba* (High King of Scotland), died in 1034, leaving the crown and country to his grandson, Duncan mac Crinan.[34] We do not know how MacBeth regarded Duncan's claim to the title of Ard Righ Alba, but he may have been forced to cooperate with him to ward off the threats from Thorfinn in the north and the English King, Canute, in the south. Duncan, however, proved to be a poor leader. He was defeated by the English at Durham and, thereafter, failed to stop Eadulf of Northumbria's successful raid into Strathclyde. There is no record of why Duncan declared war on MacBeth and invaded Moray, but his defeat there, in 1041, boosted MacBeth to preeminence in Scotland.[35]

MacBeth is not recorded as ever having assumed the title of Ard Righ Alba. This may have been because he did not exercise full authority in the south of the country. Duncan's brother Maldred became *Righ Fortiu* (King of Fortren) on Duncan's death and actively opposed MacBeth for many years. Indeed, in 1045 there was a revolt by the Cinel nGabhrain against MacBeth's rule. This revolt was successfully dealt with: Maldred's rule was limited to Strathclyde and Lothian, however, Duncan's family was scattered or killed.[36] With the dispersal of his rival's family, MacBeth felt his grasp on power secure enough to make his famous pilgrimage to Rome.

The beginning of the end of MacBeth's reign occurred in 1054 when MacBeth was defeated by Siward of Northumbria at the battle of the Seven Sleepers. Siward forced MacBeth to restore Malcolm mac Duncan to his family's position as Righ Fortiu.

Three years later, Malcolm led the Cinel nGabrain in a second attempt to oust MacBeth. This time, the rebellion succeeded. MacBeth was killed at Lumphanan in eastern Mar in 1057, while his *Tanaire-Righ* (next to the king), Lulach mac Gille-Comgain died a year later defending the eastern borders of Lorn. With the Cinel nGabnrain under Malcolm mac Duncan's authority occupying their country, the defeated remnants of the Royal House of the Cinel Lorn evacuated the more vulnerable areas of the Moray Firth for the relatively secure districts of Lorn.

The unstable political conditions in the Hebrides continued throughout the latter part of the 12th century. The Norse Kings of Man were losing their influence. The Norwegian King Magnus claimed to rule over the Hebrides, Orkney and Caithness in the north of Scotland, but could in no way control them from Norway. The right of Norway to the Western Isles was, however, confirmed by an agreement reached between King Edgar of Scotland and Magnus of Norway.[37]

Magnus was given right to the islands, while Edgar received the West Coast of the Scottish mainland. This parcelling up of the west, gave both kings land which they could not control from their capitals. Magnus could not effectively rule the Hebrides and Edgar's influence did not extend west of the Drum Alban. It is clear that both Magnus and Edgar viewed the Cinel Lorn as a threat to their influence in the west of Scotland.

Magnus was allied with Muirchertach Ua Brian, the King of Munster, and rival of the Cinel Lorn's old ally, Domnall mac Lochlainn of the Ailech, for the title of *Ard Righ Eire* (High King of Ireland). When Magnus died in 1103, Edgar attempted to keep the alliance alive by sending Muirchertach Ua Brian the gift of a camel. But there was no effective rule in the west of Scotland and local conditions continued to encourage control by semi-independent warlords.

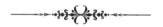

End Notes
Chapter 3

1. Laing, L. & J., *The Picts and the Scots*, Sutton, Wrens, Mid-Glamorgan, 1993, (plate 3) & 153.

2. This was where the monks who fled the Viking raid on Lindesfarn in 796 took shelter.

3. MacLean, J. P., *History of the Island of Mull*, MacLean, San Mateo 1925, 21.

4. The Vikings must have been familiar with the Gaelic culture and language to know of the relics and to be able to interrogate St. Blamhoc. They would have either spoken Gaelic themselves or had a translator with them.

5. These relics were carried by the Islanders who fought under the Lord of the Isles at the Battle of Bannockburn in 1314.

6. The son of Selbec II of Lorn.

7. Skene, *Celtic Scotland*, Edinburgh, David Douglas, 1886, Vol 1, 306.

8. Clark, H., & Ambrosiani, B., *Towns in the Viking Age*, St. Martins, New York, 1991, 217.

9. Ritchie, A., *Viking Scotland*, B.T. Batsford/Historic Scotland, London, 1993, 33.

10. The branch of the Cinel Lorn from which the MacKinnons may have been descended, was the Cinel nEchdach. The leader of the Cinel Lorn, at this time, may have been Ruadri, whose son Cathmail had a son Donald who had a son Morgan, founder of Clan Morgan. The *Genealogy of the Clan Duff* and the *Mormaers of Moray*, traces MacBeth's ancestors through Ferchar Fada to Lorn Mor, the founder of the tribe of Lorn. See Skene, W. F., *Celtic Scotland*, Edinburgh, David Douglas, 1886, Vol. III, 476.

11. The Norse generally concerned themselves with the North and West coast of Britain, whilst the Danes were preoccupied with the North Sea Coast and both sides of the English Channel. See Sawyer, P. H., *Kings and Vikings*, Routledge, London 1989, 80.

12. Raids on Scotland resumed in 892, 900 and 904, from fleets based in Ireland, but these were now on a much-reduced scale from what occurred before.

13. Arbman, H., *Vikings*, Thames and Hudson, London, 1961, 52.

14. MacNab, P. A., *The Isle of Mull*, David & Charles, Newton Abbot, 1970.

15. There has been no archeological evidence found so far which would indicate the extent of Norse settlements on Mull. We may infer, however, that, because the Norse place names are along the coasts while Gaelic names predominate the interior, the Norse stayed on the coasts. Some Norse names that are still in use are Ulva (*Wolf Island*), Scridain (*surrounded by landslide*), Staffa (*Pillar Island*), as well as Mishnish, *(Gullskerry or "Seagull Promontory")*.

16. The Scots had built both round and small rectangular houses for domestic use and large rectangular feasting halls for their warlords.

17. Sawyer, P. H., *Kings and Vikings*, Routledge, London, 1989, 110.

18. Foote, P., & Wilson D., *Viking Achievement*, Sedgwick & Jackson, London, 1990, 217.

19. Clark, H., & Ambrosiani B., *Towns in the Viking Age*, St. Martins, New York, 1991, 102-6.

20. *RCHMS, Argyll, Vol. 3, Mull, Tiree, Coll, and Northern Argyll*, Edinburgh, 1980, 199-202.

21. Kingdom of the Bar, this name is thought to refer to the Sound of Mull which barred access to the island. Ritchie, A., *Viking Scotland*, B.T. Batsford/Historic Scotland, London , 1993, 15.

22. The Earldom of Orkney was founded by the brothers, Rognvald and Sigurd, from the powerful Møre family. After the establishment of the earldom, the relationship between them and the Norse King was decidedly strained.

23. Erskine & Beveridge, *Coll and Tiree*, T. & A. Constable, Edinburgh, 1903, 13.

24. Ritchie, A., *Viking Scotland*, B. T. Batsford/Historic Scotland, London, 1993, 91.

25. Fhionghuin was a very unusual name in the Highlands. In historic times, it was used exclusively by members of the Clan MacKinnon.

26. MacLean, J. P., *History of the Island of Mull*, MacLean, San Mateo 1925, 18.

27. Cameron, A., *History and Traditions of Skye*, E. Forsyth, Inverness, 1871, 19.

28.   MacKenzie, G. M., *The Origins and Early History of the MacMillians and Related Kindreds*, Highland Roots, Inverness, 2002, 14.

29.   Maol-Coluim (Malcolm) was *Righ Beruvik* (modern Barbreck just south of Oban) and foster father for Earl Siguard of Orkney's son Thorfinn. We know that Donald Finlay's brother was in Moray at this time because of a donation of land he made to the Abby of Deer. The *Book of Deer* states *"Donald Ruadri's son, and Malcolm Culen's son, give Biffie to God and to Drostan.."* Anderson, *Early Sources of Scottish History*, Vol. II, 176.

30.   MacKenzie, G. M., *The Origins and Early History of the MacMillians and Related Kindreds*, Highland Roots, Inverness, 2002, 15.

31. Thorfinn, the son of Sigurd (who was killed at the battle of Clontarf), claimed he held both Sutherland and Caithness out of right from his grandfather, Malcolm the Ard Righ of Alba.

32. There is a town in Benderloch called Balmoadan "town of Moddan".

33. That MacBeth had the authority to call on men from Kintyre and Ireland, would indicate the close ties he maintained with his kin in these places.

34.   Malcolm II, being descended from the Cinel nGabhrain, was a granduncle to Gruoch, Macbeth's wife.

35.   Gruoch may have used her influence, as a princess of the nGabhrain, to dissuade her kin from joining Duncan.

36.   Malcolm fled to England while Donald ban fled to the *"Isles"*. Duncan's father, Crinan the Abbot, was killed.

37. The agreement between the kings of Scotland and Norway effectively divided the ancient territory of the Cinel Lorn into two. This division was never accepted by the descendants of the Cinel Lorn and was to cause centuries of conflict between the Gaels and the Scots kings.

Fionnport on the Ross of Mull

Chapter 4
INDEPENDENCE

During the early 12th century, a guerrilla war against the Norse was being carried out in the territories of what was formerly Dalriada. In the early days of the war, the raids were confined to the mainland of Argyll. There the rebellion proved very successful in loosening the Norse hold along most of the Argyll coast. As the Gaels gained the upper hand in various parts of Dalriada, their old kingdom, the numbers of their warriors increased and others were encouraged to settle in the region.

During this period there are many recorded instances in which the local population, tiring of the rule of the Norse, followed local warriors to take control of their ancestral lands. On the island of Coll, the native Gael attacked and burned Dun Acha, the stronghold of a Norse warrior known only as the son of *Anlainh* (Olaf).[1] As the revolution spread, the names of local Gaelic leaders became better known and are once again mentioned in the ancient annals. Among those named are: Giolla Bright of the Clan Cholla; Allan na Buirrche, son of Anrothan mac Aodh; and Airbertach of Lorn.[2]

The chiefs of the Clan MacKinnon are directly descended from the warrior chief, Airbertach of Lorn.[3] Airbertach is known to have held land on Mull, Tiree and Iona, which he took from the Norse by the sword.[4] He was a prince of the Cinel Lorn and an individual of note, with such influence and authority that he was mentioned by the ancient annalists.

The annals are quite specific regarding how much land on Mull, Iona and Tiree that Airbertach actually held. But, because we no longer know how to interpret the actual word used, we may never know the precise extent of his holdings. He may, in fact, have held the whole of all three islands. We can be quite sure that among the lands Airbertach held were those of: Gribun, the Ross of Mull, Iona and the region around Gott Bay on the East Coast of Tiree.[5] He may have also built Dun Airbertach, which lies just south of Oban. While nothing is known of his personal life, it is thought that Aibertach had two sons. The elder son would have been a warrior like himself and a younger son named Cormac entered the church.

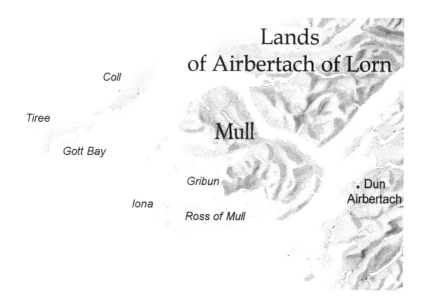

A series of events was set in motion in the North of Scotland which would have a dramatic and profound affect on the descendants of the Cinel Lorn. In particular, the consequences of these events would be felt by the distant cousins of the MacKinnons living in Argyll. Between the death of Macbeth and well into the reign of Alexander I, the men of Moray, descendants of the Cinel Lorn, continued to assert the ancient right of their leaders to the Scottish throne.[6]

These risings were not simple raids, but well-planned assaults timed to exploit moments of weakness in the central monarchy. Initially, these attacks were made only by the men of Moray, led by the MacHeaths, grandsons of Lulach, the slain Tanaire-Right. Alexander I, King of Scotland, responded to the first attack on his authority by retaliating with such savagery that he earned the name Alexander the

Fierce. It is interesting to note that the only death recorded in the ensuing campaign was that of the king's nephew--no leaders of the Cinel Lorn were reported killed nor captured. The ferocity of Alexander's attacks may have prompted the leaders of Moray to come to an agreement with him to put a stop to the fighting. Although there is no existing record of a formal treaty between the belligerents, two branches of the Cinel Lorn were returned to prominence. Angus, the grandson of Lulach, became Righ Mureb; and Cormac, the son of Airbertach, was appointed Bishop of Dunkeld.

Cormac would probably have been born in Ireland about the year 1080.[7] There are several reasons to think he may have been educated at the monastery of Derry in Ireland. At this time, Derry was the main centre of the Columban Church and the resting place of the *"Comarba Coluim Chille"* (Shrine of Saint Columba). As a prince of the Cinel Lorn, Cormac would have been related to the Ailech who held the lands just west of Derry. No more can be surmised of Cormac's early years, but he would appear to have been in his mid 30s when Alexander I appointed him Bishop of Dunkeld.

Dunkeld was an extremely important place in medieval Scotland. It was second only to Iona in importance as a religious centre and of great political value to the family of the Righ Fortriu. The diocese of Dunkeld was extensive, stretching from Dunkeld in the east, to the coast of Lorn in the West, south to the Clyde estuary and north to the border of Sutherland. This large area included most of the ancient lands of Lorn and Moray. King Alexander I appointed Cormac as Bishop of Dunkeld in 1116, which was the same year he invaded Moray. Being a prince of the Cinel Lorn, Cormac would exercise a natural authority in his ancestral territories that the Righ Alba could not.

The Leny's tradition of the Bishop Cormac calls him *"Gilleasbuig Mor"* (Great Bishop). He is remembered more as a warrior of stature than for his religious work. Although it may not have been unusual for a medieval bishop to be credited with being *"a man of very brave and warlike disposition,"* no such comment was recorded of any of the abbots of Iona.[8] The sword in the MacMillan crest commemorates the weapon that Cormac used to win his first position of prominence. Indeed, Cormac's sword made such an impression that a small silver sword engraved with the words *"Gilleasbuig Mor"* served as the charter for the estate of Leny for several centuries prior to its disappearing in 1789.

As a medieval prince and bishop, Cormac would have led a transient life, always on the move through his territories collecting tribute, renewing obligations and settling differences. One of the obligations, of which we have record, is that he acted as guarantor for the Abbey of Deer. An entry in the margin of a page of the "Book of Deer" was witnessed by his son, Gilchrist mac Cormac. The Bishop Cormac had five sons: Fhionghuin, Guaire, Gilli Christ, Farquhar and Anrias. Unlike his father, Fhionghuin mac Cormac was not a churchman. He was a warrior and became the name father of the Clan MacKinnon

Being integrated into the interregional Norse trade routes had insured that the Hebrides were, by now, well known to the outside world. They were not just an obscure appendage to a backward kingdom on the edge of the known world. By the latter half of the twelfth century, the Western Islands of Scotland were fairly well known far beyond the bounds of the Irish Sea.[9] Reginald of Durham, who compiled an account of the miracles of St.Cuthbert, was able to accurately describe the islands of Iona, Mull, Tiree, Coll and Colonsay, all of which were located within the boundary of old district of Lorn. These islands were known even in places as far away as France and the Mediterranean.[10]

In the continuing struggle against the Norse, Fhionghuin, his brother Guaire, and a warrior now known as Somerled are very likely to have been allies, or at the least, to have been known to each other. Somerled, who emerged as the leader of the Western Gael, was a member of the Clan Colla.[11] These folk were descendants of the legendary Three Collas who settled, for a time, on the island of Colonsay during the early years of Dalriada.[12] Given the long relationship between the Cinel Lorn and the Clan Colla and the small geographic area they inhabited, it would be surprising if Cormac's sons and Somerled did not know each other very well.[13]

Shortly after King David I assumed the throne of Scotland in 1124, Malcolm MacHeath again attempted to seize the Crown for the descendants of the Cinel Lorn. His efforts ended indecisively, with no clear victory for either side, thus ensuring that yet another attempt would be made.

Just six years later, Malcolm MacHeath and his brother Angus, the Earl of Moray, launched a major invasion of *Alba* (Scotland) from the Hebrides. The chances of success were great, as King David I was in England, and the MacHeaths were able to field some 5,000 men. In the king's absence, the Scottish army was led by Edward, the son of Siward of Northumbria. Edward proved to be an able general, defeating the army of Moray and killing Angus MacHeath, but Malcolm was not captured until 1134.[14] While Malcolm MacHeath was held in captivity, the fight was carried on by his two sons--Donald, and his brother whose name remains unknown.

In an effort to increase support for their cause, the MacHeaths enlisted the aid of the Gael of Argyll. The decision by Somerled of the Isles to aid the MacHeaths, made the men of Clan Cholla active partners in the struggle of their cousins. This Gaelic attempt to halt the feudalisation of Scotland was to last three years. The Scottish King Malcolm IV appeared to win militarily, but he had to come to terms with the Gael by releasing Malcolm MacHeath from Roxburgh Castle and giving him the district of Ross. Although the expedition from the Isles ended inconclusively in 1157, the remnants of the ancient Dalriada were once again united in a common cause.

The main struggle of the Gael now centred on the West Coast, pitting them against the Norse King of Man. Godred, the King of Man and the Isles, was a tyrannical ruler who had alienated most of his island subjects. In the course of his rule, he had dispossessed most of the island chiefs, spreading discontent and uncertainty through a very influential part of Hebridian society.

Thorfinn mac Ottor, a powerful but disinherited chief, invited Somerled to have his son, Dugal, named King of the Isles.[15] A naval battle between the forces of Somerled and Godred of Man, which resulted from this invitation, took place off the North Coast of Islay on the night of January 6, 1156. The battle raged all through the night and, when morning finally arrived, both sides were totally exhausted.

The outcome favoured Somerled and the Gaels, thus the power of the King of Man was broken. An agreement was quickly reached between Somerled and Godred, in which the islands were divided between them. Somerled received all of the islands south of Ardnamuchan, as well as Kintyre. Godred kept Man and those islands north of the peninsula of Ardnamuchan. With this victory, the islanders were free of the tyranny of Man and the Celtic Kingdom of the Isles was born.

Two years later, in 1158, Somerled was acknowledged in the annals by the title *"Rex Insularium"* (King of the Isles). He and his descendants were, in spirit, independent kings. Although they publicly acknowledged the authority of Norway, in practice, they were not subject to either the Norse nor their neighbouring Scottish rulers.[16]

This new Kingdom of the Isles very closely resembled the old Kingdom of Dalriada in both area and government. It may have even been an attempt to resurrect what would have been considered a Celtic golden age.[17] To effectively govern his new kingdom, Somerled quickly established a Council of the Isles, a body composed of the leading men of the kingdom. Either Fhionghuin, Guaire, or both, as representatives of the Clan Airbertach, would almost certainly have been members of this council.

As it was, Celtic practice ensured that the king ruled with the consent of the people, and these councils had real power. One of the council's first priorities was to re-establish a liberated Iona to its rightful place at the head of the Celtic Church. To accomplish this, the Council of the Isles invited the head of the Celtic Church in Ireland, Flaithbertach Ó Brolchan, to become the Abbot of Iona.[18] The invitation was summarily refused, as the re-establishment of Iona was thought, by the Irish, to threaten prestige of the Columban Church in Ireland.

There were likely a number of reasons for the host of the Isles to make the fateful invasion of Alba in the year of 1164.[19] The main body of Somerled's army was made up of men from Argyll, Kintyre, Dublin and the Hebrides. But there may also have been warriors from Galloway, Moray and Orkney as well. That Fhionghuin and Guaire, the sons of Cormac, were present could be expected, given the size and importance of this hosting.

The men of the Isles landed from a fleet of 160 ships at Renfrew, which was then a fief belonging to Walter FitzAllan. Initially, they overran and pillaged the estates without much difficulty. Only after the initial shock of the invasion wore off, was a determined defence organised and a battle ensued. The fierceness and determination with which the battle was fought is graphically described in one of the earliest written accounts of the invasion.[20] Unfortunately for the islanders, and the young Kingdom of the Isles, Somerled and one of his sons were killed in the course of the struggle.[21]

The death of Somerled, and the ensuing division of the Kingdom of the Isles among his sons, would affect the descendants of Cormac for generations. Because the Kingdom of the Isles was a Celtic polity, the feudal idea of primogeniture that insists on the eldest son succeeding his

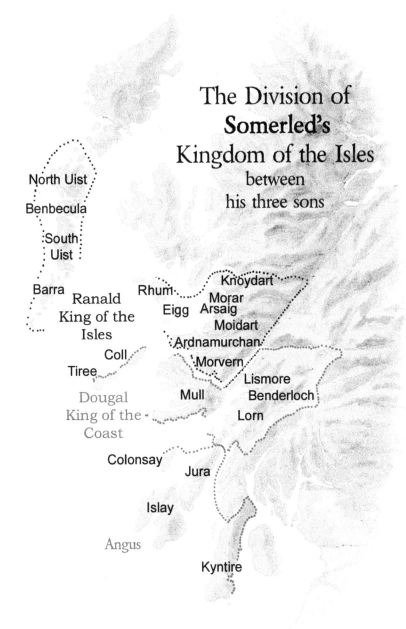

The Division of
Somerled's
Kingdom of the Isles
between
his three sons

North Uist

Benbecula

South
Uist

Barra

Ranald
King of the
Isles

Rhum

Knoydart

Morar

Eigg   Arsaig

Moidart

Ardnamurchan

Coll

Morvern

Tiree

Lismore

Dougal
King of the
Coast

Mull

Benderloch

Lorn

Colonsay

Jura

Islay

Angus

Kyntire

father was not practised. The kingdom was divided, in the Celtic fashion, equally between Somerled's sons.

Somerled had seven children; Gillebirgte and Somerled (yr) by his first marriage then by his second; Dugald, Ranald, Angus, Olaf, and a daughter, Bethag.[22] Dugal, who would be known as *Righ Airer Goidel* (King of the Coast of the Gael) inherited the mainland of Lorn with Benderloch, and the islands of Lismore, Mull, Tiree and Coll. Ranald, styled *Righ Innse Gall* (King of the islands of the Gael), received the lands of Ardnamuchan, Morvern, Kintyre, Moidart, Arsaig, Morar, and Noydart, as well as the islands of Rhum, Eigg, Benbecula, Barra, and the Uists. Angus received Islay, Jura and Colonsay. Of the remaining sons, Gillebirgte died with his father in Renfrew, and the fate of Olaf is unknown. Almost as soon as they had received their lands, Somerled's sons began an aggressive expansion of their individual territories.

Fhionghuin and Guaire, because of their interests in the islands of Mull, Iona, and Tiree, were bound to support the MacDugals of Lorn in the struggle which ensued over Somerled's patrimony. The fight for possession of Mull was destined to last several generations.

The first battles were really indecisive skirmishes and raids made by Ranald's supporters.[23] However, as time went on, the feud turned murderous as yet more of Somerled's descendants turned on each other. Somerled's sons and grandsons mustered their followers, formed formal alliances and fought bitterly against their siblings.

Both Ranald and his stepbrother, Somerled (younger), aspired to be *Thane* (governor) of Argyll, and each claimed Morvern outright.[24] Although Somerled (yr) and Ranald were able to reach an agreement relatively early on, regarding the division of their lands, other siblings did not. The strength of the understanding reached by the brothers enabled Somerled (yr) to send his son John to be fostered by Ranald.

Because of the closeness engendered by the traditional foster relationship, John eagerly took Ranald's side against his uncle Dugal. The simmering civil war intensified further when John murdered his uncle Dugal's father-in-law, Murchdanach, and Ranald's son, Donald, forced his father-in-law, his maternal uncle Gillies, into exile. John then murdered his cousin, Callum Alin. As if this where not enough, Donald would eventually murder his uncle Dugal. Dugal's estates, however, were successfully passed to his sons.[25] This internecine feud caused divisions between the descendants of Somerled and the MacDougalls of Lorn, which would colour the history of the Hebrides for years to come.

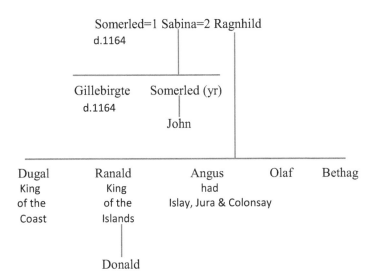

In the early years of the struggle for Lorn, Dugal was in firm control of his estates and set up an independent Benedictine monastery and a nunnery for Augustinian canoness on Iona.[26] The establishment of the monastery went ahead, despite the opposition of the Celtic Abbots of Derry and Armagh. In 1203 the last Cistercian Abbot of Iona was reconfirmed as the first Benedictine Abbot, and Dugal's sister, Bethag, was appointed to the office of the first Prioress of the Augustinian nunnery.[27]

There were now two powerful rival dynasties in the Hebrides. One dynasty was a Celtic polity, which claimed the area of ancient Dalriada, and the other was Norse, which claimed everything else. The divisions in the Somerled family provided an ideal opportunity for Godfrey, the son of Godred, to reclaim the Kingdom of Man.

In the years 1209 and 1210, Ranald's sons, along with their uncle Angus, were engaged in warfare with the men of Skye. It's not now known whether the Gael were attempting to capture the island or if the Norse King of Man was attempting to get it back but, in the end, Skye was firmly under Norse control. These raids spread to Iona in 1210 when the King of Man raided that island. Both the nunnery and the monastery were plundered, but the fate of the monastic communities is unknown to us.

The Augustinian nunnery on Iona

Five years later, the political situation of the Isles was further complicated when Kenneth MacHeath, together with Donald Ban MacWilliam and an unnamed Irish prince, resumed their war with the Scottish kings.[28] They invaded their ancestral lands of Moray with a large force of Gaels from the Isles and Ireland. This expedition was stopped in Ross by the Earl Farquhar MacIntagart, who was knighted by the Scottish king for his efforts. The end of the campaign was inconclusive, but the Scottish king was reminded of the ever-present threat to his Crown from Argyll.

At the close of this period, the Clan Cormac was scattered across the ancient lands of Lorn.[29] The MacQuarries and MacKinnons held the islands of Tiree, Ulva, Iona and Mull, and the MacPhees had Colonsay. MacCallun held the lands of Largie and Glen Orchy, and MacGregor settled in Glen Orchy. MacNab held lands in Glen Dochart, and MacMillan occupied Lenne and Glen Cannel.

MacNivens

MacGregor MacMillans ● Dunkeld
MacCullum •Cill na Charmaig
MacQuarrie   Arbeonaig
MacKinnon MacMillan ● Dun Airbertach MacNab
                                    St Catans
                                    • Abruthven

MacPhee

Lands of the
Descendants of
Cormac

St Cormac's Chapel• Eilean Mor
              Mac Cormaig   & Churches dedicated to him

MacMillan

End Notes
Chapter 4

1. Erskine and Beveridge, *Coll and Tiree*, T. & A. Constable, Edinburgh, 1903, 7.

2. Giolla Bride mhic Gille Adomnain, Chief of the Clan Geofradh (Colla), was forced by the raids of Magnus Barelegs in 1098, to flee Argyll to his kin in Oriel, Northern Ireland. Anrothan mac Aodh, the younger son of the Righ Ailech, settled in Alba about 1033. From him are descended the clans of Lamont, MacEwan and MacLauchlan, all native to the south of Argyll. Airbertach is an unusual name among the Scots but was not uncommon in Ireland. This name would indicate he may have been born in Ireland where his father Murireadach or his grandfather Ferquhar Og would have fled after MacBeth's death in 1057. See: MacDonald, *Clan Donald*, Loanhead, Midlothian, MacDonald, 1978 and MacKenzie, G. M., *The Origins and Early History of the MacMillians and Related Kindreds*, Highland Roots, Inverness, 2002, 18.

3. MacQuarrie A., "Kings Lords and Abbots", Transactions of the Gaelic Society of Inverness, LVIII, 1984, 361.

4. MacFirbis noted that Airbertach of Lorn "*Inhabited 12 treba among the Norse Greagrwghe of the warrior called Mull, and Tiree and Cruibhinis*" ("Cruibhinis" is Irish for the Scots "Eilean nan Croabh" or "Island of the Trees" an early name for Iona. See Appendix 1 for a description of ancient land measurement systems.

5. Some lands in this vicinity were later associated with the monastery on Iona, which may possibly indicate a more ancient connection.

6. MacDonald, A., "Treachery in the Remotest Territories of Scotland", *Canadian Journal of History, Vol. 33, Aug 1999*, 161-192. Between 1057 and 1085 there were several attempts against the life of Malcolm III. An attempt against Malcolm's life was made at Lodmund, where Donald's son was killed by the men of Moray. During this rising, or perhaps in another rebellion, the records aren't specific, Alexander I was attacked at Invergowrie. In answer to this attack, Alexander I chased the Moray men into Ross, where he defeated them. The MacHeaths are descended from Lulach's daughter and her husband Aedh. Most agree that Aedh was the Mormaer of Ross and a prince of the Cinel Lorn. He may have been the brother of Ladhmunn and of the Cinel nGabrain.

7. MacKenzie, G. M., *The Origins and Early History of the MacMillians and Related Kindreds*, Highland Roots, Inverness, 2002, 63.

8. Monro, R. W., & MacQuarrie, A., *Clan MacQuarrie,* Bruce MacQuarrie, Auburn, 1996, 6.

9. MacDonald, R. A., *Kingdom of the Isles,* Tuckwell Press, East Lothian, 1997, 13.

10. Robert Torigine, the Abbot of Mont St. Michael in Brittany, noted in a manuscript that the Kingdom of the Isles contained thirty-two islands.

11. Clann means children or descendants in Gaelic. Somerled was a descendant of one of the Three Collas

12. The Three Collas returned to Ireland where they won a swordland called Oriel. Men from Oriel later returned to Dalriada with Fergus Mor and settled among the Cinel of Lorn.

13. Fhionghuin and Guaire held Mull, Iona and Tiree. Somerled was on the mainland side of the Firth of Lorn. Their homes were only separated by a short 10 km galley ride. The early leaders would no doubt have considered each other close neighbours.

14. Malcolm MacHeath was imprisoned in Roxburgh Castle. He was not executed--probably because of the legitimacy of his claim to the Scottish Crown.

15. At this time, there is a great deal of rivalry between the Kingdom of Man and Dublin for dominance in the Irish Sea. Thorfinn MacOttor was definitely on the side of the Norse Kings of Dublin, in the struggle for supremacy in the region, when he made this request.

16. MacDonald, *Clan Donald*, Loanhead, Midlothian, MacDonald, 1978, 22.

17. Steer & Bannerman, *Late Mediaeval Monumental Sculpture in the West Highlands*, RCAHMS, HMSO Press, Edinburgh, 1977.

18. This occurred during the year 1158 and is an indication of how quickly the Celtic practices were reintroduced following the defeat of the Norse. Flaithbertach Ó Brolchan was the Abbot of the monastery of Derry as well as the leader of the Celtic Church. See: Steer & Bannerman, *Late Mediaeval Monumental Sculpture in the West Highlands*, RCAHMS, HMSO Press, Edinburgh, 1977.

19. Likely a conservative opposition to the rapidly-expanding number of Anglo Norman fiefs which were pushed westward by Kings David I and Malcolm IV of Alba.

20. The ancient Scots *"Carmen de Morte Sumerledi."*

21. MacDonald, R. A., *Kingdom of the Isles*, Tuckwell Press, East Lothian, 1997, 65.

22. These were the children by his second wife, Ragnhilda. The name of his first wife is thought to be Sabina but we cannot be certain. With her, he had Somerled (yr) and Gillebirgte. He also had two other natural sons, Gillies and Gal MacSgillin.

23. MacDonald, R. A., *Kingdom of the Isles*, Tuckwell Press, East Lothian, 1997, 70.

24. The eldest son by Somerled's first wife.

25. There is now some doubt that the early MacDougalls of Lorn were descended from Dougal Somerled's son. Mr. John MacConnell, the MacDonald Clan historian, told me in conversation that he believed the MacDonalds and the MacDougalls of Lorn are definitely not related. There are MacDougall families on the island of Kerrera who claim kindred with the Kings of Moray and deny any relationship to the MacDonalds. The MacDougall Lords could have been descendants of the ancient Cinel Lorn of Dalriada.

26. MacQuarrie, A., "Kings Lords & Abbots," *Transactions of the Gaelic Society of Inverness, LVIII, 1984.*

27. Bethag was prioress of Iona from 1203 until her death in 1230. She is also credited with the establishment of the Teampull na Trionaid at Carnish on North Uist. This is the most important ecclesiastical building in the Outer Hebrides and was used for the training of priests. It was rebuilt and enlarged in the 13th century by Princess Beatrice and later, during the time of Robert Bruce, by Ammie *ingean Rhuaridh* (Rory's daughter). It fell into disuse after the Reformation--but is now credited with being the first university in Scotland.

28. The MacWilliams were descended from William fitz Duncan, son of King Duncan II. They felt their line had the rightful claim on the throne rather than the sons of David I. The MacWilliams began their attempts to take the throne in 1181.There were three serious goes at the Crown before the MacWilliams joined the MacHeaths in 1215.

29. MacQuarrie, A., "Kings, Lords and Abbots," *Transactions of the Gaelic Society of Inverness, LVIII, 1984*, 361.

Chapter 5
END OF THE VIKING AGE

Of all the independent districts and petty kingdoms of ancient Scotland, only Argyll and the Western Isles, the home of Clan Cormac, remained by 1221. The representatives of the ancient Clan Cormac were scattered across an area which stretched from Dunkeld, in the east, to the islands of Coll and Tiree, in the west. Many of the older clans had dispersed and mixed freely with both native and incoming families. This dispersal was not an unusual situation for the times as families looked for land to support and sustain them. Other clans, such as Clan Somerled, whose descendants would include the MacDonalds and the MacRuairis, were already spread throughout the Hebrides. The migrations of the Clan Currie would distribute them from the Mull of Kintyre to the Long Island. Unfortunately we have no surviving traditions that would indicate which of the related kindreds of Clan Cormac, if any, provided leadership, but a common ancestry was acknowledged as late as the year 1400.[1]

The many years of independence and relative peace enjoyed by the chiefs of the Western Seaboard, would soon come to an abrupt end. The Kingdom of Scotland was about to launch a vicious and sustained attack on the Kingdom of the Isles from the east. There were several reasons for King Alexander II of Scotland's brutal attack on the territories of his Northern and Western neighbours. One of them was almost certainly the attempt by the MacWilliams of Argyll to once again assert their claim to the Scottish Crown. Another, and perhaps the dominant factor, may have been a determination to incorporate these unruly, prosperous lands into Alexander's increasingly-feudalised kingdom.

The MacWilliams' rising took place in 1221 while King Alexander II was in England marrying the daughter of the English King John. On his return home from the wedding, King Alexander II speedily raised his loyal forces from Lothian and Galloway and sailed for Argyll. Due to the severity of the storms in the Hebrides during this season, the invasion fleet was forced back to Glasgow and Alexander was not able to reach Argyll. The next year, however, his armies subjugated parts of Atholl, Cathness, and invaded Argyll again--this time by land. He defeated the local tribes in what must have been a punishing assault. Many of the inhabitants were forced to flee to safety southward toward Galloway. The surviving records of the time state much money and many hostages were taken by Alexander's raiders during this campaign.

The estates of the defeated chiefs were distributed among Alexander's followers, as a reward for their services in the campaign, thus ensuring the loyalty of the newly-conquered areas. For their service during the conflict, Sir Walter Stewart was granted Cowal, and the MacNachtans were given all the lands of Glens Shira and Aray between the Lochs Awe and Fyne. To secure his hold on these newly-acquired territories, Alexander II ordered the construction of royal castles at Tarbert, Dunoon and Eilean Donan.

The conquest of the West was not yet complete though. Several areas along the coast remained independent and Dunollie, the stronghold of the MacDougalls, was not yet taken, nor was there an attempt made at this time to take the Isles. This was the first time, however, that the authority of a King of Scotland was felt on the Western Seaboard.

Alexander II's attack on the homelands of Clan Cormac, coming first from the north then from the east and south, must have been both violent and extremely disruptive. The widely-separated descendants of Cormac were forced out of their glens and scattered as they sought safety and sustenance. Torquil mac Guare and Finlaec mac Fhionghuin remained safe on Ulva and Mull, but the descendants of Gilchrist mac Cormac were scattered between Galloway and Badenoch. The families of Finguine's nephews, Murdoch and Lorn mac Ferquhar, went on to settle areas as distant as Colonsay, Kintail and Strathfillan. These families would later be known as the clans: MacPhee of Colonsay, MacNabs of Glen Dochart and Strathfillan, as well as the Mathesons of Lochalsh, Lochcarron and Kintail.

The collapse of the Clan Cormac in its ancestral homelands of Lorn, may well have encouraged the MacDougalls to assert their authority in the eastern areas of Argyll. Adopting the title *"King of*

Argyll," the chief of the MacDougalls and his clansmen firmly established themselves as the major power in the area.[2] The MacDougall hold on these territories, which included those occupied by the MacKinnons; Mull, its adjacent islands, as well as Tiree and Coll, was gaining strength.

Clan Cormac

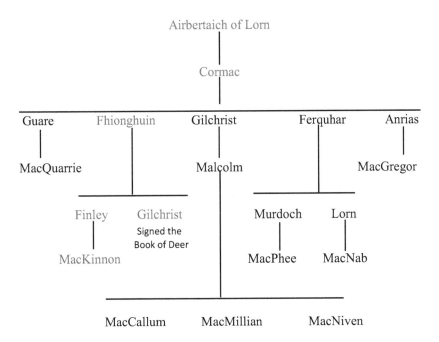

Although the descendants of Somerled had lost Kintyre to Alexander II, they did not give up their claims to the islands of Mull, Tiree, and Coll. For generations to come, they would continue to assert their right to the whole of their lost patrimony. For many years after Alexander II's invasion, the political stability of the West Coast continued to deteriorate. Violence and uncertainty increased, spreading from the mainland into the Hebrides. The Norse continued to hold Skye and the Northern Isles.[3] However, the power of the petty kings was faltering in the face of pressure from those displaced on the mainland and from the new Kingdom of the Isles to their south.

During 1223 the violence in the west increased substantially as the still undefeated MacWilliams, who had found shelter in Argyll, again launched an attack on the lands of Alexander II. This time they had the active support of Ruairi mac Somerled, the chief who had lost Kintyre to Alexander in 1222.[4] Finally by 1224, conditions on the West coast had deteriorated to such an extent that a large party of Hebrideans led by Gillichrist, Ottar and Snaekoll's son, felt it was necessary to make the trip to Bergen to ask Norway's King Haakon IV to help in restoring order.[5] Unfortunately for the Islanders, the Norse king was occupied with serious troubles of his own in Norway and was unable to send the required help.

Two years later in 1226, civil war erupted in the Hebrides as the sons of the deceased King Godfrey of Man, Olaf and Ragnvald, fought with each other for the control of that Kingdom.[6] Olaf allied himself with Farquar MacIntagart, the Earl of Ross; and Leod, the foster son of Paul Balkeson, the Norse sheriff of Skye. Although Olaf initially defeated his brother in a savagely-fought battle on Skye, the war was destined to go for another four years--a struggle that considerably weakened the Manx Kingdom.

Dugald Scrag (aka Screch), Duncan and Uspac, the leaders of the MacDougalls of Lorn whose family fortunes were rising, saw civil war as an opportunity to expand their territories at the expense of the Manx kings.[7] Taking advantage of the weakened and divided state of that kingdom, the MacDougalls were quick to dispatch raiding parties to Skye and other exposed parts of the isles.

Having finally resolved his troubles in 1230, King Haakon IV set out for the Hebrides with a fleet of 12 ships. During a brief stop at Orkney, the fleet was joined by volunteers eager for plunder and the number of ships increased to 36 well-crewed longboats. With Uspac MacDougall in command of the fleet, Haakon IV sailed for Islay where a rendezvous with the fleets of the King of Man and the other lords of the Hebrides was planned.[8]

Uspac's two elder brothers, Dugald Scrag and Duncan, had gathered a large force of Islanders, and were waiting on Islay with the other Hebridean chiefs for the king's arrival. As subordinates of the MacDougalls, it would have been likely that Finlaec mac Finguine, the Chief of MacKinnon, and his cousin, Caelbaig mac Guaire, the Chief of MacQuarrie, were there as well with their small bands of Island warriors.

During these times, the Islanders and the Norse did not share anything resembling a mutual trust or sympathy. There was, in fact, a great deal of animosity felt between the two groups. When Haakon IV's ships landed, the Islanders, in a gesture of goodwill, invited the Norse warriors to a feast. The Vikings, ever suspicious of the Islanders' motives, refused the invitation and made their own camp. Later that night after the Islanders had retired and while many of them slept, the Vikings ruthlessly fell upon their camp. Uspac MacDougall, who was sleeping aboard his own ship, was awakened by the noise of the battle. Realising what was happening, but unable to influence the Norse warriors, Uspac could only save his brothers' lives by taking them aboard his ship for protection.

We will never know how many of the Islanders were killed by their supposed allies or the number of those who managed to escape. But the Islanders do not seem to have been missed when King Haakon's fleet, which now numbered some 80 ships, sailed off to besiege and capture Alexander II's castle of Rothesay. Nor does MacDougall authority in the Isles seem to have suffered because of the murder of their men by the Norse on Islay. The MacDougall's influence remained strong on the coast of Argyll and its adjoining islands.

The MacDougalls continued to support the monastery of Iona, keeping it firmly within their own sphere of influence and authority.[9] The prestige of the MacDougall chiefs was increased significantly in 1248 when the Abbots of Iona were granted the privilege of wearing the mitre and ring by the Pope, Innocent IV, in Rome.[10] That same year, King Haakon IV honoured the MacDougalls yet again when, on receiving the news of the accidental drowning of King Harold of Man, King Haakon IV named Ewen MacDougall "King of the Isles" in his stead.[11]

The scattered remnants of the Clan Cormac fared differently in different parts of its ancient patrimony. In the islands, the MacKinnons, MacQuarries, and MacPhees seem to have supported the MacDougalls, or at least did not contest their authority or rise against them. The rivalry between the MacDougalls and the MacDonalds over Mull was far from resolved, but there is no record of open warfare. In the east of Lorn, things were different. The descendants of Malcolm mac Gilchrist had become proteges of the Comyns. The Comyns, who were the great lords of a feudal Badenoch, had become one of the most powerful kindreds in all of Scotland, holding three earldoms and many royal titles.[12] Fortunately there are extant records dating from 1234 which indicate that the Eastern branch of the Clan Cormac were enjoying a very high esteem under their feudal lords.[13]

Under Alexander II, feudalism was becoming firmly entrenched in the newly-captured districts of Argyll. By 1249 the Hebrides were all that remained of the old independent kingdoms in the north of Britain, but unfortunately they were divided between at least three petty kings who were prone to put their personal ambitions far above any collective security. Only two of these remaining kingdoms were of Celtic origin, the Kingdoms of the Isles and Argyll. The third Hebridian Kingdom, the Kingdom of Man, remained Norse.

The lack of cooperation between the island leaders and the physical closeness of their dominions, encouraged the Scottish King Alexander II to attempt to complete the subjugation of the West Coast that he had begun in 1221. In 1249, about 28 years after his first effort, Alexander II set out to finish the affair and conquer the Western Isles. While he was making preparations for an armed invasion, he simultaneously attempted to obtain the Hebrides through diplomatic means. He sent two bishops to Norway to persuade King Haakon IV to either sell or to surrender the islands to him. While these negotiations were taking place, Alexander II wrote to the King of Argyll, Ewen MacDougall, advising him to renounce his allegiance to King Haakon IV and to turn over the castles, which he held for the Norse, to the Scottish Crown.[14]

When both of these diplomatic strategies failed and as the necessary military preparations were completed, Alexander II resorted to force. The invading army marched against Ewen MacDougall during the summer of 1249. This incursion by another large foreign army, seriously unsettled the mainland territories of Lorn-enough that perhaps even Ewen MacDougall, King of Argyle, was displaced.[15]

The Hebrides, however, were saved by the sudden illness and subsequent death of King Alexander II while at his camp on Kerrera island on July 8, 1249.[16] The Scottish army, now leaderless, withdrew. By now it must have been abundantly clear to the Islanders that the policy of the Scottish kings was not just to destroy the influence of the Norse, but also the Islanders' independence. Their ultimate goal was nothing short of adding the Hebrides to Scotland's mainland dominions.

Chapter 5

END OF THE
VIKING AGE

Orkney

Cathness

Lewis

*Earldom
of Ross*

Elean
Loch   Donan
Bracadale *Skye* • Kintail

Badanoch

Coll
Tiree   *Kerrera* Strath
    Ulva *Mull* *Island* Fillan
    Iona

Glen
Shira Loch Lomond
Colonsay *Knapdale*
    Cowal
Dunoon• Loch Long
Islay Tarbart• *Bute*   *Lothian*
    Cumbraes
  Arran
Kintyre Lamlash Bay

Galloway

During the ten-year period following Alexander II's death at Kerrera, the Hebrides were left in relative peace.[17] However, it is during the decade of the 1250s that we notice the first record of the MacLeans on Mull, but whether they fled to Mull to escape Alexander II's armies or held land there previous to the invasions, is unclear.[18] The progenitor of the Clan MacLean, Gillean of the Axe, is known to have possessed some land in upper Mull and Kerrera island where he built Gylen Castle.[19] Gillian, who was a loyal follower of the MacDougall of Lorn, appears to have gained power and influence after Alexander II's raids into the west.

The security and remoteness of the islands during this period, allowed local magnets to become diverted by the politics and riches of Ireland. By 1258 any Islanders seeking adventure and wealth could have joined Dugald MacRuairi and the King of the Isles, Angus MacDonald, in their lucrative raids on that island.[20]

The peace of the isles was dramatically broken in 1261, only one year after Alexander III assumed the Scottish throne. Upon reaching the age of majority, Alexander III immediately began the completion of his father's work. He sent envoys to Norway, in an attempt to purchase the Hebrides from King Haakon IV, while simultaneously raising an army. Haakon, the Norse king, refused Alexander III's overtures as he had refused those of his father.

By 1262 Alexander III realised that diplomacy would not work and launched his armies in an attack on the Hebrides. To the north, the Earl of Ross, William MacIntagart, with some other Northern chiefs, initiated a guerrilla war against the islands adjacent to their territories.[21] The raid on the island of Skye was particularly brutal, even for these pitiless days. Alexander III's forces destroyed everything they came across--churches, villages, and people, sparing neither the old nor the young. In the south, Walter, Earl of Menteith, expelled the MacSweens from Knapdale and Arran. The Islanders, unable to oppose the onslaught by Alexander III's armies, again called on their king, Haakon IV, for help.

The response from Norway this time was fast and in great strength. Haakon IV quickly assembled a force of 120 ships at his capital of Bergen. All the preparations to enable the fleet to sail were quickly completed and, by July 1263, the fleet was on its way. While proceeding southward Haakon IV stopped only to affirm the loyalty of the men of Shetland, Orkney, and Cathness. By mid August the fleet had sailed past the island of Lewis and entered the sound of Skye. Anchoring south of

Raasay, Haakon IV was joined by Magnus, the King of Man, and the other Norse barons of the Isles.[22] The combined fleets proceeded southwards through the sound of Mull to the isle of Kerrera, where they joined the rest of the waiting Islanders.[23]

Ewen MacDougall, the King of Argyll, should have been the one appointed by Haakon IV to lead the Islanders. Indeed, he may have been asked, but his experience during the previous invasions led him to attempt a desperate policy of neutrality. He studiously avoided giving even the slightest offence to either party in the dispute. The Islanders were led, in his stead, by the brothers, Dugald and Allan MacRuairi.

It is probable that Ewen's waffling at this time may have precipitated the marked shift of allegiance by the MacKinnons, MacQuarries, and MacPhees. These ancient clans now moved away from the MacDougall *Kings of Argyll* to support the MacDonald *Kings of the Isles,* to whom the MacRuairis were related.

Not all of the Islanders willingly supported the Norse in this venture. The MacLeans on Mull would very likely have tried to remain loyal to their MacDougall overlords and not joined the northern fleet. But because this was a war host led by King Haakon IV himself, it is probable that the MacKinnons, with their cousins the MacPhees and MacQuarries, were with Dugald MacRuairi at the rendezvous on Kerrera.[24]

Once the fleet had gathered, Haakon IV divided his forces and began a coordinated assault on Alexander III's possessions. Haakon IV personally led the party which overpowered the island of Gigha. At the same time, Magnus, the King of Man, and Dugald MacRuairi took 50 ships to invade and subdue Kintyre, capturing the ancient stronghold of Dunaverty. Moving on to the island of Bute, Magnus and Dugald attacked with a small fleet of 15 ships, capturing the Castle of Rothesay. With the initial attacks successfully completed during the early days of September, Haakon IV's armada reunited at Lamlash Bay on the East Coast of Arran.

King Alexander III, who had been watching the progress of the combined fleets of King Haakon IV and the Islanders from his camp at Ayr, now moved his army to the vicinity of Largs to be able to better counter their movements. With both sides firmly encamped, the opposing kings, began a long series of negotiations. Haakon IV wanted Alexander III to recognize and respect his claim to the Hebrides, while

Alexander III simply wanted to delay Haakon IV in the Clyde Basin until the weather began to deteriorate with the onset of fall. Alexander III was able to prolong the talks for almost a month, and it was not until the end of September before they were finally broken off. On cessation of the talks, the Norse fleet moved northward to the more protected waters of the Cumbraes.

It was from the Cumbraes that King Haakon IV dispatched Dugald MacRuairi with a force of Islanders, very possibly including the MacKinnons and their cousins, on a long diversionary raid. Dugald's fleet of 60 small Highland galleys proceeded northward the length of Loch Long. Reaching its end, the Islanders carried, pushed and pulled their galleys across the portage from Arrochar to Tarbet and then launched them onto the placid waters of Loch Lomond. The island fleet plundered its way to Lennox and may even have raided as far as Menteith.[25]

By the time the booty-laden galleys could rejoin Haakon's fleet, the famous series of skirmishes, which are now known as the Battle of Largs, had ended and Haakon IV had withdrawn first to Arran and then into the Isles.[26] When the fleets reunited a couple of days later in the vicinity of the Calf of Mull, Haakon IV rewarded the island commanders, Dugald MacRuairi, his brother Allan, and Muchard MacDonald for their service.[27]

Not wanting to be caught in the Hebrides during the season of winter storms, Haakon turned his storm-tossed, but undefeated, fleet homewards only stopping at Loch Bracadale on Skye for provisions. As the Viking fleet resumed its journey homeward, they took with them all of the food the inhabitants of Loch Bracadale had gathered, leaving them to face the winter with no supplies. Unfortunately, while resting with his fleet in Orkney, King Haakon IV succumbed either to exhaustion or illness and died on December 16, 1263. Thereafter, his fleet returned to Norway, leaving the Islanders to face the aggressive Alexander III alone.

Alexander III, now styled the *"Tamer of the Ravens,"* maintained a heavy military pressure on the territories adjoining his lands for the next several years. In 1264 he again turned his attentions toward the Kingdom of Man and the Hebrides. For this purpose, a large Scottish fleet was gathered in the Irish sea. Magnus, the King of Man, intimidated by the display of force, surrendered rather than contest a fight with such a powerful adversary on his own.[28]

With the Kingdom of Man pacified, Alexander III turned his fleet on the Hebrides and Cathness. When he ordered his forces, led by the Earls of Buchan and Mar, with Alan Durward as their general, into the Isles, Angus MacDonald, King of the Isles, submitted almost immediately. Ewen MacDougall of Argyll, after years of attempting to stay neutral, now came out firmly on the side of the Lowlanders.

Only Dugald MacRuairi remained staunch in his loyalty to Norway and assumed command of the resistance.[29] The band of stalwarts led by Dugald would have consisted of the island Gael: MacKinnon, MacQuarrie, MacPhee, and MacDonald. The fight for the Isles was a long and difficult one, but Dugald was an active and stubborn leader. He won a naval engagement in the Hebrides and attacked the Lowland invaders in Cathness. In spite of the efforts by the Islanders to defend themselves, Alexander III's armies inflicted much damage. Although many of the Islanders were able to escape the worst of the onslaught, some of their chiefs were captured and hanged while the Scots took a great deal of plunder.

The strategy of sustained Scottish attacks against the Hebrides eventually wore down the will and the ability of the Gael and their Norse allies to defend themselves.[30] To end the conflict, King Magnus, who had succeeded to the throne of Norway on the death of Haakon IV, decided to come to terms with the Scots and pull out of the Hebrides altogether. The treaty of Perth, drawn up between King Magnus VI of Norway and Alexander III of Scotland in 1266, annexed the Hebrides to Scotland. Not having been consulted about terms and conditions of the treaty, the population of the Isles didn't recognize the superiority of the Scottish king and the independence of the Isles was to remain a source of conflict for centuries.[31]

The period following the annexation of the Hebrides was one of political uncertainty and confusion in the Isles. Some of the Islanders rebelled against their new overlords, while others saw opportunity and became involved in mainland politics. The Manx, under Godfrey, a natural son of Magnus, King of Man, led the first rebellion against the newly-asserted Scottish authority in 1275.[32] However, Alexander III was prepared for trouble and ordered the MacDougalls to gather their men and suppress the revolt before it spread. Alexander MacDougall, the son of Ewen of Argyll, collected a fleet of 90 ships at Galloway to transport the Scottish army in a punitive invasion of Man.[33] The uprising was quickly crushed in October by the better-armed and coordinated Scottish forces who landed at Ronaldsway. Although the rebellion was put down before it became a serious threat to Alexander III's power, his physical influence in the Isles actually remained extremely low. Indeed, it was not until the time of George II, some 400 years later, that any mainland royal power was successfully sustained in the Hebrides.

End Notes
Chapter 5

1.   The so-called manuscript of 1467 is now thought to have been compiled about 1400 as a record of the pedigree of the major families resident in the territories of the Lordship of the Isles. It lists the genealogies of ten clans, showing their descent from Cormac. Those kindreds which made up the Clan Cormac were now becoming the independent clans; MacQuarrie, MacKinnon, MacPherson, MacMillan, MacLennan, MacDougall of Craignish, MacNevin, MacPhee, MacNab, Matheson, Kenneth, and MacGregor.

2.   This MacDougall ascension to power was not unopposed by the Clan Cormac. There is a tradition in Lorn, cited by MacKenzie, G. M., *The Origins and Early History of the MacMillians and Related Kindreds*, Highland Roots, Inverness, 2002, 31, which tells of the competition between the MacMillans and MacDougalls for control of Colagin, the MacCallum seat near Kilbride.

3.   The ancestor of the MacLeods, Leod, the son of Olaf the Black, inherited land in Skye. Leod was fostered by Paul Balkeson, the Norse sheriff of Skye. On Paul's death, Leod received Uist and Harris. Olaf the Black, gave Lewis to Leod, and Leod's grandfather gave him Glenelg. By way of marriage to a daughter of the Norse Lord MacHarold, Leod came into possession of Duirnish, Bracadale, Minginish, Lyndale, and much of Trotternish. See: Nicolson, A., *History of Skye*, Glasgow, Alex MacLaren & Sons, 1930, 16.

4.   This action was lead by Gillescap MacWilliam, his sons, and Ruairi, the son of Reginald who was the son of Somerled. Reginald, the son of Somerled, was the King of the Isles whose support would guarantee the MacWilliams the help of the coastal chiefs. Ruairi lost his lands of Kintyre to Alexander II during the invasion of 1222.

5.   Haakon IV's reign is considered the beginning of medieval Norway's "Golden Age." His court was described as splendid. He improved the efficiency of the administration of the kingdom and encouraged trade treaties with England (1217), the German city of Lubec (1250) and with Russia.

6.   The King of Man, Godfrey, d.1187, had two sons who shared the kingdom; Ragnvald and Olaf. Ragnvald had a son also named Godfrey.

7. MacDonald, R.A., *Kingdom of the Isles*, Tuckwell Press, East Lothian, 1997.

8. Also called Uspac Haakon by some historians, he was the youngest son of Dugald, the name father of the Clan MacDougall.

9. MacQuarrie, A., "Kings Lords and Abbots" *Transactions of the Gaelic Society of Inverness, LVIII, 1984*, 358.

10. The Benedictine monastery on Iona was independent of outside control. In 1203 the Abbot Cellach persuaded the pope to take Iona under his personal protection, for which privilege Iona paid a sum of two byzants a year. One of the effects of Iona now following the Roman Catholic Church, rather than the Irish Celtic Church, was that Iona ceased to be mentioned in the Irish Annals after 1204. As was normal practice during this period, the monasteries, abbots, and monks would have been drawn from the families of the local aristocracy.

11. As was the custom for kings in the Isles, Ewen paid homage to King Haakon at Bergen the year he was crowned.

12. The Comyns would later be tied by marriage to the MacDougalls of Lorn and the Earls of Strathearn. Young A., *Robert Bruce's Rivals: The Comyns 1212-1314*, Tuckwell Press, East Linton, 1997.

13. These include an agreement between Walter Comyn and the Bishop of Moray involving Farquar, son of Shaw, the second refers to Farquhar as *Seneschall,* (the chief officer) of Badenoch.

14. One of the castles Ewen held for King Haakon was Cairn na Berg in the Treshnish Isles. This fort would later figure prominently in a treaty between the MacDougalls and the MacDonald Lord of the Isles, which involved the MacKinnons.

15. MacDonald, R. A., *Kingdom of the Isles*, Tuckwell Press, East Lothian, 1997, 104.

16. Kerrera is a small island in the strait of Mull, between Mull and the mainland, lying just south of Oban. Kerrera is within sight of Ewen MacDougall's castle, which was built on the site of ancient Dunollie. Dunollie was the stronghold of the Cenil Lorn of Dalriada.

17. That Alexander III was a minor during this period, helped towards the peace as well.

18. It is possible that the MacDougalls offered the MacLeans land on Mull to secure it from the MacDonald claims on the island.

19. MacLean, J. P., *A History of the Clan MacLean*, Robert Clark, Cincinnati,1889, 33.

20. Dugald MacRuairi may have been in league with Brian O'Neill, who was leading the Celtic resurgence in Ireland at the time. Angus MacDonald (the King of the Isles) seems to have been involved in a little private freebooting of his own. His activities may or may not have been related to Brian O'Neill's cause. MacDonald R. A., *Kingdom of the Isles*, Tuckwell Press, East Lothian, 1997, 129.

21.   The son of Farquhar who defeated the MacWilliams and was knighted by Alexander II for his efforts.

22.   In his book Rev. Lamont D., Strath: *In Isle of Skye*, Celtic Press, Glasgow, 1913, 53-4, the Rev. Lamont states that an examination of the Sagas will show Haakon did not sail through the Kyles. The Rev. Lamont argues that Haakon rounded Skye to the west on both this trip and his return to Norway. He argues that Kyleakin has been misnamed.   He claims, not without substance, that both Kyleakin and Kylerhea are named for two brothers, Acunn and Readh, who were ancient Celtic heroes.

23. Both Kerrera and the adjacent bay of Tobermory appear to have been popular anchorages for shipping from early times and were still in frequent use in the 18th century.

24.   At this time the MacKinnons would have been led by their chief, Finlaec mac Finguine, the MacQuarries by Caelbaig mac Guarrie, and the MacPhees by Murdoch mac Farquhar. This conflict pitted elements of the ancient Clan Cormac against one another. The Islanders would seemingly have been with King Haakon of Norway, while their mainland cousins, led by Farquhar Macintosh, supported King Alexander.

25. Alexander, D., Neighbor T., Oram R., "Glorious Victory?" *History Scotland, Vol. 2, #2, Mar/Apr 2002.*

26.   MacDonald, R. A., *Kingdom of the Isles*, Tuckwell Press, East Lothian, 1997, 114.

27. Dugald's reward were the lands which Ewen MacDougall had held from Norway. This would have been all of the islands: Mull, Tiree, Coll, Colonsay, and Iona. Thus, the MacKinnons were no longer subject to the Lords of Lorn, but now came into the sphere of influence of the Lords of the Isles. Missing from the list of prominent island chiefs, is Angus Mor MacDonald of Islay. Both Angus and his brother Merchard were reluctant to join King Haakon's force. They did join him, however, but only after the fleet's arrival at either Arran or the Cumbraes. Angus may, as some sources claim, have taken part in the raids of Loch Lomond. We do know that Angus Mor regained the island of Bute for a time, and Merchard gained control of Arran. Neither was able to keep these islands out of the grasp of the greedy King Alexander III for long.

28. Magnus swore allegiance to Alexander III in 1264 and died in 1265. With Magnus dead, Alexander, with no regard for the legal heirs, assumed sovereignty ovr his Kingdom.

29. It appears that Alexander III made considerable effort to capture Dugald. "Lord Dugald defended himself in ships and they took no hold of him" See: Rixson, D., *The West Highland Galley*, Edinburgh: Birlinn (1989), 19.

30. See Appendix 2 for other tales of the expulsion of the Norse from the Hebrides.

31. The Hebrides were divided into three independent kingdoms: Kingdom of Man, Kingdom of the Isles, and the Kingdom of Argyll. The wording of the Treaty of Perth, which is commonly understood to give the Hebrides to Scotland, actually says that Magnus gave up his right to lands on the mainland and that he would give up the Hebrides also *if they belonged to him.*

32. MacDonald, R. A., *Kingdom of the Isles*, Tuckwell Press, East Lothian, 1997, 135.

33. The other leaders of Alexander III's faction were Allan MacRuairi, John Comyn, Allan of Galloway, and John de Vesci. It is indicative of the confusion of the times that Allan MacRuairi, who was the brother of Dugald MacRuairi, allied himself with the MacDougalls of Argyll who still claimed Mull, which had been given to Dugald MacRuairi by King Haakon IV whilst under his control.

Chapter 6
WITH ROBERT BRUCE

With the increasing lowland Scottish influence on the West Coast, the Gaelic lordships of the Hebrides were doomed.[1] The loss of the benefit of direct political and commercial contact with a vibrant and expanding Norway could not be replaced by the Kingdom of the Scots and was to prove critical to the economy of the Isles.[2] The Norse trade routes through the Hebrides to Ireland, Wales, and Western England, were cut off while the southern seaways became increasingly dangerous.

Overland trade between the islands--Argyll, Lorn, and the eastern parts of the kingdom, was discouraged by the forbiddingly mountainous terrain. The Islanders' galleys continued to be the main source of transportation through the Isles and along the coasts, but after 1266 they were no longer able to keep up technologically as developments in the rest of Europe passed them by.[3] The Hebrides were thus forcibly excluded from the sphere of Europe's most vibrant and expansive commercial network to become a peripheral part of a marginal country.

The alliances of the major families on the coast diverged as they reflected the new politics and power structure of the area. By 1286 Angus Mor MacDonald and his son, Alexander Og, were members of the "Turnberry Band," along with the Bruces, James Stewart, and a couple of other Scottish earls.[4] The MacDougalls, on the other hand, supported the Baliols and Comyns, to whose families they were related by marriage.[5]

After initially coming to terms with Alexander III, both of these families took an active role in supporting England's war against Scotland. Alexander Og MacDonald was even appointed to the position of Admiral of the Western Isles by the English King Edward I in 1291. Even though both of the major island families supported the English cause against the Scottish government, their quarrels over the ownership of Mull continued to separate them.[6]

The final rift between the two most powerful families on the west coast occurred in 1292, triggered by an event which was intended to bring them closer together--the marriage of Alexander Og MacDonald and Julianna MacDougall, the daughter of Alexander of Argyll. The dispute began almost immediately after the wedding and may have come about as a simple disagreement regarding the bride's dowry. At question were certain lands on the island of Lismore. As neither party was in the mood to make concessions to the other, the dispute was at last referred to the Scottish king, John Baliol, who was related by marriage to the MacDougalls. We do not know what judgement King John Baliol actually rendered in this case, but we do know the MacDonalds were far from happy with it.

MacDonald displeasure manifested itself in the refusal, by Angus Og MacDonald, Alexander Og's younger brother, to attend the first parliament called by the new king in 1293.[7] Not willing to accept the MacDonald's defiance, King John Baliol ordered his kinsman, Alexander MacDougall, to summon Angus Og to pay the homage due a king of Scotland. Angus Og, being a supporter of the Bruce family, Baliol's rivals for the throne, and now in the midst of a quarrel with the MacDougalls, ignored the summons. The dispute, however, escalated rapidly when Alexander Og MacDonald complained to his patron, England's King Edward I, that the Scottish King, John Baliol, was occupying part of his lands without consent.

It now appears that King Edward I either needed or preferred the more powerful Alexander Og MacDonald's allegiance over that of the MacDougalls, whom there is some evidence that he distrusted.[8] The English king authorised the occupation of Alexander MacDougall's lands in 1296 and even had him imprisoned for a time at Berwick Castle. With his only local opponent in custody, Alexander Og began to retake the MacDonald lands lost during the Scottish invasions. The first of these was Kintyre, which he easily took from the Stewarts.

Almost as soon as Alexander of Argyll was released from Berwick in 1297, he began raiding MacDonald territories.[9] Gille-Iosa, the chief of the Mull MacLeans, would certainly have been one of MacDougall's captains contributing galleys to the Argyll fleet. The MacRuairis, perhaps in an effort to restore their family fortunes by recovering land also lost through the Scottish invasions, were also quick to ally themselves to the

MacDougalls. The combined fleets of the MacRuairi and MacDougall raiders swept through the Hebrides.

It is recorded these galley fleets *"plundered the greater parts of the king's lands of Skye and Lewis and killed men in the same lands and set fires."* [10] They also breached the sanctity of the church by burning the galleys placed under its protection.

Another pirate, Duncan, is said to have actually ruled, as a king, in the Hebrides for three years, even though he had no right nor authority to do so.[11] Duncan, sensing an opportunity for wider plunder, joined Lauchlan and Roderick MacRuairi who, along with Alexander MacDougall, preferred to target MacDonald settlements. However, Duncan does not seem to have been very particular regarding the loyalties of those he robbed and continued to raid indiscriminately. After living through what may have been years of intermittent raids, the Islanders raised a fleet to drive the thieves from the Hebrides.

Sean Ewen MacKinnon, then chief of the clan, mobilised a large force of Islanders who, with their galleys, proceeded against the pirates.[12] Roderick was the first of the pirates which Sean Ewen's fleet encountered. He put up a strong defence and was only captured after a determined fight in which 30 of MacKinnon's men were killed. Lauchlan and Duncan, realising their days were numbered, fled the islands making for the MacRuairi castle at Inverlochy.

Inverlochy Castle

The MacKinnon galleys stayed close behind them and the pirates had little or no chance to escape. MacKinnon and the other island chiefs must have been astonished when they approached the castle and saw two of the largest galleys ever seen in the Hebrides sitting, almost completed, on the beach beneath the castle walls.[13] These ships, if allowed to put to sea fully manned, would have been the greatest threat to the security of the islands yet encountered.

MacKinnon first demanded the MacRuairis surrender the ships but, when this was refused, the Islanders made an attempt to capture them. But the ships were too close to the castle walls to allow them to be dragged to the water without the loss of many men. Unfortunately, after much consideration Sean Ewen MacKinnon decided both ships should be burned where they lay on the beach. The two longships were destroyed, but Lachlan MacRuairi and Duncan both managed to escape.[14]

The defeat of the pirate alliance by Sean Ewen MacKinnon did not bring a final peace to the Isles. The MacDougalls, though daunted, remained a considerable sea power on the West Coast. They appear to have been particularly active against the ships supplying the English garrisons in Scotland. Edward I had ordered the judiciary of Ireland to *"procure....ships of Ireland with crews of 40 good men each"* to operate under the command of a certain Hugh Bisset and harass England's enemies in the Irish sea.[15] These enemies were almost certainly the MacDougalls and their MacLean allies.[16]

In 1299 during a visit to the English court, Angus Og MacDonald was named "Admiral of the Western Fleet" succeeding his elder brother, Alexander Og, who held the post before him.[17] Just two years later in 1301, Angus Og, in conjunction with the considerable naval power of Hugh Bisset and the displaced MacSweens, attacked the MacDougalls in the vicinity of Kintyre and Bute. The combined naval and land assault broke the will of the MacDougalls who, along with Lachlan MacRuairi, submitted to the English King Edward I.[18] The defeat of the MacDougalls was a strategic victory that ended the threat to England's naval power in the Irish sea. For the moment, King Edward's influence was secure in the Isles. The MacDonalds were allied with the English, while the MacDougalls and MacRuairies were, for the present at least, very much under his sway.[19]

Chapter 6

WITH
ROBERT BRUCE

Earldom
of
Ross

Buchan

Inverurie•

Skye

Garmoran

•Inverlochy

Lismore   Ben
Lawers

Dunstaffnage

Methven•

Cambaskenneth

Sterling Castle •

Falkirk•

Tarbert• Bute

Berwick Castle •

Loch Ranza

Saddell Castle•

Carrick

Kintyre Arran

Rathlin

•Dunaverty

Galloway

The tumultuous events now taking place on the Scottish mainland were about to spill over into the Hebrides, causing old alliances to be renewed and wrecking the fragile peace of the West coast. The terminal event was Robert Bruce's murder of John Comyn in the Franciscan Church at Dumfries in 1306. Bruce, who was then the senior surviving claimant to the throne, was subsequently crowned King of Scotland. The MacDonalds, who by that time had been allied with the Bruce family for about 20 years, did not oppose Robert's actions.[20] To the MacDougalls, however, who had been allied for just as long a time with the rival Baliol faction, the murder of John Comyn was the murder of a kinsman.[21]

For the second time in 40 years, descendants of the ancient Clan Cormac were to take up arms on opposing sides as they found themselves swept up in the struggle for the Crown of Scotland. During the days following the murder of John Comyn, Maolmhuire, the chief of the MacMillans sheltered Bruce at his home of Ben Lawers in the Highlands. Angus MacIntosh, whose people would later dominate the southeastern approaches to Inverness, was also an early supporter of the Bruce cause. In the islands, Sean Ewen MacKinnon, Torquil MacQuarrie, and MacPhee of Colonsay would follow Angus Og MacDonald. Angus MacNab of Glen Dochart was a brother-in-law to John Comyn and would ally his clan with the MacDougalls against Bruce.

Initially things did not go terribly well for Robert Bruce. He was defeated first by the English at Methven and then again at Dail Righ by John of Lorn, Alexander MacDougall's son. With his army scattered, Bruce barely escaped with his life, becoming a fugitive needing shelter and protection. Eventually he made his way to the West coast where he sought the help of his old allies, the MacDonalds. Angus Og, giving up his allegiance to the English, offered Bruce asylum in Saddell Castle, but only for a short time. For greater security, Robert Bruce was moved to Dunaverty at the south end of Kintyre, and then on to Rathlin Island off the North Coast of Ireland.[22] Angus Og was a powerful and resourceful ally who may have assigned as many as 33 galleys to Bruce's service.[23] While under Angus Og's protection, Bruce was able to spend the last months of 1306 and early 1307 safe and reasonably comfortable.

The island galley fleets gave Bruce a real strategic advantage over his English opponents. The galleys had the capacity to move large numbers of men or supplies quickly and efficiently through the islands or along the coast. With the galley fleets at sea and on the alert, the islands were almost impregnable. In an effort to stop the Islanders' increasing harassment of the English supply fleets, King Edward I ordered his admiral, Hugh Bisset, to destroy all the galleys in the Hebrides which belonged to the accomplices of Bruce. Unfortunately for the English king, his admiral, in spite of his efforts, was not able to capture nor destroy many, if any at all, of the island galleys.

Bisset's failure enabled Angus Og's fleet to transport a force of island warriors to Arran early in 1307. The Islanders dragged their sturdy galleys across the isthmus between Kintyre and Knapdale at Tarbert, avoiding the treacherous navigation around the Mull of Kintyre. Robert Bruce's rendezvous with his supporters in the vicinity of Loch Ranza, at the northwestern tip of the island, went smoothly. Bruce had no difficulty finding Douglas, who, along with his men, had been waiting on Arran for Bruce's arrival. While the command of the island warriors was given to Donald MacDonald, it is very likely this fleet was again marshaled by Sean Ewen MacKinnon, the chief who had successfully commanded the island fleets against the MacRuairis only seven years earlier.[24]

Ferried to the mainland with Douglas's men, the Islanders acquitted themselves well in the retaking of Bruce's own lands of Carrick. However, the occupation of Galloway did not proceed as smoothly. The occupying army under the command of Angus Og and King Robert's two brothers, Thomas and Alexander Bruce, was defeated by Sir Roland MacDowell, Lord of Galloway. Although Angus Og and most of the Islanders escaped, both Thomas and Alexander Bruce were captured. In spite of this early setback, the fortunes of Robert Bruce continued to rise as his influence and authority quickly spread over Scotland. By 1308 the Comyns were defeated at Inverurie, the Northeast was subdued by the "harrowing of Buchan," and Galloway was retaken.

Bruce's invasion of Argyll in 1309 destroyed the MacDougall fortunes in Scotland once and for all.[25] At the same time, this invasion once again changed the politics of the West Coast. Although the destruction of the power and authority of the MacDougalls of Argyll ended the generations' old dispute over the island of Mull, it introduced many more serious problems for the inhabitants of the West coast. Bruce went on to consolidate his authority on the Scottish mainland while the island galley fleets kept a close watch on English activity in the Irish Sea. The galleys continued to raid English supply and transport ships and harassed the Isle of Man.

The position of the descendants of Clan Cormac in the Isles was strengthened as the three island families of that kindred--MacKinnon, MacQuarrie, and MacPhee, were undisturbed in their possessions and all now supported Angus Og.[26] Those island families who had previously followed the MacDougalls, offered the Bruce their support, the most notable of these being the MacLeans. For the first time since the MacLeans arrived on Mull, they and their MacKinnon neighbours would have supported, albeit tentatively, a common lord. But, as the lands of Argyll were parcelled out as fiefs to Bruce's supporters, Skye became part of the Earldom of Ross, while the district of Garmoran became a fief held by the MacRuairies for ship service.

By early 1314 Robert Bruce had taken most of the castles in Scotland that had been held by the English. The most important Scottish stronghold that remained in English hands was Stirling Castle, and it was under siege by the Scots. Under terms of an agreement made between Edward Bruce and the stronghold's English commander, Stirling would surrender if not relieved by July 24, 1314. During the evening of the 22nd of July, England's King Edward II who had marched north with a large army to relieve the siege was camped at Falkirk.[27] The next day the two armies faced each other across the Bannock Burn, south of Stirling. King Robert I's army was numerically much smaller than King Edward II's but was much better led and held a stronger position.[28]

On the 23rd of July, the English knights made two successive assaults on the Scottish army. The first was a frontal assault led by the Duke of Gloucester, and the second was a flanking attack by the English commander Clifford. Both of these attacks were repelled by the Scottish spearmen who inflicted large numbers of casualties on the attackers.

By mid afternoon the English attack was halted and their leaders retired to hold a council of war. It was decided the English army should stay where it was and that camp would be set up somewhere between the confluence of the Bannock Burn and the Forth. Fortunately for the Scots, the English chose to place their camp between two streams, the Bannock Burn and the Pelstream Burn. The area between these streams opened toward the Scots' positions on a hill to the west of the English camp. Incredibly, the English chose to establish a camp in an area that was surrounded on three sides by water and bog or soft ground.

The next morning the Scots celebrated mass, breakfasted and, thereafter, Bruce knighted James Douglas and Walter the Stewart. The Scots then formed into a line of battle and advanced slowly, but deliberately, toward the English camp. Leading on the right was Edward Bruce's division. To its left was Randolf's division from Moray and Ross. The far left of the line was held by Sir James Douglas and Sir Walter the Stewart's Lanark men. The Islanders under Angus Og, along with the men of Carrick, made up the reserve division commanded by Robert Bruce himself.

The heavily-armoured English knights, seeing the advance of the Scottish spearmen, promptly charged the leading division. Edward Bruce's men held firm. Their lines bent with the force of the shock but did not break. Sir James Douglas and Randolf, seeing that Edward Bruce's division was in danger of being overwhelmed, ordered their divisions up to support him.

The English army rapidly became tangled and confused in its attacks as the space to manouevre between the streams steadily became more crowded before the Scots' steady advance. The English commander, in an attempt to drive the Scottish line back, ordered his archers to form on the right of Edward's army and shoot into the left flank of the advancing Scottish line. This movement was noticed by the captain of the Scottish cavalry, and the archers, unprotected by either cavalry or infantry, were promptly dispersed by the Scottish horsemen. The Scottish spearmen now pressed forward, secure there was no danger on their flanks.

Recognizing that this was a decisive moment, Bruce ordered the reserve division into the attack on the crowded English knights to the left of the Scottish line. Angus Og's Islanders, carrying the relics of Saint Columba before them, advanced steadily into the fray. With this added reinforcement, the impetus of the Scottish line increased. With each step the Scots took forward, they crowded the English army into an ever smaller area between the two streams. When Edward's lieutenants realized the battle was lost, a knight, Sir Gilles Argentine, led Edward II, who was mounted on his horse, safely from the field. When the king was safe, Sir Gilles turned to him saying, *"Sire....I am not accustomed to flee and I will continue no further. I bid you adieu."* He then turned to enter the fray. Meeting the attacking Islanders in the thick of battle, Sir Gilles was killed by MacPhee of Colonsay.

A few months after the victory of Bannockburn, Bruce held a parliament at Cambuskenneth. It was at this meeting that Bruce intended to reward those who aided him in the fight for his crown and to rebuke those who did not. An act was passed stating that all who died fighting against King Robert Bruce or who failed to come into the king's peace, were *"disinherited forever of lands...and status."*[29]

The forfeited estates were to be used to reward Bruce's followers. Angus Og was confirmed in possession of Islay, parts of Kintyre, Mull, and Tiree as well as other MacDonald territories. He was granted Lochaber, Morvern, Ardnamurchan, Daor, and Glencoe. The Campbells were granted Loch Awe and Ardscotnish and the keeping of Dunstaffnage Castle, but Bruce kept the castle of Dunaverty as a royal keep.[30] Other grants were made to the Stewarts, the Earl of Ross, and to Thomas Randolph, who led a division of spearmen at Bannockburn.

There is no record, however, of the oft repeated story of Bruce giving the MacKinnons a grant to their lands on Skye.[31] Indeed there is no mention, whatsoever, of any of the descendants of the island branch of Clan Cormac receiving any reward from King Robert Bruce. But not all branches of Clan Cormac fared well under the new regime. The MacNab lands of Glen Dochart and Strathfillan were forfeit and their charters were destroyed. The Campbell grants included much of what was occupied by the MacGregors. Those MacGregors who resisted the change in authority, were harassed, hounded, and chased by the Campbells who were based at their new castle at Kilchurn.

In the Isles, the time following Bruce's victory at Bannockburn was generally one of peace. Robert Bruce tried to win over the Islanders peacefully and, in an effort to impress them, he emulated King Magnus of Norway's earlier feat. He had himself borne across the isthmus at Tarbart in a galley with the sail hoisted.[32]

Although the armed strength of the islands was not required during this period, the galley fleet was busy. In 1315 Edward Bruce unsuccessfully attempted to drive the English out of Ireland, and in 1317 he was reinforced by his brother, King Robert I.[33] During these invasions, Angus Og's fleet was useful to the Bruces. But ominously for the MacKinnons, there is also a record from this time of the Bruces using the considerable naval power of the MacLeans.[34]

On Angus Og's death in 1318, the MacRuairis made a bid for control of the Hebrides, challenging the MacDonalds for the leadership of the Geal. The struggle for domination was intensely fought, lasting some seven to twelve bitter years. The war finally ended sometime between 1325 and 1330 with the forfeiture of the MacRuairi estates and a marriage alliance between the two belligerent families.[35]

These tumultuous years were to begin a change in the focus of the Clan MacKinnon. Their long-established influence with the Lords of the Isles would begin a slow decline, while their involvement in the affairs of the monastery on Iona increased. Finnleach, who was appointed Abbot of Iona in 1320, may have been the first MacKinnon to head the monastery on that island. Gillibride, who succeeded Sean Ewen to the MacKinnon chiefship, was destined to be the last MacKinnon master of the household to the Lords of the Isles.[36]

End Notes
Chapter 6

1. Rixson, D., *The West Highland Galley*, Edinburgh, Birlinn, 1989,12.

2. The MacKinnons may have been involved in the early commercial life of the Hebrides. Their stronghold of Dunara on the Northern Coast of Mull, overlooks an artificial harbour with a quay and jetties as well as two boat noosts. Neither the Norse longships nor the island galleys would have required jetties or a quay. Only the heavy cargo carrying Knoor would have required such facilities.

3. The importance of galleys can be shown from the fact that they were frequently put under the protection of the church. Sails were often hung to dry in churches, partly because the buildings were the largest available and partly for security.

4. Angus Mor MacDonald was the great grandson of Somerled, the founder of the Kingdom of the Isles. Angus Mor was styled Angus of the Isles. On King Alexander III's death, March 19, 1286, Scotland, as was now usual, was engulfed in turmoil. The contestants for the Scottish throne were Robert Bruce, 5th Lord Annandale, known as *"the Competitor,"* grandfather of the future king of Scotland, also named Robert Bruce, in the south, and the Comyns in the north. The situation was made worse when Robert Bruce, *"the Competitor,"* was not made one of the *"Guardians of the Peace"* who were appointed by the government of the child monarch, Queen Margaret of Scotland, *"the Maid of Norway."* Therefore, Robert Bruce, *"the Competitor,"* together with his eldest son, Robert Bruce, the 1st Earl of Carrick, and father of the future King of Scotland, Robert Bruce, led the revolt of the Turnberry Band in September 1286. The *"Guardians of the Peace,"* realizing the threat to the Scottish Crown, mobilized an army for its defense in the spring of 1287. By the time of the army was mobilized, the revolt of the Turnberry Band was no longer a threat but the Band itself continued. The Turnberry Band agreed to support Richard de Burgh, the Earl of Ulster, and Thomas de Clare against their enemies in Ireland.

5. Alexander MacDougall of Argyll was married to a daughter of John Comyn, who was married to John Baliol's sister. Thus, John Baliol's sister was Alexander MacDougall's mother-in-law and John Comyn was his father-in-law.

6. It appears that Dugald MacRuairi, who had been given Mull, Coll, and Tiree in 1230 by King Haakon IV, lost them in 1264 when Alexander III invaded the Hebrides. Mull may have reverted to the ownership of the MacDougalls as they gained the support of King Alexander III in the Isles. At the same time, Angus Og MacDonald, the younger brother of Alexander Og, also claimed to have inherited Mull. This conflict, developing as it did over thirty years, would have presented a real diplomatic challenge for Finlaec and his son Sean Eoghan who were the MacKinnon chiefs at the time.

7. MacDonald, R. W., *Kingdom of the Isles*, Tuckwell Press, East Lothian, 1997, 131 states that three sheriffdoms were created out of the old Kingdom of Man and the Isles:

    1. Skye (Skye, Lewis, Uist, Barra, Eigg, and Rhum) given to William, Earl of Ross;

    2. Lorn (Ardnamurchan to Knapdale) given to Alexander of Argyll;

    3. Kintyre (Cowal, Kintyre, Bute) given to James the Stewart,

8. Even though Alexander of Argyll joined the other Scottish nobles in swearing loyalty to England's King Edward I at Elgin in 1296, he was not trusted. King Edward I gave Alexander of Monteith, the son of the Earl Walter, a commission to take possession of all of the castles, fortifications, and lands of Alexander of Argyll. The only descendant of the ancient Clan Cormac known to have submitted directly to King Edward I, is MacNab of Glen Dochart, whose name appears on the Ragman's Roll.

9. Alexander Og MacDonald, in a complaint to King Edward I, claimed Alexander of Argyll was raiding and plundering MacDonald lands "and the men living in the same lands were killed and fires set and many other evils were done." See MacDonald, R. A., *Kingdom of the Isles*, Tuckwell Press, East Lothian, 1997, 161.

10. For more information see: MacDonald, R. A., *Kingdom of the Isles*, Tuckwell Press, East Lothian, 1997.

11. Duncan was the son of Angus, the son of Reginald, the Lord of Struan, from whom the Robinsons are descended.

12. Called Eogain Ruadh or Red Ewen by the MacDonald historians.

13. These galleys, which were of 40 oars each, were about 120 feet in length, making them twice the size of the galleys commanded by MacKinnon. Their freeboard, which was higher than that of the smaller galleys, and the ability to transport more warriors, made them a significant military threat. MacPhail, *Highland Papers*, Vol. 1, Edinburgh, T. & A. Constable, 1914.

14. Lauchlan sought the safety of his allies, the MacDougalls, and Duncan escaped to the Braes of Lochaber, where he served as prior of Killmanivais before returning to a life of crime.

15. Rixson, D., *The West Highland Galley*, Edinburgh, Birlinn, 1989, 16-17.

16. Gille-Iosa, the second Chief of the MacLeans, is known to have died c.1300. He is almost certainly to have been killed fighting either Sean Ewen MacKinnon's fleet, Hugh Bisset's fleet or during Angus Og's invasion of Kintyre and Bute. Gille-Iosa was succeeded in the chiefship by Malcolm.

17. Some records indicate Alexander Og was killed around the year 1299 fighting the MacDougalls. However, there are some MacDonald historians who indicate he was killed fighting with the MacDougalls against Bruce in 1308. If Alexander Og was not killed in 1299, then it is clear that he changed sides and joined the MacDougalls. His younger brother, Angus Og, must have had enough influence with the body of the MacDonalds to enable him to oust Alexander and lead the clan.

18. Edward I empower the admiral and captian. of his Cinque Port fleet to receive Alexander of Argyll, his sons, John and Duncan, Lauchlan MacRuairi, *and "all other husbandmen and middle-class people of the islands of Scotland."* Angus Og holds Lauchlan MacRuairi's sons hostage against his good behavior.

19. Lauchlan MacRuairi was still a powerful lord in the Isles. In 1304 he began to rebuild his shattered fleet by ordering every davoch of land in his territory to furnish a galley of 20 oars.

20. In 1286 Angus Mor MacDonald and his son Alexander were members of the "Turnberry Band" with the Bruces, James Stewart, and some others. Angus Og MacDonald continued the relationship begun by his father and older brother.

21. John Comyn was the father-in-law of Alexander MacDougall.

22. Dunaverty was the principal home of Angus Og who was styled "King of the Isles."

23. These galleys would, undoubtedly, have been under the command of Sean *Eogain* (Ewen) MacKinnon.

24. MacKinnon's involvement is mentioned in Sir Walter Scott's epic, *The Lord of the Isles*. Canto IV, verse VII

> *A summons there to war and wrath*
> *To the brave clans of Sleat and Strath*
> *And, ready at the sight,*
> *Each warrior to his weapons sprung,*
> *And targe upon his shoulder flung*
> *Impatient for the fight*
> *MacKinnon's chief, in warfare grey,*
> *Had charge to muster their array*
> *And guide their barks to Brodick-Bay*

There is some artistic licence taken by Sir Walter Scott in composing this verse. Skye was, at this time, a part of the Earldom of Ross. The MacLeods held Dunvegan, but the MacKinnons had yet to settle Strath or the MacDonald's Sleat. Barbour, in his early poem, "The Bruce" says that the landing on Arran was at Lochranza. Donald MacDonald was the son of Alexander Mor.

25. Bruce invaded Argyll, from both the land and sea, with an army of 10-15,000 men. Castles Sween and Dunstaffnage were both quickly captured and the ancient lands of Lorn were laid waste. Alexander MacDougall of Argyll and his son John were defeated and given safe passage to England. See MacDonald, R. A., *Kingdom of the Isles*, Tuckwell Press, East Lothian, 1997, 179.

26. Of the other descendants of Clan Cormac, Bruce offered Ewen ban MacMhuirich, Chief of the MacPhersons, land in Badenoch in return for his support. Ewen had three sons; Kenneth of Cluny, Ian of Pitmain, and Gilles of Invereshie, hence the name "Clan of the Three Brothers."

27. Edward II succeeded his father, Edward I, who died in 1307.

28. Brown, *History of the Highlands*, Fullarton, Edinburgh,1885, 149, gives the names of the chiefs who were present as MacKay, MacIntosh, MacPherson, MacLean, MacGregor, MacKenzie, MacQuarrie, MacFarlane, Cameron, Sinclair, Campbell, Sutherland, Robertson, Grant, Fraser, Ross, and Munro.
Rev. MacKinnon, D. D., *Memoirs of Clan Fingon*, Lewis Hepworth, Tunbridge Wells, 1899 gives the names of the Chiefs as MacNab, MacAulay, MacPhie, and MacKinnon.
MacLean, J. P., *History of the Clan MacLean*, Clarke & Co, Cincinnati, 1889 35, names 21 chiefs who fought for Bruce and says that MacNab, Cumming and MacDougall were there for the English.

29. MacDonald, R. A., *Kingdom of the Isles*, Tuckwell Press, East Lothian, 1997, 184.

30. Rixson, D., *The West Highland Galley*, Edinburgh, Birlinn, 1989, 27. The grants made in respect of Lach Awe and Ardscotnish were on condition that the Campbells supply the use of a 40-oared galley. A 40-oared ship would have been about 120 feet in length, a very large ship for the Hebrides at that time. McWhannell, D., "Ship Service and Indigenous Sea Power in the West of Scotland", *West Highland Notes & Queries, Aug. 2000, Society of West Highland And Island Historical Research, Breacachadh Castle, Coll*, 5.

31. A tale mentioned Rev. MacKinnon, D. D., *Memoirs of Clan Fingon*, Lewis Hepworth, Tunbridge Wells, 1899.

32. There was said to have been a superstition among the Highlanders at this time that the rightful king would sail over the isthmus at Tarbart. King Magnus sailed over this same isthmus when he was dividing up the Western Seaboard with King Alexander I. It may be that superstition and history were confused here.

33. Edward Bruce had use of a fleet of some 300 ships. Most of these would have been Hebridean galleys.

34. McWhannell, D., "Ship Service and Indigenous Sea Power in the West of Scotland," *West Highland Notes & Queries, Aug. 2000, Society of West Highland And Island Historical Research, Breacachadh Castle, Coll, Coll*, 8.

35. The title used to refer to the chief of the MacRuairis was Righ Innse Gall, while that referring to the MacDonalds was Righ Airir Goide. John MacDonald is thought to have been the first to have used the Latin title "Dominus Insularum." The Latin form may simply have been a rendering of the ancient "Righ Innse Gall." John MacDonald enjoyed the same authority and loyalty in the islands as his predecessor, Angus Og. Both were considered independent rulers by the Islanders, regardless of larger external alliances.

36. At this time there was no sharp division between church, political, and economic spheres. The abbots were drawn from the local aristocratic families. Abbot Finlaec was confirmed by the Bishop of Dunkeld at Tippermore near Perth. See: Macquarrie, A. & MacArthur, E. M., *Iona through the Ages*, Society of West Highland & Island Historical Research, Highland Printers, Inverness, 1992, 15.

Chapter 7
THE LORDSHIP OF THE ISLES

In the face of the volatile politics of the times, the new Lord of the Isles, John MacDonald, was determined to preserve the independence of his rule. To this end he allied himself with the English King Edward III and the Baliols--both were long-time opponents of the Bruces. The death of King Robert Bruce in 1329, along with the victories at the battle of Dupplin Moor in 1332, and Halidon Hill the next year, put Edward Baliol on the throne of Scotland.

In return for his support, Baliol granted the Lord of the Isles the island of Skye, a grant which was confirmed in 1336. Under Edward Baliol's reign, the fortunes of Clan Cormac seemed to be on the rise. The MacNabs, whose charters had been destroyed by Robert Bruce in 1314, had their fortunes partially reversed in 1336 when King Edward Baliol granted Gilbert MacNab the lands of Bothmachan or Bowain in northern Argyll.

By the time David Bruce, Robert Bruce's son and heir, reached his majority in 1343, Edward Baliol had lost the Scottish Crown. The young Scottish King David promptly pronounced John MacDonald, then Lord of the Isles, and his MacRuairi allies forfeit because of their support for the Baliols. In a vain attempt to destroy the authority of John MacDonald and his father-in-law, Ranald MacRuairi, King David granted the best part of their lands to Angus MacIain of Ardnamurchan and returned some of the MacDougall lands forfeited to Robert Bruce. Neither MacIain nor King David had the ability or the power to assert any authority over these lands, so they remained safely in the hands of their former occupants. John MacDougall, however, exercised a natural authority over the lands returned to him.

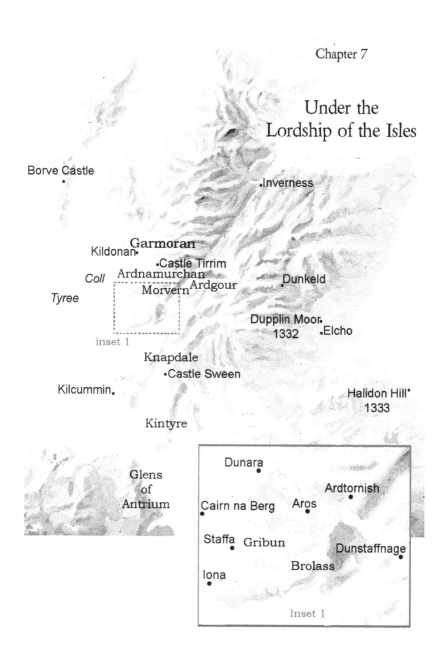

Chapter 7

Under the
Lordship of the Isles

Borve Castle

Inverness

Garmoran
Kildonan
Castle Tirrim
Coll   Ardnamurchan
Morvern Ardgour
Tyree

Dunkeld

Dupplin Moor
1332   Elcho

inset 1

Knapdale
Castle Sween

Kilcummin

Halidon Hill
1333

Kintyre

Glens
of
Antrium

Dunara

Ardtornish

Cairn na Berg   Aros

Staffa Gribun

Dunstaffnage

Brolass

Iona

Inset 1

To hold the throne of Scotland against a hostile England, King David soon realized that he would need the support of both the MacDonalds and the MacRuairis, so he returned the forfeited lands to its former owners. John MacDonald was confirmed in all of his lands except Kintyre, Knapdale and Skye. Skye was returned to the Earldom of Ross, and the feudal superiorities of Kintyre and Knapdale were held by the king. Perhaps by way of compensation for the territories that he kept, King David granted John MacDonald certain lands in Lorn, which had formerly belonged to the MacDougalls.

Feeling that the West coast of Scotland was now secured by loyal allies, King David's thoughts turned to the ongoing struggle with the English. Attempting to take advantage of the English King Edward III's absence in France, King David summoned his armies in preparation for an invasion of England.

Ranald MacRuairi mobilized his men and set off almost immediately to join the king. While on their journey, Ranald and his band of warriors stopped a little south of Perth at Elcho monastery to spend the night under its shelter.[1] The details of what occurred next have been blurred by the passage of time. At Elcho, old animosities apparently surfaced and Ranald MacRuairi was murdered by the Earl of Ross who had also decided to spend the night at the monastery.[2] With their chief murdered in cold blood, the MacRuairis naturally did not want to go on so they returned to bury their chief near his home. The Scots continued to marshal their forces and then, under King David II, marched off without the MacDonalds, MacRuairis, nor any of their associated clans, to defeat at Neville Cross in Yorkshire.

These were not normal times in the Highlands.[3] John MacDonald, having just been given a great deal of McDougall and MacRuairi land, would have to populate it with loyal men. Under normal circumstances the kin-based clan system then operating in the Isles, would allow Lord MacDonald to simply grant the key positions in these new territories to his kinsmen. But for a number of reasons, there were not enough MacDonalds to go around. Several of the leading MacDonalds had backed the wrong side in the civil wars and found it prudent to retire in Ireland. Then in 1349 the Black Death raged through Scotland. The Highlands were nearly as affected by the plague's rapid spread as were the more populated Lowlands and a great many died. John MacDonald needed allies to fill these vast territories, and he would find them on Mull.

It was about this time, and under these unsettled circumstances, that the MacKinnons were dealt one of the greatest blows, politically, they would ever receive.[4] This story concerns John MacDonald, Lord of the Isles; Gillibride, the chief of MacKinnons; and the two sons of John Dubh, then chief of the MacLeans.[5]

During the season of Lent, John MacDonald and his household were, as was MacDonald's custom, at his castle of Ardtornish on the coast of Morven. Knowing MacDonald was there, MacDougall of Lorn sent the two sons of John Dubh MacLean, Hector and Lauchlan, as ambassadors to discuss the remaining differences over the island of Mull and perhaps convince MacDonald to relinquish his claim to the island. Following their arrival at Ardtornish and an immediate but unfruitful meeting with MacDonald, Hector and his brother Lauchlan retired to dine alone.

Gillibride MacKinnon, who was master of the Lord of the Isles' household, was the officer responsible for insuring the MacLeans were properly fed and looked after during their stay at Ardtornish. For their meal, however, MacKinnon gave them bread and guthrim.[6] The guthrim was so brittle that it was not easily taken up with their only utensils, their long knives.[7] John MacDonald, who happened by and saw the difficulty the MacLean brothers were having with their meal, asked MacKinnon to give them some other food, which would have been easier for them to consume. MacKinnon, who evidently did not care much for the MacLeans, replied that, *"if they could not eat their meal as it was, they should put on the nabs of hens with which they might gather it up easily"*. This insulting reproach deeply offended the MacLeans and they resented MacKinnon for uttering it .

Later that day John MacDonald was to solemnise the festival of Pasch at his castle of Aros, which lay across the sound from Ardtornish, on the island of Mull. MacDonald left ahead of his household, taking a small boat for himself, leaving MacKinnon to organize the household's crossing in the great galley.

When the preparations were completed, MacKinnon proceeded to the shore to board the great galley and follow MacDonald to Aros. The MacLeans took this opportunity for revenge and calling MacKinnon aside as if to talk, they stabbed him to death. MacLean's men quickly boarded the great galley and set out after MacDonald himself.

The Lord of the Isles, seeing his galley approach and thinking it was MacKinnon and his household, did not speed up nor otherwise attempt to evade them. Coming alongside the smaller boat, the MacLeans and their men leaped into it, captured the Lord of the Isles and made him a prisoner. However, once they had him captive, the MacLeans found themselves at a loss regarding the best way to proceed.

Taking MacDonald's galley, they rowed down the sound of Mull towards Dunstaffnage, the home of MacDougall of Lorn. On their arrival the MacLeans found MacDougall at dinner, so they waited outside the castle with their prisoner to be called into his hall. Upon being told the MacLeans were waiting at the gate with MacDonald as prisoner, MacDougall is reported to have commented he was *"happy MacDonald was safe and was looking forward to having him prisoner."* However, he felt the MacLeans *"were over bold in this attempt and so forward in their insolence, he would have to bridle them later"*.

MacDougall had a young son who had been fostered by John Dubh MacLean and this son had heard his father's remarks. Quickly going outside, the young MacDougall told his foster brothers, Hector and Lauchlan, what his father had said. The MacLeans, realizing the severity of the situation they now faced, offered to release the Lord of the Isles and join MacDonald's service if he forgave them for their rash behaviour. When MacDonald agreed to their request, the MacLeans quickly hustled him back into his galley and rowed back to Mull.[8] The Lord of the Isles was as good as his word, for he not only gave both Hector and Lauchlan land on Mull, but made Lauchlan chamberlain of his household and allowed him to marry his daughter.

Gillibride MacKinnon was buried on Iona with his ancestors, but the consequences of his murder would take years to settle. It can well be imagined that Ewen, who succeeded the murdered chief, would not have been happy with the reduction in his clan's prestige. There may very well have been more than one attempt to revenge Gillibride's murder and a feud may even have erupted.[9]

We are left with only snippets of tradition, which appear to be from this time. One states; *"MacKinnons and the MacLeans at the commencement of this feud encountered one another at a place called Doire Shuaig, near Gribun, and the MacKinnons were victorious until one of the MacKinnons a powerful man connected with the MacLeans by marriage, deserted his Clan, and all his friends followed suit. Consequently the MacKinnons were routed and the Chief made for this*

Grave slab of Gillibride mac Fhionghuin

cave. *The descendants of this deserter were for ever after, and are to this day, called Clann Sith Ruidh (Angliĕè, "always running"), in Mull, and were despised by their brother Clansmen both in Mull and Skye"*

Another traditional story also discusses a feud saying;[10] *"MacKinnons of Gribun were at feud with the MacLeans, and the Chief was in hiding in the Gribun Cave for a long time, but MacLean was informed of where he was, and some of MacKinnon's friends came to know that MacLean was going to the cave to take him next day and afterwards put him to death; so the night before, his friends got a boat and had him taken to Staffa where he remained in a cave in that island which is still called MacKinnon's Cave, on the south side opposite Fingal's Cave. Here he remained until he made his escape to Skye."*

That Lauchlan and Hector MacLean, who had so callously murdered Gillibride at Ardtornish, had escaped the Lord of the Isles' retribution for their audacious acts, has been commented on by many historians. However, there may have been several good reasons for John MacDonald's leniency toward these murderers.

There is evidence the Lord of the Isles may have been related, by blood, to the MacLeans. Lady Margaret MacDonald, daughter of John MacDonald, married Lauchlan MacLean of her own free will, but needed a dispensation from Rome absolving them from excommunication incurred by marrying without banns.[11] The need for the dispensation would indicate a forbidden familial relationship between Lauchlan and Margaret. Besides the familial relationship which may have been close, John MacDonald also had good strategic reasons for confirming the MacLean presence on Mull.[12]

Cementing the relationship with the MacLeans would have brought one of the more important MacDougall allies firmly into the MacDonald fold and, moreover, would have ensured the whole of Mull was occupied by friendly clans. The MacLeans may also have been given their lands and offices in return for a much needed sea-service to the Lordship. The MacLeans had developed a considerable naval presence that was strong enough to have interested King Robert Bruce as early as 1317.[13] Twenty years later it may have been even greater. John MacDonald would have needed these galleys to protect the sea routes of the Lordship of the Isles. In exchange for such service, MacDonald granted Hector MacLean the constabulary of Duart. Hector's brother, Lauchlan, was granted the north end of Jura and half of the constabulary of Dun Chonnuill and Dunkerd as well as the constabulary of Cairn na Berg. As if this were not enough, John MacDonald named Lauchlan chamberlain of his house, a post which traditionally should have been a MacKinnon honor, and took him under his patronage.[14]

There is no doubt, that at a time during which he needed all of the loyal followers he could muster, John MacDonald would have made every effort to patch up the differences between these two neighbouring but hostile clans. The ill feelings between the MacKinnons and the MacLeans would likely have been strong, and it may have been no easy task to ease the tensions existing between them.

An indication of the importance that John MacDonald placed on these competing clans may be gleaned from the following, undoubtedly, politically-motivated marriages; Lauchlan MacLean married Margaret, the daughter of John MacDonald; Gillibride MacKinnon, the son of the feuding Chief Ewen MacKinnon, married Lauchlan MacLean's cousin; and Gillibride's son Neil married Maria MacLean, daughter of the murderer, Lauchlan MacLean.[15] Thus the three families, MacKinnon, MacLean, and MacDonald, were in the end joined by blood relationships.

That there were many severe and lasting concerns caused by the murder of Gillibride MacKinnon, can be inferred by the terms of a 1356 treaty drawn up between John MacDonald, Lord of the Isles, and John McDougal, Lord of Lorn. This treaty, which was ratified during Ewen's chiefship of the MacKinnons, was a formal confirmation of the authority MacDougal had been given over his lands several years before. The treaty contains several clauses that are of considerable interest.

In a direct reference to Gillibride's murder and to discourage any further acts of violence, two of the clauses read: *"anyone doing murder will be exiled by both"* and *"wrongdoers would not be allowed to transfer from the retinue of one party to the other unless willing to answer for their wrongdoings."*[16]

To protect both the MacLeans and the MacDougalls from attacks by revenge-seeking MacKinnons, another clause stipulates that the keeping of Cairn na Berg, a small but virtually impregnable castle in the Treshnish islands, *"would never be given to the keeping of anyone named MacKinnon."* Cairn na Berg situated atop a rock surrounded by ocean, was, by the means available at the time, unassailable. From such a stronghold the MacKinnons could have ravaged, with impunity, the MacLean's lands on the East Coast of Mull or MacDougall's tenants on Coll and Tiree.

By 1357 John MacDonald had become a firm supporter of the Scottish King David and a confirmed enemy to the English. There is seemingly no record that there where MacKinnons with the Lord of the Isles when he led his Highland army to France to help the French in their struggles against the English Black Prince, but the MacKinnons were very active at home.[17]

Peter, the Abbot of Iona, died in 1357, giving an opportunity for the MacKinnons to once again exercise their influence in the affairs of the monastery. Neil, the MacKinnon chief, had a younger brother, Fhionghuin, who was elected Abbot by the community of Iona and was confirmed by William Russell, then Bishop of the Isles.[18] Fhionghuin's tenure proved to be controversial from the very start.

The Bishop of Dunkeld, possibly feeling that Fhionghuin's confirmation by the Bishop of the Isles somehow diminished the

MacKinnon   MacLean

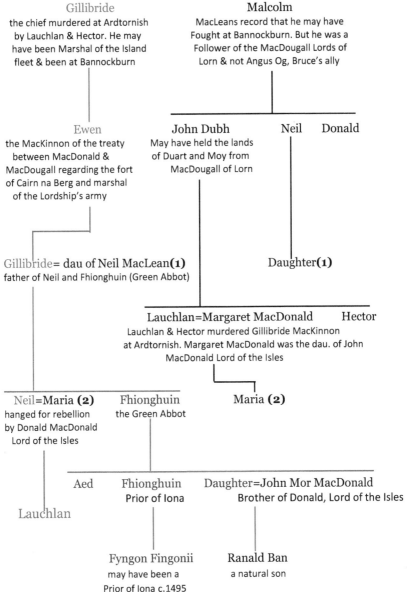

Gillibride
the chief murdered at Ardtornish
by Lauchlan & Hector. He may
have been Marshal of the Island
fleet & been at Bannockburn

Malcolm
MacLeans record that he may have
Fought at Bannockburn. But he was a
Follower of the MacDougall Lords of
Lorn & not Angus Og, Bruce's ally

Ewen
the MacKinnon of the treaty
between MacDonald &
MacDougall regarding the fort
of Cairn na Berg and marshal
of the Lordship's army

John Dubh   **Neil**   **Donald**
May have held the lands
of Duart and Moy from
MacDougall of Lorn

Gillibride= dau of Neil MacLean**(1)**   **Daughter(1)**
father of Neil and Fhionghuin (Green Abbot)

Lauchlan=Margaret MacDonald   **Hector**
Lauchlan & Hector murdered Gillibride MacKinnon
at Ardtornish. Margaret MacDonald was the dau. of John
MacDonald Lord of the Isles

Neil=Maria **(2)**   **Fhionghuin**   **Maria (2)**
hanged for rebellion   the Green Abbot
by Donald MacDonald
Lord of the Isles

Aed   **Fhionghuin**   **Daughter**=John Mor MacDonald
       Prior of Iona   Brother of Donald, Lord of the Isles

Lauchlan

Fyngon Fingonii   **Ranald Ban**
may have been a   a natural son
Prior of Iona c.1495

influence of Dunkeld, obtained a commission from Rome to replace him in 1359.[19] This effort to remove Fhionghuin from office was unsuccessful, perhaps this was because of the support the MacKinnons had from the Lord of the Isles. Because memories of Gillibride's murder were still relatively fresh, It may be probable that John MacDonald's support for the Abbot Fhionghuin was, in some measure, a way of ensuring peace on Mull.

Apart from the MacKinnon/MacLean feud, the period of John MacDonald's Lordship was generally a quiet one in the Isles. On the mainland though, because of the volatile Scottish politics of the era, life was hard for the descendants of Cormac. The MacMillans were expelled from their ancient homes in the vicinity of Loch Tay, but found a friend in John MacDonald who gave them a charter to their territories in Knapp. It was Alexander MacMillan, 5th of Knapp, who obtained Castle Sween through marriage to Erca MacNeil. Alexander renovated the castle, adding the round tower and the beautifully-carved MacMillan's Cross.

MacMillan's Cross

On the whole, for a time at least, the relationship between the Lordship of the Isles and the Kingdom of Scotland was fairly smooth. King David, who had been captured by the English at the battle of Neville's Cross some eighteen years previously, was ransomed and returned home. Shortly after arriving in Scotland, he confirmed John MacDonald in all of his possessions, regardless of how they were obtained. John MacDonald was made Constable of Edinburgh Castle, Stewart of Scotland, and special envoy to Flanders.

This was a period of political sparring between the Steward of Scotland and King David, during which time the Steward sought to increase his power by making alliances with various Scottish nobility. John MacDonald had astutely grasped the opportunity to ensure an advantageous relationship with Scotland by divorcing Amie MacRuairi and marrying Marjory, the Steward's daughter. In his divorce from Amiee MacRuairi, John MacDonald had the full support of the Steward of Scotland and the Council of the Isles. One of the councillors, in particular, MacInnis of Ardgour, who was John's foster father and closest adviser, was very forward in his support of the divorce.[20]

The dissolution of the marriage seems to have been disputed, and Amie and her sons did not forget nor forgive the part played by MacInnis in their family affairs. During the year 1358 Amiee gave a commission to Donald MacLean to kill MacInnis and his sons, for which act Maclean would receive MacInnis's castle of Kinlochaline, along with its lands of Ardgour, as his own.[21] The murders were committed in the Lord of the Isles' castle of Ardtornish, where the MacInnis' had been staying.

The loss of their chief and his male heirs, not only deprived the Clan MacInnis of its leadership and its land, but may have prompted the beginning of the MacInnis's long relationship with the Clan MacKinnon.[22] Amie MacRuairi lived for a great many years after the divorce. She was doubtless a strong-willed woman and is credited with the founding of a number of religious houses and churches as well as building the castles of Tirrim in Moidart, and Borve in Benbecula

The relationship between John, Lord of the Isles, and King David ended abruptly in 1366 when John MacDonald returned to the Isles in protest over the heavy taxes that were levied to pay King David's ransom. The commonly-held opinion of the time was that the agreed amount of the ransom was more than the Scottish nation could bear. The differences were mended three years later in 1369, without bloodshed, when John MacDonald and King David signed a treaty of friendship at Inverness.

The ascension of King Robert Stewart to the Scottish throne in 1371, for the first time created a familial relationship between the Lordship of the Isles and the Kingdom of Scotland. On his divorce John MacDonald kept the MacRuairi lands that Amie had brought with her into the marriage. John's possession of these lands was confirmed by King Robert immediately after his succession to the throne. The new king also confirmed the grant John had made to the MacLeans of the castle of Kinlochaline and the lands of Ardgour.[23]

Because John MacDonald now had two completely separate and competing families, one with Amie MacRuairi, and the other with Marjory Stewart, the succession to the Lordship was of greater complexity than usual.[24] To maintain the peace of the Isles, both families and their supporters had to be accommodated.[25]

It appears the Islanders generally felt that because John, the first son of Amie MacRuairi and John MacDonald, had died sometime before 1369, his younger brother Ranald was the legitimate heir to the Lordship. But, King Robert II of Scotland was still alive and it was considered probable, by many on the Council of the Isles, that he would have been extremely offended had one of his own grandchildren not succeeded to the Lordship.

At a special meeting of the Council of the Isles held at Kildonan on the island of Eigg in 1386, Ranald MacDonald gave over all of the rights and privileges of the Lordship to his younger half-brother Donald. Donald, who was the eldest son of John MacDonald's marriage to Princess Marjory of Scotland, appears to have had the full support of the Council of the Isles. In return, Ranald was given the charters for all of the MacRuairi lands which had belonged to his mother. Donald's inauguration ceremony was held in the presence, and with the consent of the principal men of the Isles, but apparently not all of the MacDonalds were in agreement with the outcome.

Donald's accession to the title *"The MacDonald"* and to the lordship was not entirely uncontested. Some MacDonald historians think that Godfrey, the youngest son of John MacDonald and Amie MacRuairi, may have actually been the author of a coup for which the MacKinnons would later be held responsible.[26]

John Mor, Donald's younger brother, was at this time married to the daughter of Fhionghuin, the Abbot of Iona.[27] John Mor had been given large grants of land in Kintyre and Islay as his share of his father's patrimony. But it was later said, Fhionghuin, his father-in-law, had convinced him he was actually entitled to all of the islands south of Ardnamurchan. During the years 1388/89 John Mor and Fhionghuin enlisted the aid of Fhionghuin's brother Neil, Chief of MacKinnon, as well as a number of others, including Lauchlan, Chief of MacLean; and Malcolm, then Chief of the *Siol Tormod*, (MacLeods of Harris), to help press John's claim.[28]

When Donald, Lord of the Isles, received warning of the forces uniting against him, he quickly assembled the formidable might of the Hebrides to quell the revolt.[29] There is no record of pitched battles nor valiant deeds taking place during this rebellion. John Mor, Donald's brother, seeing the size of the army gathered against him, attempted to escape from his home in Kintyre to the safety of Galloway, but he was pursued by Donald's agents. Hastily leaving Galloway, John fled to Ireland where he made a home in the Glens of Antrim. Donald, having disposed of the threat from his brother and disbursed the rebel army, returned to Islay.

After a time John Mor MacDonald, the MacKinnons, and MacLeods, seeing that their cause was lost, thought it best to save what they could of their interests by having John Mor ask for Donald's mercy. To that end they proceeded to Kilcummin on Islay, where Donald was residing. When John Mor came to his brother's seat, he is said to have prostrated himself on the ground. Donald rose from his seat, took up his brother and embraced him kindly. It was then, or shortly afterwards, that the cause of the rebellion was blamed upon sedition spread by Fhionghuin, the Green Abbot, and his brother, Neil MacKinnon. Neil, the MacKinnon Chief was tried, convicted and hanged while Fhionghuin, whose life was only spared because he was a clergyman, was confined to Iona for the rest of his days.

The execution of Neil and the incarceration of his brother Fhionghuin on Iona, would not be the end of this unfortunate affair. In either revenge or an act of defiance, the Abbot Fhionghuin's two sons, Aed and Fhionghuin, murdered their own cousin, Neil, one of the executed chief's, two sons. All we now know about this unfortunate victim is that he was fostered by Donald Ferguson who, at this time, was a well-regarded and influential individual of rank. Aed was eventually tracked down and killed by Lauchlan MacKinnon, the murdered Neil's brother, and Donald Ferguson. The abbot's other son also named Fhionghuin, however, lived to become Prior Claustralis of Iona.[30] The relationship between John Mor MacDonald and the Abbot Fhionghuin's daughter ended, leaving a natural son about whom history is silent. John Mor went to Ireland, where he married Margery Bisset, heiress to the Glens of Antrim.[31]

Following his father's death, Lauchlan MacKinnon was inaugurated chief of the clan and given charge of their lands. In about 1625 an early MacDonald writer, known only as *"The Sleat Historian,"* wrote that this was the period in which the MacKinnon lands in the Ross of Mull, and perhaps Gribun, were exchanged for those of Mishnish.

That Lauchlan MacKinnon was given a charter for these new lands by the Lord of the Isles, is demonstrated by his title, Mac Fingon of Mishnish.[32] There are no existing rental records for the island of Mull dated before 1561. It is thought that at this time the whole rent of the Ross of Mull, Gribun, and the islands of Inch Kenneth and Eorsa belonged to Iona. The removal of the MacKinnons from these districts may have been viewed by the Lord of the Isles as a way of protecting the assets of the Abbey of Iona.

Under Lauchlan's chiefship, the relationship between the MacDonalds and the MacKinnons was, to some degree, restored. However, possibly due either to the Abbot Fhionghuin's intrigue or their active part in the rebellion, the MacKinnons had lost the high status which they previously enjoyed in the Lordship. Lauchlan MacLean of Duart, who is mentioned by the Sleat Historian as one of the rebels, was rewarded with three charters granted in 1390.[33] These grants awarded Lauchlan MacLean the large estate of Brolas in the Ross of Mull, and much land in Gribun, as well as Tiree--all of which may have been traditional MacKinnon districts. MacLean was also awarded the offices of *"fargramannach"* and *"armannach"* on the island of Iona, as well as that of steward in the household of the Lords of the Isles, all offices which would have formerly belonged to MacKinnons.[34]

Although they lived transient lives, the chiefs of the Clan MacKinnon, like the other warrior chiefs of the Isles, preferred a fortified dwelling as their primary residence. Dun Ara occupies the summit of one of the prominent rock outcroppings in the vicinity of Sorn point on the Northwestern Coast of Mishnish. The view from Dun Ara is stupendous. One can see everything on the sea from the point of Ardnamurchan to the islands of Tiree and Coll in the west.

The dun was constructed by enclosing the entire summit of the outcropping by a stone wall cemented with a course lime mortar. The stone wall enclosed four separate buildings, one of which was undoubtedly a great hall. The entrance was by way of roughly-laid stone steps in a narrow rock gully on the southeast side of the outcropping. Scattered around the base of the outcropping, was a small agricultural township of at least eight buildings and their associated fields and gardens. To the southwest of the dun, lies an artificial harbour incorporating a small jetty, quay and two boat noosts. The Chiefs of MacKinnon would have made their homes at Dun Ara when they were not accompanying the Lord of the Isles on his visits to the other island chiefs or enjoying the hospitality of their tenants.

Dunara on the Isle of Mull

The Lordship of the Isles was both powerful and confident under Donald MacDonald. He was proving to be a strong, decisive, and wise leader. Donald proved more than able to defend the independence of the Isles from any foreign authority, while simultaneously expanding his own. He has been credited with bringing Skye into the Lordship of the Isles, but the campaign against that island may have actually begun several years earlier as part of the Green Abbot's attempted coup. Godfrey, the youngest son of John MacDonald and Amie MacRuairi, took control of the ancient lands of the MacRuairis on his brother Ranald's death in 1389. Between 1389 and 1390, the period of the rebellion against Lord Donald MacDonald, Godfrey styled himself as "of Sleat" and was resident at Dunscaith on Skye, which may have been taken either by force or received as gift from the MacLeods.

End Notes
Chapter 7

1. Elcho monastery was completely destroyed during the reformation.

2. Amie MacRuairi, the wife of John MacDonald, was the sister of Ranald MacRuairi. The murder of her brother made Amie heir to the MacRuairi lands of Garmoran and other northern estates. John MacDonald, was a cousin of Ranald MacRuairi, as well as Amie's husband, gaving John two claims to Ranald's estates.

3. MacLean-Bristol, *Warriors & Priests*, Tuckwell Press, East Lothian, 1995, 26.

4. Grant, I. F., *The Lordship of the Isles*, Moray Press, Edinburgh, 1935, 116.

5 The basis for this story is undoubtedly true. MacPhail *Highland Papers,* Vol. 1, Edinburgh, T. & A. Constable, 1914.

6 Guthrim was butter and curds mixed together, prepared during the harvest and preserved until Lent.

7. As spoons and forks were not commonly available, the only utensils used at this time were knives. Spoons were introduced as eating utensils by the German nobility about the mid 16th century. Before this period in time, it was common that any liquid served in a bowl was consumed by drinking. Forks did not enter into common usage in the British Isles until well into the 18th century, although they were used by European nobility as early as the 17th century.

8. For the MacLean version of this story, see Appendix 3.

9. Steer and Bannerman have called Gillibride's gravestone one of the most satisfying pieces of medieval Scottish sculpture. It gives a good illustration of the type of armour worn at the time: A high-pointed bassinet with a raised keel. The neck and shoulders are protected by mail (the throat is protected by double ring type, while the shoulders are protected by contrasting bands). The body is protected by a knee-length aketon (quilted surcoat) made of two thicknesses of linen, cotton or leather, stitched together in vertical rows. The tube-like spaces are stuffed with wool, rags, grass, or whatever was handy. They wore gauntlets on their hands, poeyns on their knees and greaves or schynbalds. On their feet they had pointed sabatons and spurs. Gillibride is shown carrying a spear and wears a sword with elongated quillions on a belt around his

waist. He carries a small heater-shaped shield painted with his arms, which are a galley with sails furled and a flag at the stern on the top half of the shield. The lower half is divided and on the left is an otter chasing a salmon, and on the right is a lion. This type of armour gave good protection against sword thrusts or blows and was well suited to use in galleys. This style of armour was in common use until about 1450, but in the Highlands may have been used as late as 1520.

10. Rev. MacKinnon D. D., *Memoirs of Clan Fingon*, Lewis Hepworth, Tunbridge Wells, 1899, 14.

11. MacLean, J. P., *A History of the Clan MacLean*, Robert Clark, Cincinnati, 1889, 38.

12. MacLean-Bristol, *Warriors & Priests*, Tuckwell Press, East Lothian, 1995, 26-27.

13. The MacDougalls were a predominant sea power in the Hebrides until their defeats by Ewen MacKinnon and Angus Og MacDonald. One could speculate here that the MacLeans had been the marshals of the fleet for the MacDougalls, making it likely that, when MacDougalls lost their authority, the MacLeans retained control of the fleet.

14. Lauchlan's descendants were to hold this post for the next century. Lauchlan was a man of considerable influence at this time. Lord John MacDonald's decision may have been influenced in part by Lauchlan being a foster son of John MacDougal of Lorn.

15. Rev. MacLean, Sinclair, A., *Celtic Review, Vol. IV*, 32, claims that Lauchlan MacLean and Margaret MacDonald were married c. 1365, which is considerably later than when the marriage was proposed. This may be accounted for, however, by the length of time required to obtain a letter of permission from the pope. Lauchlan and Margaret could easily have arranged a *handfast* union before 1356 and then legitimized it when permission arrived in 1365.

16. See Appendix 4 for this treaty and translation of the relevant clauses. Munro, J. & Munro, R. W., *Acts of the Lords of the Isles,* Blackwood, Pillans & Wilson, Edinburgh, 1986, 5.

17. John MacDonald was captured and the Highlanders suffered severe casualties when they and their French allies lost the Battle of Poitiers, September 19, 1356. The English captured John MacDonald and imprisoned him in England for over a year before releasing him on December 16, 1357, so it may have been early 1358 before he would have been back in the Western Isles.

18. See Appendix 5 for documents relating to MacKinnons and Iona.

19. MacQuarrie, A., "Kings, Lords, and Abbots", *Transactions of the Gaelic Society of Inverness, LVIII, 1984*, 363.

20. MacDonald, *The Clan Donald*, MacDonald, Midlothian, 1978, 68.

21. Donald was the son of Lauchlan MacLean who, with his brother Hector, murdered Gillibride MacKinnon.

22. MacInnis tradition believes that five galleys, each carrying a warrior and his family, escaped to Skye.

23. The Lordship of the Isles, under the leadership of John MacDonald, was now as large as it had been under his ancestor, Somerlid.

24. By the first marriage, there was: John, Ranald, Godfrey, and Mary. Children of the second marriage were: Donald, John Mor, Angus, Alexander, Hugh, Margaret, and Agnes. There are existing charters signed by Lord John MacDonald, dated 1373 and 1376, which would indicate the succession to the Lordship had been agreed to long before his death.

25. Margaret MacDonald, daughter of Amie MacRuairi and John MacDonald, was married to Lauchlan MacLean of Duart.

26. MacDonald, D. J., *The Clan Donald,* MacDonald, Midlothian,1978, 281.

27. MacLean-Bristol, *Warriors & Priests*, Tuckwell Press, East Lothian, 1995, 31.

28. Ibid, 31.

29. The MacLeods were not subjects of the Lord of the Isles. Their lands were part of the Earldom of Ross. The MacLeods would have been looked on as foreign invaders in what was otherwise a domestic coup attempt.

30. The MacDonald historian who recorded this story wrote that Fhionghuin's sons killed Lauchlan's brother. But it seems odd that, if Fhionghuin, the son of the Green Abbot, were involved in such a crime, he would have been allowed to live. It is more likely the murder was committed by Aed and the sons-in-law of the Green Abbott.

31. This was how the MacDonalds initially obtained their lands in Ireland.

32. Rev. MacKinnon, D., *The Chiefs and Chiefship of Clan MacKinnon*, Portree, 1931. Lauchlan witnessed a charter for the Lord of the Isles in 1467 and signed as Lauclan mac Fhionghuin of Mishnish. It should be noted that, because Neil MacKinnon had married Maria MacLean, his son Lauchlan would have been a cousin once removed from Alexander, Lord of the Isles. Thus, Lauchlan mac Fhionghuin of Mishnish was a second cousin once removed to John Lord of the Isles and Earl of Ross.

33. Hugh MacDonald, a Skye seannachie, wrote a *History of the MacDonalds* some time shortly after 1625.

34. In 1574 Mary MacLean, the Prioress of Iona, granted teinds of the parish of Inch Kenneth to MacLean of Duart. The Parish of Inch Kenneth consisted of the islands of Inch Kenneth and Eorsa, as well as much of Gribun--all ancient MacKinnon lands. The MacKinnons, however, did retain land which belonged to Iona. In 1665 MacKinnon of Strathswordale is recorded as having free rent of abbey lands valued at 200 pounds, for which he was expected to pay a tax for the relief of beneficial persons. With the destruction of the records of the Lordship of the Isles, it is now impossible to know exactly what these offices were or what importance was attached to them. See: Munro, J. & Munro, R.W., *Acts of the Lords of the Isles,* Blackwood, Pillans & Wilson, Edinburgh, 1986.

Chapter 8
THE ISLE OF SKYE

There are several existing accounts of the struggles for Skye and they differ significantly in detail.[1] It is difficult for us now to ascertain if there was only one large invasion of the island or several smaller ones. We also cannot now determine how long the campaign or campaigns may have lasted. What is abundantly clear, is that the MacDonalds were initially taking advantage of the divisions in the MacLeod leadership.

Owing to the youth of Chief Iain Borb, a "tutor" had been appointed to direct the affairs of the clan. Under the direction of Iain Mishealbhach, or John the Ill-Fated, as the tutor is now known, the clan was considerably weakened and could not muster adequate resources to defend itself.

Skye had been part of the Earldom of Ross almost continuously since 1309 and was held, except for the castle of Dunscaith, entirely by the MacLeods. Sometime between the years 1391 and 1395, Donald MacDonald dispatched a strong force under the command of his brother, Alasdair Carrach, to invade the island.[2] The MacDonald invasion may have been in retaliation for the MacLeod support of the MacKinnon-led coup of 1388, or it may have been an assertion of the MacDonald claim of 1332, or perhaps was the result of both.[3]

There were at least two large-scale raids during the struggle for Skye that were recorded, but undoubtedly there were many others that were not. During one of these raids the invaders evaded MacAskill of Ru'n Dunain, the constable of Dunscaith and the hereditary coast watcher of the MacLeods, enabling the MacDonalds to approach the west coast of the island without warning.

Landing at Loch Eynort in Minginish, the invaders moved rapidly north. At Carbost they turned east, moving through Drynoch, leaving a wide swath of destruction in their wake. Following the River Drynoch eastward then turning southward, the raiders came face to face with a powerful body of MacLeods who had hurriedly gathered to oppose them. The MacLeods were ably led by Tormod Coil, the son of Murdoch MacLeod of Gesto, and one of the MacAskills acted as his lieutenant.

Tormod routed the main body of MacDonalds and gave chase to the survivors. MacAskill, leading another party of MacLeod warriors across the island, seized the MacDonald galleys at Loch Eynort, cutting off the MacDonald retreat. On finding that their galleys had been captured, the few surviving MacDonald warriors scattered and fled. The MacDonalds suffered a very high number of casualties during this raid and the battle at the head of Loch Sligachan is regarded as a great victory by the MacLeods.[4]

During another raid the MacDonalds are said to have invaded Sleat and captured the castles of Camus and Dunscaith by storm. They then moved north with the intention of capturing Dunvegan. At Feorlig the MacDonald raiders again encountered a large body of MacLeods from both Skye and Lewis. Under the able command of the chief of the Siol Torquil, the MacLeods once again routed the MacDonald raiders.

Although the MacLeods had won these two engagements, the pressure on them must have been unrelenting. The young heir to the chiefship of Dunvegan, Iain Borb MacLeod, was even taken to Lewis for safety. Sometime later at the MacLeod stronghold of Rodel, he was declared chief of the clan.[5]

The results of the MacLeod victories were short-lived as they could not long withstand the forces mustered by the Lordship of the Isles. The young Iain Borb, Chief of Dunvegan, visited Donald MacDonald on Islay to acknowledge his superiority over both Skye and North Uist. At some time during the fight for Skye, Godfrey MacDonald, the son of Amie MacRuairi, was expelled from Dunscaith, possibly when the MacDonalds stormed it, and he went on to live out the rest of his life in the castle of Tirrim in Moidart.

It was either during, or shortly after, these tumultuous events that the MacKinnons moved to Skye. It is difficult for us now to ascertain how or even why the MacKinnons actually came into possession of the lands of Strath. It could have been a reward for some service rendered during the invasion of Skye or given as compensation for lands lost on

Mull since the arrival of the MacLeans. It could also have been to deliberately create a buffer zone between the MacLeods to the north and the MacDonalds in Sleat.

Chapter 8

Fight for the
Isle of Skye

Dunvegan

Feorlig

Drynoch

Loch
Sligachan

Carbost

Dunakin

Loch
Eynort

Corry

Kilmarie

Dun Ringill

Castle Camus

Dun Sgathaith

There are several interesting points to note regarding Strath. It naturally separates the MacDonald lands of Sleat from the MacLeod territories to the north. The ancient keep of Dunakin is positioned to guard access to Skye from the mainland and may be the most strategically placed of all of the strongholds on the island. Dunakin was built during this period by Donald, the Lord of the Isles. However, what is most significant for the MacKinnons is that the agricultural land in Strath is among the best on Skye.

One of the more well-known stories regarding the acquisition of these lands concerns the original owners of Strath and a young Chief of MacKinnon and is as follows:[6]

"The old chief Gillies, had one son and a nephew staying with him. The young heir to the chiefship of the MacKinnons meantime being a near relation was sent to him to be fostered. Gillies' son and the nephew were wont to go hunting together. One day they ferried over to Pabay to try the hunting in that Island of dense woods. The two hot-headed youths quarrelled. So fierce was the quarrel that words came to blows and blows to sword thrusts. And so determined was each to kill the other that each succeeded too well. Their bodies were conveyed from Pabay to Castle Ringle, and buried in Kilmaree churchyard where their graves no one can today point out. The sorrowing father made his foster child-the young MacKinnon - heir of all his estates. The lucky heir possessed Dunakin (now called Castle Moyle and Dunringle along with what we now call the Parish of Strath. which henceforth was called The Strath of the MacKinnons."

The home of the MacKinnon chiefs on Skye was indeed primitive. Dun Ringill or, as it became officially known, *Castle Findanus,* is an iron-age structure originally built some 2,000 years ago on the Southeast Coast of the Strathaird peninsula. The MacKinnons found the fort, which was situated on a cliff edge overlooking the sea, in ruins and rebuilt its defensive wall, surrounding ditch, and constructed two new buildings in its interior. They also established a small farming township just to the north of the ancient fort. This old dun, and the community it protected, would be the principal residence of the MacKinnon chiefs for the next 300 years.

The leader of one of the five MacInnis families to settle in Skye is thought to have been a Neil MacInnis.[7] Neil and his family may either have already been settled in Strath or arrived on Skye from elsewhere shortly after the MacKinnons took possession of their new estate.[8]

Lauchlan, who was the MacKinnon chief at the time, is said to have welcomed Neil into his service, giving him employment as a cowherd.

Ruins of Dun Rimgill

The MacKinnon chief, who was renowned for his physical strength, had a great bow that only he could draw to its farthest extent. Observing that MacInnis was also physically powerful, Lauchlan gave the bow to Neil and was amazed that he too could easily draw it. Sometime later when MacKinnon was entertaining MacLean of Duart and some other chiefs, he invited each of them to draw the bow. All of them failed. The MacKinnon chief then called Neil MacInnis and he again drew the bow with no difficulty. MacKinnon declared with some satisfaction, *"What a strange thing it is when even my cowherd can draw the bow."*

In return for their services as his bowmen, MacKinnon granted Neil and his descendants a farm at Surdale in Strath, where they raised a herd of Highland cattle. Henceforth, Neil became known as "Niall a'bhogha" or Neil of the Bow. The descendants of this Skye branch of the MacInnis clan later adopted the arm and bow as their symbol.[9]

Neil was a proficient archer when he arrived on the Isle of Skye and soon had the opportunity to show his MacKinnon host how great his abilities really were. A large band of MacLeods had the misfortune to raid Neil's farm and attempted to drive his cattle northwards towards Trotternish. Neil caught up with the raiders in the vicinity of Corry, where he single-handedly attacked them. Twelve of the MacLeods were quickly killed, the others fled, and Neil recovered his cattle. Neil's descendants were also gifted archers. Because of the superior abilities exhibited by the family, they were given a prominent place in the gentry of Strath as bodyguards to the MacKinnon chief. The field in which the MacInnis' practised is still known today as Archer's meadow.

Strath with a view of Beinn na Callach & Corry

With the fortunes of the MacKinnons again on the rise, the complaints against the Abbot Fhionghuin of Iona began once more. In an attempt to answer his critics, Abbot Fhionghuin issued a statement in 1397 claiming he was freely elected to his office by the community of Iona and, moreover, had been confirmed by William Russell, the Bishop of the Isles, who had died some ten years before.

Fhionghuin's response did not silence his critics, but seemed only to incite them. In 1403 one of the complaints described the Abbey as being collapsed. Then in 1405 John MacAllister, the Prior of Iona, brought the most lurid accusations against Fhionghuin.[10] John claimed Fhionghuin was living with concubines, squandering the assets of the Abbey and that he had used the Abbey's endowments as dowries for his daughters when marrying them to local noblemen. Not only were these nobles benefiting from the income of the church, but, it was claimed, they were also unlawfully holding both monastery property and land.

The charges that Iona was being allowed to fall into ruin would be repeated again in 1408, 1421, and 1428. That Fhionghuin was able to retain the office of Abbot during this period was likely due to the support of Donald MacDonald, the Lord of the Isles.

Kirkapoll Cross
The inscription reads: "This is the cross of the Abbot Fingonius and his sons Fingonius and Eage

In other areas of influence, however, the MacKinnons did not regain lost ground. But in 1409 Lauchlan MacKinnon witnessed a charter granted to Hector MacLean of Duart, giving him lands on the island of Coll.[11] The fact that Lauchlan MacKinnon was requested to witness a charter given at Ardtornish, indicates he was present, as part of the household of the Isles, and recognized as a noble of the realm, even though he may not have held an office.

It was during this period, c. 1390, that there is the first mention of clans in the Highlands by Scottish government documents. The cultures in the Highlands and Lowlands had grown apart over the last two hundred years and were now significantly different. The Highlands and Islands remained essentially a traditional Celtic society, while the Lowlands had increasingly given up its heritage to became a feudal state.

A Lowland description of Highlanders written in 1384 offers a glimpse of how they were viewed below the Highland line: *"The Highlanders and people of the Islands are a savage and untamed nation, rude and independent given to rapine, ease loving, of a docile and warm disposition, comely in person but unsightly in dress, hostile to Anglic people and language".*[12]

When Alexander Leslie, the Earl of Ross, died in 1402, his vast estates passed to his four-year old daughter Euphemia, who was under the protection of her grandfather, the Regent Albany. Donald MacDonald, who was married to *Mariota* (Mary) Leslie, did not trust the regent's motives and announced his intentions to support his wife's claim to Ross.[13] As long as the young Countess of Ross was alive and well, there was no need for either side to press their respective position.

Possibly, as the result of political maneuvering by her grandfather who wanted his son to have the earldom, Euphemia entered the secluded life of a monastery, thus giving up her title to the estates before she took possession of them. Donald's wife, Mariota, who was next in line after her niece, now came forward to claim her inheritance.

However, Albany flatly rejected her claim to the earldom on the grounds that it would be unacceptable to increase the power and wealth of Donald's already extensive Lordship. The actual ownership of the northern earldom remained in question for a number of years until the title was assigned. Because Mariota was not the head of any of the kin groups or clans then resident in Ross, there was very little sympathy or local support for her claim. The only way that Mariota and Donald could pursue the claim would be by force of arms followed by a policy of populating the territory with loyal followers. That this was the anticipated avenue Donald would take, was reflected by a meeting of the lords of Northeast Scotland in December 1410. Kildrummy Castle, where the possibility was discussed, was the largest and strongest fortification in the Northeast and the home of the Earl of Mar.[14]

During early 1411 Donald MacDonald called the island clans together and began to gather his forces at Ardtornish Castle. As the clans gathered, only the strongest men were selected to join the expedition. Surely Lauchlan mac Fhionghuin and the MacKinnons, who were renowned for their physical strength, would have been offered a place in this army. The Islanders were led by the most renowned Highland warriors of the day; Hector MacLean of Duart; Iain MacLeod of Dunvegan; and Donald Dubh, chief of the Camerons. By midsummer, Donald and his captains had completed the selection of an expeditionary force numbering some 6,000 men.

The expedition embarked in Highland galleys and sailed north to Loch Carron. Landing at Strome, they marched, unopposed, through Ross towards Dingwall. Learning of the landing and the direction taken by the Islanders, Angus Dubh MacKay, chief of his clan, hastily gathered together some 2,500 men and quickly marched to Dingwall's defense.

The two armies arrived at about the same time. Although Angus MacKay bravely maintained the offensive, he was not able to check the Islanders' advance. During the ensuing battle, which was fiercely contested by both sides, Angus Dubh was captured and his brother, Rory Gallad, was killed. The Cathness men were routed and the survivors forced to retire. Thus, after a rapid march and only one battle, Donald had captured and garrisoned Dingwall.

The Islanders now proceeded south toward Beauly. Receiving word that the Frasers were gathering at Dounie Castle, Donald moved off in that direction to engage and defeat them. On their arrival at Inverness, the Islanders found the city prepared and stoutly defended. Unfortunately, during the course of the attack the bridge over the River Ness and half of the city was burned to the ground.

Caithness

Earldom
of
Ross Beauly· ·Dingwall Strathbogie Buchan
Loch · Strome ·Inverness · Garioch
Carron Dounie Rhynie Gap· ·Harlaw
Castle Inverurie·

Mar ·Aberdeen
Kildrummy· Mearns
Castle

Angus

Ardtornish Castle

Lordship
of the
Isles Argyle Struggle
for the
Earldom
of
Ross

The thick black smoke rising above Inverness would have left no doubt, for the men out watching the tracks through the hills, as to what direction the Islanders would be approaching from. By this time the island army, which had been reinforced by volunteers from all over the North and West, numbered about 10,000 men. Although the MacKays had been beaten, the Frasers were only scattered and the MacKenzies were attempting to retake Dingwall. The Islanders' garrison at Dingwall proved too strong for the attackers and the MacKenzie chief was himself taken captive as he attempted to capture Donald's governor.

Marching south on the road to Aberdeen, the army of the Lordship marched by Enzie, Strathbogie, and Garioch. It is doubtful that Donald would have allowed much pillaging while progressing through Ross, but once south of Inverness and into hostile territory, the army resorted to its usual method of remuneration. Garioch, in particular, which belonged to the Earl of Mar, was severely plundered

Even though the Islanders' attack had been expected, the speed of their advance clearly was not. On their approach, the Earl of Mar issued a summons for the forces of the South to muster at Inverurie, which strategically covered the approaches to both the Earldom of Mar and Aberdeen. On the 23rd of July, Mar's army began assembling at the old motte and baillie of Inverurie.

Although Donald's march was expected and its direction known, the lateness at which Mar's muster was called ensured that not all of the units summoned would arrive on time and, in fact, many arrived the following day.[15] We do not know the exact numbers nor makeup of the army assembled to resist the Islanders, but it is thought to have been composed largely of spearmen and contained about 1,000 mail-clad knights and their retainers.[16] By the time Mar's forces began to gather, MacDonald's army was at Harlaw making camp only two and a half miles away from them.

On the evening of the 23rd of July, the Highland army was somewhat dispersed, perhaps confident in their numbers and the strength of their position. The next morning at dawn, the Earl of Mar ordered a general assault on the Islanders' camp. The Lowlanders formed into two battles, the first of which was made up of the men of

Angus and the Mearns, led by Sir Alexander Ogilvy, the sheriff of Angus. The second battle, led by Mar himself, was made up of the armoured gentry of the Eastern shires. With the royal standard bearer, Sir James Scrymgeour, leading the van, this army marched off on foot to meet Donald's men at Harlaw.

The Islanders, who had scattered for ease of plundering and gathering food, were caught off guard by Mar's advance. Because each man knew his place by the officers of his clan, Donald MacDonald was able to quickly marshal the clans into a line of battle. Hector MacLean led the right of the line, Callum Beg and the MacIntoshes were on the left, and Donald MacDonald, with the MacLeods, took the centre.[17] When the Islanders were ready, the Bard of the Isles, MacMhuirich, to the accompaniment of the *clarsach* (Gaelic harp), recited the battle chant to inspire the clans and give them courage.

> *O children of Conn of the Hundred Battles*
> *now is the time for you to win recognition,*
> *O raging whelps,*
> *of Sturdy bears,*
> *O most sprightly lions,*
> *O battle loving warriors,*
> *O brave heroic firebrands,*
> *the children of Conn of the Hundred Battles,*
> *O children of Conn remember*
> *Hardihood in time of battle*

As the men of Angus advanced, the force of their rush initially pushed the lightly-armed clansmen backwards as they absorbed the shock of Mar's attack. The Islanders recovered quickly, however, and counterattacked. Led by Tormod and Torquil MacLeod, and Gilpatrick MacRory of Obeolan, the charge was so fierce that the whole Scottish army was driven back a full three acres or more.[18]

As Mar's armoured knights moved forward to support the Angus spearmen, the Lowland line held, and the conflict became a battle between crowded masses of individual soldiers hacking and slashing at each other. As Forbes' Division which was the last unit to join Mar's army came up, they marched right into the fray, taking a position on the right of the Lowland line.

As the day went on, the clansmen continued to press the Lowlanders by flinging themselves forward in a series of desperate charges. The Earl of Mar, with his division of armoured gentry, penetrated deep into the heart of the massed Islanders, but eventually even the knights were overwhelmed by the sheer numbers of their opponents.

As the fighting raged around them, Hector MacLean and Irvine of Drum met face to face. They fought so fiercely that their respective friends were not able to reach them in time to offer help and the two of them collapsed foot to foot.[19] The Lowland army was slowly annihilated by the relentless fierceness of the Islanders. The fighting was stopped only by the coming of night and, with it, both sides backed away from the field.

The *Annals of Loch Ce* proclaimed this *"a great victory by MacDomnhaill of Alba over the foreigners of Alba."* If it were indeed a victory, it was dearly bought. Casualties were high on both sides. The clansmen had lost some 900 men, among whom were Hector MacLean and his son Lauchlan, Lauchlan MacMillan, Gilpatrick MacRory, Callum Beg MacIntosh, the Red Priest of Carloway, MacQuarrie of Ulva's son, three gentleman of the Monroes and two gentlemen of the Camerons.[20]

The casualties on the Lowland side may have been as high as 600 killed. One would have been hard-pressed to find a noble house in the vicinity that hadn't lost at least one member during the battle. Donald MacDonald, however, gathered his army and retired back to the Hebrides. He knew he could not hold Ross against the armoured might of the Kingdom of Scotland, but the islands were impregnable.

The Regent Albany, at the head of another Lowland army, eventually marched north. He captured Dingwall and re-established his authority throughout Ross. The next year, 1412, Albany led an ineffective invasion of Argyll, but did not attempt to take the Isles. Donald's suspicions of political manoeuvring by Albany were realized when Albany's niece, Euphemia the young heiress of Ross, renounced the earldom in favour of her uncle John, the Earl of Buchan in 1415.[21]

In 1421 Fhionghuin, the Green Abbot, was still living on Iona and there were still more complaints being made of his administration of the monastery's affairs.[22] It was still being alleged that the monastery buildings were being allowed to fall into ruin and the monastery's lands were preyed upon by *"wicked men."*[23] The wicked men the complainant referred to may well have been Fhionghuin's sons-in-law. An earlier complaint stated he had used church lands as his own, giving them as dowries for his daughters.[24]

To resolve these difficulties, but perhaps more importantly to gain the support of the residents of Ross for his claim on that earldom, Donald MacDonald appointed Dominic MacKenzie the new Bishop of Iona, thus replacing Fhionghuin.[25] To compensate the MacKinnons for the loss of the Abbacy of Iona, Donald petitioned the pope to unite certain parish churches to the Abbey and the income from these were offered to the ex-abbot. Fhionghuin, accepting the fact that he no longer had the support of the Lord of the Isles, took the offer of the parish churches. Setting Dominic MacKenzie in Fhionghuin's place was one of the last duties regarding Iona that Donald MacDonald preformed, Soon afterwards he was either retired to Iona, where he lived out his days as a monk, or died at his castle of Ardtornish.[26]

The death of the Green Abbot in 1425 did not end the difficulties the administrators of Iona were to have with his family. The very year that the Green Abbot died, his son, also named Fhionghuin, was persuaded by the Abbot Dominic to swear he would not seek to enter the monastery nor the community of Iona in any capacity.[27] To reinforce this promise and to strengthen his position in the face of MacKinnon pressure, the Abbot Dominic petitioned the pope, requesting that he not be required to receive any local noblemen into the community.[28]

Fhionghuin was active politically, as well, and seems to have been able to muster a great deal more support than did the Abbot. Also petitioning the pope, Fhionghuin asked for a papal relaxation to the promise he had given to Dominic and that he be allowed to enter the monastery. Very shortly afterward, Fhionghuin appeared with a papal mandate responding to his petition, while that of the Abbot Dominic seems to have been ignored. Fhionghuin not only secured a position in the monastery, but also succeeded in having Dominic MacKenzie excommunicated as well. Despite his excommunication, Dominic MacKenzie remained in his office as Abbot, perhaps only by the direct intervention of the Lord of the Isles, but he did have to allow the MacKinnons to resume holding positions of authority in the Monastery.

Chapter 8
End Notes

1. Although most of the stories agree on the battles which were fought, the results of the outcomes change depending on whether a MacDonald or a MacLeod recorded the event.

2. This is as related in the Bannatyne Manuscript. But Alastair Carrach was a child at the time and was very unlikely to have been the leader of this party.

3. In 1332 Edward Baloil, King of Scotland, granted Skye to the Lords of the Isles. In 1343 King David Stewart returned it to the Earl of Ross.

4. Grant, I.F., *The MacLeods: The History of a Clan*, Holmes MacDougall, Edinburgh,1959, 47.

5. Nicolson, A., *History of Skye*, Glasgow, Alex MacLaren & Sons, 1930, 32.

6. The tradition of the Gillies family having Strath is acknowledged by Otta Swire in her book, Swire, O., *Skye The Island and its Legends*, Blackie & Son, Glasgow, 1961. In her book, Swire, O., *The Inner Hebrides and their Legends,* Collins, Glasgow, 1964, 43, Otta Swire relates that the Gillies who held Strath before the MacKinnons were the descendants of Gilli who was appointed governor of Skye by the Norse Earl Sigurd of Orkney. Historically, we know that Lachlan MacKinnon was chief of the clan from 1389 until well into the 1400s, so the identity of the young man in the story remains a mystery. Rev. Lamont D., *Strath: In Isle of Skye*, Celtic Press, Glasgow, 1913, 60.

7. Nicolson, A., *History of Skye*, Alex MacLaren & Sons, Glasgow, 1930, 365.

8. The MacKinnons occupied Strath some 25 years after the MacInnis castle of Ardgour was ordered destroyed by Ami MacRuari.

9. Douglas, A., *Weekly Scotsman, 20 Sept 1962.*

10. Son of Goffred MacAlister of Ardnamurchan.

11. This same year Hector MacLean was appointed leader of the army of the Lordship.

12. Grant, I. F., *Social & Economic Development of Scotland Before 1603*, Oliver and Boyd, Edinburgh, 1930, 472.

13. Mariota was the daughter of the Countess of Ross, Euphemia, and her husband, Sir Walter Leslie. When the countess died in 1394 the earldom went to her son, Alexander Leslie. Alexander, who died in 1402, was married to Isabel, the daughter of the Regent Albany. Alexander and Isabel's four-year old daughter, also named Euphemia, was heir to the earldom on her father's death. She was under the protection of her maternal grandfather. Mariota would have succeeded to the estate if anything happened to her niece Euphemia.

14. Sadler, J., "The Reid Harlaw", *History Scotland, Vol. 2, #4, July/Aug 2002*, 35.

15. The detachment led by Sir Alexander Forbes had been securing the Rhynie Gap and only arrived during the course of the battle.

16. The Burgesses of Aberdeen only sent a small party of 36 spearmen to join Mar. It was thought at the time that one armoured knight was more than equal to a whole troop of "caterans."

17. Hector paid for the honour of leading the Islanders' right wing by granting Callun Beg MacIntosh the MacLean lands in Glengarry. Ian Borb, Chief of Dunvegan; and Ruaridh, Chief of the MacLeods of Lewis, were both present with their men. Ian Borb had threatened he would not take part in the battle unless his men were given the place of honor and he commanded the right of the center division. See appendix 6 for the Battle Chant of Harlaw.

18. Tormod and Torquil were the sons of Ruaridh MacLeod of Lewis. One account states that they, along with the Red Priest of Calloway and Lochluinn MacGillemhaoill, had marched at the head of the Highland army. The Red Priest and Lochluinn MacGillemhaoill (Lauchlan MacMillian) died in the battle, but Tormod and Torquil survived, Grant I.F., *The MacLeods: The History of a Clan*, Holmes MacDougall, Edinburgh,1959. 47).

19. Hector MacLean's body was carried to Iona for burial by *Clan Innis* (MacInnis) and MacMhuirich.

20. Although most sources claim Lauchlan MacLean was killed during the battle, others maintain he was captured and held prisoner by the Earl of Mar. During his captivity Lauchlan fell in love with and married Mar's daughter. There is a tradition, however, that claims the Maclean Chief, Hector, was the one captured and forced to marry the Earl of Mar's daughter as his second wife. See Grant I. F., *Social and Economic Development of Scotland Before 1603*, 522.

21. John the, Earl of Buchan, was the Regent Albany's youngest son. On his death in 1424, Ross was held by King James of Scotland who granted it to Donald's son Alexander.

22. The Green Abbot may have overseen the compilation of a census for Donald MacDonald. This census, now known MS 1467 or 1450, is a collection of pedigrees of the major families of the Isles and was completed during the early 1400s. It contains the earliest known MacKinnon genealogy.

23. *Collectanea de Rebus Albanicis*, Iona Club, Stevenson, Edinburgh, 1847.

24. It is interesting to note that we only know of three of Abbot Fhionghuin's children, one daughter and two sons. It seems, from the complaints against him, that he may have had a good many other offspring.

25. The MacKenzies were by now one of the dominant clans on the West Coast of Ross.

26. MacLean-Bristol, *Warriors & Priests*, Tuckwell Press, East Lothian, 1995, 50, & MacDonald, *The Clan Donald*, MacDonald, Midlothian, 1978, 89.

27. MacQuarie A. & MacArthur E. M., *Iona through the Ages*, Society of West Highland & Island Historical Research, Highland Printers, Inverness, 1992, 18.

28. The petition stated, in part, that Fhionghuin *"aspires to enter the monastery rather by reason of succession, than from devotion"* and *"the Abbot and convent at present have a bad suspicion of him because of the demerits of his predecessor since a bad tree cannot grow good fruit."*

Chapter 9
FORFEITURE OF THE LORDSHIP OF THE ISLES

On the succession of Donald's son, Alexander, to the Lordship of the Isles, King James of Scotland began a determined effort to weaken the Lordship and bring the Islanders under his authority. His first intrigue was an attempt to bribe Alexander's uncle, John Mor, to take part in a plot to overthrow his own nephew. When the clumsy effort at bribery failed, the king's envoys summoned John Mor to a meeting on Islay where he was perfidiously murdered.

King James was persistent, and in 1427 led a small army and many of the Lowland barons to Inverness where he convened a parliament. The Western chiefs, nobles, and all other vassals of the Crown were called on and requested to attend. As they arrived for the meeting, King James treacherously had the chiefs arrested; some of them were murdered on the spot, while others were thrown into solitary confinement.[1]

Alexander MacDonald, the Lord of the Isles, along with his mother, were among those captured. Alexander's cousin, Alexander MacGorrie, with whom they were travelling, was unfortunately one of those murdered. The captive Alexander Macdonald was forced to accompany the king to Perth, while his mother was imprisoned on Inchcolm in the Firth of Forth. This callous betrayal and the harsh treatment of their chiefs, aroused a great deal of resentment and anger in the islands. Alexander MacDonald was finally released by King James in 1429. Angered by the duplicity of the Crown, he immediately raised a large army numbering some 10,000 men and returned to Lochaber. The countryside was laid waste and Inverness was again burned.

In response to this invasion, King James hurriedly gathered Scotland's army and marched north to confront Alexander and the Islanders. As they watched the approach of the well-equipped and armoured Scottish army, the Macintoshes and Camerons must have realized just how vulnerable their lands were. The two clans quickly deserted Alexander's army and joined the king on the intended field of battle. The betrayal by these two powerful clans caused Alexander to reconsider his position, and he decided to withdraw his army to the safety of the Isles. In an attempt at reconciliation, Alexander surrendered himself to King James at Holyrood on Easter Sunday. Yet once again, King James showed a decided lack of good faith and had him imprisoned in the dreary Tantallon Castle.

This second incarceration of their traditional leader by King James was too much of an insult for the island chiefs to easily bear. Alexander's cousin, Donald Ballach, had no difficulty gathering the strength of the Isles at Carna in Loch Sunart during the spring of 1431.[2] This handpicked army of 6,000 men proceeded by galley to Inverskipnish where they were joined by Alastair Carrach and his 220 archers.[3]

The Islanders then moved toward the camp of the Earls of Mar, Cathness, and Huntley, which sprawled along the shore of Loch Lochy.[4] As usual, the Islanders were well-prepared and very ably led. Donald Ballach led the main battle out in front of his men, while the van was commanded by MacIain of Ardnamurchan and John MacLean of Coll. The other commanders of the body of Islanders were: Ranald Ban of Largie, Alan MacAlan of Moidart, MacPhee of Colonsay, MacQuarrie of Ulva, and MacGee of Islay. Alastair Carrach and his archers took up a position on the army's left flank as the Islanders advanced.

As the lordship's army approached the enemy camp, the Earls of Mar and Cathness, and the Chief of MacIntosh were playing a game of cards. Warned by the Earl of Huntly of the advance of Donald Ballach's men, MacIntosh replied they would play the game out and deal with the Islanders when it had finished.

They were still playing when the Earl of Huntly returned to again warn his fellow commanders of the nearness of the island army. Only MacIntosh answered, and his response was that *"he knew very well the doings of the big bellied carles of the Isles"* and made no effort to rise.[5] Angered by the arrogance and carelessness of his fellow officers, Huntly stormed out of the tent, gathered his men and ordered them safely out of the way of the oncoming fight. There is no record indicating whether the game of cards had ended or was still in progress when the Islanders' attack fell on the royal camp.

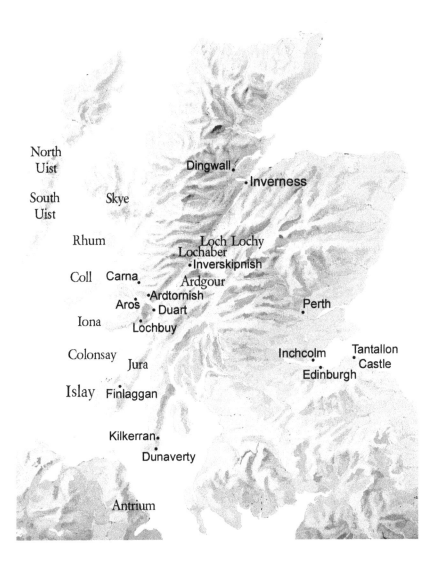

North
Uist

South
Uist

Skye

Dingwall.

Inverness

Rhum

Loch Lochy
Lochaber
Inverskipnish

Coll Carna.

Ardgour

Aros. Ardtornish
Duart

Iona

Lochbuy

Perth

Colonsay

Inchcolm

Tantallon
Castle

Jura

Edinburgh

Islay Finlaggan

Kilkerran.

Dunaverty

Antrium

The men of both sides engaged fiercely as the Scottish soldiers struggled to defend themselves. Alastair Carrach's archers fired shower after shower of arrows into the flank of the royal army. The rain of missiles was so thick that the confused soldiers were incapacitated. The battle ended almost as quickly as it had begun, and the unprepared and leaderless Scottish army was destroyed before a proper defense could be organized.[6] Donald Ballach, not forgetting the earlier abandonment of his cousin, Alexander, by the MacIntosh and Cameron Clans, ordered the merciless plundering of their lands before leading his men back to the Isles.

King James, who was under the impression that he had successfully rid the West and North of its chiefs, was furious. He raised another army and marched on Dunstaffnage Castle in Argyll but was too late to be of any use. Donald Ballach was in Ireland and the other chiefs were safely at home in the islands. King James, however, was forced to rethink his treatment of Alexander MacDonald and released him in October of 1431 in celebration of the birth of the Royal Prince James II.

Alexander MacDonald was subsequently named a warden of Scotland North by the king and spent much of his time at his castle at Dingwall. Unfortunately, Alexander continued his father's and grandfather's ill-advised policy of favouring non-MacDonalds, particularly the MacLeans, with important grants of land and offices in the Lordship. Initially this policy may have been adopted to hold the lands and status of the premier branch of the great MacDonald family undivided, but it now proved to be divisive.[7] The other branches of the Clan MacDonald and some of the smaller island clans were growing increasingly resentful of this policy and of the MacLean's almost exclusive control of the internal communications of the Lordship. There is at least one ancient story concerning a feast at Aros castle on Mull, which took place 1431, and illustrates this discontent very well.[8]

"One of the guests, John, uncle and tutor to the young Laird of Moidart, in speaking with MacLean of Duart, who was the Lord of the Isles' favourite and of whom the MacDonald kinsfolk were bitterly jealous, said that he knew that it was MacLean's office as marshal to set the MacDonalds in order tomorrow at dinner, and that he should see all the principal men there placed according to their rank and station; but if MacLean would give him a black hound that he had, he would supply his place the next day. MacLean consented to this and gave the hound.

At dinner time next day John stood at the end of MacDonald's table, and desired the laird of Ardnamurchan to sit down. Then he desired MacFinnon and Macquarie to sit, for Macquarie was an ancient Thane. Then he desired Beaton, the principal physician, then MacVurich, the poet, to take their seats. Now, said he, I am the oldest and best of your surnames here present and will sit down; as for these fellows who have raised up their heads of late and are upstarts, whose pedigree we know not, nor even they themselves, let them sit as they please. MacLean, MacLeod of Harris and MacNeil of Barra went out in a rage and very much discontented. MacLeod of Lewis remained within; the other three were determined, as soon as an opportunity offered, to be fully revenged of John MacDonald for the affront, as they thought, he had given." [9]

The MacLeans were confident of their favoured position in the Lordship under Alexander MacDonald and had became very aggressive in the acquisition of new territories. John Garbh MacLean obtained grants for the islands of Coll and Rhum as well as the districts of Ardgour, Quinish, and the old Cameron lands in Lochabar. The MacLeans of Duart are also likely to have pursued an expansionist policy of their own to supplement the gifts given them by the Lords of the Isles.

The following story may well date from this period, and discuss the defence of the MacKinnon estate of Mishnish. The first concerns a young MacKinnon clansman called Gille Reoch. [10]

"Away in the northwest of Mull, in a little boggy hollow in a loop of the Dervaig Road, just beyond the watershed at Achnadrish, there is a triangle of three small cairns, deeply embedded in the soft ground. They are reputed to mark the three leaps of the Gille Reoch-- that is, the sandy or reddish young fellow who was of the clan MacKinnon who occupied the lands of Mishnish around Tobermory. He was an expert swordsman and possessed of great agility.

One day he was surprised at this spot and hemmed in by a raiding party over from the island of Coll, all set to pay off old scores. Although defending himself stoutly he was so hard pressed that he was obliged to give the first of his three great jumps-thirty feet if it was an inch! However, he could not elude his numerous attackers except by taking a second leap, to find himself still so hemmed in that in desperation he executed his final leap, which was one of forty-five feet, and backwards at that! This landed him back at the spot from which he had originally started.

Exasperated by the agility of this nimble opponent the chief of the Coll men hurled his battle axe at the Gille Reoch who, deftly avoiding it, darted in and despatched the now defenceless chief with a cunning sword thrust. The discomfited Coll men gave up and, picking up the body of their dead leader, they retired down Glen Gorm, to their galley at Loch Mingary, leaving the Gille Reoch master of the field."

In the face of this MacLean aggression, the MacKinnons did manage to successfully hold onto their estates of Strath and Mishnish. The assault on the MacKinnons, however, took a more general turn when they lost the support of the Lord of the Isles for their control of the monastery on Iona. Much of the opposition to the MacKinnon presence in religious matters seems to have been led by Abbot Dominic MacKenzie. The Abbot, who was excommunicated during an earlier quarrel with Finguine, was now supported by the Bishop of the Isles, John Hectoris, and Alexander MacDonald.

By 1441 Alexander, Lord of the Isles, had even informed the pope by letter that he was offended that such an *"evil liver as Finguine MacFinguine, the son of an evil race of tyrants,"* should be allowed to continue as a monk on Iona. To add emphasis to his complaint, Alexander threatened to remove all relics, treasures, and the bones of his ancestors from Iona if Finguine were allowed to stay. Fyngonius Fyngonii, Finguine's son, was also removed from his office, as vicar of Saint Findoca on Coll, by the Bishop of the Isles, John Hectoris.[11]

Fyngonius Fyngonii, as it turned out, was incredibly well connected for the vicar of a small island church. He made a pact with Maritoa Suigniei, who may have been the daughter of John Garbh, the MacLean of Coll, *"that he should have her daughter as his concubine and pledged himself that he would give Maritoa and pay, the value of 40 cow lands and provide her with meat and drink and becoming raiment and treat her honorably."* [12]

The official reason given for depriving Fyngonius Fyngonii of his church, was that he had not become a priest in the stipulated amount of time. However, it may actually have had more to do with Abbot Dominic MacKenzie's efforts at curbing MacKinnon influence on Iona.[13] The MacKinnons, however, either because of support by the Council of the Isles or through sheer stubbornness, even in the face of such hostility, remained in their offices on Iona. We do not know the ultimate fate of Fhionghuin, but his son, Fyngonius Fyngonii, would eventually became the Prior of Iona.

Iona Abbey

Lauchlan MacKinnon, the son of Lachlan na Fogarach, would by now followed his father as chief of the clan. Lauchlan appears to have been an able leader, and under him the fortunes of the clan began to improve. The troubles with the MacLeans seem to have continued, new alliances were formed, and Lauchlan took an active part in the household of the Lord of the Isles. When John MacDonald, Alexander's son, was initiated as the new Lord of the Isles and Earl of Ross in 1449, it is very likely Lauchlan MacKinnon would have been present. Most importantly, Lauchlan married Margaret MacLeod of Lewis, with whom he had three sons: Neil, John, and Ewen.

As his father did before him, John MacDonald held court in both Dingwall and Ardtornish. John's administrative policies for managing the Lordship continued to encourage the promotion of clans, other than MacDonald, and particularly that of the MacLeans, to key offices.[14]

During John's rule, and not for the first time, a Lord of the Isles became drawn into the murky politics of mainland Scotland. John, ill-advisedly, took the side of the Earls of Douglas and Crawford in their grievances with the king. When the complaints led to armed rebellion, John MacDonald went with them.

The rebel plan called for Douglas to take the districts north of the Clyde, while Crawford held those to the south and MacDonald was to take the north from his strongholds in Ross. John MacDonald and his men seized Urquhart Castle, captured Inverness, and burned the royal stronghold at Ruthven.

The Earl of Huntly who, as the King's Lieutenant, was prepared, quickly defeated Crawford's southern army and then moved the whole royal army against John MacDonald in the North. The northern defences proved too strong, so Huntly redirected his forces southward against Douglas. Douglas was now having a difficult time. He faced Huntly's army and severe opposition from the local landowners. At a meeting in Knappdale, Douglas asked John's help in putting down the forces hostile to him on the islands of Bute and Arran.

Almost immediately (1452), John MacDonald dispatched Donald Ballach, in command of 5,000 men and 100 galleys, to his aid. Donald landed his force at Inverkip before moving on to Arran, where they burned Brodick Castle. Rothesay Castle, on Bute, was also easily taken by the Islanders. During this very successful raid, the Islanders suffered few casualties, but took a great deal of booty home with them.

Because John MacDonald's forces in Ross and the Isles were too numerous to be easily defeated by a royal army, the Scottish King found it expedient to negotiate a separate peace with him. As a reward for remaining neutral while the Scots pursued their campaign against Douglas, John was awarded Urquhart Castle and Glen Moriston by King James II. It was not until 1455 that Douglas was finally defeated by Huntly's royal army and the rebellion collapsed. The peace between the Lordship of the Isles and the Scottish Kingdom was to last until 1460, when King James II died during the siege of Roxburgh.

Almost immediately upon the succession of King James III, John MacDonald was again drawn into the realm of Douglas politics. The Treaty of Ardtornish was drawn up between the Lord of the Isles, the English, and Douglas. This treaty documented the plans made by these conspirators to conquer and divide the Scottish Kingdom between them. John MacDonald, in accordance with his part of the agreement, raised a considerably large army. With John's son, Angus Og, in overall command and the experienced Donald Ballach as his general, this army was a formidable force.

The Highland army marched up the Great Glen and easily took Inverness. However, the English army, which was to aid Douglas in the south, did not arrive. Realizing that without English help the war was lost, Douglas fled the country, leaving John MacDonald in the north to face the Scottish army alone. The rebellion was a failure. Angus Og withdrew to the Isles, but the Scots did not retaliate. John MacDonald was twice summoned to appear before parliament in 1463 but did not go. Wisely, there were no efforts made to force the issue and, in 1464, John MacDonald and the young King James III came to terms at Inverness.

The relationship between the MacKinnons and the Lords of the Isles had been largely repaired by the early 1450s. Lauchlan, the MacKinnon Chief, was a member of the household of the Isles. He spent time in Dingwall when John MacDonald resided there and had witnessed at least three of the charters which John awarded while at that castle.

Fyngonius Fingonii, the grandson of the Green Abbot, was still a monk on Iona, but the complaints against the MacKinnons had stopped. John, Lauchlan's second son was also involved in religious matters. John had possession of a parish church, Kilmaluaig in the diocese of Sodor, which he had held for some eight years.[15] When the Abbot, Dominic MacKenzie died in 1467, John sought admission to the community of Iona as a monk.

John MacKinnon appears to have been a man of extraordinary ability who enjoyed the respect of his contemporaries. At the request of the convent and John MacDonald, Lord of the Isles, he was made Abbot and named Dominus of the Council of the Isles.[16] John immediately proved to be more conscientious in his position than his MacKinnon predecessors had been. Two years later, June 23, 1469, there is a record that the Abbot John paid part of the annates of the monastery into the papal camera.

The end of hostilities between England and Scotland was quick to prove disastrous for the Lordship of the Isles. England, in a show of good faith toward Edinburgh, released to the Scottish government a copy of the Treaty of Ardtornish--the details of which were unknown in Scotland at that time. During the parliament of 1475, an indictment was drawn up listing all of the political crimes committed by John MacDonald, and these were ordered to be read at the market crosses of Dingwall and Inverness.

After being found guilty by the Convention of Estates, John MacDonald submitted to the mercy of the Crown. John's life was spared, but he was asked to surrender Ross, Kintyre and Knapdale, and the independence of the Lordship was no longer recognized.[17] We can only now wonder what went through the mind of John MacKinnon, Abbot of Iona, as he sat in the parliament of 1476 and heard them discuss the forfeiture to the Crown of the ancient Lordship. John MacDonald was now only a Lord of Parliament with a grant of the now empty title of Lord of the Isles.

This loss of land, power and prestige by Clan Donald was viewed differently by the various clans resident in the Lordship of the Isles and the Earldom of Ross. Some saw the fall of *"The MacDonald"* as an opportunity for more independence, power, and prestige, while others resented John's undignified surrender to the Scottish authority.

John MacDonald may have taken the loyalty of the other MacDonald families for granted, but he continued to maintain the allegiance of other clans by gifts of land or titles. Continuing the flawed policy of his ancestors only increased the resentment felt by the MacDonalds and the other ancient clans who felt slighted or neglected by it. The compensation given to the Clan MacLean by John MacDonald, for lands they lost in Ross due to the forfeiture of that Earldom, only aggravated the widespread discontent within the Isles.

John MacDonald had, ill-advisedly, granted MacLean charters to some of the best land on the MacDonald's home island of Islay. Other, resentful MacDonalds fell upon the MacLean settlers, destroyed their charters and drove them off the island.[18] John MacDonald's son and heir, Angus Og, understood the divisions and the underlying resentments developing in the Lordship and did not approve of his father's actions. In an attempt to re-establish the unity and authority of the Lordship, Angus Og met with the MacDonalds, the MacKinnon chief and some other members of the Council of the Isles on Islay.

" [Angus Og] thought to deprive him [John] of all management and authority. Many followers adhered to him [John]. His [Angus Og's] father being at Islay, he went after him with a great party, forced him [John] to change seven rooms to lodge in, and at last to take his bed, during the whole of the night, under an old boat.

When he [John] returned to his house in the morning he found his son sitting with a great crowd about him. MacFinnon [Lauchlan MacKinnon], rising up, desired MacDonald to sit down; who answered that he would not sit down till he would execute his intention, which was to curse his son.

So, leaving Islay with only six men, he went to the mainland and to Inveraray, and having waited without till one of the Argyll gentlemen came forth in the morning, who, observing MacDonald, went in immediately and told Argyll of the matter, who could scarcely believe him, saying, if he were there, he would certainly have sent some person to inform him beforehand. Argyll hurried out to receive John, exclaiming at the smallness of his retinue. "That is little, said MacDonald, to the revolutions of the times, and thou shall be the better of my coming; and so, after dinner, he bestowed on him the lands of Knapdale Rilisleter, from the river Add to the Foxburn in Kintyre, 400 merks lands, and desired Argyll to convey him to Stirling . . . and for his son's disobedience he would resign all his estates to the king." [19]

Angus Og immediately attempted to reassert the independence of the Lordship of the Isles and regain all of the territories lost to Scotland. With Donald Ballach again acting as general, Angus Og mustered the island army and launched an invasion of Ross.

The Earls of Argyll and Atholl, together with the Northern clans, the MacKays, MacKenzies, and Frasers, attempted to halt the Islanders, but instead they themselves were defeated at Lagbread. A second attempt to dislodge the Islanders was made by the Earls of Huntly and Crawford, but this fared no better than the first. A third attempt was planned in which the Earls of Argyll and Atholl, and John MacDonald, the ousted lord, with their respective forces, would invade the Isles.

John MacDonald, who had persuaded some of the island clans to support his restoration by supplying galleys and men, was to lead the attack on his own people. At the last minute, however, the Earls of Argyll and Atholl withdrew, leaving John MacDonald, and the few clans that had joined him, to battle Angus Og on their own. Angus Og was supported by his kinsmen, the leaders of the cadet branches of Clan Donald, as well as the MacKinnons, MacLean of Lochbuie, and others. John MacDonald was supported by his adherents, the MacLeans of Duart, the MacLeods, and the MacNeil of Barra. MacLean of Duart was in command of John's fleet.[20]

"The supporters of the old Lord mustered in the bay on the Mull side of the end of the Sound of Mull, now known as the Bloody Bay, in memory of the battle.

Angus Og and his followers were on the northern side of Ardnamurchan, detained by bad weather and suffering from shortage of provisions. After five weeks of waiting there the weather changed, and he sailed round the stormy point. As he came to the Sound of Mull he saw MacLean of Ardgour on his way to the rendezvous in the bay, who rashly displayed his colours, Donald Gallach (son of Hugh of Sleat) and Ranald Ban (son of Allan MacRuairi of Moidard) steered toward MacLean of Ardgour's galley.

MacLean of Dowart, William MacLeod of Harris and MacNeil of Barra thereupon left the bay to go to Ardgour's relief, the rest of the faction, seeing themselves in danger at least of losing their galleys, thought best to enter their harbour.

MacDonald coming as swiftly as he could, accompanied by Donald Gallich of Sleat, Austin's son [his first cousin], and Ranald Bain, laird of Mudort's son [the descendant of Ranald, Amie Macruari's son], the last of whom grappled side to side with MacLeod of Harris's galley. There was one called Edmond More Obrian along with Ranald Bain, who thrust the blade of an oar in below the stern-post of MacLeod's galley, between it and the rudder, which prevented the galley from being steered.

The galley of the heir of Torkill of the Lewis, with all his men, was taken, and himself mortally wounded with two arrows, whereof he died soon after at Dunvegan. Angus Ogg and Allan, Laird of Mudort, attacked [MacLean?]. Neil MacLean of Lehir earned fame with his battle axe by cutting the thumbs off of his enemies as they attempted to board him, took MacLean of Duart prisoner, with a great slaughter of his men. Angus Ogg would have hanged MacLean immediately had he not been prevented by Allan MacRuairi of Mudort saying, he would have none to bicker with if MacLean was gone. Some time thereafter, giving his oath of fidelity, he was pardoned.

John Lord of the Isles was captured as well Macneill of Barra made his escape about Coll, and three galleys in pursuit of him" 50 MacLeans who swam ashore were smoked out of a cave and slaughtered. This victory put Angus Og securely Captain of Clan Donald and in command of the Lordship. It was a barren victory for Angus Og, for the Earl of Atholl, in boats supplied by the Earl of Argyll, crossed over to Islay and captured Donald Dhu, the only son of Angus Og, and carried him a prisoner to Inch Chonail, on Loch Awe; nevertheless it effectually broke the opposition of his opponents within the Lordship."

Shortly after Angus Og's successful coup against his father, there was another campaign to rid Iona of MacKinnon influence. Perhaps more in an effort to discredit Angus Og's administration by attacking his supporters than focussing on actual problems, John Campbell, the newly elected Bishop of the Isles, made a series of lurid accusations against John MacFinguine, then Abbot of Iona. The attempt to have the Abbot John replaced was a failure. John MacFinguine retained the support of Angus Og and the Council of the Isles and so remained in office until his death circa 1500.[21] An indication of the Abbot John's high standing in the Lordship is shown by his signature on a charter (August 1, 1492) from the Lord of the Isles in favour of his nephew, Alexander of Lochalsh.

The Crown of Scotland had little respect for the independence of the Lordship of the Isles, nor did they recognise the leadership of Angus Og. In the year 1488, even before the forfeiture of the Isles, the Crown claimed a great deal of land that was integral to the ancient Lordship. This claim made the islands of Jura, Islay, Colonsay, Tiree, Uist, as well Trotternish and Sleat on Skye, and the mainland districts of Ardnamurchan, Sunart, and Morven property of the Crown. On the island of Mull, the Ross of Mull in the south was taken. In the north, Mishnish, which was occupied by the MacKinnons, was also claimed by the king. The Crown's claim to these lands, which was maintained until 1513, was ineffective as long as Angus Og was alive. After his

MacKinnon's Cross

The inscription reads: "This is the cross of Lauchlanus MacKinnon and of his son
Johannes, Abbot of Iona, made in the year of Our Lord 1489

murder at Inverness in the year of 1490, the Crown's claim and the loss of the Earldom of Ross would add confusion and bitterness to the anarchy which followed.

John MacDonald of Islay, the brother of Angus Og, did not attempt to take up the leadership of the Gael upon his brother's death. He deferred to his cousin, MacDonald of Lochalsh. Alexander of Lochalsh succeeded to the management of the Lordship, but it was not long before John MacDonald, the old Lord, had regained some influence. Although Alexander was widely regarded as the defacto leader, he and John MacDonald seem to have cooperated in the Lordship's management.[22]

It may have been Alexander of Lochalsh's disregard of the Scottish authority and his attempts to bring the Earldom of Ross back into the fold, or simply the king's greed which prompted James III to forfeit the entire Lordship during May of 1493.[23] The elderly John MacDonald, erstwhile Lord of the Isles, was personally treated with considerable kindness by King James IV, although he was deprived of all his estates and titles.

The Islanders, in general, did not recognise the authority of King James nor that of his agents and officers in the Isles. King James' agents could not perform any of their assigned duties, nor even travel in the Isles, without large military escorts as their lives were in constant danger. In an effort to legitimise his claim to rule over the West and its inhabitants, King James IV travelled to the Isles with the intent of receiving the submission of the island chiefs in person.

Initially the meetings between the island chiefs and the king appear to have gone very well for all involved, and much was accomplished. Alexander of Lochalsh, as heir presumptive to the Lordship, received a promise from King James IV that all free tenants of the Isles would be secured in their holdings. King James IV also granted charters to the chiefs for the land they had occupied under the Lordship of the Isles. These charters, which were held directly from King James IV, made the chiefs freeholders of their estates and independent of any feudal overlords.

Thus, the breakup of the large clans into their smaller constituents, which was evident during the last years of the Lordship, was officially encouraged.[24] Strategically, charters were given to Alexander MacDonald of Lochalsh, John MacDonald of Islay, John MacLean of Lochbuie, and Duncan MacIntosh of the Clan Chattan.

Government troops were promptly dispatched from King James IV's retinue to occupy and garrison all the ancient clan castles and strongholds. As the Islanders did not welcome the government soldiers, all of whom were viewed as foreigners by the native Gael, these garrisons would generate considerable ill will in the Isles. Even before King James' fleet left the vicinity of Dunaverty Castle, John MacDonald of Islay (Clan Ian Mor), hung the new royalist governor from the castle walls. Thus, James' authority was not increased as much as he may have anticipated on this first visit to the Hebrides.

By this time, the island chiefs fully recognised that the old regime of the Isles had ended and that some accord would have to be reached with the government in Edinburgh. To this end, Roderick MacLeod of Harris, and John MacDonald, known as MacIain of Ardnamurchan, both submitted to royal authority in 1494.

Unfortunately for the Islanders, however, the vengeful nature of the Scottish Kingdom soon made itself fully apparent. Whether at the request of the king or of his own accord, John (MacDonald), MacIain of Ardnamurchan, undertook to capture John MacDonald of Islay and his sons and bring them before King James IV at Edinburgh. Because MacIain was the head of one of the main branches of the Clan Donald, it was not difficult for him to gain access to MacDonald of Islay's home at the ancient court of Finlaggan. John of Islay's two younger sons escaped to Antrim and safety, but John MacDonald, with his eldest son and heir, were taken to Edinburgh where they were executed for treason.

The following year (1495), King James IV again held court on the West Coast. This time it was held at Kilkerran on the southwest shore of what is now known as Campbelltown Loch. More of the island chiefs now appeared and submitted to royal authority than had during the previous court.

Alexander MacLeod, the new chief of Harris, and Torquil MacLeod of Lewis, both submitted. The remainder of the Clan Donald; John Hughson of Sleat, Donald Angussson of Keppoch, and Allan MacRuari of Moydart, also all appeared and submitted. Other leaders submitted as well: Hector MacLean of Duart, Ewen Allanson of Lochiel, the captain of Clan Cameron, and Gillian MacNeil of Barra.

Notable by their absence from these lists of the chiefs are, Lauchlan MacKinnon and John mac Iain Abrach MacLean of Coll. There is no record of either chief submitting to James IV during the visit in 1493, nor that of 1495, although all of their neighbours did. Indeed, it seems that Lauchlan MacKinnon and John MacLean of Coll may have been the only island leaders not to submit to King James IV. If Lauchlan MacKinnon and John MacLean of Coll did not make the trip to Kilkerran because of a lack of trust in King James IV, their caution was justified. When Kenneth Og MacKenzie of Kintail and Farquhar MacIntosh came to submit, they were seized and dispatched as prisoners to Edinburgh.

With the kidnapping of MacKenzie and MacIntosh, King James was completing his savage elimination of all those descended from the direct line of *"The MacDonald."* The mothers of these two chiefs were both daughters of John, the last Lord of the Isles. With Angus Og murdered in Inverness, his young son, Donald Dubh, a captive in Argyll, and John of Islay and his heir executed for treason, there were no further direct heirs of *"The MacDonald"* who, it was felt, could rally the forces of the ancient Lordship.

King James was confident now that he could rule the Isles as he pleased. Almost immediately on the king's return to Edinburgh, he initiated numerous civil acts brought by the Lords in Council against the Islanders. Many of these new laws sought to replace the customs and traditions then current in the West, with those of Lowland Scotland.[25]

Times were difficult for the Islanders. The ancient government of the Gael had been destroyed, but the government in Edinburgh was not strong enough to replace it.

On Iona, the last of the MacKinnon clergy still held their positions and influence as Iona was to experience one last flash of brilliance.[26] The Lord of Argyll is recorded as sending a letter to the pope and the Vice-Chancellor of Scotland asking that the church on Iona be made a cathedral until the Cathedral of St. Germain on the Isle of Man could be recovered from the English. Accordingly, the Monastery of Iona was duly established as the Cathedral of the Diocese of the Isles.

On the death of Robert, Bishop of the Isles, John MacKinnon, the Abbot of Iona, was elevated to the Bishop's office in his place. It was during this period that the wonderfully-carved monuments to the MacKinnons were produced on Iona. John MacKinnon, the Abbot, realizing he was approaching the end of his life, had an elaborate grave slab carved for himself. This memorial shows a skilfully-executed likeness of the old abbot, but was evidently carved before he was promoted to Bishop of the Isles.[27]

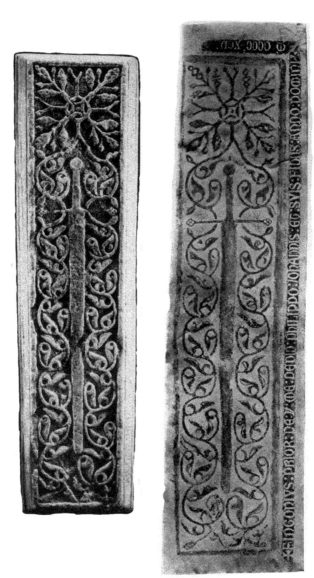

Kirkapoll, Tiree, grave slab
The inscription reads: "Fingonius, Prior or Iona, gave me to Philoppus, son
of Johannes, and to his sons in year oif Our Lord 1495"

When John's father, Lauchlan MacKinnon, chief of the clan, died in 1499, the elaborate cross raised by him and his son in 1489 still stood in front of the chapel.[28] Margaret MacLeod, Lauchlan's wife and the Bishop John's mother, survived her husband and spent her remaining years on Lewis.[29]

The Abbot, John MacKinnon's cousin, a grandson of the "Green Abbot," Fyngonus Fingonii, was prior of Iona at this time and made a gift of a beautifully-carved gravestone to his relatives in Kirkapol on Tiree.[30] With the fall of the Lordship of the Isles, other religious sites would eventually eclipse Iona in importance, it's craftsmen would scatter, and the beautiful monastery and nunnery would be allowed to fall into ruin.

The first attempt to restore the Lordship of the Isles was born out of the bad faith and the cynical approach to his relationship with his Gaelic subjects exercised by King James IV. Alexander, who had managed the Lordship since its forfeiture, raised the Islanders in 1496 to reestablish the Lordship of the Isles in the name of Angus Og's captive son, Donald Dubh.[31] The island army swept into Ross, chasing all before it.[32] The MacKenzies and Monroes rallied their forces at Drumchatt, where they met the Islanders in a rather sharp encounter. The Islanders' invasion, having lost its momentum, was stopped cold and they retreated back to the safety of the Hebrides.

The divisions between the Islanders, themselves, effectively put an end to the rebellion more completely than the reverse at Drumchatt. While travelling through the Isles recruiting for a second attempt to restore the Lordship, Alexander visited the island of Oronsay, where he was the guest of a prior locally believed to have been named Colin.[33] As fortune would have it, this prior was closely related to Malcolm MacDuffie, the brother-in-law of Alexander MacIain of Ardnamurchan. This was the same Alexander MacIain of Ardnamurchan who had earlier betrayed John of Islay and his sons to King James IV. Not surprisingly, Alexander of Lochalsh was found murdered in the prior's house. The perpetrators of the murder were never found. Later, in 1506 Malcolm MacDuffie was given a lease to the whole island of Colonsay, for which MacIain of Ardnamurchan was surety.

In 1498, two years after the Battle of Drumchatt, King James again held court at Kilkerran. This time he stayed for the better part of a month, entertaining the chiefs and receiving their pledges of loyalty.

King James IV used this opportunity to grant new charters to many of the island chiefs. Ranald MacAlan, the Chief of Clanranald, was granted lands in Uist, Eigg, and Arsaig. Torquil MacLeod and his heirs by Katherine Campbell, the daughter of Colin Campbell of Argyll, were given Trotternish on Skye. Cynically, many of the charters given out by the king contained grants of land which had been occupied by other clans for centuries. Naturally, this created a great deal of new conflict as the new owners attempted to claim the estates and were resisted by those already occupying the land. Although the MacKinnon estates of Mishnish on Northern Mull were still considered the property of the Crown, the MacKinnons never relinquished their hold on them.

Once safely returned to Edinburgh, King James IV promptly revoked all the charters he had just awarded--an act which added to the confusion and consternation he had so thoroughly sown in the Isles.

A new, tougher policy regarding the Isles was adopted by the king, which would set the pattern for government attitudes towards the Islanders for the next 250 years. King James took a number of ill-considered steps, which were to cause a great deal of anger and hostility amongst the clans of the West Coast. Firstly, the king revoked all the charters granted since the forfeiture of the Lordship, except those in Kintyre and Islay. The Hebridean chiefs suddenly had no legal claim to their ancient lands and the Lords in Council in Edinburgh actually began legal proceedings to evict the entire Gaelic population of the Isles.

Secondly, King James appointed the Earl of Argyll; Lord Lieutenant of the Isles, keeper of the castle of Talbert as well as bailie and governor of the king's lands in Knapdale. Argyll was given the authority to lease out the entire territory of the ancient Lordship to anyone he thought suitable. John MacIain of Ardnamurchan, son of the notorious Alexander, was given lands on Islay and Jura. Stewart of Appin was given Glencoe and Duror. Lord Gordon, Huntley's son, was given vast lands in Lochabar.

The new policy of the Scottish court was based on the belief that, as long as an heir to the Lordship of the Isles remained alive, unrest would continue in the Isles and that any claim to the Lordship would prove disruptive to the Kingdom as a whole. Thus, the imprisonment of the young Donald Dubh by his grandfather, the Earl of Argyll, was viewed with relief, and perhaps gratitude, by the government in Edinburgh.[34] Because the Islanders viewed Donald Dubh as the hereditary heir to the Lordship of the Isles and the natural leader of the Gael, they deeply resented his captivity and were offended by the attempts of the government to declare him illegitimate.[35]

Chapter 9
End Notes

1. James I felt threatened by the military power of the great barons of Scotland. The Highland chiefs whom James I executed or imprisoned are believed to have had a following of 70,000 or 80,000 men between them. For a good description of the power of feudal barons and their followings. See: Grant, I. F., *Social & Economic Development of Scotland Before 1603*, Oliver & Boyd, Edinburgh, 1930, 175.

2. Donald was the son of John Mhor Tanister. Because of his youth, he was called "Ballach" which is Gaelic for boy.

3. Alastair Carrach was John Mhor Tanister's younger brother and an uncle to both Donald Ballach and Alexander MacDonald, Lord of the Isles. Inverskipnish is just two miles from Inverlochy.

4. This is the same Earl of Mar who fought at Harlaw against Donald MacDonald. He and the Earls of Cathness and Huntley were in Lochabar putting down any signs of disaffection to the Scottish Crown that may have been found there.

5. MacLean, J. P., *History of Clan MacLean*, Cincinnati, 1889. 47, and Sir Robert Gordon, *Genealogical History of the Earldom of Sutherland,* A Constable & Son, Edinburgh, 1813.

6. MacDonald, *The Clan Donald,* MacDonald, Midlothian,1978, 95, and also Williams, R., *The Lords of the Isles*, Chatto & Windus, London, 1984, 200.

7. MacLean-Bristol, *Warriors & Priests*, Tuckwell Press, East Lothian, 1995, 47.

8. Formal feasts were regularly held within the Lordship and followed the ancient Irish traditions.

9. Grant, I. F., *The Lordship of the Isles*, Moray Press, Edinburgh, 1935.

10. MacNab, P. A., *History of the Island of Mull*, Jobes & Sons, Ohio, 1923.

11. This Finguine was the son of the Green Abbot. MacLean-Bristol, *Warriors & Priests*, Tuckwell Press, East Lothian, 1995.

12. That Fyngonius would have a relationship with the daughter of John Garbh, the MacLean of Coll, at a time when the MacLeans were putting a great deal of pressure on the MacKinnon estates, illustrates the political pragmatism of the period. See MacLean-Bristol, *Warriors & Priests*, Tuckwell Press, East Lothian, 1995, 52.

13. The practice of removing vicars who did not reach the priesthood on time was not an unusual one. In 1432 John MacGillian held the parish church of Strathordill in Skye for years before he was removed for not

becoming a priest within the time stipulated by the authorities.

14. Donald Ballach was head of the Council of the Isles, MacLean of Ardgour was head of the household, and Monroe of Foulis was Chamberlain of the Lordship.

15. John had demitted his diocesan church to allow the pope to *"wipe out the stain of inability because of the detention of the said church"* Steer & Bannerman, *Late Mediaeval Monumental Sculpture in the West Highlands*, RCAHMS, HMSO Press, Edinburgh, 1977, 112.

16. Ibid, A petition dated 9 Aug 1467 in the names of John, Lord of the Isles, and the Bishop of the Isles, requested that John be admitted to Iona ad Abbot. A papal provision, 9 August 1467, to admit John into the community of the monastery refers to him as a clerk in the diocese of Sodor. John is recorded as having been the son of a married noblewoman and an unmarried noble man [Lauchlan MacKinnon],

17. MacLean-Bristol, *Warriors & Priests*, Tuckwell Press, East Lothian, 1995, 67.

18. Ibid, 69.

19. MacPhail, *Highland Papers* Vol. 1, Edinburgh, T. & A. Constable, 1914, 47.

20. Ibid.

21. There is no record of when Abbot John died. Some sources claim he died before 1499. Another source claims he died sometime after 1506.

22. In 1492 both Alexander of Lochalsh and John MacDonald, with the consent of the Council of the Isles, grant a charter to Ewen Allanson, the captain of Clan Cameron, to former MacLean lands in the district of Lochabar.

23. The end of the Lordship of the Isles was cemented in 1499 by the execution at Edinburgh of John Mor "Righ Innis Gall," his son John Cathanach, and his two grandsons. This barbaric act left the Isles without a legitimate hereditary leader who represented the main line of the Lords of the Isles.

24. The Clan Donald was now divided into two parts; Clan Donald North under Alexander of Lochalsh, and Clan Donald South under John of Islay. John MacDonald of Islay would later be executed in Edinburgh for treason. By directly awarding MacLean of Lochbuie a charter, King James made the division of Clan MacLean into its three constituent parts; MacLeans of Duart, MacLeans of Coll and MacLeans of Lochbuie, permanent and official.

25. Gregory, *Western Highlands & Isles*, William Tate, Edinburgh, 1836, 91. An act of council was passed to make the chief of a clan responsible for the actions of his clansmen. *"That every chief of every clan be answerable for the due execution of summonses and other writs against those of his own tribe under penalty of being made libel himself to the party bringing the action"*

26. The Rev. Donald D. MacKinnon reports a silver chalice, said to have belonged to the Abbot John MacKinnon, was in the possession of a Miss Young during the later years of the 19th century. Charles MacKinnon of Dunakin writes *"a highly chased silver chalice is in the possession of the clan to this day. It is known to have been buried on Iona during Cromwell's ravaging of the English and Scottish churches. An expert some years ago gave its probable date as 1607, and pronounced it to be very valuable. However, the tradition behind the chalice is that it belonged to John, the last Abbot of Iona, who died in 1500."*

27. Rev. MacKinnon, D., *The Chiefs and Chiefship of Clan MacKinnon*, Portree, 1931. The name of the Bishop of the Isles listed a John in 1506, which indicated that the Abbot John MacKinnon succeeded the Bishop Robert to his office.

28. The inscription on the cross reads *"HEAC EST CRUX LACHLANI MACFINGOINE ET EJUS FILII JOHANNIS ABBATIS DE HY, FACTA AN. DOM MCCCCLXV"*

29. The memorial for Margaret is in the Church of Eye on Lewis. The stone has an interlaced foliage and animal design. The inscription reads *"Here lies Margaret, daughter of Ruaridh MacLeod of Lewis, and widow of MacKinnon, 1503."*

30. *"The stone was carved on Iona and is the first representation of a claymore. There are similarities in the lettering that may indicate that the artisan who carved this also carved the effigy of Abbot John inscribed: FINGONIUS PRIOR DE Y ME DEDID PHILIPPO IOHANNIS ET SVIS FILIIS ANO DOMINI/M CCC XCV (Fingon Prior of Iona gave me to Phillipus son of Johannas and to his sons in the year of our lord 1495) Phillip was the Latinised form of Finlag of Finlay, Johannas was John or Ian It is very likely that Finlag was related to Fingonus and was possibly a MacKinnon. Finlag and his son may have administered or leased the six merk lands of Kirkapol which belonged to Iona. A family association with this area may have gone back as far as 1350.*
The stone is in the Claodh Beg (little burial ground) at Kirkapol Near the most modern (built in or before the 13th cent.) of three chapels interior measures 37' 3" by 17' 6"originally there were doors in the south wall and west gable (round headed) and a cross in the west gable there were eight sculptured grave slabs in the yard the best preserved is that of MacKinnon" Steer & Bannerman, *Late Medieval Monumental Sculpture in the West Highlands*, RCAHMS, HM Stationary Office, Edinburgh, 1977, 102.

31. MacDonald, *Clan Donald*, MacDonald Publishers, Loanhead, Midlothian, 1978, 29.

32. Gregory, *Western Highlands & Isles*, William Tate, Edinburgh, 1836, 91. The reasons for the invasion of Ross may have been to regain the Earldom for the Lordship of the Isles or as revenge on the MacKenzies for Alexander's defeat at their hands at Blairnapark.

33. Byrne, K., *Colkitto*, House of Lochar, Isle of Colonsay, 1997, 15.

34. Donald Dubh was the son of Angus Og MacDonald, Lord of the Isles, and his wife, a daughter of Colin Campbell, 2nd, Earl of Argyll. Donald Dubh was treacherously captured after the Battle of Bloody Bay.

35. Cathcart, A., "Domhnal Dubh: The Restoration of an Ideal," *History Scotland, Vol. 2, #5, Sept/Oct 2002*, 13.

Chapter 10
FOR THE RESTORATION OF A LORDSHIP

In the early sixteenth century, the Clan MacKinnon was entering a new era with a new chief, Neil Ban, whose duty it would be to guide them through an uncertain and violent age. Neil, who was raised as a nobleman under the Lordship of the Isles, would probably have been a young man, perhaps no older than thirty, when he assumed the chiefship of the clan. Like many of the other island chiefs, it is likely that he would have preferred living under the familiar government of the ancient Lordship, rather than the uncertainty of rule from Edinburgh.

The great cultural difference between the Highlands and Lowlands was, by now, universally recognised throughout Scotland. It had even become a matter of pride to both Highlanders and Lowlanders, and the differences were used to explain the superiority of each culture over that of the other. John Major, while teaching at the University of Glasgow circa 1500, wrote disparagingly of the Gaelic way of life in his *"Historia Majoris Britanniae,"* calling the Highlanders *"Wild Scots"* and the Lowlanders *"Householding or domestic Scots."*[1] It was a generally-held view of the Scottish government that the language and culture of the Highlands and Islands caused them to resist the benefits of adopting the Lowland's feudal system. Although Scotland was officially one country, in practice, it remained two states separated by the Highland line.

In 1500 the Earl of Huntly's son, Alexander, Lord Gordon, was given a grant to a large tract of land in Lochaber, which had formerly been part of the Lordship of the Isles.[2] The grant may well have been a reward, by a thankful monarch, for Alexander's bloody expedition through the Isles during the troubles which accompanied the forfeiture of the old Lordship. The leaders of the Western clans watched carefully, and with disapproval, as Huntly's influence in the West increased. In particular, Archibald Campbell, the Earl of Argyll, who had relatives and economic interests in the Isles, would not have approved of Huntly's approach and would have had the means to engineer an opposition to him.

The following year, 1501, the last surviving heir to the Lordship of the Isles, Donald (Dubh) MacDonald, was taken from the Innisconnel Castle by a band of Glencoe men. Young Donald Dubh, who at the time was only eleven years old and a nephew of Archibald Campbell, was immediately taken to the island of Lewis and the protection of his uncle Torquil, who was chief of the MacLeods of Lewis.[3]

It would be incredible to suppose, as is widely believed, that Donald Dubh would have been in any real danger from the family of Argyll. Donald was the grandson of Colin Campbell, 1st Earl of Argyll, through the marriage of his daughter Margaret to Angus Og MacDonald.[4] After Colin's death, his son Archibald, Margaret's brother and uncle to Donald Dubh, succeeded to the earldom and continued to hold young MacDonald. Donald was born a ranking member of the House of Argyll as well as being the heir to the Lordship of the Isles. It is certain he could have counted on the full protection of both his mother and his uncle.

It was common knowledge that James IV had executed all of the other heirs to the Lordship, so it is possible that Colin Campbell and his son Archibald may have held Donald, wanting to maintain a close watch over their grandson and nephew. Donald's captivity may have been intended as much to protect him from the king in Edinburgh than it was to deprive the Islanders of a leader. It may even be possible that Donald's well-known rescue by the band of Glencoe men was a ruse orchestrated by Argyll and the Islanders to deceive the Edinburgh government.

When Donald Dubh reached Lewis, he was proclaimed Lord of the Isles and inaugurated into the position with all the ancient ceremonies and traditions. Donald was immediately accepted as the legitimate Lord of the Isles by the majority of the Western clans: MacKinnons, MacQuarries, MacNeils, MacLeans, Camerons, MacDonalds, MacLeods of Lewis, and some others--all of whom undoubtedly attended the ceremonies occasioned by his inauguration.

It was, perhaps, during these rituals that the Council of the Isles, which had been reconvened, carefully made its plans for rebellion. Word of the restoration of the ancient Lordship would have spread quickly through the Isles. As the Islanders flocked to join the cause, letters were prepared and dispatched to the courts of both Ireland and England, asking for their support against Scotland.

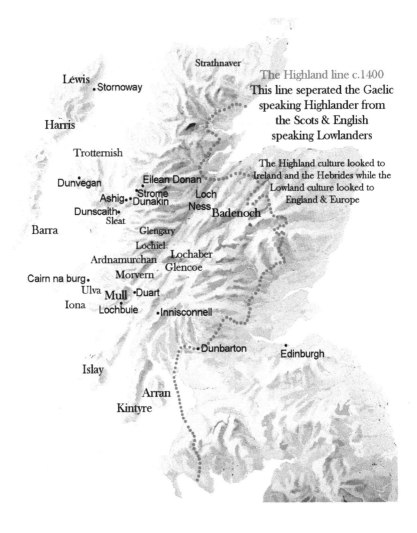

Strathnaver

Lewis
• Stornoway

Harris

The Highland line c.1400
This line seperated the Gaelic speaking Highlander from the Scots & English speaking Lowlanders

Trotternish

The Highland culture looked to Ireland and the Hebrides while the Lowland culture looked to England & Europe

Dunvegan   Eilean Donan
Ashig. •Strome   Loch
    •Dunakin
Dunscaith•   Ness
    Sleat   Badenoch

Barra   Glengary

Lochiel
Ardnamurchan Lochaber
    Morvern   Glencoe

Cairn na burg.

Ulva Mull •Duart
Iona Lochbuie
            •Innisconnell

            ••Dunbarton   Edinburgh

Islay

    Arran
Kintyre

However, not all the island chiefs favoured a restoration of the Lordship. Understandably the most prominent of its opponents were MacLeod of Dunvegan and Ranald MacAllan, the Captain of Clanranald. Indeed, as if to affirm his opposition, MacLeod of Dunvegan even assumed responsibility for the continuation of royal government in the Isles during the period of the revolt.

To protect his newly-acquired lands in Lochaber and pacify the resistive Stewarts of Appin, the Earl of Huntly rallied the Clan Chattan, while King James IV personally considered the options he had available to quell the rebellion.[5] After some discussion, the government in Edinburgh decided the best course was to reinstate King James IV's earlier policy of expelling the native population of the Isles and to lease the land to men loyal to the Crown.

In 1502 commissions to this effect were issued to the Earl of Huntly, Fraser of Lovat, and Monroe of Fowlis. The first forfeiture, that of Torquil MacLeod of Lewis, was quickly followed by those of MacLean of Duart and Cameron of Lochiel. Both Lauchlan MacLean and Ewen Cameron had rejected King James' crude diplomatic attempts to break up the island confederation and quickly paid the price of forfeiture.

King James, undeterred by the initial failure of his diplomacy and his underestimation of the Islanders' loyalty to their traditional leadership, persisted in the cynical belief that he would be able to exploit their individual greed. Personally writing to each of the island chiefs, King James attempted to bribe them into abandoning their confederation.

The Earl of Huntly was given a letter from King James IV to be forwarded to Neil Ban, the MacKinnon chief, on or about March 14, 1503. The letter ordered him to act against MacLean of Duart and Cameron of Lochiel, both of whom were forfeit. Neil Ban was insultingly offered a share of their lands if he were to help in the capture of Donald Dubh or any of his associates. Naturally enough, as his loyalty lay with his traditional overlord, this letter was ignored by the MacKinnon chief. The other chiefs, refusing to betray what they regarded as their legitimate leadership, also ignored the letters from the king.

By December 1503 the Islanders' army had assembled and was ready to strike. Toward the end of that month, they moved against the Clan Chattan in Badenoch. This assault was a response to Huntly's invasion of Lochaber and intended to punish the Clan Chattan for their part in it. All of Badenoch was plundered and burned by the Islanders as Huntly's power in the west was successfully challenged.

In Edinburgh the defiance to royal authority posed by this attack was seen by the Scottish government as a threat to the very fabric of the Kingdom. Early in 1504 the whole might of the Scottish Kingdom was called out to respond. The leadership of the assault on the West was given to a joint command comprised of Alexander Gordon, the Earl of Huntly; Alexander Campbell, the Earl of Argyll; Alexander Lindsay, the Earl of Crawford; Andrew Baird, the Earl of Marischall; and Thomas Fraser of Lovat.

Huntly, Crawford and Lovat were jointly charged with pacifying the North, while Huntly, specifically, was to take the strongholds of Strome on Lochcarron and Eilean Donan on Loch Duich. Argyll and the Earl Marischall were to attack the Hebrides from the south. A naval force under Admiral Andrew Wood of Largo and his associate, Robert Barton, would also be sent into the Hebrides. Plans were made to have this fleet supported by land forces gathered on the Isle of Arran.

While his forces were gathering, King James IV summoned Dunslaff MacQuarrie of Ulva, Gillian MacNeil of Barra, and Donald MacRanald of Largie to appear in Edinburgh to answer for their treasonable support for Donald Dubh. Once again the king sent letters to the island chiefs, advising them to take the government side. These letters offered increased rewards for those who joined the royal forces and threatened charges of treason for those who did not. The island chiefs steadfastly ignored the king's crude bribes, preferring instead to remain loyal to their traditional leadership.

With the southern army mustering at Dunbarton in April 1504, the northern army attacked. The castles of Strome and Eilean Donan were besieged and captured, but Huntly was not able to lead his forces into the Isles. The southern army, under the command of Argyll and Earl Marischall, did not make much headway against the Islanders and the invasion was stalled.

The following year King James IV led an invasion of the Isles from the south and Cairn na Berg off the Western Coast of Mull was besieged. Initially the northern invasion of 1505 faltered, as the rough terrain favoured the Islanders, but eventually Huntly's army prevailed. The two-pronged attack by the well-equipped royal army crippled the confederacy of island clans and it fell apart. MacLean of Duart, MacLean of Lochbuie, MacNeil of Barra, MacQuarrie of Ulva, and Donald MacRanald of Largie all surrendered at about the same time.[6] Seemingly, there is no extant record of the surrender of Neil Ban MacKinnon and the clan he led.

While it is likely the MacKinnons may have surrendered along with the other clans, they may also have joined Torquil MacLeod and the clans making a stand on the Isle of Lewis. Although the revolt ended in 1506, another government campaign was mounted against the clans of Lewis. Huntly captured Stornoway and Y MacKay of Strathnaver subdued the remainder of the island.[7] Again, the severity used to suppress this revolt and the subsequent rewarding of those who followed King James IV, left a legacy of uncertainty and bitterness in the Isles.

In his attempt to impose peace on the Highlands, King James IV began the process of replacing the ancient Brehon laws with the feudal laws as then practised in the Lowlands. This change of legal codes was not embraced by the Islanders as the Brehon laws were considered fairer and more just than the Lowland laws. The change in legal practice would have had a direct and immediate consequence for the MacKinnon chiefs. Indeed, as a result of the impending change, the MacKinnon chiefs would have lost their hereditary positions as judges and the income that went with it.[8] Moreover, at this time the king also supported the sons of certain Highland gentlemen at university and attached others to his court.[9] As will be seen by later events, not all the young men who were educated and supported at court preferred Lowland fashion to Highland tradition.

In the wake of the rebellion, King James IV ordered the alteration of three aspects of life in the Isles which would also have a direct effect on the MacKinnons in Strath.[10] The first of these was the royal prerogative to appoint ministers of religion to various parish churches. While it was a duty of the chief, on whose territory the churches were located, to fund and maintain these buildings, the clergy were to be appointed by the king.

On Skye in 1505, the parish church known as Kilchrist in Askimruby was the successor to the old parish church of Ashig.[11] The building, although not particularly large, could comfortably accommodate 150 to 200 worshipers. Between the church building and the east end of Loch Cill Chriosd, is a small hill called *Cnoc na hÉireann* (hill of the mass). The singular name for this hill may suggest that religious services were held in the open whenever the weather permitted. In the vicinity of the church, is the intriguingly-named area of *tir cheriridh* (land of wax or candle land). This may have been the area where the altar candles were made.[12]

It is known that, prior to 1505, Sir John MacGillibrideson (MacGillivray) was the parish priest of Strath. Sir John was replaced, for reasons unknown, when King James presented Sir Kenneth Adamson as chaplain to the rectory and vicarage of Kilchrist in 1505. Sir John Johnson was the clerk of the rectory until his death in 1508, when King James IV appointed John Rolandson to replace him.

Ruins of the church of Kilchrist

The second, and potentially much more serious, royal intrusion into the affairs of Strath was in 1507 when Alexander Gordon, the Earl of Huntly, was granted four merklands of Scalpa-Torrin in Strathordill. It is thought these lands had been forfeited by Margaret, a sister of Alexander of Lochalsh, because her husband, *Donald Makarle Maklauchlan doue* (Black Donald MacLauchlan), aided Torquil MacLeod of Lewis who had been deemed a rebel.[13] We have no way of knowing why or for how long these lands were held by the family of the MacDonalds of Lochalsh or even of their historical extent. However, this forfeiture may have been the means by which the MacKinnons eventually gained the watch tower of Dunakin and the land which surrounds it.

The third item changed by King James and Bishop John MacKinnon, now a privy councillor, was to unite the offices of the Abbot of Iona and Bishop of the Isles so that *"the Bishop of the Isles shall hold the Abbacy of Iona in commendam and receive its revenues."* [14]

Surprisingly there appears to be no mention in the official records of the forfeiture of Neil Ban MacKinnon for his part in the last rebellion. It was, after all, Lauchlan, Neil's father, who was married to Margaret, the daughter of Rory MacLeod of Lewis, and Margaret's brother, Torquil MacLeod, who was the rebel leader and the guardian of Donald Dubh. Margaret MacLeod died in 1503 during the early years of the rebellion, and only a few years after the death of her husband Lauchlan.[15]

Neil Ban MacKinnon is on record as being an early and active supporter of Donald Dubh, something that could only be expected of one with his family ties. The MacKinnon lands of Mishnish on Mull, which had been claimed by the Crown in 1488, were officially still in government hands and would remain so until after King James IV's death at the Battle of Flodden in 1513.[16] Remarkably, neither the forfeiture of Mishnish, nor the grant to Huntly, appears to have been enforced and the MacKinnons remained firmly entrenched on all of their estates.

The unease with which the Highlanders viewed the political conditions they now lived under can be seen in the appearance of the first record of the Siol-Alpin. This novel clan alliance, of which the MacKinnons were a major part, was an ingenious, if not entirely fictive, response to a perplexing political problem. How, in changing times, could the clan chiefs, who had never before relied on tangible documentation from Edinburgh, legitimize the claim to their ancient lands?

The island culture was traditionally one in which an individual or clan's descent determined their status and position in society. To legitimize their claims to the estates and to show how they were related to their new rulers, the Highlanders astutely resorted to the use of genealogy.

There is no record of when either the MacKinnons or the MacQuarries first discovered they were of Alpinian stock, but they appear to have been amongst the first to do so.[17] The first written mention of the Siol-Alpin was in a publication by the Dean of Lismore, Sir James MacGregor, and his brother Duncan in 1512, where the name appears in a new genealogy of the Clan MacGregor. This genealogy, taken from the *Books of the Genealogies of the Kings,* 'proved' that the MacGregor chiefs were descended from King Alpin, the father of Kenneth mac Alpin, the first King of Scots.[18]

The MacGregor chiefs adopted the motto, *"S'Rioghal Mo Dhream,"* meaning "My Race is Royal" to reflect their change in status. This seemingly innocuous, but not at all inconsequential, change in the clan's ancient history not only made the MacGregors new allies among the Highland clans, but showed how they were related to the present kings of Scotland and thus legitimated their right, by descent, to their traditional lands.

The death of King James IV on the battlefield of Flodden, killed by the explosion of one of his own cannons in 1513, and the subsequent naming of his widow, Margaret Tudor, as regent, did little to reassure the Islanders that their situation would improve in the near future.[19]

Donald (Galda) MacDonald of Lochalsh, the son of the murdered Alexander of Lochalsh who led the rising of 1496, returned to his estates after the battle of Flodden and almost immediately took part in a meeting of island chiefs at the great watch tower of Dunakin.[20] We are not entirely sure who held Dunakin at this time, as it was located on

154

Detail from John MacKinnon's memorial

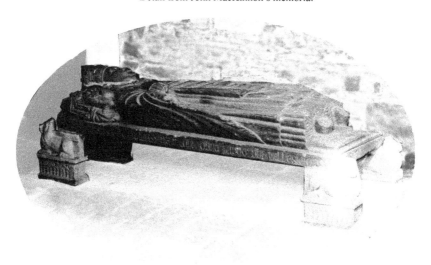

John MacKinnon's memorial in Iona Abbey
The inscription reads: "Here lies Johannes MacKinnon, Abbot of Iona, who died in
the year of Our Lord 15--, on whose soul may the Lord Most High have mercy, Amen

The grave slab of Margeret MacLeod of Lewis, the inscription reads:
"Here lies Margarete, daughter of Rodericus MacLeod of Lewis,
widow of Lauchlanus MacKinnon

the lands previously forfeit by Donald Galda's aunt, Margaret of Lochalsh, and given by the king to the Earl of Huntly, but it is likely the estate may have already been informally occupied by the MacKinnons.

In all probability, the island chiefs, along with their followers and attendants, would have presented a colourful and lively sight as they gathered inside Dunakin's grey walls. The object of the meeting was the restoration of the Lordship of the Isles and the selection of a suitable chief to lead them in that endeavour.[21]

The names of the chiefs who attended and the reported negotiations shed a good deal of light on the politics and concerns in the Isles during this period. One of the more influential leaders of the meeting appears to have been Malcolm MacLeod, then chief of the MacLeods of Lewis.[22]

The MacLeods of Dunvegan, however, had good reasons to absent themselves from the affair. The MacLeods of Lewis had allied themselves with the MacDonalds of Sleat who were, at the time, feuding with MacLeod of Dunvegan over the lands of Trotternish on Skye. However, we can be assured that, at a meeting of this import, the clan chiefs who held office under the ancient Council of the Isles; MacKinnon, MacNeil, MacQuarrie and others, would all have been present. The chief of MacLean, however, did not attend as he was occupied by the affairs of his own clan in Morvern.

Alexander MacDonald of Kintyre advocated that Donald (Gruamach) MacDonald of Sleat be selected to lead the island clans. Alexander may have had many good reasons for not wanting the closer candidate, Sir Donald (Galda) MacDonald of Lochalsh, to assume the leadership of the island Geal. Alexander of Kintyre was married to the daughter of Alexander (MacIain) of Ardnamurchan. It was MacIain who, as a favor to King James IV, engineered the murder of Sir Donald Galda's father, Alexander of Lochalsh, in 1496. It was rumoured that Alexander of Kintyre, himself, may have had a hand in that treacherous affair.

The appointment of Donald Gruamach would also have tended to divide the chiefs on the Council of the Isles as two closer candidates still lived. Sir Donald Galda was the grandson of Celestine, the second son of Alexander, the Lord of the Isles, and Donald Gruamach was the grandson of Alexander's third son Hugh. In the Gaelic society of the Hebrides at this time, these relationships would have been well known and considered extremely important. No doubt Alexander of Ardnamurchan would have preferred the leadership of MacDonald of Sleat, as presenting a better opportunity for personal profit from the civil war in the Isles, which would have been the likely result of this choice.

Malcolm MacLeod of Lewis accepted the proposed nomination of his ally, Alexander of Kintyre, and approached Donald Gruamach of Sleat with the offer. However, Donald Gruamach gave two important reasons for his refusal; first, he very much doubted all the Islanders would follow him in such a difficult enterprise and second; while Donald Dubh, the legitimate Lord of the Isles, was still alive, he would have nothing to do with such an affair.

Ruins of the old watch tower of Dunakin

Only after the refusal by Donald Gruamach, was Sir Donald Galda's nomination for the position of leadership advanced to the fore. There appears to have been strong opposition voiced to Donald Galda's nomination at the meeting, perhaps by Alexander of Kintyre. The matter was finally settled when Malcolm MacLeod and the other chiefs visited MacLean in Morvern, where MacLean agreed to support Sir Donald Galda's leadership. The Islanders were once again united, even the MacLeods of Harris (Dunvegan) had agreed to follow Sir Donald Galda of Lochalsh.

When the uprising actually began, the forces the Islanders could field were the MacDonalds of Islay and Glengarry, the MacLeods of Harris and Lewis, Chisholm of Comer and, of course, the MacLeans, MacKinnons, MacNeils, and MacQuarries.

By November 1513 the Islanders were well on the offensive. Sir Donald Galda, with Alexander MacRanald of Glengarry, and Wiland Chisholm of Comer, besieged and captured Urquhart Castle at the head of Loch Ness, laying waste to the surrounding countryside. Meanwhile in the Hebrides, the MacLeans of Duart, Lochbuie, and Ardgour, together with Neil Ban MacKinnon, Gillonan MacNeil, and Dunslaff MacQuarrie besieged and captured the ancient stronghold of Cairn na Berg[23]. With the fall of Cairn na Berg, the maritime force under MacLean of Duart proceeded northward to Skye, where it joined up with the MacLeods of Harris.

Because Donald Gruamach had long contested the district of Trotternish with MacLeod of Harris and had not joined in the rebellion, he was now seen, by the rebel clans, as an enemy. Landing on the Sleat peninsula, MacLean's maritime force captured and then destroyed Donald Gruamach's castle of Dunscaith. These were heady days for the Islanders. As their ranks were swelled by eager recruits from the islands, Sir Donald Galda was proclaimed Lord of the Isles.

By 1514 the government in Edinburgh realized the serious nature of the revolt and Colin Campbell, the Earl of Argyll, was commissioned to proceed against the Islanders led by MacLean of Duart. MacKenzie of Kintail and Monroe of Fowlis were named lieutenants in the North and ordered to contain the forces led by Sir Donald Galda and Wiland Chisholm. Not the least of the government's preparation, was to instruct the chief men of the mainland areas adjacent to the Isles, to oppose any landings by the Islanders or they too would be held guilty of rebellion.

The island clans, specifically the MacKinnons, MacLeans, MacDonalds of Islay (Clan Ian Mhor), MacLeods, MacQuarries and MacNeils, were resolute in their cause--the reestablishment of the Lordship of the Isles. It transpired that 1514 became a year of predatory warfare in the Isles and along the coasts of the mainland. There were no large-pitched battles during this time, but rather a constant series of raids and counter raids. There was a great deal plundered and much destroyed.

Unable to subdue the rebellion militarily, the government in Edinburgh turned to negotiation. In the year of 1515 John MacIain of Ardnamurchan was awarded a commission to negotiate with the less violent of the Islanders. The commission gave MacIain the authority to promise royal favour and remission to any Islander who paid restitution for the damage or injury he had caused to the king's loyal subjects.

The promises contained in the commission were not intended to apply to the leaders of the island clans. Simultaneous to this initiative, Colin Campbell, the Earl of Argyll, prevailed on the island chiefs to submit in person at the court. In this way, Colin Campbell suggested, the island leaders could discuss their terms with the Crown directly.

To satisfy the chiefs' legitimate concerns for their personal safety, Campbell promised them his protection if they wished to make the journey to Edinburgh. The islands were not subdued, but were quiet, and by August 1515, Sir Donald Galda of Lochalsh and MacIain of Ardnamurchan had their disputes settled by arbitration.

After several appearances before the Privy Council, Sir Donald Galda's reconciliation was so cordial that the government left him in power in the Isles. What became of the negotiations with the lesser island chiefs is unknown. Indeed, they may not have actually submitted at all as it may have appeared to them that the Lordship of the Isles was resurrected and they, for all intents and purposes, had triumphed. By 1516 the Edinburgh government's confidence in Donald Galda's leadership of the Islanders appeared to be complete. He was even summoned by the government to raise his forces and proceed to the southern borders to help fend off the English.

Chapter 10
End Notes

1. Grant, I. F., *Social & Economic Development of Scotland*, Oliver & Boyd, Edinburgh, 1930.

2. Alexander was the eldest son of George, the 2nd Earl of Huntly. This grant of land to Huntly, which was occupied and traditionally owned by the clans Ranald, Cameron, and Stewart, would be the cause of great strife during the early 1540s.

3. See Appendix 7.

4. Angus MacDonald was then styled the Master of the Isles. He was the son of John, the last Lord of the Isles.

5. The Stewarts of Appin held Duor and Glencoe at this time as they had formerly under the Lordship of the Isles. The Stewarts tended to follow Argyll, which put them at odds with both the island clans and Huntly. Huntly was ordered by the king to insure the Crown rents were collected, by force if necessary. Gregory, *History of Western the Highlands & Islands*, William Tait, Edinburgh, 1836, 96.

6. MacLean of Duart surrendered the person of the young Donald Dubh to King James when MacLean himself submitted. This may not have been the betrayal it appears. Archibald, the Earl of Argyll and Donald Dubh's maternal uncle, may well have negotiated the surrender to prevent Donald being captured or killed by Huntly's men

7. For their service in the Isles, the king gave the MacKays the MacLeod lands of Assint and Cogeach.

8. The Brehon was the lawyer/judge class of Celtic society. One did not become a Brehon until a very long and detailed course of study was completed. The Brehons were the appointed wise men at the top of Gaelic society, and the law they administered was extremely sophisticated and covered every aspect of life in that society. The judges would collect a set fee for every decision they gave. However, if the judge rendered a wrong decision, he was obligated to compensate the offended party for damages. Brehon law, which was based on tradition and culture, not precedence, was extremely fair and easy to live under. In fact, the English settlers in the Irish Pale preferred it to the harsher English common law. Despite being outlawed by Queen Elizabeth I, Brehon law survived until well into the 16th century.

9. King James gave Kenneth Williamson a gift of Crown land in Skye. The land was to support him while he was at school becoming a master of laws, with the intent of practicing as a lawyer in the Isles.

10. The changes affected the whole of the Hebrides, but Strath in particular, as the appointments were made immediately. Before this time, the appointments to positions in local churches were the responsibility of Iona or the Bishop of the Isles. On the MacKinnon lands of Mishnish in northern Mull, St. Mary's Chapel, at the east edge of the Clachan of Tobermory, is first mentioned in Scottish Crown rental records in 1509. By 1540 the patronage of St. Mary's was in the hands of the Scottish Crown, and in 1542 Crown records stated that certain lands in Mull had belonged to the chapel "from the time of its foundation long ago."

11. Askimruby may have referred to the area within the immediate vicinity of the church at the east end of Loch Cill Chriosd and not to the larger Parish of Strath.

12. If there was wax enough to supply altar candles, it may be wondered if the chief's family, and those other leading men of the clan, also used candles for light. Tallow or candle wax was prepared by rendering animal fat.

13. Alexander of the Isles was Alexander of Lochalsh who led the rebellion to restore the Lordship of the Isles in 1496. He was recognized as leader of the Islanders after Angus's death in 1490. His son, Donald of Lochalsh, would continue the struggle against the government after his father's death.

14. Rev. MacKinnon, D., *The Chiefs and Chiefship of Clan MacKinnon*, Portree, 1931, 7.

15. Margaret's epitaph notes that she was the "Widow of MacKinnon." Margaret is buried beneath the Church of Eye on Lewis.

16. The Crown of Scotland did not tolerate nor respect the independence of the Lordship of the Isles. The Crown claimed land in the Isles in 1476, 1488, and finally in 1493. In the year 1488, five years before the last forfeiture of the Isles in 1493, the Crown claimed a great deal of land that was integral to the Lordship of the Isles. This claim made the islands of Jura, Islay, Colonsay, Tiree, and Uist; Trotternish and Sleat on Skye; the mainland districts of Ardnamurchan, Sunart, and Morven, property of the Crown. On the island of Mull, the Ross of Mull and Mishnish, which were occupied by the MacKinnons, were also claimed by the king. The reason for the Crown claiming the lands was the insistence by the nobles of Scotland that the king should be self supporting. One of the ways in which the king could raise his income, was simply to take the land of those who had fallen out of favour through the legal process of forfeiture.

162

17. An early MacQuarrie chief named Allan authenticated the MacQuarrie descent from Alpin with the now lost "*History of the Alpinian Family.*" There is some question regarding the existence of this book, as no copies nor other quotations from the text have survived, and, in consequence, many modern scholars tend to believe that it never did exist.

18. The *"Genealogies of the Kings"* has not been seen since. The descent from Alpin may not, however, have be entirely fictive. The MacKinnons, MacQuarries, MacGregors, MacPhees, and MacNabs, who all claim membership of the Siol-Alpin, are historical descendants of Cormac, who was a descendant of the Cinel Lorn. The kings of Scotland were descended from the ancient Cinel Gabhran of Dalriada, which was headed by Alpin until 842. The two root families, that of Lorn and Gabhran, are tied by the marriage, circa 1015, of Doada, daughter of Malcolm II of Scotland, to Finlay, the son of Ruaire mac Domhnall ic Muireagain, son of the King of Moray. Thus, the descendants of Cormac could claim descent from King Alpin through Doada. It is interesting to note that, of the families of the Siol Alpin, the only two which cannot be shown to be descendants of Cormac and the Cinel Lorn are the MacAulays and the Grants.

19. King James IV invaded England after the English army invaded France. He had intended to remove the pressure on his French allies by forcing the English to divert some of their force to confront the Scots. The battle, however, was a disaster. The Scottish army was destroyed and King James IV was killed. In Gregory, *Western Highlands & Isles*, William Tate, Edinburgh, 1836 112, he reports that there was a sizable contingent of Highlanders with the Scottish army. Although no Hebridean chiefs are recorded as being killed, the Earl of Argyll and many of the senior members of his house were slain and John of Kintail, the young chief of the MacKenzies, was captured. James IV had an infant son, thereafter James V, who was too young at 17 months of age to take the throne.

20. Donald of Lochalsh was raised at court after the death of his father, Alexander. He was a favorite of King James IV and was allowed to succeed to his family's estates. Donald took part in the disaster at Flodden Field, where he was knighted by the king.

21. See Appendix 8 for the relationships of the heirs to the Lordship of the Isles.

22. Torquil MacLeod, Chief of the MacLeod of Lewis, who had played a major part in the rebellion of Donald Dubh, had died sometime before 1511. John MacLeod, Torquil's son, was excluded from the succession of Lewis in 1506 and again in 1511, when the king granted a charter to his uncle Malcolm. It wasn't until Malcolm's death, in about 1528, that John recovered possession of the chiefship and was able to hold it until his own death in the late 1530s. The times were disturbed by a tripartite fight over Trotternish in Skye. In 1498, while holding court at Kilkerran, King James

IV had granted the office of bailliary and lands in Trotternish and a heritable grant to the MacDonalds' lands of Sleat to Alexander MacLeod of Dunvegan, but within two weeks he had also made the same grant to John's father Torquil. Confusing matters even further, the king, on his return to Edinburgh, then revoked all the charters he had granted to the island chiefs. Alexander MacLeod of Dunvegan seems to have been in possession in 1528, but was feuding with Donald Gruamach of Sleat over lands in Sleat and North Uist as well as Trotternish. Donald Gruamach's mother had been married to Torquil of Lewis, so Donald could count on John's support in the continuing feud with Alexander of Dunvegan.

23. Cairn na Berg was considered a royal castle and had been garrisoned by government soldiers since its capture by King James IV in 1505.

Chapter 11
THE DAUNTING OF THE ISLES

It may have been during Sir Donald Galda's time on the borders that he met Alexander, Lord Home. At any rate, during the year 1516, Sir Donald Galda involved himself in Alexander's plots against the Scottish government. The Council of Island Chiefs appears to have been regularly consulted by Sir Donald Galda and not only approved of his actions, but were actively involved as accomplices. The plots were foiled and on the 8th October, 1516 Alexander Lord Home was executed for treason. During the investigation of the affair, several of the Hebridean chiefs were also found to be implicated and were also accused of treason.

Due to his position and stature in the Edinburgh government, Sir Donald Galda was able to effectively shelter his followers and protect the implicated chiefs from prosecution. Indeed, by 1517, in spite of being found to have been deeply involved in Lord Home's treason, Donald Galda officially assumed the Lieutenancy of the Isles and several other high offices in the government at Edinburgh.

Confident of his power within the Isles and his authority in Edinburgh, Sir Donald Galda gathered the armed might of the islands to revenge the murder of his father, which had taken place in 1496 at the hands of Alexander of Ardnamurchan. The Islanders; MacLean of Duart and Ardgour, along with Neil Ban MacKinnon, Gillonan MacNeil, Dunslaff MacQuarrie and Alexander MacLeod, quickly seized and burned the castle of Mingary and then laid waste to the entire district with fire and sword.

The savageness of the attack and its ruthless continuation, even after MacIain had fled, greatly disturbed the island chiefs. The many doubts resulting from Sir Donald's poor decisions, gave way to a deep concern regarding his suitability to lead. Eventually, Lauchlan MacLean of Duart and Alexander MacLeod of Dunvegan, after consulting with

Lewis

Harris

Trotternish

Dunvegan   Raasay

Scalpy
Lochalsh

Sleat
Glengary

Barra

Lochiel

Ardnamurchan
Mingary Castle
Coll   Morvern
Cairn na Berg
Tyree   Lismore
Ulva   Ladies Rock
Mull   Duart

Craignish

Colonsay

Roseneath

Islay

Kintyre

Fairhead
Murlough Bay
Torr Head

other chiefs, decided to take matters into their own hands. They laid plans to capture Sir Donald and turn him over to the then acting regent, John Stewart, the Duke of Albany, in Edinburgh.

Sir Donald was informed of the plot against him and immediately fled, successfully evading capture. Unluckily, his two brothers, either not alerted to the danger or not feeling the need to flee, were both captured and surrendered to the regent.[1] This affair, and the recently resurrected Lordship of the Isles, ended when MacLean of Duart, MacLeod of Harris and the Earl of Argyll each presented separate petitions to the governing Lords in Council at Edinburgh. MacLean and MacLeod requested pardon for themselves and their friends; MacKinnon, MacNeil, MacQuarrie and others, for the crimes committed while serving Sir Donald.[2]

The wily Earl of Argyll asked for the Lieutenancy of the Isles and the authority to receive into the king's favour all who should submit to him except, of course, Sir Donald Galda of Lochalsh, his brothers, and the Clan Donald of Islay. He also requested the authority to pursue the rebels with fire and sword, a move that would further Campbell power in the west. All of these petitions were met with favourable responses in Edinburgh and a "Precept of Remission" was issued "for all that passed before the date of 12 March 1516-17" to MacLean, MacKinnon, MacNeil, MacQuarrie, their kin and servants.[3]

Indeed, so favourably was the submission received, that MacLean and MacLeod were immediately granted much more than the royal favour requested in their petitions. The rewards given by the government to the two principal lieutenants of the Hebridean forces, MacLeod of Harris and MacLean of Duart, illustrate the fickleness of the government in Edinburgh and the resulting uncertainty of ownership and possession of land during this period.

Alexander MacLeod of Harris had asked for rights to the district of Trotternish, but was given the right undisturbed only for a period of 11 years. Trotternish was, after all, along with possession of Sleat, the object of the recent feud between the MacLeods of Harris and the MacDonalds of Sleat and their allies, the MacLeods of Lewis. Lauchlan MacLean of Duart was granted the four merklands of Scalpa, which had reverted to the government on the death of Archibald Huchonson, its previous owner. Scalpa or Scalpay, as it is now known, an island off the East Coast of Skye, is now considered a part of the district of Strath, which at the time belonged to the MacKinnons. Although they held the adjacent island of Pabbay, the MacKinnons did not obtain ownership of Scalpay until sometime just prior to 1664.[4]

In the wake of his renunciation by MacLean and MacLeod of Harris, Sir Donald Galda of Lochalsh strengthened his alliances with the MacDonalds of Islay and the MacLeods of Lewis. The next year, in 1518, Sir Donald, together with the MacLeods of Lewis and Raasay, descended on Ardnamurchan, where they joined forces with Alexander MacDonald, the chief of the *Clan Iain Mor* (MacDonalds of Islay). On this occasion, MacIain did not flee but, in an attempt to protect his lands, was defeated and killed at the battle *Craig an airgid* (Silver Craig) in Morvern.

It appears that many of the Islanders still considered Sir Donald the legitimate Lord of the Isles and, on hearing of this victory, flocked to his standard. The rising was very short-lived, however, as Sir Donald died of unknown causes a few weeks later on either Tyree or at Cairn na Berg.

Possibly, as a consequence of Sir Donald's attack on MacIain and in an effort to protect their lands from royal retaliation, the island chiefs met and agreed to place themselves under the protection of the Earl of Argyll. In July of 1519 the clan chiefs: Ewen MacKinnon, Lauchlan MacLean, Alexander MacLeod, Gillonan MacNeil, and Dunsleve MacQuarrie of Ulva were signatories to a bond of manrent, homage and fealty in perpetuity to the Earl of Argyll.[5]

It was about this time that Clan Donald began to establish large permanent settlements in Antrim on the Northeast Coast of Ireland. The direct involvement of the island clans in the factious Irish/English politics of the time would eventually spill over and colour the history of the Hebrides themselves. The Islesmen, however, had a natural affinity toward Ireland and contact had been maintained between the two peoples since the founding of Dalriada. The cultures of Ireland and the Hebrides were essentially similar. The two peoples shared the same customs, religion, laws, language, and experience.[6] Indeed, the Islanders may have felt that, as their ancestors had originally come from Ireland, they still retained a claim to parts of that island.

The communications between the two areas were also, for the times, extremely easy. The island galley fleets could make the trip from the Hebrides to Northern Ireland in the short space of a couple of hours. On the cliffs overlooking the landing sites of Fairhead, Murlough Bay, and Torr Head on the Irish East Coast, there were ancient signal beacons which could be seen from Kintyre and Islay. The signals sent from these sites could be quite sophisticated, indicating the need for men or ships and in what numbers.

Generations of Islanders had joined the Irish ranks during the intertribal struggles and later during the ongoing conflict against the English. The Irish chiefs knew how to make good use of the large numbers of readily-available island warriors. Although the Islanders fought for both the Irish and their English foes, even at times simultaneously, overall they preferred to aid their fellow Gaels.

The relationship between the Clan MacLean and the Campbells suffered irreparable damage shortly after they had signed their bonds of manrent in 1519, and came close to plunging the islands into war. Lauchlan MacLean of Duart, for some now unknown reason, had determined to get rid of his wife. He was married to the Lady Elizabeth Campbell, the daughter of Archibald Campbell, the second Earl of Argyll, and sister to John Campbell of Cawdor. MacLean, naively following the advice of two of his clansmen, had her put onto a rock in the sound of Mull at low tide. The rock, which lies halfway between Lismore and the coast of Mull, is still known as the *Ladies Rock*. His intention was seemingly that she would be swept out to the open sea and drowned as the tide rose. What the motivation was behind this clumsily-executed attempt to murder his wife, is not known. It may have been a domestic quarrel or due to the fact they had no children or, alternatively, as suggested in some accounts of the incident, that she had twice previously attempted to murder Lauchlan.

Fortunately for her, however, she was seen and rescued by a passing galley, the crew of which delivered her safely to her brother's house. Not surprisingly, the relationships between the two clans quickly deteriorated to the point of imminent violence. The MacDonalds of the Clan Ian Mor quickly sided with the MacLeans in the fray and, in consequence, had the island of Colonsay raided and burned by Argyll for their trouble.[7] The feud ran the risk of developing into open warfare in 1523, when John Campbell of Cawder took revenge for his sister's maltreatment by going to Edinburgh and murdering Lauchlan MacLean who was there on business.[8] The MacLeans, of course, were furious at the murder of their chief and the clan gathered for war. Fortunately, before it could develop into a full-blown conflict, this affair was ended by the swift intervention of the government, but the bonds agreed to in 1519 had been rendered meaningless.

With the coming of age of King James V in 1528, the government in Edinburgh once again revoked all the charters and grants which had been made to the island chiefs. This time, the Privy Council gave the Earl of Argyll the full authority to enforce the revocation.

The peace and relative calm of the Hebrides was broken for the second time in nine years when, in 1528, the government in Edinburgh granted the island of Uist and the district of Sleat to the court favourite, Alexander MacLeod of Dunvegan. These two districts, along with Trotternish and Strath, had belonged to the MacLeods of Dunvegan while they served the earls of Ross, but the MacDonalds had occupied Sleat since about 1390. The MacKinnons, incomers from Mull, had occupied Strath from about the same period. The struggle for possession of Trotternish began shortly after Sleat was initially occupied by the MacDonalds. By the time of the king's grant to Alexander MacLeod in 1528, the MacDonalds would have held Sleat and had been contesting the ownership of Trotternish for at least one hundred years.[9]

Donald Gruamach MacDonald of Sleat opted to take the initiative and to attack the MacLeods of Dunvegan before they could make good their claims to his estates. Along with his ally, John MacLeod of Lewis, Donald Gruamach and his clan invaded Trotternish by sea from the north. The MacLeods of Dunvegan, surprised and caught completely unprepared, were unable to mount any defence. The rout was terrible; there was much bloodshed, burning and destruction as the invaders offered the MacLeods of Dunvegan no quarter.

All the inhabitants of Trotternish were systematically driven from the district. At the southern end of Loch Snizort Beag, at the ford of the Snizort River, the MacLeods took up a strong defensive position and prepared to make a stand. All of those who couldn't fight--the women, children, and elderly, were sent to the castle of Dunvegan for safety. All the others, warriors and common folk alike, were determined to protect their homes. The defence, although fierce and determined, proved futile and was overrun by a vigorous assault by the MacDonalds and their Lewis allies.

The whole of the MacLeod lands in Northern Skye was now laid open to the victorious allies. No attempt was made to lay siege to nor capture Dunvegan as the task was deemed to be a too difficult and time-consuming undertaking. The whole of Skye north of the MacKinnon territories of Strath was plundered by the marauding MacDonalds. Great herds of MacLeod cattle and other booty were taken overland though the

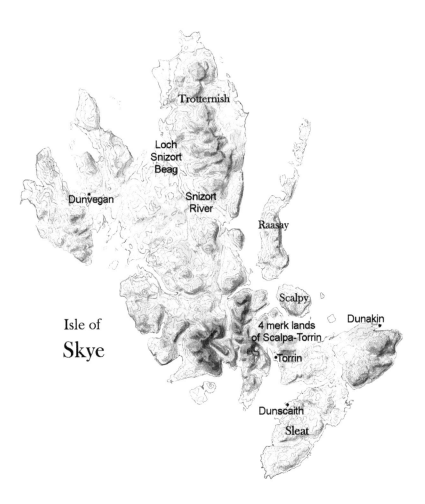

Trotternish

Loch
Snizort
Beag

Dunvegan

Snizort
River

Raasay

Scalpy

Dunakin

Isle of
Skye

4 merk lands
of Scalpa-Torrin

•Torrin

Dunscaith

Sleat

Cuillins and across Strath to Dunscaith in Sleat. One wonders what thoughts passed among the MacKinnons of Strath as they watched the great herds of captured cattle being driven through their country. The MacKinnons would have witnessed almost the entire wealth of the northern part of the island being taken southwards.[10] Consequent to this affair, the MacLeods of Dunvegan not only lost Trotternish, but were also effectively prevented from occupying Uist and Sleat.

John MacLean of Coll who had lost the estate of Lochiel under the previous government, had it returned by King James V. Well aware of the transient nature of royal charters, MacLean of Coll strengthened his position in the North by marrying a daughter of Lord Lovat. While Lovat and his daughter were on the difficult journey to the island of Coll, they met two MacKinnon brothers, Donald Ban and Alastair Mor. Lovat knew both of these gentlemen well as they were *"real MacKinnons out of his own family"* and he had often visited MacKinnon's house.

Because Donald Ban and Alastair Mor had recently refused their chief's request to go into Sleat and apprehend their brother-in-law, they were, at present, not on good terms with him. The MacKinnons suggested they accompany Lovat and his daughter to Coll *"and get a situation as they could not live comfortably where they were."* The offer was accepted and Donald Ban accompanied Lovat and his daughter to Coll, but Alastair Mor decided to go to Glengarry instead. As Alastair Mor had quarrelled with and defeated some MacDonalds, he was not able to stay very long in Glengarry. He, therefore, offered his services to MacLean of Duart who gave him a farm at Killiechronan.[11]

Argyll, whose carefully negotiated web of alliances was now torn apart, eagerly undertook his assigned task of enforcing the revocation of royal charters, quickly turning it to his own gain. The MacDonalds of Islay, the MacLeans, MacKinnons, and a few other clans had little choice but to immediately rise in rebellion to protect the claims to their lands. As the Earl of Argyll was actively enforcing the cancellation of charters, his lands were attacked in force.

The island clans descended on Roseneath, Craignish, and other Campbell districts, which were first plundered and then burned. In retaliation, the Campbells laid waste to Mull, Tyree, and the whole district of Morvern. When news of the magnitude of the fighting in the west reached Edinburgh, it was eventually realized that the ill-omened situation in the Isles was escalating. It was felt that perhaps the Earl of Argyll's selfish actions were a factor in the discontent caused by the repeal of the charters. The Privy Council, in an attempt to bypass Argyll, dispatched a herald to treat directly with Alexander of Islay, the rebel leader.

The attempt to settle the dispute without the involvement of Argyll failed miserably. King James V, perhaps exasperated, ordered Argyll to immediately and forcefully reduce the Isles to obedience. A military stalemate soon developed, which lasted throughout 1529 and was broken only by small-scale predatory raiding by both sides. Early in 1530, in an effort to break the deadlock, the Earl of Argyll issued an order to the effect that all the tenants of the Isles were required to personally appear before the king on 24th of May and were not to support the rebels in any manner. To encourage compliance with the order, Argyll promised his personal protection for all those appearing before King James V and throughout the hazardous journey to Edinburgh.[12] As might have been expected, none of the rebellious chiefs, and precious few others, accepted Argyll's offer of protection.

Edinburgh Castle

With the Isles still defiant, King James ordered the gathering of a large force from the Lowlands and Eastern Highlands to assemble under the direction of Argyll. In May of 1530, as they watched the king's massive army assemble, the island chiefs decided to yield. Hector MacLean of Duart was elected to carry offers of submission from the other principal chiefs: John MacLean of Lochbuie; John Moydertach,Captain of Clanranald; Alexander MacIain of Ardnamurchan; Alexander MacLeod of Dunvegan; John MacLeod of Lewis, and Donald Gruamach of Sleat.

Hector MacLean appears, in this instance, to have dealt through the offices of the Burgess of Ayr, bypassing Argyll altogether. The king offered protection from Argyll to MacLean and any of the island chiefs who might accompany him to Edinburgh by the 20th of June. As an additional assurance, the king offered to take two of the following hostages from Argyll; Duncan Campbell of Glenurchy, Archibald Campbell of Auchenbreck, Archibald Campbell of Skipness or Duncan Campbell of Ilangerig, who were to be held at Edinburgh castle.

It is a significant indication of frustration with Edinburgh's polices that the names of the MacLeods of Lewis and Dunvegan, along with MacDonald of Sleat and MacIain of Ardnamurchan, are all listed as supporters of the rebellion. Notably absent from MacLean's list, are Alexander of Islay, Ewen MacKinnon and the MacNeils of Barra. As Colin Campbell, the Earl of Argyll, died while the negotiations were taking place, the surrender of these chiefs did not materialize. Although Argyll's aggressive stance was taken up by his son, who was of age, support for the king's service in the Isles withered, the Lowland army dispersed, and the condition of stalemate resumed.

By November 1530 Scotland's rulers resolved that two armies would be required to conquer the Isles; one personally led by King James V, and another led by his brother, the Earl of Moray. Orders were given for the assembly of both armies by June 1, 1531.

In the meantime parliament was called on to pass a sentence of forfeiture against any of the chiefs who remained in rebellion. Parliament proceeded diligently and, on April 26, 1531, Ewen MacKinnon was charged with rebellion. The Skye chiefs, Ewen MacKinnon and Donald Gruamach of Sleat, were both summoned to appear before the Privy Council in Edinburgh to answer the charges against them. But there is no indication, from surviving records, that they complied. As the preparations for the invasion of the Hebrides progressed, Hector MacLean of Duart and Alexander MacDonald of Islay decided to submit.

The surrender of the two principal leaders of the rebellion greatly reduced tensions as the government immediately saw the rebellion, without its leaders, as less of a threat to the stability of the Kingdom. The Privy Council decided that Argyll and Moray could competently handle the submission of the Isles without the direct involvement of the king. The two armies assembled for the planned invasion of the Hebrides had gathered by the end of June, and Argyll and Moray took charge of their commands. Fortunately for the Isles folk, these forces were never used and, by summer's end, all of the island chiefs had submitted and the rebellion was over.[13]

End Notes
Chapter 11

1. Although the Privy Council was split on their fate, it appears that both of Sir Donald's brothers were executed.

2. See appendix 9, MacLean promised his allegiance to the king and regent and promised his assistance to the Earl of Argyll in keeping peace in the Isles. He also gave a bond of manrent to Sir John Campbell of Cawdor.

3. The Remission issued by the Edinburgh government (1517) is the last official mention of Neil Ban, the MacKinnon chief. The next mention of a MacKinnon Chief occurs two years later (1519), and names Ewen as chief of the clan. There is no documented indication of when Neil Ban died, nor when or under what circumstances his son Ewen assumed the chiefship. There is not a great deal known of Neil's descendants. All we know is that he had two sons, Ewen and Lauchlan. Lauchlan's son, another Ewen, was alive in 1558 and is thought to have been the progenitor of the MacKinnons of Torrin.

4. *Origines Parochiales Scotiae,* Vol. 2, Part 1, W. H. Lizars, St James Sq., Edinburgh, 1854, 345. Because the herring fleet rendezvoused here, this was a valuable island. Ownership of Scalpay is given as:
    1. Margaret MacDonald, sister of Alexander of Lochalsh
    2. 1507 Alexander, Earl of Huntly, let to Archibald Huchonson, captain of the MacDonalds of Sleat
    3. 1517 Lauchlan MacLean of Duart
    4. 1540 Hector MacLean of Duart
    5. 1603 Hector MacLean of Duart (grandson of the above Hector), sold or otherwise obtained by Sir Roderick MacKenzie of Coigeach
    6. 1662 Sir George MacKenzie of Tarbet (from his grandfather), obtained by Ewen MacKinnon
    7. 1664 Lauchlan MacKinnon

5. This bond was also signed by John MacLeod of Mingonish and John MacLean of Coll. Bonds of this type between clans in the Highlands or noble families in the Lowlands were outlawed by King James I in 1425. He wanted to eliminate any alliances which might have undermined royal authority. That the Highland clans should resort to the use of these bonds

and agreements between families during the 16th century, reflects the uncertain nature of the times and their distrust of the ineffectual government in Edinburgh.

6. Both peoples had experienced the Viking and later cultural invasions in which their neighbours attempted to impose foreign values on the populations. In Ireland, the English were trying to replace the traditional Celtic way of life with a more feudal one. In the Western Highlands. the central government in Edinburgh was also attempting to replace accepted traditions with more feudal values. In both places the changes were resisted. Thus, the two peoples could understand and sympathise with each other's experience and motives very well.

7. Alexander MacDonald had just (1520) obtained leases for the islands of Islay, Colonsay, and Jura in exchange for a bond of manrent and gossipry with John Campbell of Cawdor. Cawdor legally held the islands by right of grants from the government in Edinburgh. By taking sides with the MacLeans, MacDonald broke his agreement with the Campbells.

8. Campbell, A., *History of Clan Campbell*, Edinburgh University Press, 2002, Vol. 2, 10. This account claims that MacLean was dirked by his brother-in-law, Cawdor, while at the king's residence, which would imply that Maclean was on official business of some kind.

9. For a good summary of the ownership of Trotternish, see: Gregory, *Western Highlands & Isles*, William Tate, Edinburgh, 1836, 130.

10. Alastair Crotach, the Chief of the MacLeods, had notified the government of the raid and submitted a list of the losses with a request for compensation.
    For MacLeod 100 cows,
        Talisker, 300 cows,100 horses, 2000 sheep 2000 goats
        Donald Roy of Carbost, 200 cows, 80 horses, 500 sheep, 500 goats
        Ferchar Liath, 100 cows, 60 horses, 200 sheep, 400 goats
        John MacAngus of Borreraig, 120 cows, 100 sheep 100 goats
        Donald Glas 80 cows 100 sheep, 100 goats,100 horses.

11. MacLean-Bristol, *Warriors and Priests*, Tuckwell Press East Lothian, 1995, 96.

12. Neither King James V, nor any of his nobles, could have been trusted to let a Highland chief pass unmolested. The nobles and government of the time were convinced that the trouble in the Hebrides was due to the fact that they were occupied by the Gael. It was commonly believed that, if the Gael could be gotten rid of and the Hebrides settled with civilized folk, the Isles could become a productive part of the Kingdom.

13. Archibald, the new Earl of Argyll, not caring to see his opportunities for gaining royal favor and reward so easily thwarted, did all he could to provoke the island chiefs. Argyll, when all else failed, even brought charges against MacDonald of Islay. MacDonald, to Argyll's surprise, appeared in Edinburgh in his own defense. MacDonald explained himself so well it appeared that Argyll was, in fact, the cause of the trouble in the West. MacDonald then offered the king his loyal service, stating he could bring many more men out in his service than Argyll could. Should the king desire it, MacDonald even offered to drive the Campbells out of Argyll so that the king would find it easier to watch him.

Chapter 12
FROM DONALD GALDA TO DONALD DUBH
THE LORDSHIP RESURRECTED

The 1530s were relatively quiet years in the Hebrides. There were, of course, scattered outbreaks of violence as old scores were settled, but these were generally on a small scale. The Islanders were being attracted to Ireland in increasing numbers. There was unrest in the native Irish community as the local chiefs sparred with each other and with the English for power. These struggles created many opportunities for the employment of island warriors and they were eager to take them.[1]

By 1533 English officials in the northern parts of Ireland were dispatching notices to the governing council in Dublin that the number of Islanders settling in Ulster was increasing daily. In an effort to discourage passage between the Hebrides and Ireland, the English instituted a coastal patrol. A fleet of English ships was stationed off the coast of Ulster with orders to intercept all island galleys making towards Ireland. It was reasoned that, if the Islanders could be kept from crossing the North Channel in large numbers, the conflict in Ireland could be more easily dealt with.

As the English navy of the time was racked by both corruption and incompetence, the coastal patrol proved to be very ineffective. The galley traffic between the Hebrides and Ireland does not appear to have been impeded in any way by the deployment of English ships. It would have been no surprise to the English government in Ireland when the first recorded clash between Islanders and English troops was reported in 1538. At Lecale a body of English soldiers intercepted a party of

The
Lordship Resurrected

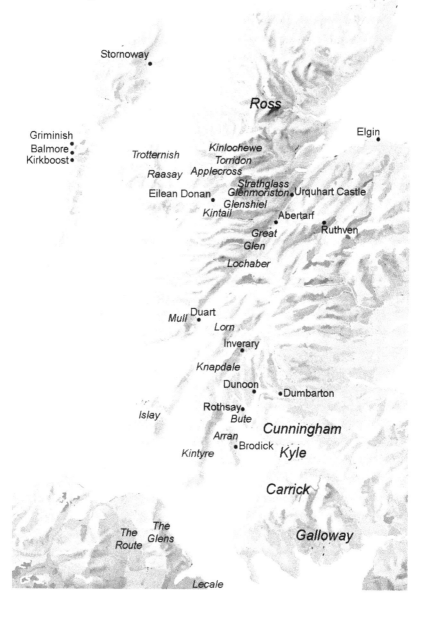

Stornoway

Ross

Griminish   Elgin
Balmore
Kirkboost

                 Trotternish   Kinlochewe
                              Torridon
              Raasay   Applecross
                        Strathglass
              Eilean Donan Glenmoriston Urquhart Castle
                         Glenshiel
                   Kintail   Abertarf
                                         Ruthven
                         Great
                         Glen

                      Lochaber

                   Duart
              Mull
                     Lorn
                       Inverary

                Knapdale

                    Dunoon
                              Dumbarton
                  Rothsay
            Islay   Bute
                            Cunningham
                  Arran
                      Brodick Kyle
            Kintyre

                              Carrick

          The   The
          Route Glens   Galloway

                      Lecale

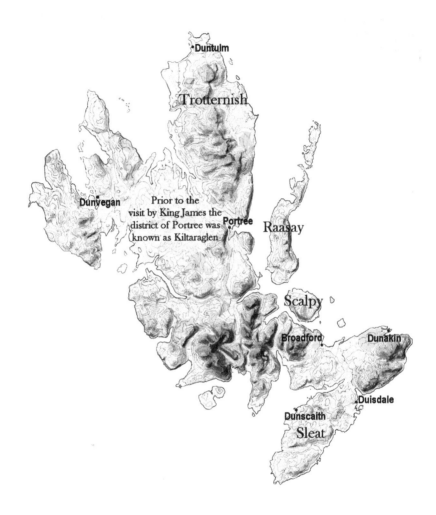

Prior to the visit by King James the district of Portree was known as Kiltaraglen

Islanders returning from a raid with their booty and a sharp skirmish resulted. The Islanders evidently escaped with the plunder as there is no report that any of them were captured nor that the booty had been recovered.

It was during the late 1530s that a MacKinnon became involved in a fatal MacDonald intrigue on the Isle of Skye itself.[2] Donald Gruamach, who was chief of the MacDonalds of Sleat at this time, made his home at his castle of Dunscaith, which is perched high on a lofty rock on the southern shore of Loch Eishort. Over the years the castle of Dunscaith had been extensively repaired following its destruction during the rising of 1513.

It transpired that Donald Gruamach and his wife, Catherine of Clanranald, were each visited by relatives at the same time. Ronald Herrach, a favourite cousin of Donald's, took great umbrage with Catherine's relatives. He was offended by their attitude and bearing and what he saw as the licence they took with the courtesy shown them by his cousin. One night in a fit of revenge, Ronald Herrach killed twelve of Catherine's family and had the bodies dumped outside the castle so that they lay on the ground below her window.

Then taking a hurried leave of his cousin Donald, Ronald left the castle just hours before Catherine was due to rise in the morning and discover what he had done. As can well be imagined, Catherine was indeed furious when she awoke and witnessed the awful deed perpetrated by Ronald the night before. Vowing to avenge her family's injuries, Catherine hired Black Finnon MacKinnon who agreed to take on her task.[3]

Ruins of Dunscaith Castle

Having the use of a galley, MacKinnon followed Ronald to the Long Island and eventually trailed him to North Uist. On New Year's Day, Donald Gruamach sent Black Finnon to the farm of Griminish to fetch Ranald Herrach so he could spend the New Year in Kirkboost with his cousin. As the two men approached Druimard, Finnon drew the dirk he had stolen from Donald Gruamach and killed Ranald where the cairn on Druimard in Balmore now stands. Finnon left Donald Gruamach's dirk with Ranald's body as a token to the people that Ranald's death was by Donald's orders.[4] That there appears to have been no repercussions felt by the MacKinnon clan for Ronald's murder, can only be attributed to the desire to maintain the peace by the leaders of Clanranald and the MacDonalds of Sleat.

When Donald Galda of Lochalsh, the last of his race, died in 1517, the captive, Donald Dubh, was viewed as the senior legitimate sucessor to the Lordship of the Isles. The claim of the MacDonalds of Sleat to lead the Lordship of the Isles was wildly recognised as subordinate only to that of Donald Dubh. Donald Gorm, the son of Donald Gruamach of Sleat and a daughter of Alastair Crotach, the MacLeod of Dunvegan, was recognized as the legitimate leader of the Islanders by all branches of the Clan Donald and by the other clans of the old Lordship.

With the exception of only two chiefs, Donald Gorm was welcomed by the clans to take the leadership of the ancient Lordship. The MacKenzies and MacLeod of Dunvegan both had good reason not to support his leadership. For some time now, the Mackenzie chiefs had been aligned with the government in Edinburgh, while the MacLeods of Dunvegan were still disputing the ownership of Trotternish with the MacDonalds of Sleat. In May of 1539 Donald Gorm had the consent of the Council of the Isles to lead another attempt to restore their ancient government.

Unfortunately, MacDonald family politics were to again interfere with and sidetrack the greater goal. Donald Gorm was married to Margaret, daughter of Iain mac Torquil MacLeod who had, with the blessing of the Edinburgh government, usurped the chiefship of Lewis. On the death of Donald Gruamach, Donald Gorm's father, the legal rights to Lewis should have passed to Ruairi MacLeod his accepted successor, but government interference ensured they did not.

The rift in the family of the MacDonalds of Sleat became apparent when Iain mac Torquil, Donald Gorm's father-in-law, refused to support his son-in-law's efforts to return Trotternish to MacDonald ownership. But the deposed Ruairi MacLeod did agree to lead his men in support of Donald Gorm's claim to those estates if Donald Gorm would, in turn, support the restoration of the chiefship of Lewis to him.[5] The invasion of Trotternish, by the combined forces of MacLeod and MacDonald warriors, was an overwhelming success and resulted in the total and final expulsion of the MacLeods of Dunvegan from that district.

Now that he had Trotternish, Donald Gorm turned his attention to his real challenge, the restoration of the Lordship of the Isles. The MacKinnons of Strath, led by Ewen, their chief, joined Donald Gorm, replacing the MacLeods of Lewis who went home to take the chiefship back from Iain mac Torquil.

When Donald Gorm led the MacDonalds of Sleat in an invasion of Ross, the only ally with him was Ewen MacKinnon at the head of his clan.[6] There is an old tradition which claims that, during this time, the MacKinnon's hereditary standard bearer was the head of a cadet family and tacksman of the farm of Duisdale.[7] The Islanders were transported across the Inner Sound by a fleet of 50 galleys, which landed the army at Applecross. They quickly ravaged Torridon and Kinlochewe and then attacked Kintail. In their effort to defend themselves, the MacKenzies and their MacCrae allies suffered very high casualties, one of whom was Sir Dugald MacKenzie, the priest of Kintail, who resided in Glenshiel.[8]

Hoping to surprise the Chief of MacKenzie, the Islanders moved quickly against the castle of Eilean Donan. As it was garrisoned by only three men, the castle should have been easy prey; however, as the invaders approached, the castle's defenders put up an extremely lively defence which lasted for more than an hour. As the limited stock of arrows in the castle was diminished, they were fired with less and less frequency. When he thought the defenders had at last run out of projectiles, Donald Gorm stepped out into the open to survey the easiest way to assault the castle.

By a twist of fate, what was possibly the last arrow in the castle, found its mark, striking Donald Gorm in the thigh.[9] Perhaps more annoyed than hurt by the wound, Donald reached down and roughly pulled the arrow out himself. The arrow, however, was barbed and, in its extraction, an artery was severed.

Eilean Donan Castle

Although they tried with the utmost of their ability to save their leader, there was not much Donald's followers could do to help him. Bleeding profusely, Donald was carried to a crude hut by a nearby inlet where he died shortly afterward.[10] The Islanders, distraught at the sudden loss of their leader, revenged themselves by burning every house, barn, and boat in the district. The rising, led by Donald Gorm, began with the potential to be the most serious threat yet faced by the government in Edinburgh, but was ended before it had a chance to develop.

King James, realizing the magnitude of discontent in the west, thought it best to personally appear in the Isles and awe the clans with a display of his wealth and power. A number of the principal nobles of Scotland were asked to accompany the king and each bring a large body of men.[11] A fleet of twelve, well-provisioned and armed ships left the Firth of Forth in May of 1540 and sailed northward along the East Coast of Scotland.

The fleet made a stop in the Orkneys before proceeding on to Strathnaver, where Donald, the Chief of Clan MacKay, was seized by the royal company. Continuing on to the Outer Hebrides, the fleet put into Stornoway, where Ruairi MacLeod of Lewis and his principal kinsmen were also taken prisoner and forced to accompany the expedition. A few days later while the fleet was off the north of Skye, Alexander MacLeod of Dunvegan visited the king on his ship but was not held as a prisoner for reasons of court.[12] In Trotternish, most probably at the MacDonald castle of Duntulm, John of Moidart, Chief of Clanranald; Alexander of Glengarry, and several other MacDonald chieftains were invited aboard to see the king. Then in a betrayal of royal honour, they were captured and held as prisoners.

Proceeding south between the islands of Skye and Raasay, the fleet put into Loch Chaluim Chille, where it anchored for several days. A great many mainland chiefs and gentlemen, who had come to wait on the king and ask royal favours, met and welcomed the fleet. The local people were so impressed by the spectacle, that the district, which was then known as Kiltaraglen, began to be referred to as *Port Righ* (Portree-Port of the King).

Sailing on to Kintail, the fleet made its way past Broadford and the watch tower of Dunakin to anchor in Lochalsh, where it was joined by the MacKenzie chief. Proceeding south through the Sound of Sleat, the fleet visited Mull, Knapdale, Kintyre, and Islay, stopping along the way to make prisoners of Hector MacLean of Duart and James MacDonald of Islay. As the fleet passed, and to insure his grasp on the islands, the king left garrisons, captained by men of his own choosing, in several of the more important Hebridean strongholds. It is certain that Dunakin, which was the single most strategically-placed tower on Skye, was garrisoned by royal troops at this time.

Landing at Dumbarton, the king proceeded overland to Edinburgh, while the captured chiefs made the same journey, but they travelled around the north of Scotland by ship.[13] Upon reaching Edinburgh, the king and council acted to legislatively strengthen royal authority in the Isles. On December 3, 1540, the king passed acts through parliament which annexed, inalienably to the crown, all the lands which had once belonged to the old Lordship as well as North and South Kintyre. After giving hostages to insure their good behaviour, several of the captured chiefs were released. Others, however, who were perhaps seen as more of a threat, would be detained for a considerably longer period.

Incredibly, there is no record of Ewen, the MacKinnon chief, having being made prisoner on the king's fleet at this time. Subsequent events suggest that he may have been taken but used the opportunity to make good his peace with the government. On March 22, 1541, Ewen MacKinnon received a remission for his role in the attack on Eilean

Donan. Just four months later, on the 2nd of August, Ewen received a charter, now known as the *"Carta Engenii mac Fingone"* (Ewen MacKinnon's Charter), from King James V.

This charter, which was the first royal charter held by a MacKinnon chief, signified that the clan lands, comprising of twenty merklands of Mishnish on Mull and twenty merklands of Strathardill on Skye, were held directly from the king. The merklands mentioned in this charter were not a measure of land area, as is acre or hectare, but rather they measure its productivity. The rent due the king for each 20 merklands was about 34 cattle, 34 wethers, 255 stone of cheese, 255 stone of ground flour, £8 and 10/ (eight pounds 10 shillings) in silver, and 16 bolls of malt. The amount of the king's rent was produced above what was required to support the clan chief, gentlemen, and their tenants and does not include the profit of the rent collectors.

The charter gave the lands in free tenantry and sasin to Ewen MacKinnon and to the lawful heirs male of his body, failing whom to the nearest lawful male relatives. The role of the MacKinnon chief was now substantially changed from what it had traditionally been. As clan chief, he was no longer merely the guardian of the clan lands, but was now their sole legal owner.

The attention of the Hebridean chiefs was now focusing away from mainland Scotland and more often wandered toward their ancestral home.[14] With the MacDonalds of the Clan Ian Mor leading the way, the island clans were quickly being drawn deeper into the affairs of Ireland. The MacQuillins of the Route, which is roughly the region of Antrim to the east of the Bann River and southwest of the River Bush, had asked for MacDonald's help against the O'Kanes and the Clan Sweeney.

The MacDonalds, who had possessed the Glens of Antrim since the 1380s, cheerfully aided the MacQuillins in the defeat of both rival clans. The MacDonalds, however, then turned on their allies, the MacQuillins, and drove them from the Route as well. Thus the MacDonalds of Islay came into possession of both the Route and the Glens of Antrim. This Hebridean colony in Ulster would soon act as the open gateway for the involvement of all the major island clans into the affairs of that ill-fated island.

188

Meanwhile on the Isle of Skye, the Edinburgh government's interference and involvement in land ownership was to cause more trouble. The MacDonalds of Sleat suffered a severe legal setback in 1542 when Alastair Crotach, Chief of the MacLeods of Harris, was granted a charter to the lands of Uist and Sleat. Incredibly, the very next year King James V also conferred Trotternish on Alastair Crotach in life rent.

Irish dress during the reign of Englands King Henry VIII

The island of Uist, at this time, was occupied by the MacDonalds of Clanranald, while Sleat, as well as Trotternish, were both occupied by the MacDonalds of Sleat. As the MacDonalds remained in actual occupation of the lands, the generosity of King James V was of faint value to the MacLeods.

It was about this time, and perhaps because of the royal grants to MacLeod, that the MacDonalds of Sleat moved their principal residence from Dunscaith in Sleat to Duntulm on the Northwest Coast of Trotternish. This constant shuffling of charters by the central government in Edinburgh along with the political and economic instability that it brought, was the greatest single cause of the discontent in the Isles.

When James V died in 1542, his daughter Mary, then only six days old, was too young to take the throne. In her stead, Lord Hamilton, the Earl of Arran, was to rule as regent in her name. Arran was a weak, manipulative leader and the government of Scotland soon dissolved into a great many competing factions as the nobles became entangled in self-serving squabbles.[15] Early in the regency during 1543, Donald Dubh, the last heir to the Lordship, escaped from custody in Edinburgh and was to ignite a sentiment and fervour in the Hebrides greater than any yet seen. The ties between the Gaels of Ireland and the Hebrides would be strengthened and, for the first time, the English were invited to play a major role in the politics of the Isles.

On making his way back to the Hebrides, Donald Dubh was immediately recognized and welcomed by Ewen, Chief of MacKinnon; Alastair Crotach, Chief of MacLeod of Dunvegan; Archibald the Clerk, then captain of the MacDonalds of Sleat; Alexander MacIain of Ardnamurchan; and Angus (the haughty) of the MacDonalds of Islay. Donald Dubh's leadership was soon endorsed by most of the island clans, the most notable abstentions being Angus MacDonald's brother, James MacDonald of Antrim, MacDuffie of Colonsay, and MacLean of Duart.[16]

Many of the Highland chiefs and other hostages taken by King James V in 1540, were still held by the Scottish government in Edinburgh, so the Islanders proceeded carefully. Donald Dubh, who had revived the Council of the Isles and his claim to the Earldom of Ross, even opened communication with England.[17] The Council of the Isles, not feeling free to act out of concern for the safety of the captive chiefs, agreed to a truce with Argyll, which was to last until May 1543.[18] Through the duration of the truce, Argyll did his best to keep the uncommitted clans from joining the rebellion.

On the 23rd of May at Illanagawen, Argyll and MacLean signed a bond of manrent in which Duart promised to be the earl's man in exchange for 40 merklands. In the end, however, all of the earl's diplomacy was undone when the Earl of Arran, in a gesture of either goodwill or, as some claim, an act of vengeful cynicism, released all of the hostages and the captive chiefs. Arran took only a worthless bond of good behaviour from them.[19] Donald Dubh and the Islanders were now free to act.

With the chiefs safely back in the Isles, the preparations which had been made to drive both Huntly and Argyll from their acquisitions in the West and assert the Islander's claim to Ross, were put into motion.

To this end a small, but sturdy, force of 1,800 Islanders was immediately gathered. In May of 1543 the Islanders struck. They invaded Argyll with determination and speed.

There was much livestock and other plunder taken as the Islanders ravaged the whole of Campbell's country from Lorn to Knapdale. By June Argyll managed to organize a hurried defence and mobilized his forces in hopes of driving the invaders from his estates. Donald Dubh, however, was able to maintain the initiative and all Argyll could manage was to protect the district around his castle at Inverary. By now Hector Maclean of Duart had changed his mind and actively joined the rebellion. For his trouble, Argyll's men raided the MacLean island of Tiree, killing some 10,000 oxen and kyne (cattle) and taking 1,800 horses and mares.

In the North, John of Moidart, Chief of Clanranald and one of the chiefs released by Arran, stripped the usurper, Donald Galda, and his Fraser supporters of the authority they exercised over his clan.[20] Then, with the blessings of Donald Dubh and the Council of the Isles, he began a campaign to drive the strangers from his clan's traditional territories. The other northern leaders, Ewen mac Allan of Lochiel, Chief of the Camerons, Alexander MacDonald of Glengarry, and Ranald MacDonald Glas of Keppoch, all eagerly joined the fray. It wasn't long before the interloping Frasers and Grants had been driven back toward their ancestral lands in the east and completely out of the MacDonald and Cameron country.

The Earl of Huntly could not let this expulsion of his vassals go unpunished. In the late spring of 1544, Huntly returned with a large body of Gordons, together with Lord Lovat and his Fraser clansmen, to reclaim Lochaber. The Camerons and the MacDonalds, however, were not willing to fight a pitched battle with such a large and well-equipped force. They simply slipped away into the mountains, vanishing like shadows before Huntly's advance. Consequently, after proceeding as far as Inverlochy, Huntly found he was not able to bring the local chiefs into a pitched battle and, rather than spend the summer chasing them fruitlessly across the hills and through the glens and straths, he decided to take his own forces home.

During July of 1544 Huntly ordered his army to withdraw. Marching back up the great glen, Huntly's army divided when they reached Glenspean. Huntly, Grant, and the bulk of the army proceeded on to Strathspey by way of the Braes of Lochaber, while Lovat and the

Frasers continued up the glen. The MacDonald and Cameron chiefs, watching from the protection of the hills, were well aware of the separation of Huntly's army. As the Frasers marched along the South shore of Loch Lochy, they could plainly see the MacDonald and Cameron banners, followed by seven companies of clansmen, proceeding in the same direction along the North Shore.

Upon reaching the head of the loch, the MacDonalds of Clanranald and Glengarry, along with the Camerons, quickly fell upon the isolated Frasers.[21] The opposing clans first discharged their bows and then fell on each other with swords. Being very fiercely fought, the battle ended only on the coming of night. There were heavy casualties on both sides, but Lovat and his son, along with some 300 of the name of Fraser, were killed.[22] Word of the victory spread rapidly throughout the whole of the Highlands and islands as it was claimed there were no men left alive with the name of Fraser.

Following up on their victory, Alexander MacDonald of Glengarry, along with Angus, son of Ewen Cameron of Lochiel, marched along the Great Glen, proceeding northeastward where they raided the Laird of Grant's properties of Urquhart Castle and the districts of Glenmoriston. They then turned their attention to the Fraser estates of Abertarf and Strathglass.[23] The ancient estates of the Grants and Frasers were devastated before the raiders withdrew, taking much booty with them.[24]

This devastating eastward raid into the Earl of Huntly's home territories, was too much, even for the government of Arran to ignore, so on the 3rd of August, summonses were issued for MacDonald of Glengarry and Ewen Cameron to appear in Edinburgh to answer charges laid against them. The summonses were, of course, ignored and both chiefs were consequently declared rebel and their lands forfeit to the Crown.[25]

The Earl of Huntly took the earliest opportunity he could manage to retaliate. Returning deep into the Great Glen, he laid waste to all of Lochaber. Eventually, through the treachery of Keppoch's brother-in-law, William MacIntosh, many of the Western leaders were captured. Ewen Cameron of Lochiel and Ranald MacDonald Glas of Keppoch, along with several of the ranking men from their clans, were betrayed to Huntly. After a long period of confinement at Ruthven, the chiefs were taken to Elgin, where they were tried for complicity in the death of Lovat. After being found guilty of rebellion against the Crown of Scotland, the two chiefs were beheaded in 1547 and their heads placed above the town gates.[26]

While Huntly and Argyll were occupied with defending their estates and vassals from the wrath of angry Islanders, Scotland was attacked again, this time by the English. King Henry VIII, in an attempt to force the nobles of Scotland to agree to the marriage of his son Edward, born in 1537, to the young Scots Queen Mary, ordered several attacks made on that country. In May of 1544 the Earl of Hertford burned Edinburgh, and in August, Matthew, the Earl of Lennox, undertook to deliver up to the English the island of Bute, along with its castle of Rothsay and the castle of Dumbarton.[27]

Lennox, with a small well-armed force, sailed from the English port of Bristol with a fleet of ten ships.[28] Arriving off the West Coast of Scotland, they were joined by a large force of MacFarlanes, MacLeans, MacKinnons, and other Highlanders.[29] The islands of Arran, where the MacLeans razed Brodick Castle to the ground, and Bute were attacked and plundered. Rothsay Castle was captured and the army moved east to capture Dumbarton. Some of the Islanders, most notably Hector Maclean of Duart, now returned home with their galleys heavy with plunder.

Lennox fully expected Dumbarton to be handed over to him easily because the constable of the castle, Stirling of Glorat, was his vassal and in his employ. However, the constable, being of an independent mind, refused to surrender the castle and indeed had joined a plot, led by the Earl of Glencairn, to capture Lennox. The castle was well provisioned and the garrison strongly reinforced, so it remained in government hands.

Lennox and his army, after abandoning any further action against Dumbarton, retired to Bute where they held a council of war. While at Lennox's base at Rothsay, the English force was reinforced by a further unknown number of Highlanders and Islanders. It was decided to attack the militias that Argyll was mustering at Dunoon.

Argyll, who was able to assemble some 700 men and artillery, was ready for the attack. As the landing by Lennox's force was covered by cannon fire from the ships, it went smoothly. After a sharp skirmish in which Argyll lost some 80 men, he was forced to retreat before the advance of Lennox's Highlanders and Islanders with their English allies. The village of Dunoon was burned and the church, in which the common people had put their goods for safekeeping, was pillaged. As Lennox's men returned to the safety of their ships at night, Argyll harassed their retreat. Some five days later Lennox again landed 500 men on the mainland of Argyll. They plundered and laid waste the country for a full day before retreating to their ships.

The skilful deployment of this small force by Lennox's officers protected it from any attack so that, although the Earl of Argyll had assembled some 2000 men, they could only watch helplessly as the Islanders and their English allies undertook the destruction of his lands. Lennox then moved on to plunder Kintyre, carrying off great numbers of cattle and other property. Moving eastward, the Islanders struck Carrick, Kyle, Cunningham, and Galloway with such speed and fury that, for many gentlemen resident in these areas, the only escape was to put themselves under the personal protection of Lennox himself. During these raids particular attention was given to the estates of the Earl of Glencairn. By December 1544 the Islanders all would have returned to their homes and Lennox was back in England.

End Notes
Chapter 12

1. The Earl of Argyll was imprisoned in 1531 for his lack of accounting for the king's revenue collected in the Isles, and Alexander of Islay was awarded many of his offices and duties. In 1532 King James IV dispatched Alexander of Islay to Ulster at the head of 7,000 men to support the O'Donnells who were fighting the O'Neills. The O'Neills were supporting the English at this time. The invasion was intended to divert English troops from attacking Scotland, with whom they were at war.

2. Nicolson, A., *History of Skye*, Alex MacLaren & Sons, Glasgow, 1930, 51, & Cameron, A., *History & Traditions of the Isle of Skye*, E. Forsyth, Inverness, 1871, 33.

3. Some accounts state that Ronald Harrach had just returned from Ireland and that MacKinnon was the steward for Donald Gruamach.

4. MacKenzie, A., *Celtic Magazine, Inverness, 1880, Vol. 5*, 424.

5. Iain MacDonald of Sleat had resigned the rights to Trotternish to Clan Ranald in 1506, but the estates were physically occupied by the MacLeods of Dunvegan. In 1528 Donald Gruamach of Sleat, along with the MacLeods of Lewis, drove out the occupying MacLeods of Dunvegan. Trotternish, however, may have been returned to Dunvegan to obtain his support for the rebellion of 1530, or may have been retaken by the MacLeods by force. Now Donald wanted it back.

6. Ross was invaded because the MacKenzies not only declined to aid Donald Gorm but were hostile to a restoration of the Lordship of the Isles

7. Nicolson, A., *Guide to the Isle of Skye*, Glasow, (nd). Alastair Campbell of Airds in his article "The Nearest Guard" West Highland Notes & Queries, Aug. 2007, claims that the hereditary standard bearers for MacDonald of Sleat were the MacKinnons of Duisdale Beag in Isleorsay.

8. Cameron, A., *History and Traditions of the Isle of Skye*, E Forsyth, Inverness, 1871, 34.

9. Nicolson, A., *History of Skye*, Alex MacLauen & Sons, Glasgow, 1930, 56, says that Donald Gorm was struck in the thigh.

Gregory, Donald, *History of the Western Highlands & Isles*, William Tate, Edinburgh, 1834, 145, says he was struck in the foot. The exact location of the wound isn't so important as the result.

Cameron, A., in his *History & Traditions of Skye*, E Forsyth, Inverness, 1871, 34, relates a MacKenzie tradition that the fatal arrow was the last one loosed by Duncan MacCrae.

10. The remains of the hut can still be seen and are known as Larach tigh Mhic Dho'uill.

11. The men accompanying King James were:
    1. Cardinal Beaton with 500 men from Fife and Angus
    2. Earl of Huntly with 500 men from the North with a number of gentlemen
    3. Earl of Arran with 500 men from the West and a number of gentlemen

12. Although Alexander MacLeod was well known and liked at court and was a victim of Donald Gorm's rising, he was required to give a hostage to ensure his good behavior. MacLeod of Dunvegan gave his 3rd son Norman as a hostage.

13. It is interesting to note that Argyll had no command in this expedition, indeed, he may have had no part in it at all. This would have been a royal snub of monumental proportions, indicating the extent to which Argyll was out of favor.

14. The rise of the Islanders interest in Ireland corresponds with King Henry VIII of England's declaration of himself "King of Ireland" and his attempts to stamp out the native Irish customs and practices.

15. Scotland was divided both politically and religiously. The Scottish nobles who supported religious reformation tended to support Henry VIII of England, while those who supported the Roman Church tended to oppose the English pretensions. Individual loyalties changed rapidly as opportunities to exercise power or influence changed. The reformation of the church was gaining popular support, as even now old order churches in the Lowlands were being sacked. For a good description of these divisions see Gregory, *Western Highlands & Isles*, William Tate, Edinburgh, 1836, 151.

16. It is likely that Hector MacLean of Duart was made Steward of the Isles. The stewardship was a post held by the MacLeans under the old Lordship.

17. See appendix 10.

18. James MacDonald of Islay was married to Lady Agnes Campbell, the daughter of Colin the 3rd Earl of Argyll. The MacDuffies had been involved in the murder of Alexander of Lochalsh in 1496 and had not had a change of heart. See Byrne, K., *Colkitto*, House of Lochar, Isle of Colonsay, 1997, 17. The unanimity of the clans, however, can be seen from the inclusion on the Council of the Isles of Angus MacDonald, brother of James of Islay. James MacDonald, who led the most powerful of the island clans, was keeping his options open. While not openly supporting Donald Dubh, he did not oppose him either. Archibald the Clerk was administering the affairs of the MacDonalds of Sleat because the young chief, Donald Gormson, was a minor and had been sent to the English court for shelter from the government in Edinburgh.

19. The chiefs were released by Arran at the instigation of the Earl of Glencairn. There seems to have been no other motive than to embarrass the Earls of Argyll and Huntly by increasing the resistance to their territorial ambition in the west

20. Donald Galda was made Chief of Clanranald by the Lovat Frasers during John of Moidart's imprisonment. Much of Clanranald's lands were settled by Frasers and Grants. Both the Grants and Frasers were vassals of the Earl of Huntly. They had been settled on lands in Lochaber that was traditionally held by the Camerons and MacDonalds. King James had given the land to Huntly for his previous service against the Islanders

21. This battle known as "Blar nan Leine" is described in: Gordon, *A Genealogical History of the Earldom of Sutherland*, A. Constable, Edinburgh, 1813, 109-110, but the most complete descriptions are in: Keltie, *History of the Scottish Highlands*, A. Fullarton, Edinburgh, 1875, Vol. 1, 87, and Gregory, Donald, *History of the Western Highlands and Isles*, William Tait, Edinburgh, 1834, 160-162

22. Of the party led by Lovat, only one gentleman, James Fraser of Foray, who was badly wounded and left for dead, and four common men are said to have survived.

23. MacDonald, Donald, *Clan Donald*, MacDonald Publishers, Midlothian, 1978, 331, Keltie, *History of the Scottish Highlands*, A. Fullarton, Edinburgh, 1875, Vol. 1, 87.

24. Booty taken from Grants: 1,188 full-grown cattle, 392 young cattle, 525 calves, 383 horses and mares, 1978 sheep, 1099 lambs, 1410 goats, 794 kids, 122 swine, 3,006 bolls of oats, 1,277 bolls of barley, and furniture, linen and cloth valued at £500. In addition, the Laird of Grant lost 200 bolls of oats, 100 bolls of barley, 100 big cattle, 100 calves, 16 horses, 300 sheep, much furniture and household goods, 3 great boats, and other goods as well as money.

25. Glengarry remained in possession of his estates by right of his sword. The Crown gave them to Grant of Freuchie but he was unable to occupy them. Eventually, because the government could not oust Glengarry, he was granted full remission for rebellion and restored to his estates. Glengarry, however, remained unrepentant and aloof from the government until his death in 1560.

26. The other MacDonald and Cameron gentlemen were either imprisoned or banished.

27. The Earl of Lennox was Matthew Stewart, and thus could claim a kinship with both Donald Dubh and the Stuart kings. He was also a great feudal baron in the West Highlands, whose forfeited estates had been granted to Argyll and Huntly. He was married to Margaret Douglas, a niece to King Henry VIII of England. See: Gregory, *Western Highlands & Isles*, William Tate, Edinburgh, 1836, 152-153, for an interesting, but brief, account of Lennox's politics.

28. The English troops were led by Sir Rise Mansell, Sir Peter Mewtas, and Richard Broke and consisted of 200 hackbuteers, 200 archers and 600 pikemen. Walter MacFarlane of Tarbet led seven score light footmen wearing coats of mail, each being armed with bows and arrows and two-handed swords.

29. This is generally recorded as an English invasion as the MacFarlanes were vassals of Lennox. But the large number of remissions given to Island clans for their parts in this raid, would indicate a role by Donald Dubh and his army. While it is clear that a large numbers of Islanders took part in the attack, we do not know exactly when or where they joined Lennox. See Mackenzie, *Highlands & Islands of Scotland*, Moray Press, Edinburgh, 1949, 135, and MacLean Bristol, *Warriors and Priests*, Tuckwell Press, East Lothian, 1995, 117.

198

West Highland galley under sail

Chapter 13
END OF THE DREAM

During the spring of 1545 Argyll and Huntly continued to be occupied by the affairs in the Highlands. On the 18th of March they agreed to a truce with Donald Dubh when he asked for safe conduct to visit the Queen Dowager in Edinburgh. Nothing, however, appears to have materialized from the proposal. Expanding his diplomatic offensive, Donald Dubh persuaded the Earl of Tyrone to petition Henry VIII to take Donald and his army into his service.

In spite of the considerable help given by the island clans during the Dumbarton campaign, the English appear not to have fully trusted them. In April of 1545 the English government was worried that Donald Dubh had offered to aid the Irish chief, Tyrone, in his rebellion against them. Fearing an invasion by a large force of Islanders, possibly reinforced by French auxiliaries, the English authorities in Ireland were ordered to fully provision and garrison their strongholds. The Earl of Lennox also began a concerted diplomatic effort to win the Council of the Isles over completely to the English side. Employing an emissary named Patrick Colquhoun, who was a distant kinsman to Donald Dubh, Lennox was able to successfully obtain bonds of service from several of the island chiefs.

The decisive defeat of an invading English army at Ancrum Moor, and the arrival of French reinforcements, did much to increase the Scottish government's confidence. The Regent Arran and the Scottish Privy Council felt confident enough to turn their attentions against Donald Dubh and the unrepentant Islanders.[1] On the 4th of June the English Privy Council informed Dublin that Donald Dubh had entered the king's service and was to receive a pension. That same month the government in Edinburgh issued a proclamation against Donald Dubh and the clan chiefs who followed him. They were ordered to cease their rebellious activities or face an invasion by the whole body of the realm of Scotland and its French allies. The proclamation was naturally ignored by the clan chiefs. However, Donald Dubh answered for them all in a letter to the Earl of Lennox, by disclaiming any allegiance to the realm of Scotland to which he and his ancestors were *"auld enemies."*[2]

Waiting only one month after its initial proclamation, until July 1545, the Privy Council began proceedings of treason against Donald Dubh and the principal island chiefs. Summonses were promptly issued for Donald Dubh to immediately appear in Edinburgh to answer the charges against him.

The ineffectual threats, charges and bluster from Edinburgh only encouraged the negotiations between the Islanders and the English. At a meeting of the Council of the Isles on the 28th of July on *"Ellan Charne"* (Ellan Charrin), it was decided to initiate talks directly with the English Crown.[3] The council and barons of the Isles who met at this historic meeting were: Hector Maclean of Duart; John MacAllister, Captain of Clanranald; Rorie Macleod of Lewis; Alexander Macleod of Dunvegan; Murdoch MacLean of Lochbuie; Angus MacDonald, the brother of James MacDonald of Islay; Allan MacLean of Torloisk, brother of Hector MacLean; Archibald MacDonald, Captain of Clan Huistein; Alexander MacIan of Ardnamurchan; John MacLean of Coll; Gilleonan MacNeil of Barra; Ewen MacKinnon of Strathordill; John MacQuarrie of Ulva; John MacLean of Ardgour; Alexander Ronaldson of Glengarry; Angus Ronaldson of Knoydart; and Donald MacLean of Kingerloch.

Two envoys were commissioned to negotiate under the guidance of Lennox: Rory MacAlister, Dean of Morvern and Bishop-designate of the Isles; and Patrick MacLean, the Consular and Chief Justiciar of the Isles. The Council of the Isles hoped these envoys would soon conclude a treaty with the English.[4] Through the course of all of this diplomacy, the Islesmen acknowledged Lennox to be the true Regent of Scotland and made it clear that it was under his direction that they offered allegiance to England.

The week following the Council of the Isles' commissioning its emissaries, the Lord of the Isles appeared in Ireland. On August 5th, 1545, Donald Dubh, with Ewen MacKinnon and the other members of his council, landed at Knockfergus leading a force of some 4,000 warriors transported by a fleet of no less than 180 galleys. Three thousand of the

Islesmen were recorded by witnesses as being very tall, clothed, for the most part, in habergeons, long coats of mail, armed with two-handed swords and long bows, but with very few guns. The remaining 1,000 men, those who rowed the galleys, are described as tall mariners.

This army, as impressive as it evidentially was to the witness, did not constitute the whole strength of the Isles. There was an equal force left in the Hebrides to insure that Huntly and Argyll remained in check.

The landing place at Knockfergus, on the north side of Belfast Lough, was not the closest nor most convenient site for a Hebridean army to disembark in Ireland.[5] However, it was only a few short miles from Belfast and the mouth of the Lagan Valley. Although Belfast was under English control at this time, the Lagan Valley was firmly under the control of the O'Neills from their stronghold in the Castlereagh Hills. The landing of such a large force at Knockfergus was undoubtedly intended to impress upon the English the ease with which the Hebridean Geals could reinforce their Irish cousins if they so chose.

Knockfergus Castle is now known as Cerrickfergus

At the monastery church of Grey Friars, Donald Dubh and the members of the Council of the Isles took an oath of allegiance to King Henry VIII of England. This ceremony, in all of its color and splendor, was officially witnessed by the constable of the castle, the mayor, the town magistrate, and Colquhoun and Walter MacFarlane who were Lennox's two commissioners. Watching with the gathered crowd, was John Carswell, who would later be the first Protestant Bishop of the Isles and translator into Gaelic of the Book of Common Order.[6]

The Council of the Isles and its army remained encamped at Knockfergus, while the emissaries, Rory MacAlister and Patrick MacLean, hurriedly shuttled back and forth between Ireland and England. Finally having concluded the negotiations, an agreement was signed between Henry VIII and Donald Dubh on September 4, 1545, at Oatland Manor.[7] The commissioners returned to Knockfergus with a personal letter to Donald Dubh from the English king expressing satisfaction at the results of the negotiations and advising Donald to *"proceed like a noble man"* and revenge the dishonours committed by their common enemies. [8]

While the negotiations between Donald Dubh and Henry VIII were in hand, the Earl of Hertford was preparing to invade the border districts of Scotland. The Earl of Lennox was requested to join him, and together they devastated the area around the Merse. While the Earl of Lennox was occupied with Hertford in Scotland, Donald Dubh and the Islanders waited at Knockfergus for him and the Irish army he was to command.

The Governing council of Ireland had run through the £6000 in gold which had been sent from London and, consequently, there were difficulties raising the required numbers of Irish troops.[9] Many of the English transport ships dispatched from Chester and Beaumaris did not all arrive and the crews of those that did had not been paid, so the sailors were demanding their wages in advance before agreeing to go on. There were ordinance problems as well. Although the army was not supplied with full cannons, it had a range of weaponry including 1 demi-cannon, 1 saker, 2 falcons, and 50 demi-hakes.[10] The logistics of moving these weapons would have been daunting. The black powder sent for the guns was of very poor quality and had to be returned while the bows sent to arm the archers were so worm-eaten, they were not usable.

The government of Scotland, having had somehow obtained knowledge of the dealings between Donald Dubh and the English, attempted to undermine his strength by offering remissions to several of the island chiefs in return for their support. To the credit of the individuals concerned, they ignored this offer and were quickly charged with treason by the government. Indeed, on September 9, 1545, while he was still in Ireland, Ewen MacKinnon was summoned to appear before the Scottish parliament to answer charges of rebellion which had been brought against him.

After waiting at Knockfergus for the better part of two months, Donald Dubh, the Council of the Isles, and the army were all tiring of the delay in Lennox's return. Naturally no one wanted to tarry unnecessarily in Ireland while Huntly and Argyll continued to threaten their homes. Concerned about the welfare and security of the Isles, Donald Dubh, in either late September or early October, ordered his army back to the Hebrides.

The Islanders' return home did not bode well for the success of the coming campaign. On the island of Mull, MacLean of Duart hosted a meeting of the clan chiefs to recompense them for their services, past and future, to the English. The meeting at Duart is the object of the often repeated story of a disagreement between the chiefs over the dispersion of the English gold, which led to the immediate breakup of the Hebridean army.[11] Although there may be some truth in the tale, it is not likely to have been the only reason for the dispersal of the island clans.

The Islanders had been standing under arms in Ireland for months, waiting for Lennox to return. It's likely that, appreciating the difficulties faced by the Governing Council in raising Ormonde's Irish army and naturally inpatient for spoil, the island chiefs did not want to wait any longer. They simply may have just picked up their wages and gone home.

Toward the end of October 1545, Lennox was finally ready to invade Western Scotland. The diplomat, Patrick Colquhoun, was sent into the Isles in the warship *Salop* to find and meet with Donald Dubh and to aid in coordinating the movements of the two armies. Colquhoun requested Donald Dubh gather the Islanders and be ready to join Lennox at a previously determined place. The bustle of activity in the Irish Sea and the gathering of the island clans is likely to have alerted the government spies to the impending invasion. Before the month of October had ended, the government in Edinburgh had warned the garrisons of both Dumbarton and Renfrew castles of the impending threat, thus giving them plenty of opportunity to be provisioned and strengthened.[12]

When, belatedly, Lennox and his Irish army sailed from Dublin on November 17, 1545, the seasonal storms and winter cold were at hand. In spite of the short notice, Donald Dubh and a force of Islanders made the rendezvous with Lennox and a joint attempt may have been made to capture Dumbarton.[13] However, the well-garrisoned, but hastily provisioned castle, was impregnable to the weapons brought by the invaders. Having brought no artillery to bring down the walls, the only alternative was a long, and probably futile, winter siege. Neither Donald Dubh's men nor Lennox's force was equipped for such an undertaking. The attack on Dumbarton was called off and the clans returned home. Lennox, along with Donald Dubh and the Irish army, returned to Ireland.

Probably having been disembarked at Knockfergus, Donald Dubh was making his way south to meet with the Governing Council in Dublin when he was struck down by a fever at Drogheda, just a few miles north of his destination.[14] When the news of Donald Dubh's death reached the English court, Henry VIII decided he should have a funeral which suited his office and high birth. To this end, Henry VIII sent funds to Ireland and Donald Dubh was buried with all of the honor and dignity of a Lord of the Isles.

James MacDonald, of the Clan Ian Mor, was the most powerful Hebridean clan chief at the time and, although not a member of the Council of the Isles, he appears to have been the designated successor to Donald Dubh and readily assumed the title of Lord of the Isles.[15] During the month of January 1546, James had, through the services of Patrick MacLean and Roderick MacAlistair, proposed to the Governing Council of Ireland that the cooperation between Lennox and the Islanders be renewed. Not receiving a response from that agency, James wrote directly to the king. In a letter dated the 24th of January, James suggested the English and Hebridean armies again be united and rendezvous on the island of Sanda for an invasion of Scotland. However, it appears there was no further English interest in an official relationship with the Islanders.[16] Furthermore, only a few of the island clans supported James MacDonald's assumption of the leadership of the Gael. For the others, all hope of resurrecting their ancient patrimony had died with Donald Dubh.[17]

Those clans which did not support James MacDonald began a process of reconciliation with the regent in Edinburgh. Although the MacKinnons had always been among the staunchest supporters of the Lordship, they were now numbered with those who did not support James. Sensing changes in the power base of the Isles, it appears that Ewen MacKinnon quickly approached the government in Edinburgh. On February 16 , 1546, he was given a respite of 19 years for the treasonable assistance he had given to the Earl of Lennox. Even James MacDonald, and those clans which supported him, soon found it prudent to make their peace with the government. The long struggle by the Islanders, for their independence under the Lords of the Isles, was finally over.[18] There was no longer anyone one left who had the ability to unite the island clans in the cause.[19]

The English policy of involvement in the Hebrides remained active, in spite of the island clans' movement toward reconciliation with the government in Edinburgh. The fact that the English were supplying arms and money to the clans until at least 1547, when King Henry VIII died, and possibly even later still, during the reign of his daughter Elizabeth I, is documented in English state papers.[20]

What influence English policy actually had when Ewen MacKinnon was discussing clan interests with his durbfine, can never be determined.[21] The MacKinnons, along with the other island clans, despite their surrender to Edinburgh, appear to actually have continued in opposition to the central government, albeit on a lesser scale. But the attention of the Edinburgh government was directed toward more important matters elsewhere. Following the defeats of the Scottish armies at Musselburgh and Pinkie Cleugh by the English, there was little need for the Islanders to fear retaliation.

During the summer of 1548, it was recorded in the Privy Council records that on the 4th of August all summonses against Ewen MacKinnon were deserted. There is no record of what the abandoned summonses pertained to, but they are likely for acts or felonies committed after Ewen's surrender to the government in January 1546. It may never be possible for us to know the full extent of outside involvement, meddling or intrigue in the Hebrides. However, we do know that, without a doubt, the Islanders remained very well armed with a goodly supply of modern weapons for generations to come.

End Notes
Chapter 13

1. Neil MacNeil of Gigha was with the English army at Ancrum Moor. Whether he was an ambassador from Donald Dubh or leading a party of Islanders, is unknown.

2. MacDonald, *Donald, Clan Donald*, MacDonald Publishers, Midlothian, 1978.

3. National Library of Scotland, MS 1307, #83

4. Rory MacAlister is the brother of John of Moidart, Chief of Clanranald, and Patrick MacLean was the brother of MacLean of Duart. There followed a considerable amount of diplomatic correspondence between Donald Dubh and the English Court. See appendix 11 for the letter they brought to Lennox.

5. Knockfergus *(Fergus's hill)* was the site of a stronghold built circa 1177 by the Norman invaders of Ulster. The capital of the Norman earls of Ulster, it later became an important English stronghold called Carrickfergus *(Fergus's rock)*.

6. Called *Foirm na n-Urrnuidheadh*, this work was added to the Protestant Catechism and was the first book printed in Gaelic.

7. Gregory, Donald, *History of the Western Highlands and Isles*, William Tait, Edinburgh, 1834, 173. "The pension of two thousand crowns was confirmed to the Lord of the Isles by letters patent; and Henry engaged that that nobleman and his followers should be included in any treaty made between England and Scotland. On the other hand, the Lord of the Isles became bound, with all his adherents, to serve the King of England truly and faithfully, to the annoyance of the Regent of Scotland and his partisans. He engaged to make no agreement with the Earls of Huntly or Argyll, nor with any of the Scots, to the prejudice of the King of England; but, on the contrary, to continue steadfast in his opposition to them and in his allegiance to Henry. It was arranged that the Earl of Lennox, with a body of two thousand Irish under the Earl of Ormond and Ossory, should lead an expedition from the west against Scotland, in which he was to be assisted by the Lord of the Isles with eight thousand men. As long as Lennox should remain in the country of the Earl of Argyll, the whole eight thousand men were to be placed at his disposal; but, in the event of his proceeding to

208

another part of Scotland--and a march to Stirling was seriously contemplated--it was provided that only six thousand of the Islanders should follow him, while the remaining two thousand should be employed in occupying the attention of the Earl of Argyll. Lastly, three thousand of the Islesmen were to receive pay from the King of England for two months." Later that same month King Henry VIII showed his pleasure with the agreement reached with the Islanders by richly rewarding the envoys, R. MacAlister and P. MacLean, for their service to the English cause. If there had been no agreement reached with the English, it is possible the Islanders would have marched westward and joined Tyrone O'Neil in his fight against them.

8. MacDonald, Donald, *Clan Donald*, MacDonald Publishers, Midlothian, 1978, 145.

9 The 2,000 Irish soldiers to be raised by Ormonde were to be *"of the most wild and savage sort"* whose absence from Ireland *"would do good rather than hurt"* MacKenzie, 139.

10. The demi-cannon with its 6½" bore would have weighed 6,000 pounds and required a load of 28 pounds of powder to fire a 30-pound ball. The smaller saker had a 3½" bore, but still weighed 1,500 pounds, and utilized a 5-pound charge to fire a 5-pound shot. The falcon, with its 2½" bore, needed 2½ pounds of powder to shoot a 2½-pound ball. Demi-hakes were a very primitive handgun.

11. Gregory, Donald, *History of the Western Highlands and Isles*, William Tait, Edinburgh, 1834, 174. This story was just one of the many which focuses on the greed, simplicity, and lack of fidelity exercised by clan chiefs. It should be noted that the island chiefs always displayed the greatest loyalty to the Lordship and those whom they saw as their rightful leaders. They seldom displayed any affection toward the government in Edinburgh, with whom they were generally hostile.

12. Mackenzie, *Highlands & Islands of Scotland*, Moray Press, Edinburgh, 1949, 140. Also to ensure that Dumbarton remained in Scottish hands, Huntly and the Cardinal Beaton bribed the constable to allow them to garrison it with their own men.

13. Lennox was advised of the government's control of Dumbarton Castle while he was at sea. Because of the obscurity of events during this part of the campaign, it's not known for certain if the forces under Lennox actually attempted a landing at Dumbarton or not.

14. Just before he died, Donald Dubh commended the care of his natural son to the English court. It is not known if this boy was ever actually under the protection of the English court, but he was living on Lewis in care of Rory Macleod in 1551. No claim to the Lordship of the Isles was ever made on behalf of the boy.

15. Under normal circumstances, the succession would have gone to the MacDonalds of Sleat on Skye. But, as Donald Gorm had died in 1539 and his son, another Donald, was an infant, the succession passed to the Islay MacDonalds.

16. The envoys, Patrick MacLean and Roderick MacAlister, remained in Dublin, pressing the Governing Council for a treaty and an army. In May the envoys had indicated they wished to return to Scotland, so they may have actually been held by the English against their will. By the end of July the Lord Justice of Ireland was instructed to deliver the bodies of the envoys and their servants to the representatives of Lennox.

17. James' claim was supported by: the MacDonalds of Islay and Sleat, and MacIan of Ardnamurchan, and the Camerons and MacNeils of Gigha. He was not recognized by the MacKinnons, MacQuarries, MacNeills of Barra, MacLeod of Harris and Lewis, nor the MacLeans.

18. The sentimental value of the title, *"Lord of the Isles,"* remained strong in the territories of the ancient Lordship. Both the Scottish and English governments were quick to recognize the esteem which the title to the Lordship still carried in Scotland and Ireland. In 1563 the Scottish government proposed to promote James MacDonald to the title, *"Lord of the Isles,"* and Queen Elizabeth I used the term when referring to MacDonald of Sleat, while encouraging him to oppose James MacDonald. Although the Scottish government did not claim the title for itself, the English royalty did. The *"Lord of the Isles"* is one of the official titles taken by the successor to the British throne. The real Celtic dignity and title of *"Lord of the Isles"* now resides with Lord MacDonald of Sleat, a direct descendant of the ancient lords themselves.

19. In December of 1545 Archibald Campbell, the Earl of Argyll, signed an agreement to marry Katherine MacLean, sister of Hector MacLean of Duart. Hector had signed a bond of manrent with Argyll two years previously in 1543, the same year as the escape of Donald Dubh from Edinburgh. It is interesting that the intervening rebellion, which saw them on opposing sides, did not harm their relationship nor interfere with their status as allies.

20. In a letter to the Lord Deputy of Ireland, Cameron of Lochiel pointed out his services to the English in raiding the lands of Argyll and Huntly. The letter was written to remind the deputy to send the arms and money promised by King Henry VIII. Henry VIII was followed in 1547 by his son Edward VI who, in turn, was succeeded by Mary in 1553 and Elizabeth in 1558. Edward, Mary, and Elizabeth vigorously continued Henry's policy in Ireland.

22. Interestingly, it is from this turbulent period that we have first notice of cadet families of MacKinnon. The Chief Ewen's brother, Lauchlan, had a son also called Ewen who was alive in 1546. Tradition states that this Ewen is the progenitor of the Torrin family of MacKinnon. But this is disputed by the Rev. MacKinnon, D., *The Chiefs and Chiefship of Clan MacKinnon*, Portree, 1931.

Chapter 14
INTO IRELAND

T he first surviving eyewitness account we have of life in the Hebrides was recorded by Sir Donald Monro, Dean of the Isles, during his tour in 1549.[1] In writing of his Hebridean tour, Sir Donald took care to mention the names of the clan chiefs who had lands in the areas he visited. It is from this account of Monro's visit to Skye that we know the MacKinnons by now officially held the tower of Dunakin, and his account of Mull indicates the continued MacKinnon hold on Mishnish.[2]

During this period most chiefs led transient lives living among their people or visiting other chiefs. It may have been Monro's account, however, that caused some modern authors to believe MacKinnon chiefs actually lived within the now ancient watch tower of Dunakin.[3] Donald's short descriptions generally portray the islands as reasonably prosperous. Nowhere does he mention want or a lack of food in his account. The lands and resources of the Hebrides appear to be fully utilized but well able to support the local populations.

Celtic customs were still dominant in the Isles and the adjacent mainland but were slowly giving way before the incessant pressure on the clan chiefs to adopt the feudal practices of the Lowlands. The traditional social structures of the island clans were, for the most part, unchanged. The chiefs and their families still provided the hereditary rulers and nobility of the Isles and each merkland of property still sustained a gentleman in food and clothing. These gentlemen of the clan who did no physical labour were regarded as the chief's household men, ready to follow him at a moment's notice. As individuals, these men were admired by the society that supported them, and they enjoyed a status which was deeply embedded in the Gaelic culture.

The professional Highland warriors of this period could overawe almost any opposition, and there was a lucrative market for their swords in Ireland.[4] The tenant farmers who supported and armed these gentlemen were not allowed to leave their district, except under special circumstances, and were only called to arms when the clan lands themselves were in danger.[5] Ewen MacKinnon, holding 20 merklands in each of Mull and Skye, would have had a force of at least 40 warriors he could call up instantly.[6]

The decade of the 1550s was mostly one of peace in the Isles. The territorial wars and rebellions which divided the clans and mainly characterised the 1540s had, in general, subsided. The competition between clans for control of food-producing land remained important and may have been the cause for friction between the MacKinnons and the MacLeans. Hector MacLean, whose position in the Isles had been strengthened by the acquisition of a chest of English gold and his position as Argyll's father-in-law, appears to have turned his eyes on the MacKinnon lands of Mishnish. Thus, surviving tradition claims that, instead of peace, Ewen MacKinnon *"fought many battles against the Macleans...in defence of his lands in Mull."*[7]

This story which may date from this period tells of a MacKinnon chief who may have been Ewen Ruadh nan Cath, who succeeded to the chiefship during the early decades of the 16th century.[8]

"A large share of the lower part of Mull belonged to the MacKinnons of Mishinish, and the MacLeans, who held most of the Island, were very anxious to get hold of MacKinnon's share also; with this view they took advantage of MacKinnon's youth and absence from the Island, and also of the fact that MacDonald, of Sleat, to whom he was maternally related, was too old and infirm to help his youthful friend.

Therefore the families of Duart and Lochbuy seized and divided MacKinnon's lands among their own friends, driving all MacKinnon's friends away. A short time afterwards MacKinnon made up his mind to regain his ancestors' soil, and to this end he set sail for Ireland to solicit aid from his friend the Earl of Antrim. The Earl received him with kindness, and on his return allowed 40 young gentlemen to accompany him.

On his way to Skye he thought he would make a call in Mull to see how matters stood before proceeding to raise followers in the northern island. Landing at Bloody Bay (Camus-na-fola) on a very dark night, he ascended the cliff alone, and with difficulty, till he arrived at a small hut in a lonely glen (Glac-Naomhaig) a little above his own house at Earay, a short distance from Tobermory, where an old woman of his Clan lived. This old woman being shrewd and intelligent had the reputation of being a witch and through fear of her powers the MacLeans did not banish her with the rest of the Clan.

Here he entered and opened up his mind, asking her advice in the matter. She enquired "How many men are with you?" "Only 40," he answered. "Enough," said she, "and if you take my advice you will be in possession of your own and fully avenged on MacLean long before to-morrow's sun will rise. Duart and Lochbuy are to-night in Ledaig House (Tigh-a-phuirt) without any suspicion or sentry, and their men after much jolification are lying drunk and asleep in their birlinns, and if your men are men, and if you are a son of your father, the whole business is easy to settle."

He returned to his men and desired them to follow him to the woods, where he said "Let every man of you cut a fir caber for himself and snick off every knot and branch. Also choose for me a long straight caber but leave it with all its branches on." The men did so, when he asked them to follow him to Ledaig House which they surrounded, and each man struck his caber into the ground, MacKinnon planting his own opposite the front door.

Then he entered the house and after hanging his bare sword above the door of the room in which Duart and Lochbuy were sleeping, he and his men left. In the morning when Lochbuy heard what had happened and saw his people troubled and amazed, he said, "I now see plainly how matters are. MacKinnon has been here last night, of whom this caber with its branches are an emblem, with his 40 men and his sword which is hanging there above the door, and this proves that had MacKinnon wished to take our lives his work was easy. We have found him an honest and valorous man, send for him, and let his lands be returned to him, and let peace be established between us."

The Edinburgh government remained alert to any disturbance in the Isles, which could indicate further risings in support of the MacDonalds, and was determined to prevent the island clans from uniting once more. One such incident occurred when Rory MacLeod inadvertently attracted the government's attention by leading raids on the Shetland and Orkney Islands.

Further inquiry in 1551 reported him to have *"taken ane pupill,"* a child rumoured to be the son of Donald Dubh, whom Rory was raising to become the next *Lord of the Isles.* The government's response to this news was swift and sure. Argyll was immediately issued a commission to seize the infant *"using that name will be occasioun of grat troubles and inconvientis to us,"* and Hamilton dispatched two warships to Lewis, where 160 men were *"justified."* Donald Dubh's son does not appear to have been taken during that expedition. The Edinburgh government issued orders to Argyll, MacLean, and James MacDonald to apprehend Rory MacLeod, but he subsequently made good his escape. History makes no further mention of Donald Dubh's son nor of the Lordship of the Isles.

The Edinburgh government was in the last years of the regency of the Earl of Arran, which was still unsuccessfully struggling to make its policy felt in the Highlands and Islands. Arran, probably under the advice of the Dowager Queen, Mary Guise, summoned all of the Highland chiefs to meet at Aberdeen during June of 1552, where he would hold justice courts in the course of a tour of the country. For those chiefs either not able or unwilling to travel to Aberdeen, the courts would also be held a month later in Inverness. The purpose of this meeting of chiefs was not to punish past transgressions but to prevent future difficulties. Most of the Highland chiefs on the mainland seem to have appeared before the courts and complied with the conditions asked of them by providing for their good behaviour.[9] Some of the island chiefs either neglected to appear before the courts or simply disregarded the conditions imposed on them.

By April of 1554 the Dowager Queen, Mary Guise, had assumed the regency from the Earl of Arran and began to take measures to subdue the chiefs who had not submitted. Two months later in June, the Earls of Argyll and Huntly, along with MacLean, were ordered to proceed into the Isles and exterminate the Clanranald, MacDonalds of Sleat, MacLeods of Lewis and all of their associates.[10]

While Clanranald was being punished for not attending the Privy Council when summoned, MacLeod of Lewis still had the pupil, thought to be the son of Donald Dubh, and MacDonald of Sleat was known to be an active agent for the English. The attitude of Ewen MacKinnon and his clan to these events is unknown, but it is likely the MacKinnons were alert to the changing politics in the Isles.

Neither incursion was successful, so the peace enjoyed by the Islanders was not severely disturbed. In the atmosphere of quiet now prominent in the Hebrides, the island warriors and their chiefs again began to look seriously toward Ireland for adventure and profit. As early as 1551 the English in Ireland were taking measures to protect themselves against inroads by the Islanders. The English forts along the Ulster coasts were provisioned to resist raids from the Hebrides, and in Connaught the Irish were ordered not to employ nor to otherwise allow Islanders to settle there.[11]

The meagre measures taken by the English to dissuade them were not enough to deter the island Gaels from involvement in the affairs of their Irish cousins. Before the Irish leader, Calvagh O'Donnell, attempted his bid to secure the chiefship of the O'Donnell clan from his father in 1555, he first sought a formal treaty of cooperation with the Earl of Argyll and an alliance with MacDonald of Islay.[12] The treaty, which allowed Calvagh to recruit large numbers of Campbell warriors, was witnessed by MacLean of Duart.[13]

The ties between the Islanders and the Irish were immeasurably strengthened in 1558 when Katherine MacLean, the widow of Archibald Campbell, the 4th Earl of Argyll, married Calvagh O'Donnell who had, by then, secured the chiefship of the powerful O'Donnell clan.[14] The greatest fear the English rulers of Ireland entertained during this time was the possible union against them by the Irish, the Scots Gaels, and the French.

In July of 1556 when the English Lord Deputy of Ireland, Sir Henry Radcliff, Earl of Sussex, ordered an attack on Shane O'Neill, Earl of Tyrone, who had MacDonald allies, a large part of his army were Hebredian Gaels.[15] The Gaels, recruited on Skye and led by Donald (Gorm) MacDonald of Sleat, are likely to have been warriors representative of most of the island's surnames. We can only speculate on the number of MacKinnon gentlemen who may have left Strath to earn a little English silver in Ireland. Not only did the Islanders fight on both sides on this occasion, but the opposing leaders were both chiefs of Clan Donald. The English army led by the Earl of Ormond quickly scattered Tyrone's force, then out-manoeuvred the allies led by James MacDonald of the Clan Ian Mor. James MacDonald and his brother Coll barely escaped with their lives, being forced to flee to Kintyre by galley.

James' son, Alastair Carrach, who actually commanded the MacDonalds in Ulster, was captured a short while later when the English moved on Glenarm to recover booty taken from them by the MacDonald raiders. To end the campaign, Ormond proceeded against the Islanders near Knockfergus and Dundalk. Although the Clan Ian Mor's leadership had fled or had been captured, the clan was not routed and so remained a strong force in Ulster. Indeed, in the very next year, 1557, the lord deputy complained that James MacDonald had been allowed to overrun Ulster and that he had some 7,000 men there.[16]

Margaret MacKinnon, the daughter of Lauchlan MacKinnon of MacKinnon and sister of John the last abbot of Iona, married Donald MacLeod of Waternish and thus tragically became a victim of the ruthless internal politics practised by the Clan MacLeod.[17] The tragedy began with John MacLeod of Waternish, Donald's father. He is described in the MacLeod manuscripts as tall and handsome, his fair hair clubbed, a fashion not in vogue at that time among the gentlemen of the Isles, and a capable man of affairs. He was popular with his fellow clansmen and had the respect of the MacLeod chief, Alastair Crotach.

Alastair Crotach's son and successor, the Chief William MacLeod, died in 1551, leaving an only child, a daughter named Mary. William's two brothers, Donald and Norman, had been away from the Isles for some time, and the MacLeod clansmen did not know whether they were dead or alive. The absence of the rightful heirs was a cause of consternation and confusion.

After William's funeral at Rodel, the customary funeral feast was held. As was the custom, the family bard, Roderick Morrison, recited the genealogy of the departed chief, praised his achievements, and lamented his loss. Having done this, he *"expressed the hope and expectations of the clan in the virtue and valour of the next chief whose duty it was to stand in his place and demand his father's or predecessor's sword, which was always placed in his hand by the first man of the clan."*

In the absence of the last chief's brothers, John MacLeod of Waternish, father-in-law to Margaret MacKinnon, was the nearest male relative present. When Roderick Morrison went on to address the clansmen, each head of a family drew his sword and held it naked before him. Then the bard recited the descent of John MacLeod of Waternish, claiming that his grandfather Norman was the elder and not the second son of Chief Iain Borb. The bard's statement took the assembled clansmen by surprise. As Islanders, they were born genealogists and knew full well that Morrison's assertion was not true.

The bard hailed John MacLeod of Waternish as chief by right of blood and, when Norman, John MacLeod of Waternish's eldest son, stood up holding Iain Borb's sword by the point, he offered it to his father who, standing up amidst some commotion, accepted it. John MacLeod of Waternish knew very well that the chiefship was hereditary, not elective. Therefore, he may have accepted the dignity to which he was elected by the majority of the clansmen at Rodel as being merely a tutorship of the clan until one of the brothers of the deceased chief could return to claim the estates and his place a chief of the clan.

When Donald, the younger brother of William, the late chief, returned to the Isles in 1557, John MacLeod of Waternish immediately resigned the office he had accepted at Rodel six years previously. He then summoned the MacLeods of the Siol Tormod and Siol Torquil to a meeting to discuss the chiefship. The meeting of the clansmen was duly held in March 1557, and Donald's claim was widely recognised.

John MacLeod of Waternish had a large family, seven sons and three daughters, all of whom were grown with families of their own in 1557. Margaret MacKinnon had married John's third son Donald, who was known as Domhnall Breac, and between them they had several children. Domhnall Breac was viewed by the family as a man of sense and ability, so when his eldest brother Norman died, Domhnall Breac was asked to tutor his brother's son, also named Norman, the heir and successor to Waternish.

But unfortunately for the Waternish family, Domhnall Breac's elder brother and Margaret's brother-in-law, Iain Og of Minginish, was prepared to wade through the blood of his relatives to gain control of the MacLeod clan.

Iain Og had participated in the March 1557 meeting of the clan to consider Donald MacLeod's claim to the chiefship. The clansmen evidently regarded Donald's claim favourably and dispatched Iain Og to fetch him from Kingsburgh, where he was waiting for their decision. But Donald never arrived at the Lynedale meeting. He had been murdered by Iain Og, either on the track or at Kingsburgh. There appears to have been some doubt regarding the circumstances of Donald's death, and Iain Og was outlawed rather than executed for it.

Dunvegan Castle

Iain Og's father, John of Waternish, who once again would have been the natural leader of the clan in the absence of its chief, died a few months later. Taking advantage of his father's death, Iain Og immediately took possession of Dunvegan Castle, where he slaughtered his young nephews, the sons of his deceased elder brother Norman, who were in the care of Domhnall Breac and Margaret. He also murdererd any other clansmen who he felt opposed him. It is likely that Domhnall Breac, Margaret's husband, was also killed because, as tutor to the heir of Waternish, it would have been his duty to protect his pupil. However, Margaret and her children survived.

Iain Og managed to maintain his grip on Dunvegan for almost two years. However, when Norman, the youngest brother and only surviving heir of the last chief, William MacLeod, returned to Skye, the situation changed. Norman must have been told of the murders of his brother Donald; Margaret MacKinnon's husband, Domhnall Breac of Waternish; and of the youths Domhnall Breac was responsible for. Norman wasted little time in gathering a body of men and proceeded to Dunvegan Castle. There, the warden, who evidently did not care for Iain Og, immediately admitted him to the castle.

Iain Og's foster brother warned him that Norman had returned and was in the castle. Iain Og barely had time to slip out of his chamber through a passage in the wall. Once on the beach, he took a galley to a MacLeod castle on the island of Pabbay in the Sound of Harris. The warden of this castle refused to admit Iain Og and the crew of his galley, so they proceeded on to Ireland. Here Iain Og wandered destitute about the country until he was captured and executed by the O'Donnells.

Norman, the newly acknowledged chief of the MacLeods, was understandably angered by the murders committed by Iain Og and by his the occupation of Dunvegan Castle. To prevent any further attempts on the MacLeod chiefship by any future member of the Waternish family, Norman thought it best to have them all killed. In the course of a single night, the surviving sons of John of Waternish, along with their families, were all killed at Norman's request. By morning only Norman, the youngest son of Alexander MacLeod, warden of MacLeod castle, was the sole male survivor of the once influential Waternish family.

There is no record of what became of Margaret MacKinnon but, when her husband had been murdered by Iain Og in 1557, she may have gone to Strath to seek shelter with her relatives. There is little doubt, however, that her children were all killed on that fateful night when the Waternish family ceased to exist.

Ewen MacKinnon, the chief who had so strenuously supported all attempts to restore the Lordship of the Isles, died in 1557. In accordance with legal practice then current in the whole of the Scottish Kingdom, on the death of a feudal land holder, the estates reverted to ownership by the Crown. The MacKinnon estates were duly taken and held by Mary, Queen of Scots.

In theory, the land became the personal property of the monarch and she could dispose of it as she wished. In practice, it was expected that any estates which passed into the hands of the monarch should be transferred as quickly as possible to the legitimate heir of the deceased chief. However, before any transfer of lands could be made, hearings were held in which the merits of various claimants to the chiefship were examined and weighed under the laws of escheat and sasine.[18]

The first government-sponsored hearings in relation to the MacKinnon lands were held at Inverness in 1557. Before this type of examination, known as retours, was held, the care of the clan's estates was an obligation of the chiefship, and the chief was chosen by his durbfine in the traditional manner. The focus of the hearing at Inverness was to determine the legal suitability of Lauchlan, Ewen's son, to take possession of the lands, not his ability nor his right to lead the clan.[19] A jury was called to hear the claim, and Donald MacLean of Dochgarroch represented Lauchlan's interests. As could be expected, the investigation went smoothly and, in July 1557, Queen Mary granted Lauchlan Dubh (Black Lauchlan) the estates and dues of both Mishnish and Strath.

By 1558 nothing remained of the alliance between the island clans and the English, which had been so carefully forged by Donald Dubh and the Earl of Lennox. Even the alliances between the clans were now generally being formed by expedience and just as easily broken. There were raids and counterraids throughout the area of the Irish Sea and beyond.

A large body of Campbells, who had been serving O'Donnell under the leadership of two of Argyll's young cousins, invaded Connaught at the invitation of the Burkes.[20] This unfortunate expedition ended when its leaders and most of its 1,200 men were surprised and killed in their camp on the River Moy. The rout of the Campbells signalled the start of a determined effort by the English, under the Earl of Clanricarde, to drive the Highlanders completely out of Connaught and Ulster.[21]

During the following September, the Lord Deputy of Ireland sailed from Dublin with a large force to attack Kintyre, landing near Campbelltown on 19th of September. The Lord Deputy burned some eight miles of MacDonald lands and the house at Saddell. The following day the English burned another 12 miles and several more houses as they marched south to Dunaverty. After burning their way back north to Campbelltown, the English proceeded on to Arran and the Cumbraes, which were also burned. Bute and Islay were only spared because a storm blew up which damaged the English fleet and forced it to retire to Ireland, where raids were mounted on the MacDonald estates in Antrim.

The MacDonalds of Islay and the MacLeans were, during this period, arguably the two most powerful clans in the Isles.[22] However, there were territorial frictions between them which erupted into an ugly spat of violence in 1562. The island of Jura was, at this time, occupied by the MacLeans, and the MacDonalds were aggravated by the lack of sympathy felt for their rights to the island. The main point of contention though was the ownership of the Rhinns of Islay. The MacDonalds held Islay by a charter from the government, but the Rhinns were occupied by the MacLeans as MacDonald's tenants. The MacLeans, however, demanded that they held the right to the Rhinns of Islay directly from the Crown and refused to recognise its MacDonald ownership.

When the inevitable fighting started, it appears that, while the MacLeans were initially the aggressors, the MacDonalds of Islay quickly invaded Mull and burned both Tiree and Coll. As the fighting raged in the Isles, James MacDonald explained his case before the Privy Council in Edinburgh. Even though the Privy Council recognised MacDonald's claim to the land and issued a statement that MacLean really did occupy the Rhinns as his tenant, the feud continued.

The government was extremely quick in issuing remissions to the MacDonald party, thus by the year's end, December 7, 1562, MacDonald of Sleat, Donald McKynnon, Niell Achwayne Mckynnon, and Lauchlan Dhu McKynnon were all given remission for the devastations they committed on Mull, Tiree, and Coll.

This feud, whose origins were a legal dispute over land ownership, would eventually develop into the most devastating inter-clan war the Isles had ever seen. By the time the feud was over, it would have involved most of the island clans and occupied a great deal of the Edinburgh's government's time and energy. The power and influence of the main combatants would be destroyed and the Campbells, almost by default, would supercede them both in power and influence. MacKinnons would fight on both sides, managing a balancing act that both preserved the clan and maintained its estates. For the moment, however, although the feud still simmered, both belligerent clans were distracted by events in Ireland.[23]

In the four years since Shane O'Neill assumed the title, Earl of Tyrone, he had alienated his Hebridean allies who now viewed him as an enemy who had to be firmly dealt with. The Earl of Argyll, perhaps encouraged by his English allies, formed a confederation with James MacDonald of Islay and Calvagh O'Donnell, Lord Tyrconnell, to move against the O'Neills.[24]

The forces led by Calvagh O'Donnell were quickly defeated by their O'Neill enemies. The Earl of Tyrconnell was captured in an abbey where he had taken refuge and was later executed. Tyrconnell's widow, Katherine MacLean, was also taken, but she was not killed nor was she ransomed. She joined Shane O'Neill, who kept her as his own wife.[25] The MacLeans, desperate to get Katherine safely back, negotiated a plan with the MacDonalds that would see Shane O'Neill married to the daughter of James MacDonald of Islay and made foster father to James' son, Sorley Boy mac James.

Sorley Boy, for his part, would provide O'Neill with 508 horses, furniture, and an escort of 400-500 men for his travels if he gave up Katherine. Shane O'Neill refused this offer, which only further inflamed the emotions of the Islanders against him. In 1563 James MacDonald and the English Queen Elizabeth, signed an agreement by which they would cooperate in deposing the troublesome O'Neill.[26] O'Neill, upon learning of the pact, immediately went off to England, where he threw himself on the mercy of the queen. Not only did Elizabeth not honour her agreement with MacDonald, but she offered O'Neill a commission to drive the MacDonalds out of Ulster.

During 1564 O'Neill, now with the hearty blessing of Queen Elizabeth, gathered his army and attacked Ulster. O'Neill's forces were victorious.[27] The triumphant O'Neill ravaged the MacDonald estates in Antrim, leaving nothing of value behind. This defeat severely crippled the leadership of the MacDonalds of Islay. James MacDonald and his son, Sorley Boy, were captured and James' brother, Angus (the Haughty), with 600-700 warriors, had been killed.[28] Efforts to secure the MacDonald's release were even made by Mary, Queen of Scots; Argyll, and several other lesser persons. None of these attempts were successful and James MacDonald, who remained a captive died of his wounds.

MacDonalds (MacDonnells) of Antrim

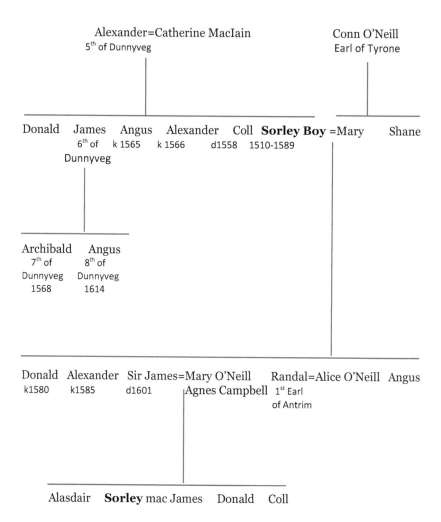

Alexander=Catherine MacIain
5th of Dunnyveg

Conn O'Neill
Earl of Tyrone

Donald   James   Angus   Alexander   Coll   **Sorley Boy** =Mary   Shane
       6th of   k 1565   k 1566   d1558   1510-1589
       Dunnyveg

Archibald   Angus
7th of   8th of
Dunnyveg   Dunnyveg
1568   1614

Donald   Alexander   Sir James=Mary O'Neill   Randal=Alice O'Neill   Angus
k1580   k1585   d1601   Agnes Campbell   1st Earl
                                  of Antrim

Alasdair   **Sorley** mac James   Donald   Coll

A French illustration of Highland dress c.1560

The victory swelled O'Neill's pride, and he demanded recognition of his title, Earl of Tyrone, and the *"tribute due in old times to kings."*[29] O'Neill had less than two years to enjoy his newly-aquired prestige and status in Ulster. Alastair Og, the Captain of Kintyre, succeeded his brother, James MacDonald, to the chiefship of the Clan Ian Mor. One of the first undertakings of the new MacDonald chief was to vigorously attack the O'Neills, driving them completely out of Ulster. Shane O'Neill, was tracked down, found and killed. During 1569, almost five years later, an Act of Attainment was passed by the English parliament which posthumously attainted Shane O'Neill, abolished the name and title "O'Neill" and the inauguration that went with it.[30]

The English desire to rid Ulster of the Hebridean settlements was only inflamed by these events. The Islanders did not regard the English authority in Ireland as a deterrent to settlement, and they poured into Ulster by the thousands. In 1567 urgent warnings were hurriedly issued to the English commanders when Argyll alone threatened to invade Ireland with 5,000 men unless Queen Elizabeth gave aid to Mary, Queen of Scots.

Two years later the English may have believed they were gaining the upper hand when in 1569 a large party of some 400 Islanders and their Irish allies were defeated near Castlereagh. But any semblance of English superiority in Ulster was swept away that same year when Lady Agnes Campbell, the widow of James MacDonald, arrived with 1,000 warriors to reinforce the MacDonalds in Antrim.[31]

Katherine MacLean, now the widow of Calvagh O'Donnell, was also raising men in the Isles and reinforced Ulster with a large party of MacLeans. Even the Earl of Argyll was regularly sending large numbers of well-armed men in support of the O'Neills. Although they tried desperately, the English could not long prevail against the steadily increasing numbers of Islander warriors.

Walter Devereux, the Earl of Essex, came to prominence in Ireland during the early 1570s. He was to become well known by both sides for his duplicity and ruthlessness. In 1573 Essex advised Turlough O'Neill that his mission was to expel all of the Scots from Ulster. Turlough was requested to break off his alliance with Sorley Boy and from that time forward to actively aid the English with Essex's mission.

What little influence Essex had with the O'Neills was undermined in 1574 when he treacherously seized and executed Sir Brian MacPhelim, Chief of the O'Neills of Clandeboye. However, Essex's ultimate undoing came in 1575 when he ordered a raid on Rathlin Island. The small narrow island off the Northeast Coast of Ulster was where the families of the Hebridean solders traditionally fled for safety during times of trouble. Essex ordered Captains Norris and Thornton, with a force of 3000 men and a fleet of six frigates, to take the island. Captain Thornton distinguished himself on the voyage north when he became one of the very few English naval officers to capture a Highland galley at sea.

The frigates opened the attack on Rathlin by bombarding its small fort. The bombardment was immediately followed by an assault, which the MacDonald garrison fought to a standstill. After the failure of the first assault, the English called for a parley with the garrison commander. Shortly after the meeting, the English resumed their assault.[32] The second assault carried the fort. The garrison of 200 men was slaughtered, as were the wives and children who had sheltered there for safety.

MacDonald warriors witnessed the attack from the shores of Antrim but, because their galleys were stored on the unfortunate island, they could only helplessly watch in horror. Sorley Boy and the MacDonalds, furious at the cowardly murder of their families, vowed revenge. A few weeks later, after reinforcing the estates with another 600 warriors from Islay and Kintyre, Sorley Boy struck. He attacked Knockfergus, plundered the town, and routed the larger English column sent against him. This infamous slaughter of the Highland families was also too much for the London government and Essex was recalled for an interview by Queen Elizabeth herself.

End Notes
Chapter 14

1. In 1498 the Earl of Argyll petitioned the pope, requesting the Abbey of Iona be erected to the bishop's seat of the Isles. Rather than make Iona a cathedral, the pope granted the abbacy of Iona to the bishops of the Isles in *commendam,* thus subordinating Iona to the cathedral of Snizort (Skeabost on Skye). With the fall of the Lordship of the Isles, the MacKinnons no longer had any influence over the affairs of Iona, leaving it to the MacLeans and Campbells to squabble over its remains. Vestiges of the old order on Iona lasted until being swept away in the revolution against King Charles I in 1638. Sir Donald Monro was Dean of the Isles- -a dignitary of the Cathedral of the Isles on Skye.

2. See Appendix 12, *Dean Monro's account* and MacKinnon, D., *How to see Skye, A Guide*, Moray & Nairn, Elgin, 1937, 11.

3. MacKinnon, D., *How to see Skye, A Guide*, Moray & Nairn, Elgin, 1937, 11.

4. Ireland would have been seen as a land flowing with milk and honey, where the island warriors could easily take whatever they wanted. However, for the most part, the Islanders chose to live under Hebridean chiefs in Ireland because the Irish chiefs and English lords taxed their tenant farmers far more than was customary in the Isles. Ireland had always been considered a place of refuge for the Islanders. After the relationship between the Campbells and the MacGregors soured in the mid 1560s, the latter clan fled to Ireland for safety. Argyll then ordered the island chiefs not to transport anyone by the name of MacGregor. The Clan Gregor only returned to Scotland with much difficulty.

5. Gregory, D., *History of the Western Highlands and Isles of Scotland*, William Tait, Edinburgh, 1836, 128.

6. This number would not include the family of MacInnis who provided archers for the MacKinnon chief's bodyguard. For this service, the MacInnis clan was provided with the farm of Dal na Saighdear located just south of Surdal in Strath.

7. MacLean-Bristol N., *Warriors and Priests*, Tuckwell Press, East Lothian, 1995, 145.

8. Rev. MacKinnon, D. D., *Memoirs of Clan Fingon*, Lewis Hepworth, Tunbridge Wells, 1899, 10-11.

9. The two holdouts were John MacDonald of Clanranald and Ewen Cameron of Locheil. The Earl of Huntly was immediately ordered to deal with the disobedient chiefs. But due to his followers' lack of confidence in Huntly's leadership, the expedition was not launched and Huntly was imprisoned.

10. These clans had been ordered by Arran to deliver hostages, which would be held by the Edinburgh government to insure their good behavior. None of the clans complied. The Queen Mother made another attempt to control the Isles in 1555 when she brought charges of treason against MacLeod and made Argyll and Atholl royal commissioners over the Isles.

11. The relationship between England and the government of Scotland was one of guarded hostility. In December of 1552 the Scottish government ordered Huntly to raise two regiments of Highland soldiers for service to the King of France.

12. The O'Donnells of Tyrconnell (Conall's land) in Ulster descend from Conall, the son of Niall of the Nine Hostages. Over time, Tyrconnell became known as Donegal. This clan was often at feud with their neighbours, the O'Neills.

13. Argyll supplied O'Donnell with a huge cannon and the use of a large body of soldiers, which was led by the earl's son. The Campbell warriors were in Ireland for about one year. See: MacLean-Bristol N., "The MacLeans from 1560-1707: A Re-Appraisal" 17th Century in the Highlands, Inverness Field Club, John G, Eccles, 1986, 78, and Campbell, A., *History of Clan Campbell*, Edinburgh University Press, 2002, Vol. 2, 42.

14. Katherine MacLean was sister to MacLean of Duart. She is described as sober, wise and social. She spoke Latin, French, Italian and English as well as her native Gaelic.

15. Shane O'Neill was the chief of the O'Neills, elected by the O'Neill durbfine. Shane's father, Conn Bracach, had accepted the feudal title of Earl of Tyrone from King Henry VIII on the condition that he give up the ancient Irish title of *The O'Neill*. Shane would spend his life working to reinstate the ancient title and restoring his family to their ancient position as High Kings of Ireland.

16. In 1557 James MacDonald receives a grant of Bar in Kintyre from the Scottish government for his services against the English. James also asks a pardon from Queen Mary and Phillip of France, offering to share with them the fishing off the Bann. Galleys from Kintyre and Jura frequently fished there. In 1611 the salmon fishing in Lough Foyle & Bann was valued at £800-£1000 yearly.

17. Margaret, the daughter of Roderick MacLeod of Lewis, married Lachlan MacKinnon of MacKinnon. Margaret and Lachlan had two children: John, the last abbot of Iona, and a daughter called Margaret who had the ill luck to marry Donald MacLeod of Waternish.

18. *Escheat* is the Scottish legal term for property reverting to the Crown in the event there are no legal heirs to an estate. The law of escheat determines who is and who is not a legitimate heir, determined by feudal relationships. *Sasine* is the term for the actual legal holding of the estate. The law of sasine defines which claims of use, access, or ownership of land is legitimate and will be recognised.

19. When a Scottish landowner died, the heir could not succeed to the lands until his claim had been formally recognised and he had been served nearest lawful heir. The procedure to do this began with a brieve of inquest (writ) sent from the Chancery (the office of the Lord Chancellor, later the Director of Chancery) to the sheriff of the county in which the lands were situated. The brief [brieve] instructed him to appoint a jury and hold an enquiry [inquest] into the claimant's right to succession and into other questions related to the value of the land, the feudal superior, and the feudal service of the land holding. The findings of the enquiry were then sent back to the Chancery (i.e. retoured) and recorded in the Record of Retours [Returns]. When the land itself was transferred, this record was in the Register of Sasines (property register).

20. The Burkes were known as the Clan William by the Islanders. They may have been descended from the MacWilliams who led the fight against the Scottish kings during the 12th century. The identity of the leaders of the Campbell force is known only by their names, Donald and Donough, who are supposed to have been grandsons of the second Earl of Argyll. There is no doubt they were Campbells of rank.

21. In spite of the loss of such a large number of warriors by English hands, Argyll still favoured the English over the government in Edinburgh. The bulk of the Hebridean chiefs remained fiercely independent and did not give their allegiance to either government. As the MacDonald settlements in Connaught contained the largest numbers of armed men in the district, there was no attempt by the English to remove them.

22. Archibald, Earl of Argyll (1558-73) would eventually build up the largest personal armed force, backed by his own artillery, in either Scotland or England.

23. James MacDonald, Chief of the Clan Ian Mor, died of wounds received defending his lands in Ulster from O'Neill in 1565. After his death the MacLeans escalated the raids on MacDonald territory. On April 28, 1567, Queen Mary issued a commission to the Earl of Argyll to act

against MacLean of Duart for his ravaging with fire and sword of the island of Ghiga.

24. Argyll and MacDonald had been allied with Shane since he took the chiefship of his clan. But now there may have been some English pressure on Argyll to unite the Islanders against O'Neill. The English had agreed to help Argyll against the French garrison at Leith in return for help in Ireland. Scotland was now in civil war, the Queen Mother, Mary of Guise, was employing French troops to support the Roman Catholic Church against the Protestants.

25. She lived with Shane O'Neill long enough to bore him three children. Another version of events states that both Katherine and her ex-husband, Calvagh O'Donnell, were released in 1566. This version also states that Calvagh O'Donnell died from a fall from his horse shortly after his release. Katherine would eventually marry Stewart of Appin.

26. MacDonald may have been pressured by Argyll to sign an agreement with the English, but he had reason enough of his own for such an understanding. Shane O'Neill had either murdered two of his kinsmen himself or he had ordered the deed committed.

27. English policy had changed and they regarded the Scots in Ulster as a greater threat than Shane O'Neill.

28. On the 22nd of April the MacDonalds were defeated at the pass of Knockboy. Sorley Boy lit the signal fires on the coast, calling for help from Islay and Kintyre. The galleys quickly put to sea and by the 1st of May, the MacDonald forces in Ireland were united. They were however defeated with great loss at Glenshesk and the Clan Ian Mor was, for the moment, shattered. The English agents who had accompanied O'Neill's army reported that the Scots fought like mad men. By November of the same year, in an attempt to pressure the English government to actively support the Reformed religion in Scotland, Argyll offered Shane O'Neill 4,000 men to use against the English. Argyll's support for Shane O'Neill was authorized by Queen Mary, who likely misunderstood Argyll's true motives. After this, Argyll worked against the English.

29. MacKenzie, W. C., *The Highlands and Islands of Scotland*, Moray Press, Edinburgh, 1949, 150.

30. Shane O'Neill's successor, Turlough, assumed the titles "O'Neill" and Earl of Tyrone in 1567, but neither title was recognized by the English nor the Scots. Almost immediately upon assuming the leadership of the clan, he took up the fight against the English.

31. Lady Agnes also married Turlough O'Neill on Rathlin Island. This dynastic marriage gave the Irish nationalists an army of 3,000 Scots-- mostly Campbells, MacLeans, and MacDonalds, and as many Irish as any

O'Neill had ever led. Lady Agnes' son, Sorley Boy, had another 32 galleys and 4,000 men ready at a moment's notice to sail from Islay to Loch Foyle. Lady Agnes returned to the Hebrides to raise men several times--the most notable being in 1570 when she returned to Antrim with a large force of some 700 Campbells. That O'Neill's rising against the English may have, in part, been in support of Queen Mary of Scotland, may be seen from a letter written to Queen Elizabeth by Lady Agnes. After Queen Mary's supporters were defeated in Scotland, Lady Agnes wrote London offering peace. A treaty was concluded and Turlough O'Neill dismissed his island mercenaries.

32. An English report of the attack on Rathlin says that, "during the parley, the constable of the fort was given his life for betraying his fellows".

Chapter 15
AGE OF THE RAIDS

A lthough Ireland was in turmoil and would remain so for some time, life in the Hebrides had, on the whole, been relatively quiet since Donald Dubh's death. The relationships between the clans were, for the most part, civil but there was little in the way of formally-imposed law or order, and relationships were at times fragile.

During the summer of 1568, the Earl of Argyll attempted to unite the Western clans in support of the captive Queen Mary but failed miserably. A meeting attended by the island chiefs was rancorous and little of value was accomplished.

The Hebrides were now regularly plied by English ships as agents attempted to gain the support of island clans for their war in Ireland. The clans did not wholly support, nor trust, the English, and the high level of intrigue alone would have been somewhat unsettling.

It was during this period that the first Campbells arrived on Skye. They were sent by the Earl of Argyll to serve as a bodyguard for the young heiress, Mary MacLeod of Dunvegan. One of these families was granted land on the island of Scalpay, just off the East Coast of Strath, which at the time belonged to Hector MacLean of Duart, then an ally of Argyll's.

Although for the last several years Iona had actually been held by the Bishop of the Isles, there was a spirited competition between the MacLeans and the Campbells for the control of the abbacy. Neither clan was able to maintain a position of influence for long, and control alternated between the two families.

As a result of the continuing confusion and constant reorganisation of Iona's affairs, the MacKinnon estates on Mull were exempted from the yearly penny rental due to the abbot in 1561.[1] The money to maintain what remained of the religious establishment had to be obtained from other sources. Donald M'Kynnine, the tacksman of Ostage, witnessed an obligation for funding between James MacDonald of Castle Camus and the Bishop of the Isles.[2]

During the episcopate of Bishop John Campbell, who succeeded John Carswell as head of the Reformed Church in the diocese of Argyll and the Isles, the first Reformed service is recorded to have taken place in the ancient abbey of Iona.[3] This service, which took place in 1573, fittingly occurred under the ministry of Fingon mac Mullen. But from about 1556 the church on Iona had become little more than an empty shell. Its lands and wealth had been usurped by the MacLeans and the Campbells, and very little remained of its ancient glory.

Leading the church in the Isles during these times presented many unique challenges. Bishop Campbell repeatedly complained of the MacLeans lifting his rents and was, for a time, even forced to leave the country as Hector MacLean attempted to dispossess him of his office.

The Reformation in Scotland began in earnest in 1560 when the country formally broke from the papacy. Starting in the burghs that had contacts with Europe, acceptance of the new doctrines spread from merchants and traders to the Lowland gentry. From its beginning, however, the Scottish Reformation had political overtones. During 1572 the Convention of Leith inaugurated a Reformed Episcopate to replace the many Catholic bishops who had, until then, retained their positions and influence.

In the Western Isles it was Bishop Campbell who attempted to win the support of the clan chiefs for the Reformed Church by engaging them in legal agreements. He had some success, but most of the clan chiefs appear to have preferred not to commit themselves. By 1573 Macleod of Lewis had formally agreed to adhere to the laws and constitution of the Protestant Church. In 1580 MacDonald of Sleat agreed to accompany the bishop through the Isles to aid him in collecting the church's rents.[4]

During the year 1577 the peace of the Isles was violently broken by the resumption of what was rapidly developing into the most fiercely-contested feud in the entire history of the Scottish Highlands. The feud was ostensibly over the rights of occupancy to what the MacLeans claimed were Crown lands in the Rhinns of Islay but would grow to involve revenge for cattle theft and murder.

The MacLeans had been leasing the land for several years, as tenants of the MacDonalds of Islay, who were its legal owners. Lauchlan MacLean, who had spent his youth at court in Edinburgh and had returned to take the chiefship of the clan in 1576, was well aware of the legal status of Islay but was determined to right what he saw as an historic wrong against his clan.[5] Lauchlan demanded that the Rhinns of Islay should belong to him by charter directly from the Crown and that MacLeans would no longer occupy it as tenants. The MacDonalds of Islay stood firmly by their position that the MacLeans were only welcome on Islay if they agreed to hold the land there as their tenants.

The fighting erupted during March of 1577 when Colin Campbell, the Earl of Argyll, and John Dubh, the young MacLean chief's uncle, sent a party of Campbell warriors to attack the MacLean holdings on the island of Luing.[6] The island was plundered and many depredations committed. The booty taken by Argyll included large numbers of cattle, sheep, horses, and even the clothing worn by the inhabitants.

Although the MacLean fort in the middle of Loch Gorm on the Rhinns of Islay was also attacked by a combined party of MacDonalds and Campbells, it appears not to have been taken. In retaliation for these assaults, Lauchlan rallied his supporters and struck at Argyll, causing a great deal of damage. In turn, the Campbells again struck at the island of Luing. This time they even carried off George Smollett, the captain of the island.

Colin Campbell was determined to isolate Lauchlan MacLean and his clan in the Isles and so refused to allow any of his people permission to cross the territory of Argyll which provided the easiest, most direct, road eastward. While attempting the trek across these districts to reach the Lowlands for trade or other reasons, several MacLean clansfolk were caught. One of those captured, a servant to Lauchlan MacLean, may have been a messenger sent by his chief to request help from the court in Edinburgh. The servant, who was being held by Campbell of Lochgoilhead, was imprisoned for ransom on orders received directly from Argyll himself.

The MacLeans needed allies to maintain their security in the Isles, but none were forthcoming. In December of 1577 Lauchlan MacLean visited the court in Edinburgh in person and, no doubt, explained to the king the dire position his clan now occupied in the

Hebrides. There is seemingly no record of help being offered by the government at this time, so Lauchlan began the journey home empty-handed.

On his return home, the MacLean chief stopped at the house of Walter Cunningham, Earl of Glencairn. During his brief stay with the Cunninghams, Lauchlan met and married the earl's daughter Margaret. The MacLean histories put a rather romantic turn to this story, but the alliance with such a powerful family was just what the young MacLean chief was looking for.[7]

How the feud escalated from here is not entirely clear, but early in the following year, 1578, the MacLeans made several predatory raids on MacDonald lands and these, of course, were promptly answered. Angus MacDonald, of the Clan Ian Mor, quickly raised a force of about 1400 men comprised of his Irish allies, the MacDonalds of Sleat, some MacKinnons, and a party of Campbells.[8] Angus first moved against the MacLean holdings on Islay. They besieged the fort at Loch Gorm and plundered the MacLean-occupied Rhinns of Islay. MacDonald next proceeded against the MacLean holdings on Tiree, Coll, and the island of Mull itself.

The MacLeans, still a formidable naval power, were far from idle. A powerful force was dispatched to Ireland, where they laid waste the lands of Shane O'Dochtrie in retaliation for his aid to the MacDonalds. Because of its great strategic importance to both sides, the MacDonald island of Colonsay, in particular, suffered from many hit-and-run raids.

Any traffic from Mull to the MacLean possessions on the Rhinns of Islay or Jura, would have to pass along the east coast of Colonsay. Passage along the Western coast of the island would subject the galleys to the heavy Atlantic swells and the danger of being wrecked on Islay's bleak northern coastline. This, and the consideration that the closest landfalls to Colonsay were settled by MacLeans, made that island very important to them. The Clan MacDonald needed control of the island because its three lookout points, still known as Cnoc-na-Faire, could monitor all galley movement south of Mull and west of Jura. With a strong base on Colonsay, no hostile galleys could enter the Sound of Islay without danger of interception from galleys based on Colonsay itself or dispatched from Islay.

A West Highland galley in the Hebrides

The government moved as swiftly as it could to stem the rising level of violence. On January 12, 1579, all of the chiefs involved in the feud were threatened with charges of treason unless they quickly gave pledges for their good behavior. There does not appear to be an extant record of what pledges were actually offered by the chiefs to the government if, in fact, any were. But the fighting stopped for the moment and the clans appeared to reach an accord. Angus MacDonald married Mary MacLean, Lauchlan's sister, and Lauchlan and Colin Campbell also came to terms. However, the causes of the feud had not been addressed, so the ill feeling between the clans festered, waiting for another opportunity to erupt.

During about 1580 the Edinburgh government granted a licence enabling a fair to be held at Portree on Skye. The market would be held twice a year, lasting from Wednesday until Saturday. All the produce of the island was displayed during this event: ground grains, butter, cheese, poultry, sheep, cattle, horses, hides, wool, linen, and dried fish-- especially salmon and herring. As it was very rare in those days for a stranger to venture far in the islands, most of the goods would be bartered between the Islanders themselves.

Later that same year an incident occurred which sheds a little light on how Edinburgh viewed the clan alliances of the time. For some reason now long forgotten, the Earl of Argyll gathered his clan to attack the MacDonalds of Glengarry. The Privy Council in Edinburgh, alerted to trouble in the West Highlands, quickly dispatched orders to MacKinnon and MacLean not to aid Argyll in this project.[9] The government, perhaps knowing how little weight its writ carried in the west, also ordered the MacKenzies and the Frasers of Lovat to aid Glengarry in the event of a Campbell invasion.[10] The threatened violence, however, does not appear to have taken place.

It may have been partly because of Argyll's demonstrated restraint in this instance that the government appointed him Chancellor and Justice of Scotland on August 20, 1579. One of Argyll's first acts in his new post was to compel Lauchlan MacLean to deliver pledges for his later appearance at trial for the damage done during his raid on Shane O'Dochtrie's territory of Glach. There is no record that the trial actually took place and an accommodation between the parties may have been reached out of court.

On May 27, 1580, Lauchlan MacLean surrendered lands, with a yearly rent of 200 merks, to Argyll as a final settlement of the dispute. With the last conflict newly resolved, Argyll was again ordered by the Privy Council to proceed against Lauchlan MacLean for his pirating of the English ship "White Hart."

When the MacKinnon chief, Lauchlan Dubh, died in July of 1586, he was succeeded by his eldest son also named Lauchlan. Even though he was about 40 years old and had been married to Janet Fraser of Guisachan since about 1583, three years before assuming the chiefship, the new chief would be known as *Lauchlan Og* or Young Lauchlan in MacKinnon tradition.[11] The new chief had two brothers and a sister, of whom little is known. Lauchlan's brother, *Iain Cannach* (John of Canna), whose descendants would be known as *Sliochd Iaic Cannaich,* were the founders of the Torrin and Kinloch families. Ewen, Lauchlan's youngest brother, would die in 1618, leaving no descendants, and Fionnghal, his sister, married Iain MacLean of Grishipol on the island of Coll.[12]

Between 1580 and 1585 the Islanders' involvement in Ireland had risen to such a high level that it threatened English rule on that island. During this period there were thousands of Hebridean soldiers

240

Highlander
Drawn by Lucus de Here
c1577

serving in Ireland under various Irish lords and, at times, even their own clan chiefs.[13] The politics of the Hebrides were, to a large extent, reflected in Ireland as the various island clans allied themselves with differing Irish rebel factions for reasons of familial relationships or gold.

In 1581 William Nugent, the Irish nationalist, negotiated with Turlough O'Neill and Sorley Boy for Hebridean aid. It was agreed that 8,000 Islanders would land at Ards and Lecale in County Down. Angus MacDonald of Islay did lead 4,000 men, MacLeod of Harris was to lead 2,000, and MacLeod of Lewis would lead the remaining 2,000. It is not now known if this proposal was acted upon as there is no record of such a large multi-clan force actually landing in Ireland during this time.

Although Angus MacDonald did much damage to the English cause. The English did not lose every contest, however, and in December of 1582, it was reported that a large force of English soldiers succeeded in forcing a galley fleet to put to sea into a storm with the estimated loss of 140 galleys. The influx of island warriors to Ireland was not at all slowed even by such a considerable loss of transportation. Lauchlan MacLean, with 2,000 well-appointed men, is reported to have landed in MacSweeney's country in Ulster, taking every cow in the territory.[14]

The pressure on the English increased during 1584, with concerns in Dublin and London that the Scottish King James VI was actively backing a concerted and well-coordinated rising in Ulster, Connaught and Munster. English spies reported that the Islanders would support the rising in Ulster, while the rebels in Connaught and Munster would be supported by Spanish troops. These reports were seemingly verified by sightings of *"inland Scots"* (Lowlanders) among the Islanders in Antrim.[15]

The English were determined to end this threat by dividing the Islanders and driving them from Ulster once and for all. In a report offered to Queen Elizabeth by Sir Geoffrey Fenton, it was stated that:

"the people which most annoy Ulster from Scotland are the Clan Donnells (MacDonald) who are ever in continual wars with another sept of the people of the Isles named MacAlanes (MacLean) and if on MacLean, Her Majesty, would bestow some convenient pension, he will I think, undertake to keep the MacDonalds continually engaged as they shall be able to send none of their people to disturb Her Majesty's subjects in Ulster."[16]

There is no doubt that the MacLeans and the English Crown were in contact during this period, but the details of any pacts between them are unknown. The English goal of provoking the long-standing ill feeling between the clans into open warfare was to be accomplished not by the English but rather by a party of renegade MacDonalds.

Donald Gorm Mor (MacDonald) of Sleat had recently returned from Ireland and, as befitted his rank, was accompanied by a large number of his clansmen. He set out from Skye with the intention of visiting his kinsman, Angus MacDonald of Islay, at his castle of Dunnyveg. Beset by bad weather, Donald Gorm's party was forced to land at Inbhir cnoc Breac, a part of Jura which belonged to MacLean of Duart.

The storm also forced a renegade MacDonald; MacDonald Terreagh; and Eachuinn an Clireach Beag MacLean, 5th Laird of Coll, to land at a neighbouring harbour.[17] We will never know for certain whether the pirates knew of or even considered their chief's whereabouts on that night. It is, however, very well known that, using the storm as cover, they made off with large numbers of MacLean cattle, leaving their chief to shoulder the blame. The MacLeans noticed the cattle were missing and naturally assumed that Donald Gorm's party was responsible for the disappearance. The following night, under cover of darkness, the MacDonalds, still waiting out the storm, were attacked by a larger body of MacLeans led by Lauchlan MacLean of Duart himself. The slaughter was horrendous, the unsuspecting MacDonalds lost some 60 men and Donald Gorm only survived because he slept aboard his galley. Escaping to his home on Skye, Donald Gorm immediately sent word of the attack to Angus MacDonald of Islay.

Once again the English showed an interest in exploiting the rift between the island clans. In a letter dated August 22, 1585, Walsingham, Queen Elizabeth's secretary, received a letter from the Agent Wotton, who again suggested the English hire MacLean to act against the MacDonalds and keep them out of Ireland *"Hee [King James] ys presentlye to direct his lettre to Sorle boy, and Agnus Maconell, to commaunde theym to revoke their Highelande followers which ar passed into Irelande ... yet these Highelanders (as farre as I can see) care but little for the King, and will obeye him at their owne pleasure. But the thing that gevethe mee most hope of their revocation, ys a quarrell that ys latelye fallen out between Agnus and Macclan [MacLean], who have ben together by the eares within these 2 dayes (as I am informed) and Makklan hathe slayne 140 of Agnus his men. I am (for myne owne parte) of opinion, that yf her majestie wolde bestowe a yerelie pension of one hundred or two hundred poundes upon Makclan, yt wold save her 4000 or 5000 poundes everye yere in here Irish expences, — for this Makclan (being a great Lorde in the Highelandes) and having a deeidly fewde against Agnus, upon whom hee borderethe, were hee her majesties pensioner, wolde be redye at all tymes, whensoever eyther Agnus or Surleboy sholde sterte into Irelande, to spoyle and burne their countryes. So that the feare thereof wolde (as I thincke) keepe theym from goyng (or yf at any tyme they dyd go) wolde quycklye call theim home agayne.*

As knowledge of the attack spread through the Hebrides, the various branches of the Clan Donald united and were joined by MacNeil of Giga, MacFie of Colonsay, and MacLeod of Lewis.[18]

The MacDonalds, in retaliation for the attack on Donald Gorm, wasted no time in wreaking havoc on any exposed MacLean lands they could reach. The Hebrides were now awash in blood as the long-simmering feud broke into open warfare. The MacKinnons, MacQuarries, and MacNeil of Barra joined the MacLeans while, for the moment, MacLeod of Dunvegan attempted to remain neutral.

By the end of September 1585, King James, himself, had requested that MacLeod of Harris actively aid MacLean against the MacDonald onslaught. Thus, with the onset of winter, all of the Hebridean clans were engaged on one side or the other; there were no neutral parties.

Angus MacDonald of Islay, realising the danger to the Isles posed by escalating the feud to an all out war, thought to calm events by intervening personally with his brother-in-law, Lauchlan MacLean. After a visit to Sleat, Angus proposed that he stop at Duart castle, which he would pass on the way home to Dunnyveg.

Angus was sure that once he met with Lauchlan a peaceful settlement could be found. The proposed visit, though, was strongly opposed by Angus's kinsmen, who expressed a distrust for Lauchlan and would have preferred Angus open the negotiations through a messenger.[19] Angus, however, placed a great amount of faith in his position as Lauchlan's brother-in-law and was determined to have the visit proceed.

In accordance with his intentions, Angus, accompanied by his brother Ranald and a small party of his clansmen, landed at Duart on their way south through the Sound of Mull. Lauchlan MacLean was not one to let an opportunity to capture such a powerful opponent pass and ordered the whole party detained. In order to save his own life and those of his compatriots, Angus was made to renounce his claims to the Rhinns of Islay in favour of MacLean. Lauchlan also demanded that Ranald, Angus's brother; and James, Angus's son; be left at Duart Castle as hostages. As the MacDonalds were released and made their way homeward to Dunnyveg, the enraged Angus became determined to avenge the indignity that he and his party had been subjected to.

During the early months of 1586, the Clan Ian Mor was fully occupied in both the Hebrides and Ireland. Angus MacDonald's brothers, Donald Gorm and Alastair Carrach, were leading a large party of MacDonalds who had aided the rebellious Burkes and then themselves settled in Connaught.[20] In Ulster, Angus's uncle, Sorley Boy, was depending on the promise of 2,000 men to help him fend off the English, who were still trying to drive him from Ireland.

On Islay, Angus MacDonald was negotiating with Lauchlan MacLean who came to take formal possession of the Rhinns of Islay.[21] Lauchlan brought one of the hostages, James, Angus's son, with him from Duart but left Ranald behind as surety for Angus's goodwill. Lauchlan MacLean initially made the old fort in the middle of Loch Gorm his principal residence. Angus MacDonald, on learning of Lauchlan's landing, invited him and his party to reside with him at his home, a place called Mullintrea.

Because of the distrust and animosity between these two chiefs, all communication between them was conducted by way of messengers. MacLean was initially adamant that he did not trust MacDonald's offer of hospitality. However, Angus MacDonald persisted, stating that, as MacLean still held two hostages and since his aim to reconcile the relationship was sincere, Lauchlan MacLean had nothing to fear. Eventually Lauchlan relented and, accepting MacDonald's offer, arrived at Mullintrea with 86 men during July of 1586. Preparations had been made and, on the very day the MacLeans arrived, a great feast was held. As the feast ended, the MacLeans, for security, elected to pass the night all together in one blackhouse which was set a little apart from the others.

Unknown to Lauchlan MacLean, Angus MacDonald had summoned all of the principal men on Islay, about 300 in number, to gather with their arms at Mullintrea in the late evening or shortly after nightfall. These men now completely surrounded the blackhouse occupied by the MacLeans. When all was ready, Angus called out to Lauchlan that there was one more drink prepared which they had forgotten to take before retiring. Lauchlan replied he had drunk enough that night and he desired nothing more. Angus's insistence that he come out alerted Lauchlan to the danger he and his men were facing.

When Lauchlan did emerge from the blackhouse, he carried young James MacDonald, Angus's son, on his shoulder. As James's eyes adjusted to the moonlight, he recognised his father with his men gathered around and, noticing their swords drawn, he cried out that his Uncle Lauchlan's life be spared.

The MacLean chief was immediately arrested and placed into a secure place for the night and a strong guard posted on the blackhouse which contained the remaining MacLean warriors. The next morning, when Angus MacDonald called on the rest of the MacLeans to surrender, 84 of them came out of the blackhouse together. Only two men refused to surrender--one was a prominent MacLean who was famous for his wisdom and valour in battle, the other was the renegade, MacDonald Terreagh, who had stolen the cattle on Jura and provoked the violence. Angus asked once more for the two warriors to come out of the blackhouse and, when they refused, he ordered the house burned on top of them.

Word of the capture of Lauchlan MacLean and his men was not slow in reaching Mull. Most MacLeans found the news disastrous; however, it could not have been better for Allan MacLean, a close relative of Lauchlan's and the guardian of Lauchlan's young son.[22] In hopes that Angus MacDonald would execute the MacLean chief, Allan put out the rumour that the hostage, Ranald MacDonald, had been killed. This rumour reached Islay, causing great anguish to both of Ranald's brothers, Angus and Coll MacDonald. Coll, in revenge for his brother's death, had two of the MacLean prisoners beheaded each day in the presence of their chief. Finally only Lauchlan remained of the prisoners and he too was led out for execution. The beheading of his rival was of great interest to Angus and he intended to watch from horseback. MacLean's life, however, was saved when an accident occurred as Angus MacDonald mounted his horse, and the execution was called off.

The feud, as violent as it was, did not seem to interfere with the normal livelihood of the chiefs of Skye. On November 11, 1586, the Burghs of the Realm of Scotland registered a complaint with the government in Edinburgh. The complaint, made by Lowland fishermen likely after many years of hard treatment by the Islanders, was a request for the government to intervene and stop what the fishermen viewed as harassment.

The list of charges brought against the leading men of Skye is quite lengthy and includes: charge of exorbitant fines for anchorage, high payments required for stances for huts and barrels, and the constant theft of nets and boats.[23] The Islanders, of course, would have regarded this as merely as an assertion of their territorial rights. Some of the individuals named in the complaint are John MacKinnon of Loch Slapin, Donald Gorm of Skye, MacLeod of Harris, and Rory MacAllan of Gairloch. These individuals were all summoned to appear before the Privy Council in Edinburgh to answer the charges brought against them. In the usual manner of the Islanders, the summons was ignored and the individuals were put to the horn and charged with treason.

News of Lauchlan MacLean's capture and the execution of his men quickly made its way to Argyll and from there on to Edinburgh. There was a flurry of diplomatic activity as various Campbell chieftains were employed by the king to mediate between the warring clans.[24] The government dispatched a herald of arms to Islay carrying a summons for Angus MacDonald. He was to answer the several charges brought against him in Edinburgh and the government's demand that MacLean be released into Argyll's care.

However, the herald was recalled as he was about to embark for Islay and therefore was unable to deliver the summons. The mediation which was carried on by the Campbell chiefs proved more fruitful. Angus agreed to suspend the feud, provided certain conditions were met: that he be pardoned for any crimes committed during the feud, that promises of their good behaviour be made by the chief men of MacLean, and that he be given hostages of rank by the MacLeans and each of their allied clans. These conditions were all met about April 16, 1587, with the handing over of eight hostages. The hostages given to Angus MacDonald were: Lauchlan MacLean's eldest son, Hector; Donald, son of Hector MacLean, the constable of Cairn na berg; Lauchlan and Neil, sons of Lauchlan Og MacKinnon of Strathardill; Alexander, brother to William MacLeod of Dunvegan; John and Murdo, sons of Ruari MacNeil of Barra; and Allan, son of Ewen MacLeod of Ardgour. With the settlement achieved and peace between the clans declared, Angus MacDonald felt secure enough to visit his lands in Ulster.[25]

Lauchlan MacLean was not satisfied with the settlement and, on hearing of Angus's absence from the Isles, struck at the very heart of his territory. In an orgy of revenge, Lauchlan savagely attacked the islands of Islay and Gigha, laying great parts of them waste with fire and sword.[26] Angus MacDonald, on being told of the attacks, was quick to respond and *"Yit great preparations on men and shipping,"* attacked Tiree and Mull.[27] On Mull the MacDonalds easily progressed to the very foot of Ben More, where *"they chased and killed the Clan Lean at Pleasure."*[28] While the MacDonald invasion of Mull was being carried out, the MacLeans were ravaging Kintyre. The fight was carried on in an utterly ruthless manner by both sides. The MacDonalds spared nothing belonging to the MacLeans as they burned all of the buildings and slaughtered with equal abandon all the people and animals they could catch. The MacLeans, in a similar manner, killed whatever they encountered and burned or otherwise destroyed all they could not carry off.

Shortly after the invasion of Mull, the MacLeans regrouped and, along with the MacKinnons, MacNeils, and MacQuarries, intercepted a massing of MacDonald warriors from both the Northern and Southern Hebrides. The MacDonalds were gathering on the small fortified island of Bachea, which lies almost in the middle of the sound of Mull being just southwest of Kerrera.

To facilitate a landing on the island, MacLeans invasion force was divided into three parts; two groups of archers led by MacNeil of Barra and MacLean of Borreray, and the main body of warriors led by

Lauchlan MacLean. During the fleets approach to the island, the MacLean galleys carrying the archers flanked and thus protected those which transported the main body of the army.

As the landing began, the archers opened the assault from their galleys by laying down a withering barrage of arrows on the large party of MacDonalds who had rushed to the west side of the island, intending to dispute the invasion. The MacDonalds' advance guard was driven off by the severity of the barrage and the invasion force successfully landed. Rushing inland, the MacLeans, MacKinnons, MacQuarries, and MacNeils appear to have caught the MacDonalds unprepared.

After a short fierce fight about the stronghold at the centre of the island, the MacDonald defence broke. Retreating to their galleys, the great majority of Bachea's defenders escaped. Their casualties, however, were so great that the threat of another MacDonald invasion was ended.[29] Among the many warriors captured were; MacDonald of Sleat, MacIain of Ardnamurchan, MacLeod of Lewis, and MacPhee of Colonsay. This attack, and subsequent capture of so many prominent leaders, may have prevented a MacDonald invasion and the widespread devastation of MacKinnon lands on both Mull and Skye. Incredibly, the MacKinnon territories were apparently unscathed throughout the entire duration of this war .[30]

King James, now worried about the violent escalation of the feud, ordered all captives taken by both sides to be freed. The hostages held by Angus MacDonald were to be turned over to Argyll for safety. As a consequence of the government interest, Lauchlan MacLean declared himself an obedient subject, releasing the prisoners taken at Bachea and was immediately welcomed into the king's favour. Angus MacDonald, on the other hand, was declared an outlaw because he steadfastly refused to release any of the hostages which he held.

The chiefs of all of the feuding clans were ordered not to gather their men under arms nor to launch an attack on any of the opposing clans. To isolate the two major combatants, the Earl of Huntly was asked to insure that the clans in the North: MacKinnons, MacLeods, and MacDonalds of Sleat, remained peaceful. Simultaneous with these measures, the Scottish parliament passed a bond called the "General Band." All chiefs, landlords and bailies were to give sureties for the peaceable behaviour of those under them. These sureties were determined to be quite large and proportioned according to the wealth and number of followers of the individual chiefs. Any individual injured by a member of one of the clans mentioned in the bond could seek compensation from the surety provided by the chief. The chief of the offending clan was then bound to make up his surety to its original amount.

The lull in the fighting provided an opportunity to mend the relationships between the MacLeans, the MacDonalds of Ardnamurchan, and the Campbells. It was agreed that Lauchlan MacLean's widowed mother, a Campbell by birth, was to be married to John MacIain of Ardnamurchan. The arrangements for the wedding were attended to by the MacLean chief who was of the opinion that, after the ceremonies, MacIain would be firmly won over to his side in the dispute with the MacDonalds.

In April of 1588 the wedding, at the bride's residence of Torloisk House on Mull, proceeded as planned, even though it was becoming increasingly apparent that MacIain would not be siding with MacLean against his kinsmen.[31] On the wedding night Lauchlan, having fully realised the nuptials would not gain him an ally, ordered all of MacIain's party killed and MacIain himself was dragged from his wedding bed, his life being spared only by the pleadings of his new wife.

MacIain was imprisoned within Duart Castle, where he was reportedly tortured daily. However, by some means MacIain managed to notify his kin and get a written message through to the government in Edinburgh complaining of his maltreatment. The Privy Council immediately summoned Lauchlan to personally appear before it, explain his conduct, and release his prisoners. Lauchlan appears not to have been too concerned about what action Edinburgh might be considering against him as he was very slow to release John MacIain. He was, however, well aware of his clan's weakness against the united forces of the now angry MacDonalds of Ardnamurchan and Clanranald. MacLean was determined to strike them before they had a chance to unite and marshal their forces against him.

Only one short month after MacIain's wedding, events would unfold in Spain which would give the alliance, of which the MacKinnons were a part, their greatest military advantage over their MacDonald rivals. During May of 1588 an armada of 130 Spanish ships sailed north toward a rendezvous with a battle-hardened professional army which waited for them on the coast of Flanders. By July the Spanish fleet was making its way up the English Channel against a largely ineffective, but mounting, English resistance.[32] The weather soon turned against the

Spanish and, although they were able to maintain fleet discipline, the fleet was blown into the North Sea. The army in Flanders was not ready to embark for England and even, if it were, it could not break the Dutch blockade of the shallow embarkation ports. The weather proved to be the decisive factor, and it was ultimately the wind direction which prevented the Spanish fleet from embarking Parma's army at Dunkirk. The commander of the Spanish fleet decided the most prudent action, under the circumstances, would be to sail northward around Scotland, swing wide into the Atlantic, then proceed southward and east back to Lisbon.

In Scotland preparations had been made which may indicate prior knowledge of the armada's sailing and that some men of influence considered the Spanish to be allies in their affairs. In the West the Maxwells garrisoned Caerlaveroch Castle and seized the castles Morton and Lochmaben. In the North the Gordons attempted to take the Sinclair stronghold of Girnigoe. We may never know all of the preparations made by Francis Hay, Earl of Errol; George Gordon, Earl of Huntly; or Archibald Douglas, the Earl of Angus, to welcome the Spanish fleet but they may have been considerable.[33]

It was about the 12th of August when the Armada, which still counted some 120 ships, passed north of the Firth of Forth and the English fleet returned to its home ports. The passage of the Spanish fleet was hampered by the worst storms witnessed in decades. In its progress northward, the fleet's numbers were only slightly diminished by the severe and unexpected weather. Two ships were wrecked off Tantallon Castle and another off Old Slains, while two more were lost off Fair Isle, which lies between the Orkneys and the Shetland islands.[34] Once in the Atlantic, the fleet sailed well out to the west, gaining sea room for its return to Lisbon. Not all of the ships, however, proceeded into the mid Atlantic, some were blown into the Hebrides and others were forced onto the Irish coast.[35]

It was shortly after September 10, 1588, when the armed merchant ship, *San Juan de Sicilia,* and perhaps a larger companion, sailed into Tobermory Bay.[36] The progress of the rich Spanish ships into the Sound of Mull must have presented a wonderful sight to the residents of the MacKinnon farms at Ardmore, Teanga Mheadhoin, Rairaig, Erray, and finally the old clachan of Tobermory itself. Tradition relates that, in exchange for food and allowing the refitting of the ship,

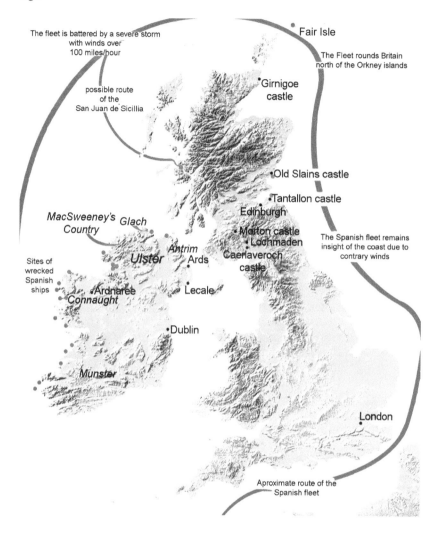

The fleet is battered by a severe storm with winds over 100 miles/hour

Fair Isle

The Fleet rounds Britain north of the Orkney islands

possible route of the San Juan de Sicillia

Girnigoe castle

Old Slains castle

Tantallon castle

Edinburgh

MacSweeney's Country

Glach

Morton castle

Lochmaden

Antrim

Ulster

Ards

Caerlaveroch castle

The Spanish fleet remains insight of the coast due to contrary winds

Sites of wrecked Spanish ships

Ardnaree

Connaught

Lecale

Dublin

Munster

London

Aproximate route of the Spanish fleet

the Spanish captain gave Lauchlan MacLean the service of some 100 Spanish marines.

Lauchlan, confident in his newly-acquired technical advantage, immediately lashed out at his MacDonald enemies. Along with his allies, the MacNeils and MacKinnons, he struck the islands of Rum, Eigg, Muck, and Canna.[37] The four small islands lying in the Hebredian Sea between Mull and Skye were completely ravaged. No one of any age or sex was spared and everything of value was carried off. These attacks were closely followed by an attempt to capture Mingary, MacIain's castle in Ardnamurchan.

A Spanish Galleon
The armed transport that arrived off Tobermory would have been a smaller ship

The attack on the castle was broken off after just three days because of the sudden appearance of a large, hostile force of MacDonald warriors, reinforced by men of the neighbouring clans. As the Islanders and their Spanish allies retreated, they sacked the lands in the vicinity of Mingary Castle, burning everything they could not carry off with them. The long simmering feud had once again erupted into open warfare. The Clanranald and the MacIains of Ardnamurchan ravaged MacLean lands with abandon as their galleys carried well-armed warriors throughout the Hebrides.

The clan alliance led by the MacLeans, however, had the Spanish on their side. The ships, high-sided and armed with cannons, were the most powerful vessels in the Irish sea. The slow awkward cogs employed by the English would have been no match for them, and they were invincible to the galley fleets employed by the MacDonalds. Toward the end of 1588 the MacLeans and their Spanish allies struck at Angus MacDonald's castle of Dunnyveg on the east end of his home island of Islay. The details of this attack are sketchy at best, but it is known that the raid failed.[38] There is a local tradition on Islay of the wreck of an armada ship in the vicinity of Dunnyveg, although no traces of it have been found by modern archeologists.[39] If a second Spanish ship did, in fact, aid the attack on Islay, the MacDonalds would have had much cause for concern. Although the MacDonald chiefs and the English government were on opposing sides in Ireland, they would no doubt have shared a mutual anxiety regarding the Spanish aid to MacLean in the Hebrides.

MacLean tradition relates that, during the attack on Mingary Castle, Lauchlan MacLean received a message from the captain of the Spanish ship requesting the return of the marines. Almost simultaneously, Lauchlan received a message from MacLean of Treshnish stating the Spanish ship was preparing to depart without paying for the provisions or materials received from the farms on Mull.

To prevent the ship's sailing, Lauchlan took three of the principal officers ashore, as hostages, but permitted the marines to return to the ship. An agreement was reached and the Spanish captain promised the ship would not sail before payment was made. Donald Glas, the son of MacLean of Morvern, was sent aboard by his chief to receive the money, but he and his servant were seized and made prisoners by the Spanish.

Donald found that the cabin in which he was being held was close to the magazine. Being determined that the ship carrying him would not escape, if his chief did not wish it, Donald made a plan for its destruction. That night he made his way into the magazine and laid a trail of powder in as inconspicuous a location as possible from the magazine to his cabin. The next morning, on the 5th of November, Donald Glas was called to the deck to bid farewell to Mull as the ship prepared to leave Tobermory Bay. Slipping a note into his servant's hand, Donald Glas advised the servant to take it to the chief as quickly as possible. Shortly after the servant was a safe distance from the ship, it exploded killing all but three of the persons aboard. Two of the survivors are said to have eventually recovered from their injuries, but the third was so badly injured that he died the next day.[40] With the ship now destroyed, the officers who were held by MacLean were of no further service and they were released. Making their way to Edinburgh, the Spaniards lodged an official complaint before the king and his council against Lauchlan MacLean for their imprisonment and the destruction of the ship.[41]

As the war in the islands expanded in both ferocity and scope, the MacDonalds of Clanranald and Ardnamurchan were joined by the MacDonalds of Islay and Sleat. The savagery exhibited by both sides in the conflict exhausted all of the combatants in just a few short months. As the clans sought a way to end the mutual slaughter, negotiations were carried on by Katherine MacLean in Ireland, who was welcomed in both camps. A settlement was agreed to and, by the end of 1588, the eight hostages held by Angus MacDonald were traded for MacIain and the other prisoners held by MacLean. A semblance of quiet soon fell over the Hebrides.

Taking advantage of the calm which had fallen over the Isles, the focus of the chiefs of the smaller clans once again turned to Ireland. The MacNeil of Barra, with an estimated force of 600 men, made a cattle raid on Erris in Mayo.[42] During the same year Calvagh MacDonald, a younger brother to Angus MacDonald of Islay, led a rather larger raid, some 1,500 warriors, in revenge for the MacDonald defeat at the hands of the English at the Battle of Ardnaree.[43] This band raided throughout Connaught with impunity. MacDonald only returned to the Isles after defeating the large body of English soldiers who had been sent after him. Then during 1591 there was another large raid on Connaught. The raiders this time appear to have been members of the clan alliance headed by the MacLeans and may well have included the MacKinnons. This raid was repulsed by the Burkes (Clan William) but with heavy losses.[44] There would, no doubt, have been many smaller and perhaps less successful raids carried out between 1589 and 1591, but these are not recorded.

The Islanders' interest in Ireland was not simply commercial or mercenary but also was also largely political. Because of their longstanding relationships with Ireland and the intermarriages between the Irish and Hebridean chiefs, the Islanders were at this time invited to take an active role in Irish dynastic struggles. In 1589 Hugh O'Neill, the Earl of Tyrone, who had defeated Turlough O'Neill in battle the year before, claimed the right to succeed him as *"the O'Neill"* even though Turlough still lived. This claim was disputed by Hugh Geimhleach, one of the seven sons of Shane O'Neill, a previous Earl of Tyrone, and the last Irish leader to be widely recognised as "The O'Neill". Hugh Geimhleach O'Neill, who had been staying in the Hebrides with his MacLean relatives, returned to Ulster with nine galleys to assert his claim. A short time later Lauchlan MacLean, or one of his sons, followed with 2000 island warriors to support him.

Meanwhile, Hugh O'Neill, the current Earl of Tyrone, worried by his opponent's increasing strength, approached the MacDonalds of Antrim and Angus MacDonald of Islay for help. Sorley Boy's sons agreed to lead a force of some 500 MacDonalds on his behalf and Angus MacDonald pledged his friendship in Ulster. The division of clans in Ireland soon began to mirror their political alignment in the Hebrides. However, the war, which appeared to be developing in Ireland between the island clans, did not materialize as it was prematurely stopped by the capture of one of the major antagonists.

Hugh Geimhleach was captured through some deceit by the MacGuires who sold him to the Earl of Tyrone. Because of the reverence still felt in Ireland for his ancient family, no hangman could be found to execute him. Not to be undone, Hugh O'Neill, Earl of Tyrone, took the part himself and, with his own hand, executed his rival. This single fateful act would alienate Hugh O'Neill from the Islanders and eventually be seen as one of the steps which led to his downfall.[45]

The Scottish King James granted all parties in the late Hebridean feud remissions under the Privy Seal for any and all crimes committed during the conflict. To ensure the animosities could be set aside the island leaders: Angus MacDonald, Donald Gorm MacDonald of Sleat, and Lauchlan MacLean were invited to Edinburgh the next year, in 1589, to discuss ways of reaching a lasting peace.

King James, in what was by now an all too typical display of bad faith by the government, revoked the remissions he had given earlier and the island chiefs were arrested and taken captive. The MacDonalds were arrested because they had employed English mercenaries and MacLean was held because he had employed the Spanish marines. After several months of captivity, the chiefs were brought to trial but refused to enter a plea or appear before a jury. Rather, the Islanders threw themselves on the king's mercy, an act which no doubt flattered the vanity of King James. The chiefs were freed only after the payment of large fines, for which they needed financial guarantees, and an agreement to a series of undertakings regarding their future behaviour and the leaving of hostages.[46]

In what may have been a show of his displeasure and an intentional insult towards the MacDonalds, King James knighted Lauchlan MacLean just after his release in 1591. Angus MacDonald was not released until 1592.

End Notes
Chapter 15

1. Since the fall of the Lordship of the Isles and breakdown of the old church, much of its wealth had been taken by the Western nobility by way of grants or purchases. By the 1550s there was very little remaining of the once vast church lands.

2. Now called Knock Castle, it is located at the north side of Knock Bay on the Southern Coast of Sleat. The farm of Ostaig is located almost four kilometres southwest of Knock Castle on the Bagh a Mhuilinn.

3. John Carswell, who witnessed the alliance between Donald Dubh and King Henry VIII in Ireland, had a distinguished career in the Reformed Church in the Isles. He was the notary of the Isles, treasurer of the cathedral of Lismore, parson of Kilmartin, and the Reformed superintendent of the diocese of Argyll and the Isles.

4. The Reformed Church continued to slowly staff the large Western Diocese. It was church policy to staff churches in Gaelic areas with Gaelic speaking ministers. In 1580 Hector MacAlister was presented to Kilmorie in Arran and Kilcalmonell in Kintyre; 1589 there is Reformed Church staff in Rothesay and (1597) Kingarth in Bute; 1592 Colin Campbell is presented to Gigha, Alexander MacDougall is presented to Kildalton and Kilnachtan, and Daniel Chalmers is presented to Kilchoman, Kilarow, and Kilnachtan in Islay. It should be noted that, even in these early days, ministers were generally graduates from a university.

5. Lauchlan was 18 when he returned to Duart to succeed to the chiefship of the MacLeans. Lauchlan's stepfather, Hector MacLean, led the clan during Lauchlan's minority and didn't want to relinquish it on his return. To this end, while awaiting a favorable opportunity to kill him, Hector MacLean endeavored to make Lauchlan appear incapable of leading the clan. Lauchlan, realizing what was afoot, had Hector kidnapped, taken to Coll, and beheaded by some loyal clansmen. With Hector out of the way, Lauchlan assumed the chiefship. It is interesting to note that Lauchlan's durbfine was opposed to his succession. It was traditionally the durbfine who chose the chief from among its membership, but by now the chiefship was seen in a feudal context and the lineage given legal recognition by the government.

6. MacLean, J. P., *History of the Clan MacLean*, Cincinnati, 1889, 93, indicates that official documents claim John Dubh confessed to assisting Argyll in the raid. Gregory, D., *History of the Highlands and Islands*, Edinburgh, 1836, 216, claims complaints were made to the government that John Dubh MacLean and one John MacDonald, son of James MacDonald of Castle Camus, were being unlawfully held prisoner by Argyll the year prior to the raid. Shortly after his release, John MacLean signed a bond of manrent with Argyll.

7. For the full account of this event, see MacLean, J. P., *History of the Clan MacLean*, Clarke & Co, Cincinnati, 1889, 94.

8. The MacKinnons who supported MacDonald of Sleat in 1562 may have supported him again 16 years later. It is very likely that support for the MacDonalds was not the policy of Lauchlan Dubh, the MacKinnon Chief. Possibly those MacKinnons who served the MacDonald chief were tacksmen who held farms from the MacDonalds of Sleat.

9. It is interesting that the Edinburgh government would think the MacLeans would support a clan with whom they were at war with the year before. The MacKinnon position may be more ambiguous in that the clan may not have been allied with either the MacLeans or the Campbells. We know that some individual MacKinnons had recently taken arms against the MacLeans, as did Argyll, but we do not know how much this reflected the political position of the clan.

10. In 1581 Colin MacKenzie and Donald MacDonald of Glengarry were at each other's throats over parts of Lochalsh, Lochcarron, and Lochbroom. The feud was likely caused by MacKenzie incursions into the MacDonald-held areas. The incursions, of course, were fiercely resisted by the MacDonalds. In the course of the feud, Donald MacDonald and many of his kinsmen were captured by MacKenzie. Donald was released after a long captivity, but his relatives had been executed. The complaints to the Privy Council on Donald's release resulted in MacKenzie's arrest and MacDonald's castle of Strone being put into the care of Argyll.

11. Janet was the daughter of Hugh Fraser of Guisachan. Her first husband was Thomas Chisholm of Chisholm and her second was Patrick Grant of Glenmoriston.

12. On some charts she is called Finovola. Her husband, Iain MacLean, was the third son of Eachuinn an Clireach Beag MacLean, 5th Laird of Coll. Canna is an island just northwest of Rum and southwest of Strathaird. It is probable that John MacKinnon of Canna held a tack on that island from MacIain of Ardnamurchan.

13. Turlough O'Neill led a force of 4,000 Irish and 1,900 Islanders, and Angus MacDonald had a force of 2,000 men operating in Ulster. By this time there are records of MacDonald, MacLean, MacLeod, Campbell, and MacNeil-led incursions into Ireland.

14. The two sons of Shane O'Neill were with the MacLeans, who intended to set them up in succession to Turlough O'Neill. Shane O'Neill's wife was a MacLean, so their fortunes were of great interest to the clan.

15. The Lowlanders were all reported to be good shots, well equipped, and trained. They were reported to have a good supply of artillery of both large and small calibre.

16. MacDonald, D., *Clan Donald*, MacDonald, Midlothian, 1978, 246.

17. Huistein MacGillespick and MacDonald Terreagh had belonged to the MacDonalds of Sleat before being expelled from that clan. By this time, they were well known in the Hebrides as pirates.

18. The united forces of Clan Donald are composed of: MacDonalds of Islay and Sleat, Clanranald, MacIain of Ardnamurchan, and MacAlister of Loup.

19. Angus's kinsmen who most vehemently opposed the visit were his brothers, Coll and Ranald, as well as his cousin, Coll mac Ranald. See: Byrne, K., *Colkitto*, House of Lochar, Isle of Colonsay, 1997, 27.

20. On entering Connaught, the MacDonalds were questioned by the governor, Sir Richard Bingham, who wanted to know the purpose of their coming. The MacDonalds answered that they had come at the invitation of the Clan William and the Clan Donald who were their cousins. They were to have entertainment and the spoil of Connaught. They warned the governor they would contest, with arms, any who hindered their advance into the district. The MacDonalds began building a fort on the River Earn, which was to be their headquarters. In an attempt to chase them out of Connaught, the governor mobilized what forces he could. But the English soldiers were skillfully eluded as the MacDonalds gathered a great deal of booty. Being well served by spies, Sir Richard Bingham was able to surprise the MacDonalds at one of their camps on the River Moy. Guided by a treacherous priest, the governor made a night march and found the MacDonald camp unguarded as they slept without fear of attack. The sound of the English advance alerted some of the MacDonalds who raised the alarm and rushed to defend the camp. The Islanders had scarcely discharged their first shower of arrows before their vanguard was pushed back into the hastily assembling main body. The English maintained the pressure, forcing the Islanders back toward the river. Many MacDonalds were killed in the pursuit but many more were drowned trying to escape. The MacDonalds were almost wiped out, some

2,000 men women and children were killed during the slaughter. To the English, this became known as the Battle of Ardnaree and was the greatest defeat of island arms suffered in Ireland

21. Gordon, R., *Genealogical History of the Earldom of Sutherland*, George Ramsay, Edinburgh, 1813, 186-88.

22. In the event of Lauchlan's death, Allan MacLean would have been the guardian of the chief's son, Hector, who at this time was a minor. Allan would then have enjoyed all of the privileges and honor of the chiefship. For a very different version of these events. See: MacLean, J. P., *History of the Clan MacLean*, Clarke & Co, Cincinnati, 1889. 99-137.

23. See appendix 13 for the complaint. The Western fishery was lucrative during this period. Fishermen came to the Hebrides from Glasgow, Aberdeen, Edinburgh, and other East Coast ports as well as Northern and Western Europe. The government had tried, unsuccessfully, since at least 1566, to regulate the West Coast fishery for the advantage of the Burghs and East Coast fishermen.

24. The Earl of Argyll was a minor at this time, so the heads of the various Campbell families were dispatched to address the rival clans.

25. MacLeod of Harris allied himself with the MacLeans because the mother of the chief, William MacLeod of Dunvegan, was a MacLean. During the month following the intervention by the Edinburgh government, Angus MacDonald concluded agreements of mutual aid in the event of aggression with Donald Gorm MacDonald of Sleat and the chief of the Clan MacIntosh. These treaties would have insured the safety of Angus MacDonald's northern borders. It is difficult to understand Edinburgh's position in the Hebrides at this time. In October 1587 MacLean was given a gift under the privy seal of the life rent of the lands of the chief of Dunnyveg as they were forfeit because he refused to release his hostages as ordered in April 1587. A short time later Edinburgh granted more MacDonald lands to Hector MacLean, Lauchlan's son and heir.

26. There is no record of attacks on Colonsay at this time, so that strategic island must have been adequately garrisoned.

27. Gordon, R., *Genealogical History of the Earldom of Sutherland*, George Ramsay, Edinburgh, 1813, 191.

28. Ibid
For a differing account of events, see: MacLean, J. P., *History of the Clan MacLean*, Clarke & Co., Cincinnati, 1889. 101-105. It should be noted that the Sutherland account was contemporary with the events it recorded and agrees with most other major sources.

29. Casualty figures from these battles are unreliable. The MacLean historians claim that of about 2,500 men defending the fortified island, the MacDonalds lost 340 killed or wounded and 360 who were captured. The MacLeans claim to have had only one killed and one wounded. The MacKinnon, MacQuarrie and MacNeil casualties are unknown.

30. There is no surviving record of either the MacKinnons or the MacLeods of Dunvegan raiding farms belonging to MacDonald of Sleat, so perhaps there was an understanding of sorts between the Skye clans.

31. See: MacLean, J. P., *History of the Clan MacLean*, Clarke & Co, Cincinnati, 1889, 105-6 for full accounts of both MacLean and MacDonald versions of this affair.

32. The purpose of the Spanish fleet was just to escort Parma's army from Flanders to England. It was not designed to destroy the English navy. As the Spanish fleet progressed northward up the channel, it was attacked twice by the English fleet. The English, however, were not able to break the Spanish fleet's formation. The Spanish defensive formation was strong; the main body of the fleet, it's center, was led by the flagship and was flanked by the remaining ships arranged in an extended horn formation. To insure the formation was not broken, it was made a capital offence for a ship's captain to leave his position in relation to the flagship. A select group of 20 powerful ships disbursed though the formation were responsible for fending off any attack on the fleet and were the only ships allowed to move about at will.

33. Letters between Huntly and the Spanish court were intercepted by the English early in 1588. Huntly, of course, denied any knowledge of the correspondence and was held for a time at Edinburgh Castle. But on his release, Huntly and Errol united and raised a force of 10,000 men which did not stand down until forced to by the king in February of 1589. After the armada had sailed around Scotland, an English force took Lochmaben Castle. The Maxwell garrison was turned over to the Edinburgh government and the Spanish troops who were captured there were taken into England. Sprat, A., *The Scots Lords and the Spanish Armada 1585 to 1597*, 2000.

34. The only wrecks on the East CXoast of Scotland were those off Tantallon and Slains castles, which have often been attributed to poor Spanish seamanship. It is interesting to note, however, that Tantallon belonged to Archibald Douglas, Earl of Angus, and Slains belonged to Frances Hay, Earl of Errol, which may suggest the ships intended to visit these castles for some reason when they were caught by the storm which sank them. The survivors of the Barca Amberg and the El Gran Grifon, which sank off Fair Isle, taken were first to Orkney by their Scots rescuers. From Orkney the Spanish were taken via Anstruther in Fife to Edinburgh, where they were entertained as guests.

35. It is estimated that some 35 ships were lost off the West Coast of Ireland and Scotland. Only one wreck is known in the Hebrides, while the rest are off the coast of Ireland. Of those wrecks identified; the *San Juan de Sicilia* which blew up in Tobermory Bay the isle of Mull, is the only Spanish ship which has been found in the Hebrides

36. On the 10th of September there were four ships from the armada fighting a storm off the North Coast of Donegal. These were the *San Juan de Sicilia, Trinidad Valencera, El Gran Grifon, Castillo Negro,* and the *Barque of Hamburg.* Of these, the *Trinidad Valencera* was grounded on the 16th of September on Kinnagoe rocks, Donegal, *El Gran Grifon* stranded on rocks east of Fair Isle on the 27th of September, *Castillo Negro* foundered at sea, and *Barque of Hamburg* was abandoned and sank during the storm on the 10th of September. *Girona* sank off Lacada Point, Antrim; and the *Santa Maria de la Rosa* sank at Blasket Sound on the southern end of Ireland.

37. Canna and Muck belonged to MacIain of Ardnamurchan, Rum and Eigg belonged to Clanranald. The fluid Hebridean politics of this time produced two strange alliances. Lauchlan MacLean, whose feud with the MacDonalds was possibly supported by the English Queen Elizabeth I, employed one of the queen's most powerful enemies. Lauchlan had the use of at least one Spanish ship and the service of 100 Spanish marines. The MacDonalds, who supported the Irish in their struggle against the English Crown, employed English mercenaries against the MacLeans. John MacKinnon of Canna must have given up the rental on the island or perhaps his lands were spared.

38. There may have been a party of Campbells supporting the MacLeans during this raid. Campbell, A., *History of Clan Campbell,* Edinburgh University Press, 2002, Vol. 2, 102, mentions that Campbell of Glenorchy and Campbell of Cawder quarreled at Tarbert while on an expedition in support of MacLean against the MacDonalds of Islay.

39. We know the *San Juan de Sicilia* did not leave Tobermory Bay. If a Spanish galleon did support the attack on Islay, there must have been two of them in the inner Hebrides at this time--both of which were in contact with Lauchlan MacLean. This second galleon may have been the *Florencia* commanded by a Captain Pereija, which may have given rise to the *Florida* legend. Looking back, it is easy for us to understand how, over the centuries, the name Florencia could have become corrupted and finally remembered in lore as Florida. The *Florencia* was one of the largest and most powerful ships which sailed with the armada.

40. Another survivor is said to have been a small dog which, on a piece of the deck, was thrown a mile and a half by the force of the explosion. The dog was found near death but was nursed back to health by farmers

in the area and returned to a spot on the shore opposite where the Spanish ship was anchored. The dog is said to have remained on that spot gazing into the bay the remainder of its life.

41. The ship blown up at Tobermory has been identified as the *San Juan de Sicilia*. (*British Archaeology #64, April 2002*) an armed merchant ship of 800 tons and 26 guns. The *San Juan de Sicilia* was not a galleon but rather a smaller ship. Local tradition, however, has it that the ship was a galleon named the *Florida* commanded by a fellow named Don Fareija. This is evidentially mistaken as there is no ship named *Florida* listed in Spanish records as having sailed with the armada. The closest listing to tradition is the *Florencia* commanded by a Captain Pereija, which is extremely close and may be significantly pointing out the presence of two ships. It is difficult to understand how the names *Florida* or *Don Fareija* could have entered Mull tradition unless they actually made an appearance. It was only during the very late 19th century that British scholars were able to examine the extensive armada archives in Spain. It was the listing in the Spanish archives of the names *Galeon de Florencia* and *Pereija* that first brought them to the attention of British historians. The *Galeon de Florencia,* with 52 guns on two decks, was one of the largest, most impressive ships of the armada. A ship of this calibre in the Hebrides would undoubtedly have attracted much attention and caused a great deal of alarm. The *Galeon de Florencia* was one of the ships which successfully returned to Spain.

42. The raid proved to be resoundingly successful as the MacNeils carried off some 1,100 head of cattle. Because of the large amount of cattle taken, they could not all be loaded into the waiting galleys, so 600 of them were slaughtered on the ,beach with only their hides and carcasses being taken. The remaining 500 head of cattle were moved by galley out to an island where the raiders could skin and render the carcases for tallow without fear of retribution. A raid on this scale was almost certainly a commercial venture. MacNeil may have had a contract for the hides and tallow with a passing merchant ship from either the Low Countries, France or Spain. At the prevailing rate of 6/ (shilling) for a hide, MacNeil would have made £330 sterling for the hides alone. This would represent a very large sum in those times. MacNeil, who had the reputation as a summer wanderer, had a great interest in Ireland. In 1593 Sir Richard Bingham reported to the Council of Deputies in Dublin that *"galleys and boats from the MacNeil of Barra usually make their summer course and steal what they can."* That same year the English discovered a fleet of MacNeil galleys off the coast of Munster making towards the North. The MacNeil fleet was expected to proceed to Kockpatrick in Mayo to make "offer" to St. Patrick. Both St. Patrick and St. Columba were revered in the Hebrides at this time. See MacKenzie, 25-26.

43. This small army is recorded as having been made up of 600 archers, 600 well-armed infantry, and 300 Lowland Scots.

44. Details of the raid are sketchy, but it appears to have been led by Angus MacLean and Rory MacNeil. A full list of the clans involved does not exist, but the Islanders' casualties included Ewen MacLean and MacLeod's son. We don't know if this was MacLeod of Lewis or Harris. On the Burke side, the two sons of their chief, the Blind Abbot MacWilliam, are known to have been killed. The Islanders, on putting out to sea in their galleys, were pursued by Grace O'Malley, (Graine O'Maille) the famous female chieftain of the Burkes, in 20 large boats.

45. The MacLeans and Argyll resented the execution of Hugh Geimhleach as a murder of a kinsmen. Hugh's mother was Katherine MacLean, sister to Lauchlan MacLean and widow of Archibald Campbell, the 4th Earl of Argyll. Angus MacDonald was angered by Tyrone's support for Sorley Boy in a family dispute over the Glens and the fact that Tyrone had jilted his daughter, thus dishonoring her. Angus's sons had sworn to avenge their sister and so actively opposed Tyrone. After his release from captivity in Edinburgh, Angus MacDonald supported the English in Ireland vowing that "he would kindle such a coal of fire in Scotland as would keep the King of Scots so busy that he would have no time to disturb Elizabeth." Angus reported to his English allies the plans prepared by Argyll and MacLean to support a rebellion against them. The rebellion by Maguire, O'Rourke and O'Donnell was to have been supported by 4,000 Islanders under Argyll and MacLean, while Sorley Boy led his own men. Angus also agreed to support the English against any invasion by the other Islanders.

46. Angus MacDonald and Lauchlan MacLean were fined £20,000 each and Donald Gorm was fined £4,000. John Campbell of Cawder was surety for the MacDonalds and John Campbell of Ardkinglas was surety for MacLean. Angus MacDonald left three hostages, one of whom was his son John. These hostages were all to be held until Donald Gorm delivered up a hostage of his own. Lauchlan MacLean was released on the promise that he would later deliver a hostage of rank. This promise was of course forgotten.

The Cliffs of Gribun on the island of Mull

Chapter 16
THE END OF AN ERA

There was a significant change in island alliances during the year 1594. For the first time the island clans would act together under Campbell command. On the 3rd of June, because of their support for the Roman Church, the Earls of Angus, Huntly, and Errol had their coats of arms torn from their coats and their estates forfeited.[1] A little more than a month later, on July 15, 1594, a royal commission of fire and sword was given to the Earl of Argyll, Lord Balveney and Lord Forbes. The commission was against all who opposed the Reformed religion in the Northeast of Scotland, among whom the most prominent were the followers of Huntly. Between the 3rd of June and the 15th of July, there had been some preliminary raids by both sides as armies were gathered and preparations made for the fighting that seemed eminent.

By Lowland standards, Argyll's force appeared to be poorly organized and lacked the professional look of a uniformed army. It was described by contemporary witnesses as *"five thousand naiked Heeland men"* but its leaders would have gained experience fighting in Ireland or the Isles.[2] Along with a good number of Campbell lairds, there was O'Donnell from Ulster, Lauchlan MacLean of Duart, MacNeil of Barra, MacGregor of Glenstrae, Murray of Tullibardine and very likely Lauchlan MacKinnon, and MacQuarrie of Ulva.[3]

At Blair Atholl, Argyll's force was considerably reinforced by some 2,000 men as some of those who missed the initial rendezvous caught up with the main body of the army.[4] Turning northward, the army marched to Ruthven Castle, which was then held by the Clan MacPherson. After a short siege it was apparent the MacPherson garrison was determined to hold the castle and were not at all intimidated by the size of Argyll's force.

After being joined by the MacIntoshes and Grants, Argyll abandoned the siege and on of September 27 and proceeded northwards up Glen Avon. As they marched north, Argyll hoped to be joined by Lord Forbes, who had raised a considerable force of horsemen for the king.

On the 2nd of October Argyll's army marched out of Badenoch toward Strathdown. The army remained camped near Drum on the River Avon while Argyll and his senior commanders attended a council of war at Huntly's castle of Drunin. It was decided at this meeting that Argyll's force not engage Huntly's army until being joined by Forbes' cavalry. Orders to that effect were given to all of the army's leaders.

While the Highlanders were marching north, Huntly and Errol had met in Strathbogie before marching to Carnborrow, where their forces assembled. From Carnborrow the predominantly mounted force moved to Auchindoon, where they met the infantry which was mostly composed of MacPhersons and Camerons. The appearance of Huntly's army differed greatly from that of Argyll's. Numbering between 1,200 and 4,000 men, the greatest percentage of the army were horsemen and professional soldiers and they also had six field pieces.[5] Also, unlike Argyll, Huntly was determined to engage in battle as soon as possible, preferably before Argyll was joined by Lord Forbes' cavalry.

By now both sides knew the other was in the vicinity but, as the opponents moved slowly toward each other, the exact dispositions of the armies were in doubt. Unknown to Argyll as he sent his vanguard of 4,000 men under MacLean, MacIntosh, and Auchenbreck to the top western slopes of Tom Cullach, Huntly's vanguard made for the same location. It is possible that MacLean considered the hill too steep for a cavalry assault and Huntly was attempting to close the route to any reinforcement by Forbes should he arrive during the battle.

MacLean's men made it to the top first and quickly took up their positions. Huntly's men, realizing that MacLean was already in place, began the battle with artillery fire directed at the Islanders on the top of the hill. The Islanders saw the first ball coming and nimbly moved out of the way, letting it pass harmlessly between the files of crowded soldiers. Gillonan MacNeil, the son of MacNeil of Barra, then rushed forward and, taking a position in front of the line, shouted abuse at the enemy and waved his sword in the air. MacNeil evidently did not see the second shot coming and it took off his head.[6]

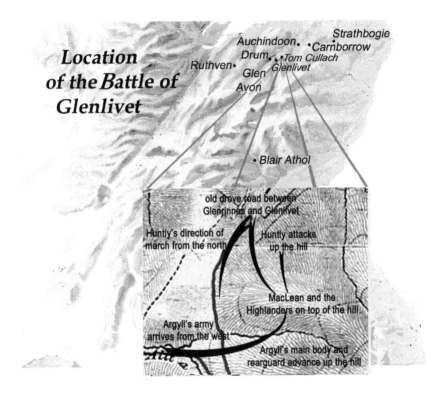

On the crest of the hill, the Highlanders, who were formed with their clans for battle, took Gillonan's death to be a bad omen. Confusion reigned as the common soldiers didn't know if they should stand and fight or if they should turn and run. As a third shot passed harmlessly by, the Highlanders fell to the ground and steadfastly refused the orders of their officers to stand up and prepare for battle. Argyll, seeing his vanguard on the ground, ran among the men shouting, kicking, and beating them to their feet. The main body of Argyll's force was still pressing forward, the whole of the army becoming more and more entangled with the vanguard as it became increasingly crowded on the top of the hill.

The Earl of Errol, shouting the war cry, *"The Virgin Mary,"* ordered a mounted charge, with spears levelled, up the steep hillside. Sir Patrick Gordon of Auchindoon led Huntly's vanguard of 300 cavalry straight up the hill toward the Islanders as the bulk of the horsemen under Errol followed. The Highland archers are said to have loosed such a volley of arrows at the struggling cavalry that the sky was blackened for a moment. The arrows and the rough climb up the hill broke the momentum of the charge, which wheeled toward the right to engage Argyll's main body and his rearguard.

The Islanders led by MacLean met Auchindoon's charge firmly at the top of the hill. Auchindoon was quickly killed and his men retreated after a short, but savage, hand-to-hand fight. After dispatching Huntly's vanguard, the Islanders were quick to strike Errol's now exposed flank and almost surrounded the main body of horse. Seeing Errol's force disappear in the crowded mass of Islanders and in danger of being wiped out, Huntly ordered the bulk of his army forward. The remainder of the horsemen, the MacPhersons, Camerons, and Lowland infantry, surged forward and up the steep slope.

The battle raged on for some two hours. Gradually Huntly's cavalry broke the cohesion of Argyll's main force and small parties of Campbells reluctantly began to leave the fight. After some time MacLean and the Islanders, realizing they stood alone on the field, retreated in good order back into the safety of the mountains. Huntly and Errol insured a victory by pursuing the retreating army until the hills became too steep for the horses.

While Argyll was trying to recover from the loss at Glenlevit, Ireland once more offered Hebridean warriors the opportunity for wealth and fame. During the year 1594 the hard-pressed English Lord Deputy of Ireland had less than 1,000 men under his command, but the Irish nationalist chiefs had many thousands of men under arms.

The supply of Highland mercenaries was not the only concern the English had. As long as the Irish chiefs had money, there were merchants ready and able to supply them with arms, ammunition, and other sundry goods from Glasgow, Inverness, and Caithness. To monitor these threats, the English intelligence officer for Ireland, John Colville, set up a network of spies with orders to scrutinize the Hebrides and inform Dublin of any occurrences of note. James Campbell, younger of Lawers, was recruited as the chief agent and would be kept very busy in that capacity.[7]

During the month of January 1595, messengers from Tyrone were sent to the seats of all Hebridean chiefs, offering to pay double wages for anyone willing to fight in Ireland. The smaller clans were approached but, because the Hebridean alliances had already been forged in blood, they preferred to wait until they could act in concert with the chiefs of the larger clans.

Donald Gorm MacDonald of Sleat was offered a £300 advance and £600 more once his men landed in Ireland.[8] MacLeod of Dunvegan was offered £500 for raising his men. Argyll was also approached, but he remained uncommitted, waiting to see if he could coax a better offer out of the English queen. The MacKinnons, MacNeils, and MacQuarries were militarily allied with the MacLeans who, in turn, were very close to Argyll. Thus, these clans waited with Argyll for the English to offer better terms.

It was not until March that parties of the Clan Ian Mor began to make their way towards Ulster to join Tyrone's growing army. The Irish chief had engaged some 6,000 men of the Clan Ian Mor, but Angus MacDonald and the bulk of his clan had concerns regarding what MacLean might do if Islay and Kintyre were left unprotected.

The Earl of Huntly, who also supported Tyrone, increased the diplomatic pressure on MacLean to join the expedition to Ireland. If MacLean's men and those of the allied clans were in Ireland, it was reasoned that the MacDonald lands of Islay and Kintyre would be safe. Angus MacDonald even went so far as to offer Lauchlan MacLean the Rhinns of Islay outright if he would join them at the side of Tyrone. MacLean, however, had other plans. He proposed to Argyll that they unite and together do whatever was necessary to delay MacDonald joining the Irish. MacLean's proposal went so far as to suggest that, once MacDonald was successfully delayed, the MacLeans and Campbells land on Ulster to trap Tyrone's force between themselves and the English Lord Deputy's army.

Towards the end of May, Argyll was still waiting for an offer from the English. The pressure from the Irish was increasingly difficult to resist and Argyll allowed a party of volunteers, under Duncan Campbell of Danna, to travel to Ireland and join Tyrone.

The Clan Ian Mor and the MacDonalds of Sleat had now united their forces somewhere along the Coast of Kintyre and waited for the MacLeod galleys to join them. The MacLeods, however, did not make the rendezvous until after the 11th of July. On that date they were sighted off the coast of Mull. The combined fleets of the MacLeods of Harris and Lewis were transporting some 2,500 armed men southward.

Lauchlan MacLean was so alarmed at the sudden appearance of such an armada off his coast that he immediately dispatched messengers to determine their intentions. MacLeod of Dunvegan assured MacLean they were not joining the MacDonalds with the intention of attacking him, rather their sole motive was the wages offered by Tyrone.

A short while after the MacLeods had passed southward, a large party of MacDonalds of Clanranald, Ardnamurchan, and Knoydart landed on Mull in order to rest while in transit to join the fleet assembling off Kintyre. This time MacLean was ready and his clan was alert. Moving quickly, he surprised the unprepared MacDonalds, and the MacLeans captured the whole party seemingly without a struggle and no bloodshed. The leaders were made captive and the 900 warriors were ferried back across the Sound of Mull to the mainland, where they were released to make their way home as best they could.

Despite what MacLeod had told MacLean of his intentions, there seems to have been no fixed plans for the large island fleet gathered off Kintyre. Leaving Angus MacDonald with a sizeable force to watch MacLean and Argyll, the fleet proceeded to Arran where a council of war was held. There is no doubt that all that had been agreed between the chiefs was that the assembled fleet was out for plunder. However, where and how this was to be gained was the subject of much debate at the camp on Arran.[9] In the end it was decided to proceed to Ulster and join Tyrone's steadily-growing army.

The fleet sailed from Arran late in the day of July 22, 1595. This fleet, which consisted of galleys, birlinns, eight-oared boats, and a few larger cargo vessels, must have stopped for the night somewhere along the coast of Kintyre. The 3,000 men led by Donald Gorm of Sleet, MacLeod of Lewis, and the MacLeod of Harris embarked the next day, making for Belfast Lough on the Northeast Coast of Ireland.

It appears the English had advance warning from either their spies in the Hebrides or from MacLean of the fleet's intentions, and were thus able to position their ships on the Islanders' route.[10] On the 23rd of July, Captain George Thornton, of the *Popinjay;* and Gregory Riggs, captain of the *Charles,* encountered elements of the fleet still at sea.

The accounts differ in the details of the meeting, some claim six galleys, others say 26 galleys were encountered. But it is agreed in all accounts that a large number of Donald Gorm's galleys were sighted and engaged in the vicinity of the Copeland Islands. It is also agreed that two or three of the galleys were sunk, with huge loss of life. The remainder of the galleys made for the safety of the Copeland Islands where they were trapped.

After a lengthy negotiation in which Donald Gorm offered to change sides and join the English against Tyrone, he and his officers gave Captain Thornton pledges of their good conduct. The English refused the MacDonald's offer of service but did accept their pledges of good behaviour. Donald Gorm and his men then returned to Skye to rest and repair their battered fleet. The MacLeods, with the bulk of the Northern warriors, escaped the trap and, after successfully landing in Belfast Lough, moved inland to join Tyrone.

By early August Captain Thornton anchored the *Popinjay* beneath the walls of Duart. There he met with Lauchlan MacLean and one of Argyll's representatives. The conversation between these three men must have been interesting indeed. Thornton later reported to his government that MacLean had told him Donald Gorm's pledges were worthless and that he, Thornton, had been hoodwinked on the Copeland Islands. More importantly, Lauchlan MacLean explained both his and Argyll's desire to avenge Tyrone's murder of Hugh Geimhleach O'Neill, whom they both regarded as kin. MacLean went on further to explain the composition of the forces that he and Argyll could call upon and their mutual desire to serve Queen Elizabeth.

Initially Thornton was offered 2,000 men, provided that Queen Elizabeth agreed to the wages asked and obtained permission from Argyll.[11] During this same series of meetings, MacLean proposed the English sponsor a joint MacLean/Campbell raid on Angus MacDonald's Clan Ian Mor. MacLean indicated to Captain Thornton that MacLeod of Lewis and MacLean's captives, the Captain of Clanranald and MacIain of Ardnamurchan, could easily be persuaded to join the English side if approached properly. Thornton apparently did not have the authority to accept the offer but did make a full report to the Lord Deputy.

That the English interest in negotiating directly with MacLean had not diminished, is shown by Thornton's return to Duart on the 9th of September. Thornton's quick return was evidently unexpected, as Lauchlan MacLean had to be summoned from Inveraray, where he was visiting Argyll, to once again discuss the Irish question with Captain Thornton. During these discussions MacLean now offered the service of 3,000 of his and Argyll's men if the queen wanted them.

If Thornton could promise MacLean's galleys the protection of the English fleet, MacLean offered to lead the joint English/Hebridean expedition himself. Likely because of the necessity of having Argyll and Queen Elizabeth personally approving any arrangements for the intended invasion of Ulster, MacLean's offer of men could not be accepted at this time. However, as a show of good faith, MacLean did agree to prevent Donald Gorm of Sleat from sending reinforcements to Tyrone's army in Ulster.[12]

None of MacLean's nor Argyll's schemes for riches were to bear fruit. During the month of October 1595, a truce was negotiated between the English government and the Irish nationalist leaders. Angus MacDonald and MacLeod of Harris, who had both spent the summer fighting with Tyrone against the English, were quick to return to the Isles and to make their peace with Argyll. All parties bordering the Irish Sea did their utmost to take what advantage they could of the ceasefire.

Tyrone, who now ruled Ulster as an independent monarch, opened negotiations with Spain for men and supplies.[13] Argyll, with the support of MacLean's galley fleet, sent 2,000 men to deal with the troublesome Clanranald and the Camerons on his northern boarders. The MacDonalds likewise used the opportunity to reinforce their territories in Antrim. By now the English government was actively courting MacLean and Argyll's armed support in Ireland. But MacLean, and probably Argyll as well, was becoming increasingly frustrated by the lack of English gold that actually crossed their palms.

It was about May of 1596 when the government in Edinburgh again became aware of the Hebrides. King James, who was having financial difficulties, decided it was time to once again bring the Isles to good order. The main objective was, of course, Angus MacDonald of the Clan Ian Mor. Angus MacDonald, alone, of all of the Island chiefs, had not submitted to Edinburgh and had been legally forfeit since 1594. In early 1596 Edinburgh began a series of proceedings against Angus to bring him to submission and collect the several years' of outstanding taxes which he owed.

The first step made by Edinburgh was to release James MacDonald, Angus MacDonald's son, who had been held hostage in

Edinburgh since 1587. James was sent to Kintyre to convince his father to submit peacefully to the Crown. Anticipating that James would fail in his mission, the government issued a proclamation for the "Reduction of the Isles and Highlands of Scotland" and ordered an army to assemble at Dumbarton by the 1st of August. Simultaneous to these two measures, and perhaps to cause the failure of the first, King James cynically awarded Lauchlan MacLean a royal lease to the Rhinns of Islay. The Rhinns of Islay is the district over which the MacLeans and the Clan Ian Mor had been fighting for the past 18 years.

As King James' army assembled for the invasion of the Isles, Sir William Stewart of Houston was given command of the force.[14] On this occasion Edinburgh appears to have thought that, for political reasons, a large percentage of the army should be made up of Highlanders and Islanders. Lauchlan MacLean of Duart; Kenneth MacKenzie of Kintail; and Francis Stewart, Earl of Atholl and High Constable of Scotland, were all ordered to muster their forces and join the gathering army at Dumbarton.

It is not stated in the official records of this affair that the MacKinnons, MacNeils or MacQuarries were called out to bolster Lauchlan MacLean's contingent. If these three clans were not raised in arms for the muster, they would surely have been on alert and ready to join MacLean at a moment's notice if required. While the king's army was gathering, the royalist Spies were reporting that Angus MacDonald was raising a large force of Irish, said to number some 3,000 men, to reinforce his defence of Kintyre and Islay.

For some reason, by early September when the army was ready to proceed, the original plan of reducing the Isles was given up. Instead it was determined that MacDonald's farms in Kintyre should be targeted and Argyll be ordered to aid in the attack. The attack on Kintyre was violent and swift. Within a very few days almost 30% of MacDonald's holdings are laid waste by fire and sword and the remainder were sacked. All record of the intended invasion of the Isles and the army itself now completely vanishes from history and we can only assume the army was disbanded later in September or early October.

King James' quest to subdue MacDonald was not fulfilled by the invasion of Kintyre. However, the invasion did make apparent the divisions within the Clan Ian Mor which, before the event, had been private affairs. James MacDonald of Dunluce, the son of Sorley Boy and leader of the MacDonalds of Antrim, wrote to King James in October explaining he was actually the rightful leader of the Clan Ian Mor and not Angus of Islay. Argyll immediately saw MacDonald of Dunluce's bid to replace his cousin Angus as leader of the Southern branch of the Clan Donald as a direct challenge to his own authority and opposed it strenuously. It may have been because of Argyll's intervention that James' attempt to unseat his cousin eventually failed, but he was called to Edinburgh, knighted and given a royal lease to 30 merklands in Kintyre for his efforts.

The challenge by his cousin and concern of aggravating the now obvious weakness of his clan, likely prompted Angus to submit on the 1st of November. Angus, thinking his son James, who was recently a hostage in Edinburgh, could negotiate better terms from the king than he could, signed all of his estates over to his son. Although this transfer was not recognized by the Privy Council, as Angus had been forfeit for some time, it would further split the clan.

The king again asked James to speak with his father and convince him to peacefully give up the Rhinns of Islay and Kintyre. Although the Rhinns of Islay had recently been granted to Lauchlan MacLean by the king, it was occupied by MacDonald clansmen. The meeting on Kintyre between Angus and James was initially cordial enough. James stayed at his uncle's house of Smerly and Angus stayed at his house of Askomel.

The negotiations between father and son grew increasingly difficult and James was getting impatient. At the moment that James' patience ran out, Gorrie MacAlister, the chief of the MacAlisters of Loup, arrived at Smerly at the head of 300 men. Gorrie MacAlister, the young chief of the clan, had just killed his guardian in a quarrel. To prevent the guardian's sons from taking their revenge in the future, he was pursuing them with the intention of killing them also. The guardian's sons, however, had taken shelter with Angus at Askomel.

James MacDonald, Gorrie MacAlister, and his men immediately proceeded on to Askomel to confront Angus and settle the score with the guardian's sons. Shortly after the armed party, with James at its head, arrived at his father's house, it caught fire. There is no way for us to determine whether the fire was accidentally set or not, but James must have known that both his parents were inside the house at the time. When Angus and his wife appeared out of the flames they were immediately captured and taken back to Smerly, where their son held them.

With his father injured and secured as his prisoner, James MacDonald assumed the chiefship of the Clan Ian Mor. James spent the next couple months consolidating his hold on the estates and trying to increase his support among his clansmen. It appears that most of James' support was centred on Islay and was much less in Kintyre and Antrim. The aggressive stance adopted by James since becoming the clan chief did not please either the king nor the Privy Council in Edinburgh, so it was decided to send another royal expedition to the Isles.[15]

The Rhinns of Islay from Beinn Tart A'Mhill

Before the Edinburgh government had a chance to act against the MacDonalds, Lauchlan MacLean gathered his men to settle his claim on the Rhinns of Islay once and for all. With the Clan Ian Mor effectively split into three parts, this was the opportunity Lauchlan had been waiting for.[16] On August 5, 1598, Lauchlan MacLean, with a large body of well-armed clansmen, landed at Loch Gruinart on the North Coast of Islay. The landing was witnessed by local farmers who immediately sent word to James. On being told of the unexpected landing, James MacDonald hurriedly gathered his warriors and made his way to meet MacLean. As the two clans met, it was obvious to both that the MacDonalds were by far the larger force and would have the advantage of numbers in a fight.

Lauchlan MacLean, however, appears to have intended to intimidate his opponents--not to spill their blood. During the meeting between the chiefs, Lauchlan MacLean was firm. He demanded the MacDonalds give up all claims to the island of Islay. James was as conciliatory as could be expected, under the circumstances, and offered the MacLeans half of the island for the duration of Lauchlan's lifetime. MacLean would, of course, have to agree to the normal conditions of military service and acknowledgment of MacDonald as his superior. If this were not satisfactory, James offered that the dispute be settled by an arbitrator of MacLean's choosing.

As neither side was happy with the outcome of the negotiation thus far, they parted, perhaps intending to resume talks at another time. It appears at this point that James MacDonald received a message advising him that the bulk of the MacLean warriors were stranded by the rising tide on nearby Nave Island and would not be able to get to Islay for several hours.[17]

The MacDonalds, who were then withdrawing to the top of a small hill, stopped, turned, and suddenly rushed down the slope into the bunched group of MacLeans. Lauchlan, who was armed with a rapier and pistol, quickly dispatched three of the attackers. Telling his son, Lauchlan Barrach, who was severely wounded in the first crush, to flee, the MacLean chief stood his ground. A moment later Lauchlan was fatally pierced by a bullet from one of the few gunmen taking part in the battle. Seeing their chief go down, the MacLean bowmen turned and fled toward the safety of their galleys. Savagely pursued by the MacDonalds, the MacLeans left 80 gentlemen and some 200 common soldiers dead on the field. The MacDonald casualties were 30 killed and 60 wounded. One of the more severely wounded was James MacDonald.

Hector MacLean, Lauchlan's son and heir to the MacLean chiefship, appealed to King James for justice and asked that the proposed invasion of Islay be reconsidered and go forward as initially planned. King James managed to lightly brush the affair aside with a vague comment that justice will be done and went on to other business.

Hector, who was not satisfied with the outcome of his encounter with the king, returned to Duart. Angry and still thirsting for revenge, Hector convened a meeting of local chiefs to discuss this matter. The impromptu council agreed with his view of the events and gave him a commission of fire and sword against the MacDonalds of Islay. In a relatively short time the MacKinnons, MacNeils, MacLeods of Harris, and Cameron of Lochiel had united with the MacLeans for a proposed invasion of Islay.

MacLean's preparations were keenly watched by the MacDonalds, who used the interval to prepare the best defence they could. The MacDonalds of Islay were joined by the MacLeans of Lochbuie who, at the time, had a dispute of their own with their cousins from Duart.

The landing of Hector MacLean, Lauchlan MacKinnon, and the other allied clans on Islay was unopposed, so they were able to quickly proceed inland looking for James and his warriors. The two forces met at Ben Bigrie near Dunnyveg on the Southeast Coast of Islay. The ensuing struggle was tremendous in its ferocity. No details of the battle were recorded, but the warriors of Islay were annihilated and the whole island ravaged. James MacDonald, being severely wounded for a second time, was rescued from the field by a couple of MacDonald gentlemen and was taken to Kintyre for safety. The long feud between the MacDonalds and the MacLeans had ended with both clans substantially weakened and Argyll's power unopposed on the Western Coast of Scotland.

After a chiefship of some 18 tumultuous years, Lauchlan Og MacKinnon died in 1598. Although the circumstances of his death may never be known, the year in which he died offered plenty of opportunity for the 58-year old chief to have died leading his warriors in battle. Lauchlan Og's son, also a Lauchlan, was duly examined by the government under the its laws of echat and sasine and inaugurated chief by the clan. It would be up to Lauchlan to guide his clan through the difficult first years of the 17th century.

End Notes
Chapter 16

1. At the same, time MacDonald of Islay and MacLean of Duart were also forfeit. Campbell, A., *History of the Clan Campbell*, Vol. 2, Edinburgh University Press, 2002, 111.

2. Ibid 112.

3. Argyll had bonds of manrent with all of the clans of the MacLean alliance, so it would be very probable that the MacKinnons would have taken part. The only details we have of this force is that O'Donnell brought 500 harquebusiers from Ireland. The king was not happy with the inclusion of MacLean in Argyll's army and called on the young earl to justify including in his number a chief who had so recently been forfeit. There were many others summoned to the rendezvous but who were late for one reason or another. Among the late were MacDonald of Islay with 500 Irish archers, MacKenzie, and the Frasers.

4. At Blair Atholl, Argyll named MacLean of Duart general of the army, only second in authority to himself. It is interesting that the young earl would have more confidence in Lauchlan MacLean than in any of the leaders of the Clan Campbell. The Campbell clan had been divided into many hostile factions for almost a generation, so much so that even the life of the young chief was in constant danger. This does, however, illustrate the close ties between the MacLeans and the Campbell chiefs during this time.

5. Some of these horsemen were Irish troops who had been sent by Tyrone to help Huntly. *Dean of Limerick's account of the Isles of Scotland.* & Campbell, A., *History of the Clan Campbell*, Vol. 2, Edinburgh University Press, 2002, 127.

6. The accounts mention a large body of Islanders and only MacNeil of Warray's son's death is specifically mentioned. If Gillonan MacNeil had not been killed, we would not have known the MacNeils participated in this battle. It is probable that the large body of Islanders was composed of MacLeans, MacNeils, MacKinnons, and MacQuarries, as this alliance was by now firmly established, and each of these clans had a bond of manrent with Argyll.

7. James Campbell spent late 1594 and early 1595 visiting the island chiefs to determine their intentions and, if possible, to dissuade them from joining Tyrone. James duly reported on the preparations made in the

Isles for the Irish invasion and offered to lead 500 men for the English, but this was declined. On the 7th of March James visited Tarbart, where 2-3 companies of MacDonalds were gathering to sail for Ulster. It was only with the greatest difficulty that James was able to get them to delay their departure for a couple of days.

8. Half of the £600 would be in horses, armour and clothing.

9. In a History of the Clan Campbell, it is stated that the object of the council of war was to decide how the fleet was to proceed. The proposals reportedly included an attack on Argyll and MacLean, an attack on the Isle of Mann, or an immediate attack on Ulster. It is clear that Tyrone expected sizeable reinforcements from the Isles because the English agents reported he had ordered cattle gathered in Clandeboye. In July 1595 Sir G. Fenton reported that 1,600 Scots were conducting devastating cattle raids in Ulster. See: Campbell, A., *History of the Clan Campbell*, Vol. 2, Edinburgh University Press, 2002, Vol. 2, 118-157, for a good description of the politics of the Isles during this period.

10. Under ordinary circumstances, the lack of speed and manoeuverability of the English warships could not catch the island galley fleets on the open sea. Because the smaller galleys were no match for the high-sided and well-armed English ships in combat, this was always avoided by using oars and sail to speedily leave the area. To catch the galleys off the Copeland Islands, the English must have been warned of their coming, took up a station, and waited for them. There must have been sufficient wind blowing that day to manoeuver the heavy English ships. The more agile Highland galleys could use their oars for propulsion or escape when the wind was light or contrary. There are very few, if any, other reports of the English successfully engaging a galley fleet at sea. In an official report dated October 1595, Captain George Thornton, who now had 30 years' experience in the Ulster patrol, stated that, due to the speed of the island galleys under oars, they could not be caught by the larger English warships.

11. Rixson, D., *The West Highland Galley*, Edinburgh: Birlinn, 1989, 48, and Campbell, A., *History of the Clan Campbell*, Vol. 2, Edinburgh University Press, 2002, Vol. 2, 123, the wages asked were; 13s 4d /month composite (including food etc.) for longbowmen and halbardmen, 16s 8d/month composite for those with firearms. That Queen Elizabeth had to obtain Argyll's permission, indicates that, while MacLean was doing the dealing, the decisions were made elsewhere.

12. It was well known by now that Donald Gorm had almost completed repairs to his galley fleet and would attempt to reach Ulster again.

13. By May of 1595 Tyrone was asking for 6,000 Spanish soldiers and had offered the throne of Ireland to the Archduke of Austria.

14. He was also made Lieutenant and Justiciary of the Isles. This appointment would have been a direct snub by the king, of Argyll's position in the West. Sir William Stewart, (1540-1605), was initially a soldier in the Netherlands, rising to the rank of colonel. In the year 1582 he was in Scotland, where James VI made him captain of his guard. Having visited the English court in 1583, Stewart helped to free James from William Ruthven, Earl of Gowrie, and to restore James Stewart, Earl of Arran, to power. He was made a privy councillor and for a time assisted Arran in governing Scotland. In 1584 he captured Gowrie at Dundee. In 1585 Stewart went to Denmark and France on secret errands for the king.

15. It may well be that King James was not satisfied with the outcome of this affair because he was still broke. An act of Parliament was passed which required all landholders in the Highlands and islands to produce the deeds and charters for their estates by May 15, 1598. The clan chiefs were also required to find surety for their good behavior and to produce it simultaneously with the charters. These tasks would have been difficult for many chiefs, including Angus or James, to perform. It is doubtless that King James was looking forward to filling his coffers with the spoils of many newly-forfeited estates. King James ordered the royal army to be assembled at Glasgow by August 20, 1598.

16. The support for James MacDonald was principally on the island of Islay. Angus MacDonald, who was still alive, had a great deal of support in Kintyre. Sir James MacDonald of Dunluce had a firm hand on the MacDonald estates in Antrim. As the situation had developed, it was now certain that, in the event of hostilities, none of these divisions could expect help from another.

17. Hector MacLean, Lauchlan's eldest son, was trapped on Nave Island with the bulk of the MacLean warriors.

Chapter 17
INDEPENDENCE ENDS

The first years of the of the 17th century brought a new order to the Hebrides. The power of both the MacDonalds and the MacLeans had been dissipated by the lengthy feud. The Campbells, who continued as agents of the government, were now the most powerful clan on the West Coast. With the defeat of the Clan Ian Mor of Islay by the MacLeans and their MacKinnon allies, an era of Hebridean history had ended and new forces were mustering to dominate the Isles.

The long nagging aggravation felt by the king at his Hebridean subjects' reluctance to pay him rent still rankled the monarch. The Scottish kings had always been self sufficient, meaning they were not supported financially by the nobles of the Kingdom nor from general taxation. Because of the need to independently support the costs of the royal court, it was important that the rents of the king's lands be collected as regularly as possible.

Even after the Scottish king had physically moved to England and took up the English Crown, he relied on the rents collected on his lands in Scotland to support the Scottish court. For the most part, the clan chiefs who inhabited the Isles saw themselves as independent of the kings in either Edinburgh or London. Although the Isles had been the subject of many vicious raids by government forces, they had never been conquered nor joined into the administrative network of the Kingdom of Scotland. Neither the king's authority nor his ownership of land was widely recognised by the Islanders, so rents or taxes from these areas could be collected only intermittently and with much difficulty.

In the meantime, the government in Edinburgh continued to be frustrated by its consistent lack of authority in the Hebrides. King James, whose finances were in an abysmal condition, increasingly turned to rentals from the Isles as a means of raising his personal income. The Royal Commission, which had been granted to the Duke of Lennox and the Marquis of Huntly in 1599, was intended to rectify the matter but ended in complete failure. The Northern Isles were not pacified and, more importantly to James, a reliable method for the collection of the king's rents was still non-existent.

Lennox and Huntly had imprudently ordered their feudal armies to muster for yet another invasion of the Isles during the harvest season which, no doubt, greatly contributed to the low response. It also appears that, in general, the Lowland militia was becoming impatient with the frequent mustering to ensure the collection of taxes or the policing of what they viewed as petty inter-clan squabbles. There can be little doubt that Edinburgh was experiencing increasing difficulties as it continued to rely on a feudal army to maintain its interest in the Western Isles.

Undaunted by the failure of his lieutenants, King James proposed that he, himself, visit the Hebrides and personally enforce his royal authority. Consequently, on April 2, 1600, a proclamation was issued for the gathering of the Western militia at Dumbarton on the 10th of July and on Kintyre on the 12th of July. The boatmen on the Clyde and the adjacent coasts were all warned to be ready to transport the army as required.

Unfortunately, the Western burghs that were to supply the ships and the bulk of the men did not have adequate resources available to produce either. It quickly became apparent that not enough men could be mustered to ensure His Majesty's safety and that other arrangements would have to be made. Thus, on the 6th of June the king ordered another proclamation to be issued: this time to all of the burghs of Scotland. Yet again the required number of ships and men could not be raised. The expedition was finally abandoned on July 14, 1600, by the issue of another proclamation, this one officially cancelling the muster of Scotland's militia.

This would be the last effort by a reigning Scottish monarch to visit the Hebrides in an attempt to win the Island chiefs support by personally asserting his influence. From this time onward the methods used by the government to suppress the Isles would rely less on direct intervention and more on the resources of a few wealthy, well-disposed clan chiefs.

The change in the government's attitude toward the Islanders was not lost on the MacKinnon chief. On January 8, 1601, Lauchlan MacKinnon and Archibald Campbell signed bonds of manrent and maintenance.[1] In spite of being considered illegal by the government, bonds of this nature were typically created by clans of differing military capacities. The contract entered into by the militarily weaker clan was a true bond of manrent, while the stronger clan agreed to a bond of maintenance.

Thus, in return for the protection of a more powerful friend, the smaller clan promised to serve the stronger with its full might on both land and sea. MacKinnon's bond with Argyll begins by commenting on the age-long friendship that had existed between the two clans and that both parties wished to continue that relationship. Argyll promised *"to protect, maintain and defend the said Lachlan MacKinnon and his dependents"* as he would his own kindred; and in return MacKinnon binds himself to serve Argyll *"as his master and protector."*[2]

Sometime during the year 1599, a marital disagreement, that became known as the "War of the One-Eyed Woman," arose between the MacDonalds of Sleat and the MacLeods of Dunvegan. The feud would end by involving the MacKinnons in one of last clan battles to take place on Skye.[3]

For some reason now long forgotten, Donald Gorm MacDonald of Sleat had a falling out with his wife Margaret, the sister of Rory Mor MacLeod of Dunvegan. Margaret apparently suffered from the loss of sight in one of her eyes and Donald Gorm MacDonald unfeelingly exploited this injury to insult both her and her family in a most humiliating manner.

He mounted his wife on a grey, one-eyed horse, led by a one-eyed servant, accompanied by a dog which also had only one eye, and sent her back to her brother at Dunvegan. Soon after Margaret's arrival at the castle, her brother Rory dispatched a remarkably civil letter to Duntulm asking Donald Gorm to reconcile with his wife and allow her to return home.

Duntulm

Dunvegan

Lewis

Bracadale

Glen
Sligachan

Harris

Portnalong

North Uist

Coolins

Dunakin

Minginish

Strath

Carinish

Harta Corrie

Applecross

Slochd Altrimen

Sleat

Strome Castle

Loch Carron
Plock of Kyle

Loch Alsh

Breachachadh
Castle

Aros

Carnaburg

Duart

Mull

Argyle

Sterling Castle

Dumbarton

Islay

Tarbert

Clyde
River

Blackness
Castle

Renfrew

Dunyveg

Kintyre

Ayr

Kilkerran

Carrick

Galloway

Donald Gorm refused to take Margaret back and, instead of accepting the requested reconciliation, he demanded a divorce, to which the MacLeods reluctantly agreed. As soon as the divorce was pronounced, Donald Gorm further incensed the MacLeods by marrying the sister of Kenneth MacKenzie who, at the time, was Rory's bitterest enemy.

Rory Mor MacLeod and the clan which he led were so offended at the callous treatment given to his family by MacDonald that there was no difficulty rallying his warriors and invading the MacDonald lands of Trotternish. Open warfare between the clans ensued as the MacDonalds struck the MacLeod clachans on the island of Harris.[4]

Ruins of Duntulum Castle
The Trotternish home of the MacDonalds of Sleat

Rory MacLeod responded by sending some 40 men, under his cousin Donald Glas MacLeod, to raid the MacDonald holdings on North Uist. The MacLeod warriors caught the MacDonalds by surprise and the entire island was quickly looted. Even the goods and cattle which had been placed in the church of Killtrynad for sanctuary were taken. The MacLeods gathered their booty at the ancient monastery of the Trinity at Carinish, where they feasted on MacDonald cattle.

Unknown to the raiders, the senior MacDonald on the island, Donald mac Iain mhic Sheumais, had gathered some twelve warriors and made for the MacLeod camp. Catching the MacLeods by surprise, the MacDonalds attacked them savagely with bows, arrows and swords. The skilfully-placed MacDonald archers wreaked havoc on the MacLeod counterattack before withdrawing to let loose their arrows yet again. The leaders of both parties were in the thick of the fighting; Donald Glas MacLeod was killed and Donald mac Iain mhic Sheumais was severely wounded.[5]

Thirty-eight of the MacLeod raiders were killed at Feitheadh na fola. Their heads were placed in the windows of the Church of the Trinity, where the skulls remained until the mid 19th century as a grim reminder of the battle. The two surviving MacLeods brought news of the defeat to their chief, Rory Mor, who was then with his galleys at Portalong. On hearing of the defeat and not knowing the numbers of the MacDonald clansmen whom he faced, Rory Mor retired to Skye to raise more of his warriors and to ponder the strategic difficulties he now encountered.

Having considered the situation, Rory Mor decided he needed help to fend off the MacDonalds. Consequently, during the summer of 1601 he travelled to Inveraray to ask assistance of the Earl of Argyll.

Donald Gorm of Sleat received news of Rory's departure almost immediately and thought it in the best interest of his clan to strike while the enemy chief was away from Dunvegan. The MacDonalds struck Minginish and Bracadale, where they burnt houses, destroyed crops, and stole most of the cattle. The invaders proceeded south, gathering their booty in the shelter of the Coolins as the MacLeods rallied under the chief's brother, Alexander MacLeod of Minginish.

The MacLeod warriors gathered at a camp deep in the Coolins, at the mouth of Harta Corrie where it joins Glen Sligachan, effectively blocking the route the MacDonald raiders had to take as they made for their homes in Trotternish.

The MacLeod camp was located on the northwest boundary of the MacKinnon lands of Strath, so it is possible that the MacLeods sent messengers south into Strath to ask for help. Tradition suggests that John Og MacKinnon, younger brother of the clan chief, was present at the battle. There is some disagreement, however, on which side the MacKinnons actually fought and whether or not John Og survived the encounter.[6] Because of the alliances and inter-clan marriages which bound the MacKinnons at this time; they were closely allied with the MacLeans, MacQuarries, and MacNeils and had just signed a bond of manrent with Argyll, so it appears likely that in this instance they would have supported the MacLeods, rather than the MacDonalds of Sleat.

The MacDonalds attacked late the next afternoon. The clans fought ruthlessly, the tide of battle flowing back and forth, with neither side able to hold the advantage. Sometime well after the battle had started, the MacDonald hero of Uist, Donald mac Iain mhic Sheumais, and his band joined the fray. Donald was a large man and his sword, *Lainnire Riabhach,* is said to have wrought terrible havoc among his foes. The battle, fought hand-to-hand, lasted until nightfall, with terrible slaughter on both sides. Late in the evening the advantage favoured the MacDonalds and, in the end, they claimed the victory.

Fairy pools, Glen Etive, Corie na Creiche

Alexander MacLeod of Minginish, who was said to have been wholly encased in armour, Neil MacAlister Roy, and some thirty other leaders of the MacLeods were captured. The MacLeod casualties included many leading members of the clan, including two near relations of the chief, John mac Tormond and Tormond mac Tormond, both of whom were killed. John Og MacKinnon was seriously wounded and would later die of his injuries.[7]

This battle, known as *Bruach na Frithe* or more commonly *Coire na Creiche* (Ravine of the Spoil), was renowned for its fierceness, which is still testified in local legend.[8] It has been rumoured that the ghosts of those killed still haunt the site, while local fairies continue to make bolts from the bones of the slain.[9]

MacKinnon tradition claims that for some reason, possibly related to the ill-will engendered by the battle, Neil, the year-old son of John Og, was in danger. To save him from harm, his aunt Jane, the sister of Lauchlan MacKinnon, is reputed to have hidden him in a cave called *Slochd Altrimen*, the Nursing Cave, in Strathaird. After the danger subsided, Jane took the child to live with her in the old tower of Dunakin. Not a great deal more is known of Neil's early life. That he did spend some time with the Earl of Argyll, either for his continued safety or as a foster son, has long been MacKinnon tradition.

It did not take long for news of the feud between the MacDonalds and MacLeods to make its way to Edinburgh and the ears of the Privy Council. Orders were promptly issued to both chiefs to disband their warriors and leave Skye immediately. Rory Mor was to surrender himself to the Earl of Argyll, and Donald Gorm was ordered to surrender to the Earl of Huntly. Under pain of charges of treason, the belligerent chiefs were to stay with the nobles they were assigned to until their quarrel had been settled.

The other Hebridean chiefs, Angus MacDonald, MacLean of Coll, and some others, were assembled to act as mediators between the two warring sides and a reconciliation was achieved after a series of meetings at Eilean Donan and Glasgow.[10] It was acknowledged thereafter by all of the chiefs that Margaret MacLeod had indeed been spurned by her then husband and was free to bring whatever legal action against him as she might be advised to do. Thus, as the violence stopped, the two parties continued to pursue their differences through the courts.

With reconciliation accomplished between the MacLeods, MacKinnons, MacKenzies, and MacDonalds, Rory Mor invited Donald Gorm, his people and their neighbours to celebrate at Dunvegan. MacLeod's piper, Donald MacCrimmon, met the MacDonalds some distance from Dunvegan, welcoming them with the specially composed tune, "MacLeod's Salute."

On reaching the castle, MacArthur, piper to MacDonald of Sleat, answered with the pibroch "MacDonald's Salute."[11] The festivities continued for six days filled with feasting, strong drink, athletic and piping competitions, and composition exercises by the bards.

The year following the reconciliation at Dunvegan, the relationship between the MacKenzies and MacDonalds of Glengarry took a turn for the worse over a disagreement regarding the ownership of some lands in Ross. During 1602 the simmering undercurrents of animosity between these two clans violently erupted. Kenneth MacKenzie, who would be made Lord of Kintail in about 1610, used his political connections in Edinburgh to engineer a commission of fire and sword against Donald MacDonald of Glengarry.

The MacKenzies devastated the MacDonald lands of Morar, for which Glengarry retaliated by plundering the ancient sanctuary of Applecross. The feud appeared to be rapidly escalating out of MacKenzie's control, so he journeyed to Duart Castle on Mull to ask for help from Hector MacLean.[12] The primary concern that MacKenzie discussed with Hector MacLean was how to keep the old enemy of the MacLeans, the MacDonalds of Islay, from joining forces with their MacDonald cousins. In an effort to help his brother-in-law, Hector MacLean led a preemptive raid on the MacDonald lands in Ardnamurchan.

Kenneth MacKenzie was still with his brother-in-law on Mull when a very large force of MacDonalds of Glengarry invaded and plundered the district around Loch Carron. During the previous century, Lochcarron had belonged to the MacDonalds of Clanranald, but their influence was reduced and now they held only the castle of Strome, while MacKenzie held the surrounding land. The surprised and leaderless MacKenzie clansmen fled the district as the MacDonalds drove deeper into their territory.

Angry MacKenzies, uniting with their cousins from Lochalsh, gathered in strength and prepared to ambush the MacDonald galleys as they passed through the Kyles. The Kyles, which separated Skye from the mainland narrowed considerably before joining Loch Alsh. The MacKenzie clansmen had no intention of letting the raiders escape unscathed. MacKenzie archers and musketeers hid themselves among the rocks and undergrowth along the west side of the Plock of Kyle and waited for the MacDonald galleys to make their way home.

The galleys made their appearance at night, moving leisurely and expecting an easy passage into the Kyle from the north. As the fleet came into bow and musket range, the MacKenzies began their assault with devastating effect. Glengarry's heavily-laden galley was hit particularly hard. The surprised crew rushed to the opposite side of the vessel, capsizing it and tumbling them all into the water. The crewmen who made it to the mainland shore were quickly dispatched by the MacKenzies, who maintained a heavy fire on the MacDonald fleet.

In the face of such determined opposition, the galleys attempted to escape by making for the MacKinnon lands of Strath on the opposite side of the Kyle. Landing on the coast of Skye, somewhere northwest of the old tower of Dunakin, the MacDonalds abandoned their galleys and headed southward toward Sleat. It would have been a long and difficult night for the fugitive MacDonalds as they skirted Sgurr na Coinnich and Beinn na Seamraig on their 14-mile trek to safety.

The warriors who reached the safety of Sleat were all transported home by their Skye cousins. We have no record of what the MacKinnons did with the abandoned galleys, which would have represented a considerable value during those times. Any of the booty from the rape of Lochcarron, which was left behind during the trek through Strath, would still have been the property of the MacKenzies. There is seemingly no extant record or tradition indicating whether the MacKinnons returned the stolen property or kept some or even all of it.

The largest change that would ever take place in the political and cultural sovereignty of the Hebrides was about to occur. To understand these momentous events, we must go back to 1503 with the marriage of Margaret Tutor, daughter of Henry VII of England, to James IV of Scotland. The consequences of this union wound their way through the life of Mary Queen of Scots, to her son, James VI. On the death of Queen Elizabeth I in the spring of 1603, James would succeed to the throne of

England.[13] James reigned thereafter as Ist of England and VIth of Scotland and, having moved to London, never again returned to live in the country of his birth.

King James VI's journey south to London began on April 3, 1603, and it would have an immediate and significant impact on the Western Isles and the folk who lived there. The differing English and Scottish policies toward Ireland now quickly became one and the Privy Council would take the lead in determining the future of the Hebrides.[14] In the Isles, themselves, this meant that the lucrative annual employment of its warriors and their involvement in Irish affairs came to an abrupt and unwelcome end. The Scottish Privy Council, although not concerned with affairs in Ireland, wanted the Hebrides civilized and finally fully incorporated into a feudal Scotland.

In October of 1603, Archibald Campbell, the Earl of Argyll, and now His Majesty's Commissioner in the Isles, was ordered to ensure that the Islanders' rents were regularly paid to the king. To give real teeth to the order, the Earl of Argyll was also given a commission of fire and sword against the MacDonalds of Islay and Sleat, the MacLeods of Harris and Lewis, Clanranald and some others.[15]

The Privy Council was soon dissatisfied with Argyll's progress against the Islanders and issued orders that, on pain of being declared rebel, the keepers of the great castles in the Isles turn them all over to Argyll. MacKinnon was to surrender his castle at Kyle; MacDonald of Islay, Dunnyveg; MacDonald of Sleat, Duntulm; MacLean of Duart, Duart and Carn na Berg; and MacLean of Coll was ordered to give up his home of Breachachadh.

The Island chiefs seem to have ignored the Privy Council's request to surrender their castles and, by May of 1604, none of them appear to have been in government hands. Orders were again issued, but this time a limit was given to the length of time the government was prepared to wait for compliance. On the 8th of May the Privy Council issued two warrants in the amount of £1,000 each to Archibald Campbell of Argyll for keeping the castles of Dunnyveg and Duart. These warrants were made payable by Angus MacDonald and Hector MacLean, even though they had not yet surrendered their castles. It is probable that similar warrants were also issued regarding the castles of MacKinnon, MacDonald of Sleat, and MacLean of Coll who, at the time, had also not surrendered their properties, but additional warrants have not been found in the record.

By the spring of 1605, it seemed obvious to the Privy Council that they had no real authority in the Isles and no prospect of collecting any of the king's rents. The Earl of Argyll's commission of fire and sword and the orders to surrender the island strongholds had all come to naught. Another attempt to assert the king's authority in the Isles had to be made. On July 20, 1605, Sir David Murray, Lord Scone, the comptroller of Scotland, had arranged to meet with the chiefs of the Southern clans at Kilkerran in Kintyre. Those summoned to the meeting were: Angus MacDonald of Dunnyveg, MacLean of Duart, Cameron of Lochiel, MacIain of Ardnamurchan, MacDonald of Keppoch, MacIan of Glencoe, Stuart of Appin, MacDonald of Largie, and MacAlister of Loup.[16]

It is likely that MacKinnon and MacQuarrie were either also summoned or they may have been represented by MacLean of Duart, as their spokesman, as they both held land on Mull. Should any chief fail to appear, Lord Scone held the authority to revoke all titles held for the clan lands and to pursue that clan with fire and sword. At the meeting it was expected the chiefs would show the title deeds to their lands and provide surety for payment of the king's rents and duties. The chiefs again ignored the orders of the Privy Council and none of them made the trip to Kilkerran. The only chief who showed any interest at all was Angus MacDonald of Islay, who met with Murray at Glasgow.

The results of his first attempted meeting being far from satisfactory, Lord Scone tried again. He was back in Kintyre on August 8, 1605, preparing to hold court the following September. In Kintyre, Murray issued a proclamation to all inhabitants of the Isles, ordering them to surrender their boats and forbidding their use without his specific permission.

This meeting also proved to be a disappointment for the government as again only Angus MacDonald and his tenants from Kintyre appeared.[17] Angus paid all the arrears in rents and duty for his lands in Kintyre and Islay and left his son Archibald as hostage. Yet again Murray was unable to either compel the island chiefs to attend his courts or to punish them for their non-attendance. Moreover, at this time there is some indication the Lowlanders, who had traditionally provided men to enforce the edicts of the Privy Council in the Isles were now tiring of these tasks.

The Privy Council maintained what pressure it could on the island chiefs and now summoned them to Edinburgh to appear before it in person. Lauchlan MacKinnon was one of those who did make the journey to Edinburgh and personally appeared before the Privy Council on February 25, 1606. Lauchlan is recorded as promising to reappear again in 60 days under a penalty of 10,000 merks, but does not seem to have paid his rents nor to have left a hostage.[18]

What compelled the MacKinnon chief to respond to this particular summons is not known. He clearly disregarded the reluctance shown by some of the other chiefs to comply. By now Lauchlan may have appreciated Edinburgh's determination to take control of the Isles and was attempting to protect his estates as best he could.

The tension between the men of the Isles and Edinburgh continued to increase as summer and the campaign season approached. On July 12 , 1606, Lauchlan MacKinnon and Finlay MacNab of Bowaine met and signed bonds of manrent and maintenance between their respective clans. This document, dated at Uir, July 12, 1606, reads in part: *"happening to foregadder togadder with certain of the said Finlay's friends in their rooms in the Laird of Glenurchay's country, and the said Lachlan and Finlay having come of ane house, and being of ane surname and lineage, notwithstanding the said Lachlan and Finlay this long time bygone oversaw their awn duties till uders in the respect of the long distance and betwixt their dwelling-places, quhairfore baith the saids now and in all time coming are content to be bound and obleisit, with consent of their Kyn and friends, to do all sted, pleasure, assistance, and service that lies in them ilk ane to uthers; the said Finlay acknowledging the said Lachlan as ane Kynd Chieff, and of ane house; and like the said Lachlan to acknowledge the said Finlay MacNab, his friend, as his special kynsman and friend."*[9]

The witnesses to this bond were John McDonnell reache MacKinnon, Ewen MacKinnon and five MacNabs. The MacKinnon chief signed his name, *Lauchland mise MacFingon*, indicating that he could both read and write, skills unusual for even a chief in those days. Too little is known of his early life to indicate whether he was schooled away from home or simply in command of better intelligence than many of his fellow chiefs.

During the same month that saw the signing of the bond between MacKinnon and MacNab, the Privy Council stepped up its efforts to subdue the Hebrides. They appointed a committee to meet with Lord Scone and the Southern chiefs to hear offers made by the Islanders on their obedience and the payment of His Majesty's rent. Again Angus

MacDonald appears to have been the only chief to have responded. The meeting, not surprisingly, was decidedly biased against the interest of the Islanders and the committee refused to answer any of Angus' questions or to allow him to petition the king in London.

The Privy Council had clearly decided their best option would be the forfeiture of all clan lands in the Isles as well as the total destruction of the two most influential of the island clans. By November an agreement was reached between the Earl of Argyll and the Privy Council, in which Argyll agreed to take in feu as many of the king's lands in the Isles as Lord Scone thought necessary for the regular payment of their rents. At the same time Argyll bound himself not to rent any of the lands over which he was to receive feudal superiority to any named MacDonald or MacLean

By now the Presbyterian Church was making itself known on the West Coast of Scotland. By 1606 there were some 20 presbyteries operating in the Highlands. Athough not yet strong nor influential in Argyll and the Isles, presbyteries did exist in some measure in these areas but did not threaten the established Episcopalian Church. One of the uses of the fledgling Episcopalian Church by the government of Scotland was to promote its control of the Isles. It was the policy of King James to promote candidates to the church whose loyalties were primarily to the monarchy and the kirk.

By early 1607 the Privy Council, with the support of Clan Campbell, had begun plans for what they hoped would be the final government effort to subdue the Isles. This collaboration between the Privy Council and Argyll would begin a major period of the expansion of Campbell power in the inner Hebrides. During February of that year, the Earl of Argyll and Campbell of Cawdor ensured their hold on Iona by reaching an agreement which would see Cawdor named Abbot of Iona.[20]

With plans completed for the final subjugation of the Isles in July of 1607, Argyll was given a Commission making him Justiciar over the Southern Isles. Initially the plan had called for an attack on both the Southern and Northern Isles, with regular troops brought over from Ireland to support the efforts of the local militias. However, due to several unanticipated events, this plan was to change somewhat before it was implemented.

Argyll was ordered to proceed against MacDonald of Islay, in spite of the fact that Angus MacDonald, Chief of the Clan Ian Mor, had paid his rents and indeed, when called upon, appears to have been the only Hebridean chief to attend the government meetings. The pretext for action against him was that the MacDonalds had failed to turn over the castle of Dunnyveg to the government.

The MacDonalds, on receiving word of the imminent attack, prudently took steps to defend themselves. Angus MacDonald and his allies began to gather their men and galleys in the vicinity of Islay. The Privy Council was also alarmed by reports from its spies that the MacDonalds intended to strike at Carrack and Galloway. In March of 1608 the militias of Argyll, Tarbert, Renfrew, Ayr, and Galloway began to muster their forces, but reports of a planned MacDonald attack effectively slowed the raising of local militias as their leaders did not want to dispatch troops that may be needed for their own district's defence.

While Argyll was preparing for war in the South, the second thrust of the government attack on the Isles was being readied in the North. King James, who considered the Highlanders *"barbarous for the most part and yet mixed with some show of civility"* and the Islanders *"utterly barbarious without any sort or show of civility"* could think of only one solution to his difficulties in the West.[21] The Marquis of Huntly was given a commission to subdue the Northern Isles, with the exception of Skye and Lewis.

The agreement between Huntly and the government stated that he would receive grants to all islands of the North provided he extirpated their entire population within one year.[22] Huntly seems to have readily accepted these conditions and was more than willing to negotiate a suitable rent for his new estates. However, when Huntly appeared before the Privy Council on the 23rd of June to finalize arrangements for the expedition, he was arrested.

Huntly, who was a Catholic, followed the Church of Rome and the militant Presbyterians on the council wanted his power and authority greatly reduced. The arrest and detention of Huntly caused the abandonment of the attack on the Northern Isles and consequently saved the lives of thousands of innocent Islanders.

Preparations for the invasion of the Southern Isles continued; the Privy Council wanted Islay occupied no later that the June 1, 1608. By now the Privy Council had appointed two special commissioners to meet personally with Angus MacDonald and Hector MacLean of Duart for the purpose of obtaining their submissions. The special commissioners were men of note: Andrew, Lord Stewart of Ochiltree; and Andrew Knox, Bishop of the Isles. A month later another special commissioner, James Hay of Beauly, was appointed to join them. The special commissioners were to report the island chiefs' offers of submission to the Privy Council no later than the 20th of May so the proposed invasion could proceed as planned.

Several orders were issued to the Islanders and mainland chiefs to ensure their good behaviour in the event of a war. Proclamations were also issued to the mainland chiefs forbidding them, under penalty of death, to harbour or give supplies to any of the Isles men. Angus MacDonald was ordered to surrender Dunnyveg to the king's representative within 24 hours of his landing on Islay. By this time, however, Huntly had been released by the Presbyterians so that command of the expedition was now, as initially intended, split between the lieutenants of the North and the South.

As the 1st of June approached, the army's muster date was postponed for a month to accommodate the raising of additional Lowland militia. This time military preparations proceeded vigorously. The burghs now had little difficulty fitting out and provisioning the required number of ships. Lord Ochiltree was given overall command of the expedition and authorisation to either garrison or destroy the various castles in the Isles.[23] Andrew Knox, Bishop of the Isles, made the arduous journey south to London, on behalf of the Privy Council, to obtain King James' final approval of its draft conditions for submission of the island chiefs.

During the following August, the royal expedition finally sailed towards Islay. On the island, the Scottish militia rendezvoused with the regular soldiers under Sir William St. John who had been dispatched from Ireland. To protect the army's artillery from the Islanders' galleys, an English galley escorted the ship carrying the artillery train. On being advised of the royalist landing, Angus MacDonald surrendered both Dunnyveg and the fort at Lochgorm. Lord Ochiltree ordered the Lochgorm fortification demolished, and Dunnyveg was garrisoned by 24 of his men.

Leaving Islay on the 14th of August, the royal army was off the East Coast of Mull the next day. Hector MacLean knew his castle of Duart would never withstand a modern artillery bombardment so, on the

the 17th of August, he too surrendered his keep to the royalists. That same day Lord Ochiltree ensured the castle was garrisoned by his own men.

With both the strongholds of Dunnyveg and Duart in his hands, Lord Ochiltree summoned all the island chiefs to a meeting at the ancient castle of Aros. Conferring at length with the chiefs, Ochiltree, Knox, and John Hay hoped to get the chiefs to agree to seven statutes which were as follows:

1. Each and every one was to find surety for the payment of His Majesty's rents;
2. The chiefs and their vassals were to strictly observe the laws of the realm;
3. They were to surrender all garrisoned houses to the king;
4. They were to renounce heritable jurisdiction and submit to the sheriffs or other officers appointed by the Crown;
5. All galleys were to be burned, except such as were required for essential services, e.g., conveyance of goods to the mainland or from island to island as the rents were then paid in kind;
6. Children of the chiefs were to be sent to school;
7. The use of two-handed swords, guns, and bows and arrows were to be prohibited.

The chiefs put up a great deal of resistance to the fifth statute as the destruction of their galleys would leave the island clans defenceless in the event of raids by their mainland cousins. Lord Ochiltree's response to the Islander's concern was to immediately send a note requesting the Privy Council also order the destruction of the boats on the mainland as well. The Privy Council agreed and in September issued orders to the mainland chiefs to destroy their galleys. With the objections to clause five removed and the invasion still threatened, the island chiefs felt confident enough to sign Ochiltree's document.

The signatories to these seven statutes were: Angus MacDonald of Dunnyveg, Hector and Lauchlan MacLean of Duart, Donald Gorm MacDonald of Sleat, Donald MacAllan of Clanranald, Ruairi MacLeod of Dunvegan and his brother Alastair MacLeod, Neil McIlduy and Neil MacRurry. In addition to the placment his own signature, Hector MacLean also agreed to answer for MacNeil of Barra who was absent. The only island chiefs who seemingly did not appear at this meeting were the Chiefs of MacKinnon, MacQuarrie, and MacLean of Coll. Both MacKinnon and MacQuarrie had land on Mull, so the reason for their not signing the statutes personally can only be guessed at. It is odd, however, that MacLean would offer to answer for MacNeil and not MacKinnon and MacQuarrie if, indeed, they were absent.

The meeting ended with both the chiefs and government parties seeming to have agreed to all of the statutes or conditions for submission laid before them. Angus MacDonald, who had pressing matters on Islay, gave a pledge of his good behaviour and left Aros almost immediately. The other chiefs were invited to dine aboard Ochiltree's pinnace, the *Moon*, and to hear a sermon preached by Andrew Knox. The only chief who refused the invitation was Ruari MacLeod of Dunvegan, who may have dined at Aros. After the meal and sermon had ended and, as the chiefs made ready to leave the ship, they were advised that they were all made prisoner by the king's orders. The *Moon* sailed from Mull, either that evening or early the next morning, to Ayr, where the prisoners were dispersed for confinement to Dumbarton, Blackness, and Sterling castles.[24]

As far as Ochiltree was concerned, the meeting at Aros was a complete success. In his report to the Privy Council, he stated he had destroyed all the boats he could find in the areas visited; secondly, he returned both the castles of Aros and Duart to MacLean as he had been instructed to do; thirdly, he had taken surety for the delivery of Mingary Castle in Ardnamurchan; and lastly, that he had wanted to proceed against MacLeod of Lewis but was prevented from doing so only by the lateness of the season.

Having so many chiefs and high-ranking clansmen in his custody was a great opportunity for King James to add to his royal estates. The king hoped the captive chiefs would voluntarily give up large parts of their lands, thus enriching the King's Majesty and simultaneously reducing their power in the Isles. Orders were issued to the special commission from London that the submission and obligations agreed to by the individual chiefs would each have to be approved personally by the king. Thus, although the chiefs had all agreed to the government's terms at Aros, the king continued to hold them in confinement, making conditions for their release that were continually more difficult for them to meet.

There was a flurry of communication between the Commission of the Isles and the island chiefs, both captive and free, during the months of January and February 1609, regarding the conditions of submission to be demanded by the government. If appears as if the government had not yet decided exactly what it wanted from the chiefs. The offers of submission made by the Islanders were considered by the commission and then forwarded to London for the personal approval of the king. However, it was not until sometime during the four months of February to May that the government finalized the demands it would make to the chiefs, and preparations were made to pressure any who might attempt to reject them.

Apparently Lauchlan, Chief of MacKinnon, was not among the unfortunate Islanders captured at Aros or, if he had been taken, he was soon afterward released. Lauchlan evidently appreciated the change in the political climate and took great care to maintain an appearance of good terms between himself and the Privy Council. When he was summoned to renew his obligations and to appear before the Privy Council again on February 6, 1609, Lauchlan made the journey to Edinburgh. However, the preparations and perhaps the weather delayed him by forty days, so he didn't arrive before the Council until the 12th of May. The Privy Council seems to have accepted Lauchlan's explanation for the delay and renewed his obligation to appear on 60 days' notice. They also reduced his penalty for non-appearance to 5,000 merks, from the previously stipulated amount of 10,000 merks.

It was not until the end of June that Andrew Knox returned to Scotland from London. He carried with him the terms of submission that had been accepted and instructions from the king on how to proceed.[25] The Bishop of the Isles was deputed to go to the Hebrides, as the sole commissioner, with authority to issue commissions of fire and sword against reluctant chiefs.[26] Before proceeding, Bishop Knox used his own authority to arrange the release of the clan chiefs and gentlemen captured at Aros. These prisoners were required to find surety that they would appear before the Privy Council at a later date and to concur with the conditions for their submission.[27]

Toward the middle of July, Andrew Knox set out to meet with the Hebridean chiefs on the island of Iona. Knox may well have taken a month and a half to visit some the chiefs in their own lands and discuss the agenda with them before proceeding to the meeting. The meeting was evidently very well prepared and took place on August 24, 1609. The assembled chiefs immediately accepted the bishop as the royal representative and agreed to submit to the king's terms. Taking advantage of the unanimity between the chiefs, the Bishop of the Isles held court and, with their mutual consent, passed eight statutes.[28]

The preface to these articles which are now known as the *"Statutes of Iona"* is an interesting commentary of the state of religion then prevalent in the Isles and formed a kind of bond of its own. The Islanders seem to have largely abandoned the Roman Catholic Church during the Reformation but had not yet adopted the new Protestant faith.

The island churches were in ruin, stipends were not paid to the ministers, and a callous indifference to spiritual matters prevailed. The preface was a declaration of religion, which stated that the chiefs *"Profess the true religion publicly taught within the realm of Scotland, and embraced by his Majesty and his estates, as the only and undoubted truth of God."*[29] This bond was signed by Lauchlan MacKinnon, MacDonald of Sleat, Ruari MacLeod of Dunvegan and others.[30]

Once the Declaration of Faith was signed, the assembly dealt with the statutes themselves. The statutes were signed on August 24, 1609, by the chiefs who each gave their solemn oath that they and their followers would honour them to the effect that:

1. The chiefs would provide security for His Majesties rents;
2. The chiefs and all of their followers undertook to be obedient to all laws;
3. All houses of defence, strongholds, and crannogs were to be placed at the king's disposal;
4. The chiefs renounced all jurisdiction to which they claimed, heritably or otherwise, and agreed to submission to the jurisdiction of sheriffs, bailies, justices, or other officers appointed by the Crown;
5. That they should be satisfied with such lands and possessions and under such conditions as the king might appoint;
6. That all their birlinns, lymphads, and galleys should be destroyed, with the exception of those required to carry His Majesty's rents in kind to the mainland or for some other necessary purposes;
7. That they, and such of their kinsmen as could afford it, should put their children to school under the direction of the Privy Council;
8. That they should abstain from using guns, bows, and two-handed swords and should confine themselves to the use of single-handed swords and targes.

A very significant event occurred during the meeting at Iona that is illustrative of the goodwill now existing between the Skye chiefs. This was the signing of a bond of friendship between Ruari MacLeod of Dunvegan and Donald Gorm MacDonald of Sleat. This bond, in which the chiefs pledged themselves to *"forget, forgive and abstain from quarrelling in the future being certainly persuaded of their dread sovereign's clemency, and to live here after in Christian society and peace"* was witnessed by Lauchlan MacKinnon and his uncle Ewen.[31] This was the first document signed in friendship by all three of the chiefs of Skye and ended the two-hundred year fight for control of the island.

With the statutes signed, Bishop Knox made his report to the Commissioners of the Isles and then made the long journey south to advise the king of the outcome of the meeting and to seek his final approval for the various submissions.

End Notes
Chapter 17

1. Campbell, A., *History of the Clan Campbell*, The Bath Press, Bath 2000, 140, See Appendix 14.

2. Nicolson, *History of Skye*, Alex MacLaren, Glasgow, 1930, 139-140.

3. Nicolson, *History of Skye*, Alex MacLaren, Glasgow, 1930, 139-140, and Cameron, A., *The History & Traditions of the Isle of Skye*, Inverness: Forsyth, (1871), 57-62. Although it is commonly believed this was the last clan battle to be fought on Skye, it was not. In 1626 the MacDonalds of Clanranald and the Clan Iain of Ardnamurchan invaded and plundered the MacLeod lands in revenge for the MacLeods having been awarded a commission of fire and sword against them.

4. Several of the inhabitants were killed and the MacDonalds took a great deal of booty in this raid.

5. Donald Glas was killed by Donald Mor mac Neil mhic Iain MacDougall at a place still known as *Ottar Mhic Dhomhnuil Ghlais*

6. MacKinnon, J., *The MacKinnons of Kyle and Other Connections*, Longformacus, (1981), 11, indicates that John fought with the MacDonalds. That John Og was married to an aunt of MacDonald of Clanranald, would not necessarily obligate him to support the MacDonalds of Sleat in a raid on the MacLeods, especially since John Og had two sisters who had married prominent MacLeods. The elder sister, Mary, married Sir Roderick MacLeod of Talisker, Rory MacLeod's son, and the youngest sister, Jane, married Donald MacLeod of Waternish, a senior member of the clan who was twice declared chief of Dunvegan. To support the MacDonalds of Sleat at this time, would have put the MacKinnons in the position of opposing their own blood relitives. John Og was the progenitor of the Torrin, Kinlochslappen, Borreraig, and Kyle families.

7. See Appendix 15 for another version of the story of this battle and a contemporary song written in commemoration of it.

8. MacKinnon, D., *The MacLeods*, J. & G. Innes, Cupar Fife, 1950, 14.

9. MacCulloch, J. A., *Misty Isle of Skye*, Eneas MacKay, Sterling, 1946, 142. The site is marked by a stone now, known as the Bloody Stone, which stands at the entrance to Harta Corrie.

10. It is likely that MacKinnon, MacLean, MacQuarrie, and MacNeil were also involved to act as mediators.

11. There are several other pipe tunes composed to celebrate the feast at Dunvegan, two of them being *Failte nan Leodach,* which was played during the feast, and *Cath Gailbheach* written to commemorate the peace.

12. MacLean of Duart was the brother-in-law of Kenneth MacKenzie, being married to his sister Janet. It should also be noted that Rory MacLeod's son, Iain MacLeod, was married to Sibyl, Kenneth MacKenzie's daughter. Should matters worsen, these alliances would put the MacKinnons on the side of the MacKenzies.

13. See Appendix 16 for the relationship between the Scottish and English royal families.

14. King James wanted the Irish question settled, with Ireland existing quietly under English dominion. With their major source of fighting men and supplies no longer available, the Celtic lords of Ireland could not expect to maintain the struggle against the English settlers as well as they once did. It could be argued that it was the lack of Celtic reinforcements from the Hebrides which stalled the Irish quest for independence.

15. The only other island clans are MacKinnon, MacQuarrie, MacLean, and MacNeil. These clans may have had recent bonds of manrent with Argyll. The determined attempt to collect the king's rents led to a complicated manoeuvre within the Clan Ian Mor, which again changed the chiefship and once more propelled it to prominence. Sir James MacDonald, who had been defeated by the MacLeans and MacKinnons on Islay in 1598, liberated his father, Angus, from confinement and proceeded to solidify his own power base in Kintyre. Angus MacDonald, fearing that his son, Sir James, was actually plotting in secret against him, had his son arrested and held firstly by Argyll and then by the government. Thus Angus MacDonald again assumed the leadership of the MacDonalds of Islay. The repercussions of these events, which occurred within the Clan Ian Mor, would be felt by all of the clans throughout the Hebrides in a very short time.

16. Gregory, *History of the Western Highlands & Isles,* William Tait, Edinburgh, 1834, 307.

17. The tenants were the MacAlisters, MacNeils, MacKays, and MacEacherans.

18. Rev. MacKinnon, D. D., *Memoirs of the Clan Fingon,* Lewis Hepworth Tunbridge Wells, 1899, 23. The sum of 10,000 merks would have been a very large amount for a chief of MacKinnon's relatively minor financial stature.

19. The reference to being of one house and one surname refers to clans belonging to the mythical Clan Alpin. The story of descent from the Clan Alpin was first circulated by the MacGregors who were under threat by the Campbells just prior to 1512. By 1606 it appears to have become established tradition and a useful tool in the hands of those with uncertain claims.

20. At the first sitting of the parliament in 1607, Argyll was to purchase the abbacy of Iona. Campbell of Cawdor, who had been granted Iona by his kinsman, Alexander Campbell, Prior of Ardchattan, would then be named Abbot of Iona. There is much written of the MacKinnon mishandling of Iona and its wealth, but after the MacLeans and Campbells obtained the island, both the abbey and its possessions were completely looted.

21.   Kirk, J., "Jacobean Church," *17th Century in the Highlands, Inverness Field Club*, 45.

22. These conditions may not have been demanded by King James, but he most certainly approved them. Huntly offered the Privy Council a rent of £400, which was thought to be too low, so acceptance of the offer was left to the king himself.

23. It appears that both Argyll and Huntly were removed from command of the expedition, although they seem to have retained their offices as royal lieutenants.

24.   MacLean, J. P., *History of the Clan MacLean,* Robert Clark, Cincinnati, 1889, 148.   Andrew Knox does not appear to have been comfortable with his part in the kidnapping of the chiefs. He wrote to King James offering to resign his special commission as he had no credibility remaining in the Isles.

25. Ibid 150, for details of the king's instructions.

26. The government was reluctant to once again commit Lowland militia to enforce its will against the clans. Instead, it was decided to order the chiefs, who had submitted to act against the other chiefs who were reluctant to do so.

27. Clanranald was released when Knox and Ochiltree agreed to stand surety for him to the amount of £5,000. Donald Gorm of Sleat was released on condition that he: (1) find surety for his appearance yearly at Sterling on a fixed date; (2) he was to declare his adhesion to Protestantism; (3) he was to maintain order in his dominions; (4) he was to give help in the surveying of the Isles. With Donald Gorm's help, the work was completed in 1609.

28. Campbell, A., *History of Clan Campbell*, Edinburgh University Press, 2002, 149; Gregory, *Western Highlands & Isles*, William Tate, Edinburgh, 1836, 330; MacLean, J. P., *History of the Clan MacLean*, Clarke & Co, Cincinnati, 1889. 150-152.

29. Nicolson, *History of Skye*, Alex MacLaren, Glasgow, 1930, 131; Rev. MacKinnon, D. D., *Memoirs of Clan Fingon*, Lewis Hepworth, Tunbridge Wells, 1899, 26 see Appendix 17 & 18.

30. It should be noted that the prevalent religion taught in the realm of Scotland was Presbyterianism, but the ministers of Skye at this time were Episcopalian. The Reformation proceeded slowly, but steadily, in the Isles. In 1605 there were Reformed *Episcopalian* ministers active in Rodel, Harris and Barra. The minister to Barra was murdered in 1609. The first Reformed ministers to Skye were appointed in 1609--one was appointed to Durnish and the other ministered to Sleat.

31. MacLeod, R. C., *The Book of Dunvegan I*, Spalding Club, 1939, 47. See Appendix 19

The Ross of Mull from Iona

Chapter 18
A NEW BEGINNING

While Bishop Knox was away from Scotland, the affairs of the Isles were attended to by the Lords Commissioners of the Isles. The commissioners heard a complaint lodged by the island chiefs that a proclamation had been issued prohibiting the inhabitants of mainland Argyll from purchasing cattle, horses or other goods produced in the Isles. It is not now known who issued the proclamation, but it was immediately withdrawn.[1] The commissioners also issued orders that the island chiefs appear in Edinburgh on February 2, 1610, but this command was later postponed this until the 28th of June.

Once again Lauchlan MacKinnon made the trek to appear before the Privy council. There were twelve chiefs and gentlemen who made an appearance that year. The Privy Council specifically called six of the assembled chiefs: MacKinnon of Strathswordale, MacDonald of Dunnyveg, MacDonald of Sleat, MacDonald of Clanranald, MacLeod of Dunvegan, and Cameron of Lochiel, to hear His Majesty's pleasure declared to them through the Privy Council.

The six selected chiefs were advised that the king approved of the actions of the bishop and of the statutes signed on Iona. The island chiefs solemnly promised they would:

1. concur with the king's lieutenants, justices, and commissioners in all matters connected with the Isles;
2. live together in peace, love and amity,
3. finally resolve any difficulties that might arise between them by course of ordinary law and justice.

Difficulties and ill feelings between the chiefs were forgiven as they heartily embraced each other and clasped hands together in the presence of the council. All twelve of the assembled chiefs and gentlemen were then required to provide sureties for their next appearance, which was ordered for May of 1611.

Unfortunately, the spirit of friendly reconciliation established on Iona and confirmed before the Privy Council was not to last. Almost immediately on their return to the Isles, the MacLeans, MacKinnons, and MacQuarries carried out a devastating raid on MacNeil of Barra. It seems that Roderick "the Turbulant" MacNeil had been handfasted to a daughter of MacLean of Duart.[2] This relationship had lasted considerably longer than the customary year and a day and the couple had a number of grown sons. As the relationship had never been legitimised, there was little in the way to prevent MacNeil from leaving his MacLean wife to marry the sister of the captain of Clanranald. The second relationship also lasted long enough to produce a number of grown sons.

When the eldest son of the second family came of age, a rift appeared in the Clan MacNeil. The sons of the second family would become the legal heirs to all of the MacNeil estates because their parents had legitimised their relationship through a more formal marriage. The sons of the first family refused to give up their rights to the estates until they were forced to do so by Clanranald. The raids in April of 1610 on Mingulay, Barra, Fladda, Sanda, and Vatersay by the MacLeans, with their MacKinnon allies, was clearly conducted in support of the claim to the MacNeil estates by the MacLean of Duart's grandchildren.

This unfortunate split in the ancient alliance of island clans was not easily mended. In 1612 the eldest son of Roderick MacNeil's first family was implicated in an act of piracy against a ship from Bordeaux.[3] Clanranald captured young MacNeil and brought him to Edinburgh, where he died under very mysterious circumstances. Young MacNeil's brothers, with the support of MacLean, MacKinnon, and MacQuarrie captured the eldest son of Roderick's second family, claiming he was also implicated in the piracy, and sent him to Edinburgh. The charges against the heir to the MacNeil estates could not be substantiated, but he was, nonetheless, held for a considerable period. Clanranald was eventually able to have his nephew released on the promise that he would appear on demand before the Privy Council on penalty of 10,000 merks. Clanranald's influence in Edinburgh also secured his nephew's succession to the MacNeil estates.[4]

The sons of the first family grew desperate now there was little chance of inheriting their father's estates. MacLean's surviving grandsons seized their father, the old chief of MacNeil, and held him in irons. Orders were sent from Edinburgh that Roderick MacNeil was to appear before the Privy Council, but of course this was not done. A commission of fire and sword was promptly granted to Clanranald, enabling them to act against the MacNeils, but this proved unnecessary. Clanranald was able to negotiate a peaceful settlement in favour of his nephew.

The affair was thought settled when, on December 18, 1612, Sir Dougal Campbell of Auchenbreck was ordered to act against MacLean, MacKinnon, and MacQuarrie for the raid they had committed two years previously.[5] It appears that nothing of note came of Auchenbreck's order and the episode disappeared into history.

Despite the island chiefs' appearances before the Privy Council, it appears the government was still having trouble collecting the rents it claimed as due from the Isles. In 1611 Andrew Knox, who had been appointed Steward and Justicar of all of the Northern and Western islands and constable of Dunnyveg in June 1610, was given the the rents of certain island chiefs to support his office. "*At Quhythall, the fifth day of Novenber 1611*" King James granted Andrew Knox "*all and quhatsumever soumes of money sall be found rest and auentand to his Majestie, by Donald Gorm of Slaitte, Rorye MacCloyd of Hereis, Lauchlane MacKennie of Strathorrodill, Alexander MacGillichallom of Rasa*" "*for yair parties of quhatsomever taxationes grantit to his Majestie, within his said kingdom, at any tim proceeding the first day of July 1606,*"[6]

The islands were once again quiet. The strife between the MacKinnons and Clanranald had been completely set aside. It was on February 15, 1613, that Lauchlan MacKinnon witnessed the bond of marriage between John of Moydart, the son of Clanranald, and Moir, daughter of MacLeod of Dunvegan.[7] By July 1613 Donald Gorm and Rauri Macleod had settled their accounts with the exchequer--perhaps even Lauchlan MacKinnon did so as well. The Bishop of the Isles, Alexander Knox, still influential at court and thankful for the income, may have recommended that Lauchlan MacKinnon, Ruairi MacLeod, and some of the other island chiefs be knighted by the king. Where the ceremony took place is not known, but it seems likely the Islanders would have made the long and difficult journey to London to receive the honour.

The castle of Dunnyveg was held by the Bishop of the Isles with only a token occupation force. The significance of holding the castle was purely symbolic, in that its occupation represented the physical possession of the MacDonald estates on Islay by the king. The small garrison had, however, grown careless over the four quiet years it had been on watch. In April 1614 this carelessness would prove fatal for the MacDonalds of Islay when Ranald Og MacDonald, the son Angus MacDonald, succeeded in capturing the castle with the help of only four men.

The danger to the Clan Ian Mor, by the rash taking of the castle, was not lost on its leaders. The younger brother of Sir James MacDonald, Angus Og, roused the MacDonalds of Islay with the fiery cross and took the castle back from Ranald. Angus Og then immediately offered to return the castle to the royal garrison, but they stoutly refused to take it. Angus Og was then obligated to hold Dunnyveg himself until a representative of the government arrived to take command of the garrison and once again occupy it for the king.[8]

Other than the continuing power struggles within the Clan Ian Mor, the affairs in the Hebrides remained relatively quiet, but Edinburgh maintained its watch on the island chiefs. Sir Lauchlan MacKinnon once again made the journey to appear before the Privy Council during July 1614. At the meeting which took place on the 3rd of August, Sir Lauchlan ratified the statutes he had agreed to at Iona in 1609 and accepted further obligations from the Privy Council. The additional obligations, which were imposed on all of the island chiefs, specified that the chiefs, now give due obedience to their kirk ministers and assistants, punish offenders according to the discipline of the kirk. They were also ordered to appear in Edinburgh when next summoned by the council.

Andrew Knox, Bishop of the Isles, was finally able to tend to the recovery of Dunnyveg for the government in September--some five months after it was occupied by Angus Og. While journeying to Islay, the Bishop of the Isles met MacDonald of Sleat and Aulay MacAulay. He asked them to act as intermediaries between himself and Angus Og MacDonald in the forthcoming negotiations for the surrender of the castle. When the negotiations ultimately failed, Knox believed it was because of interference by the Campbells.[9] The bishop's opinion was confirmed when the Privy Council, apparently angered at what they saw as Angus Og's treachery, agreed to grant all of Islay to Campbell of Cawder. In return, Cawder was expected to subdue the MacDonalds at his own expense and maintain order on the island thereafter.

There were many and varied rumours of plots and counterplots regarding Islay circulating among the Hebridean clans and the officials in Edinburgh. Sir James MacDonald, who was still a prisoner in Edinburgh, heard some of these from his cell and made suggestions to the government regarding settling the island's affairs in a peaceful manner. All of Sir James' advice was dismissed out of hand and ignored. It seems clear that it was well known at the time that the MacDonalds were about to be deprived of Islay, but who the Privy Council would ultimately award it to was still the matter of much speculation.

The Chancellor of Scotland, in a bid to have Islay granted to himself, sent a private message to Angus Og ordering him to hold Dunnyveg at all costs. He specifically advised MacDonald not to let it fall into Campbell of Cawder's hands. In this way the chancellor hoped to foil Cawder's plans and have the castle surrendered to himself.

During the early days of 1615, Campbell of Cawder's army, reinforced by some 200 soldiers and a train of artillery from Ireland, landed on Islay.[10] By February both the castle of Dunnyveg and the fort at Lochgorm had fallen. The feud was spreading and, during the months of March, April, and May the MacDonald warrior, Colkitto, with his ally Malcolm MacRuairi MacLeod, ravaged the whole of the coasts of Argyll.

In a futile effort to contain the feud, the government issued orders to Sir Lauchlan MacKinnon and seven other chiefs to proceed against Colkitto's rebel force.[11] Sir Lauchlan and the clans with him were to be supported by a Royal Navy ship, *Phoenix;* and a pinnace, *Moon*, under the command of Captains Wood and Monk, and a hoy which carried a train of artillery. The Hebridean chiefs fully understood the complicity of the Campbells, in what was being done to the MacDonalds of Islay, and appear to have been in no hurry to aid either the government or the Campbells in displacing fellow Islanders from their ancestral homes.

At about the same time that Islay was invaded, Sir James MacDonald, aided by Alastair mac Ranald MacDonald of Keppoch and the captain of Clanranald, escaped from Edinburgh castle.[12] The Privy Council, now very much in a state of excitement, offered a £2,000 reward for Sir James either dead or alive. However, Sir James was spirited safely to Skye where he met Donald Gorm of Sleat with whom he signed a bond of friendship.

Travelling on to Eigg, he joined the forces led by Colkitto, bringing with him bonds of friendship with Ruairi MacLeod of Dunvegan and the Captain of Clanranald. Even Hector MacLean of Duart was moved to publicly state that, if he were however, ordered to move against the MacDonalds, he *"would not be very earnest in the service."* The government, which now estimated that Colkitto had some 300 men under arms, knew that many more MacDonalds, especially from Ardnamurchan, were joining him daily.

Mingary Castle was known to have been fortified and held for Sir James by Donald Mac Iain MacDonald, its constable. There was a growing fear in Edinburgh that this rising would unite the various branches of the Clan Donald and eventually envelope the whole of the Highlands.

Reports from the West began to reach the Privy Council that large parties of warriors from Clanranald,

MacLeod of Harris, MacDonald of Sleat, and MacLean of Duart were serving with Sir James.[13] The desperate government responded by raising the reward for the MacDonald leaders: Sir James to £5,000; Keppoch and Colkitto would fetch 5,000 merks each; Ranald Og, Keppoch's son; and MacLeod were worth 3,000 merks each.

By June 20th, 1615, the Privy Council realised that neither Cawder nor itself had the power to subdue the MacDonalds. The best the Privy Council could now do was to write to the king in London requesting he send Argyll back to Scotland so that he might personally take command in the West.

Mingary Castle, home of the MacDonalds of Ardnamurchan

Estimating the government would need at least 500 Isles men to adequately deal with the threat posed by the MacDonalds, they ordered the island clans to mobilise with provisions for 40 days. This was the first time the government in Edinburgh ordered the Celtic might of the Isles to muster against one of their own tribes. The clans ordered out were: MacKinnon and MacLean of Coll, who were to raise 100 men; Campbell and the MacLeans of Duart and Lochbuie, raising 250 men; MacLeod of Dunvegan with 50 men; MacDonald of Sleat and the Tutor of Kintail, raising 50 men, Campbell of Cawder was to hold Dunnyveg and defend Islay at his own expense.[14]

It was decided the Privy Council's priority should be the defence of the coast of mainland Scotland south of Skye. To this end, a disposition was drawn up as follows. MacLeod of Dunvegan, MacDonald of Sleat, and Clanranald were to defend their estates with 200 men each. Earl of Enzie, the son of Huntly, was to defend Lochaber with 100 men. MacKinnon and MacLean were to defend the point of Ardnamurchan, south to Lorn, with 200 men. Campbells of Lochnell & Barbreck were to defend Lorn, with 150 men from Lorn and Glenorchy and any of Cawder's men who were not employed on Islay. Campbell of Auchenbreck was to defend mid Argyll, Knapdale, and Kintyre with 200 men. Campbell of Ardkinglas was to defend Cowel with 100 men. The Marquis of Hamilton and the sheriff of Bute were to defend Arran and Bute. The total force the privy planned to muster for the defence of the coasts was in excess of 1150 men.[15]

The clans were ordered to take up their assigned positions by the 6th of July. How many of these clans actually deployed to their assigned positions is unknown. But, from the surviving orders which were subsequently issued by the Privy Council, we can be sure that neither the MacKinnons nor the MacLeans actively supported the government.

Just a few days later, on the 18th of June, a worried Rory Mor MacLeod of Dunvegan wrote to the Privy Council, advising them to order a general mobilisation of the island clans.[16] His letter suggested that MacLean of Duart and Lochbuie form one company; MacDonald of Sleat and Clanranald form another; MacLean of Coll, MacKinnon, and Kintail would form the third. It was suggested these companies, along with the MacLeods of Dunvegan, could expel the MacDonalds from the Hebrides altogether. However, not all of the island chiefs shared MacLeod's sentiments.

Indeed, Sir Lauchlan MacKinnon does not appear to have raised his clan for either side, but it is likely that his sympathies were with the Clan Ian Mor. MacLean of Duart had already spoken openly of his feelings and had many close relatives who actually joined the MacDonalds in their struggle against the government and its Campbell allies.

The campaign escalated on the 22nd or 23rd of June when James MacDonald and his men landed on Islay. MacDougall of Raray's brother, as the constable of Dunnyveg, commanded the castle's garrison for the king. When MacDougall and his men were ambushed, only 12 survivors managed to reach the safety of the castle. However, because there was no water within the castle, the survivors were forced to surrender the next day.

Sir James honourably released Campbell of Ardchattan, along with his two sons, and Cawder's surviving men, ferrying them back to the mainland. Sir James also dispatched several letters to the king, Bishop Knox and other members of the government. The letters explained that Sir John intended to remain a loyal subject and that his only wish was that his lands be kept from falling into the hands of the Campbells.

To raise the remainder of the Clan Ian Mor, Colkitto sailed to Kintyre and Sir James visited Jura. Reinforcements soon began to arrive and Sir James returned to Islay, where he strengthened the defences of Lochgorm and awaited the arrival of MacDuffy of Colonsay and Donald Gigach of Jura with their men.

Leaving his son, Donald Gorm, in command of Islay, Sir James proceeded to Kilkerran Castle in Kintyre. The "Special men of Islay," Donald MacIan of Jura, MacDonald of Keppoch, and a large body of men from the Outer Isles accompanied Sir James. The MacDonald galleys landed off the West Coast of Kintyre on the island of Cara, where they were placed under heavy guard. Sir James once again summoned the clan by sending the fiery cross around the peninsula. By the end of July, Sir James had some 1,000 warriors under arms.

The Privy Council must now have been in a state of near panic at the news of developments in the West. Writing to the king in London, they once again pleaded that Argyll be sent back to Scotland. They specifically mentioned he was needed to keep the promise to maintain order that the

Campbells had made when they were granted Kintyre in 1607 and Islay in 1613.

Campbell of Auchenbreck had been held as caution for the Earl of Argyll and, upon his release from prison, he was placed in command of the militia of Argyll and Tarbert. From the North, Campbell of Ardchattan dispatched news to the Privy Council that the people of Ardnamurchan and Lorn were greatly discouraged by rumours that now all of the island chiefs were preparing to rise against the government. Realizing their plans for utilising the island clans to defend the seaboard would not materialize, the Privy Council ordered out the militias of Ayr, Dumbarton, Renfrew, Bute, Inverness, Argyll, and Tarbert. The Marquis of Hamilton and the captain of Arran were charged with protecting that island from the MacDonalds and if necessary, the other island clans.

By the end of July, the king had decided it was prudent to rely wholly on the Earl of Argyll to pacify and civilize the Isles. The court declared that, in return for this service, all of the forfeited lands in Argyll and Kintyre would be given to the earl. Campbell of Ardkinglas and Lord Lorn, Argyll's eldest son, were ordered to raise militias from Cowal and Argyll.

Out of fear of a general rising in the Isles, the men of Argyll and Lorn, however, still hesitated to follow their leaders. Incredibly, even MacLean of Duart was again ordered to be ready in the event his forces were needed. This second order to MacLean indicates that the orders issued to the clans earlier in the month had not been obeyed. It was widely recognised in the Isles that the MacDonalds had only occupied their traditional lands and had not invaded Argyll, so the sympathies of the other island clans rested with them.

From our distant prospective, it seems incredible that the government was unaware of the views of the island chiefs. Indeed, the clans that the Privy Council were attempting to mobilise for the protection of the coast were the very clans which it worried were rising against it.

The Earl of Argyll arrived at Duntroon in early September of 1615. With him he brought four companies of professional soldiers and a lieutenancy which had been extended to all of the Western Isles.[17] Preparations were started for Argyll to begin his pacification of the Isles. As part of that provision, letters were sent out to the island chiefs advising them not to rest any of the fugitive MacDonalds.

That Sir Lauchlan MacKinnon received his letter about the 6th of October, once again indicates he and his clan may not have responded to the orders of July in which they were to take up defensive positions on the point of Ardnamurchan. If there were a general rising of island clans against the government, the MacKinnons were almost sure to have been with it.

Argyll, who now commanded some 2,000 men, a good part of them mercenaries, began military operations against the MacDonalds. In an effort to isolate Sir James on Kintyre, Argyll first attempted to capture or destroy the galleys on Cara.[18] However, the watchmen on Cara were warned of the danger when MacDonald of Largie's folk on the Kintyre Coast set signal fires ablaze. The escaping MacDonald galleys were hotly pursued by the Campbell fleet. Campbell of Lochnell followed Keppoch to Kintyre, while Cawder chased Sorley mac James to Islay. Shortly after scattering, but not capturing nor destroying the MacDonald galleys, the Earl of Argyll, with his chief lieutenants and some 800 men, moved toward Tarbert to join the militia waiting there under the command of Campbell of Auchenbreck.[19]

Events began to change quickly. Sir James had dispatched his uncle Ranald with 400 men to counter Auchenbreck's advance on Tarbert, but now realised this small force was not large enough to defend Kintyre against the Campbell onslaught. Sir James ordered a general retreat and the MacDonalds began to move southward. Campbell of Ardkinglas followed the retreat, but was not fast enough, and the bulk of the MacDonald army was evacuated to the safety of Rathlan Island. Once Kintyre was overrun, the Earl of Argyll ordered his entire force to move to Jura in preparation for the invasion of Islay.

Sir James, whose reorganised army had left Rathlan and had by now landed on Islay, was camped at Orsay near Portnahaven in the Rhinns of Islay. The leaders of the Clan

Donald do not appear to have expected an immediate Campbell invasion of Islay. When it did occur, and Argyll's force was united with that of Cawder, Sir James found his army outnumbered and, because of unfavourable winds, unable to escape.

Attempting to stall his inevitable defeat, Sir James asked Argyll for a four-day ceasefire, after which he would surrender. Argyll publicly agreed to the ceasefire but secretly had other plans. He ordered a 1,000-man seaborne expedition, led by Cawder and Captain Boswell, to capture Sir James and the other MacDonald leaders that night. Luckily for Sir James, there happened to be a full moon and the Campbell embarkation was witnessed by the people of the Oa of Islay. Sir James and his army, being warned by the signal fires lit along the coast, barely managed to escape.

Sir James, with one of his sons and several of his men managed to escape through Ireland to Spain. Many other MacDonalds were given refuge among their cousins in Antrim. Keppoch, with the MacAlisters and Mckays of Kintyre, found refuge in Lochaber. Unfortunately, as the various strongholds surrendered, other MacDonalds and their allies were tried for treason and executed.[20]

By January 1616, although the rebellion was officially over, many of the MacDonald leaders were still at large in the Hebrides. One of Sir James MacDonald's sons, and MacRuairi MacLeod, continued to command large bands of well-armed men. The Campbells were ordered to subdue the remaining MacDonalds and their allies as soon as possible.

Lord Gordon, Huntly's son, was likewise given a commission to clear the rebels from Lochaber and the districts surrounding Argyll. The inhabitants of Mull, Tyree, Morvern, Inverness, Banff, and Perth were all ordered to assist Lord Gordon against the fugitive MacDonalds. Mull and Tyree were inhabited mainly by MacKinnons and MacLeans, so it would be surprising if any of the inhabitants actually left home to chase fugitive MacDonalds through Lochaber. Even though the government offered a reward of 5,000 merks each for Keppoch and his son, either dead or alive, they were not captured.[21]

During July of 1616 the island chiefs again answered a summons to appear before the Privy Council in Edinburgh. MacKinnon, Clanranald, MacLeod, and the MacLeans of Duart, Coll, and Lochbuie made their initial appearance on the 11th of July. It seems that the only chief who was summoned and did not attend was MacDonald of Sleat.

Records indicate that it was due to sickness that MacDonald was excused. When he later regained his health, he ratified of all the obligations imposed by the council. The gathered chiefs were observed to be demoralised by the complete and unwarranted destruction of the Clan Ian Mor at the hands of the government and the resultant growth in the power of Clan Campbell. The Privy Council, taking advantage of the situation, moved quickly to assert its control over the disheartened Islanders. Ordering them to appear a second time, the council prepared new demands.

The second appearance before the council took place a couple of weeks later on the 26th of July. At this meeting the statutes agreed to on Iona were reviewed and strengthened. The new clauses added by the Privy Council were to forbid the chiefs from bearing arms under any circumstances and required the chiefs to free their lands of sorners and others without lawful occupation. They were also asked to agree to a set of *"Regulations of the Chiefs,"* which set out the behaviour the government wanted from the chiefs themselves.[22] These regulations demanded:

1. Annual provision of hostages. Sir Lauchlan agreed to produce his uncle Ewen.
2. The men of the chief's household were limited. MacKinnon was allowed three.
3. The chiefs were to reside in named houses and to supervise the cultivation of home farms. MacKinnon was to reside permanently at Kilmorie.
4. No chief was to maintain more than one berlinn.
5. Education of the chief's children; schools were to be established in every parish so that *"the Irishe language which is one of the chief and principall causis of the continwance of the barbaritie and incivilitie among isthe inhabitantis of the Iles and Heylandis, maybe abolisheitt and removit"*[23]
   Chiefs were to send all children over nine years of age to

be educated in the Lowlands and sons who had not received such schooling would not be allowed to succeed their fathers.
6. Limitations on the consumption of wine.
   MacKinnon was allowed one tun.
7. By martinmas next, they were to lease all of their lands except the home farms, to their tenants at fixed rents, not the vague traditional extractions,
8. The penalty for an infraction of these Statutes was set at 5,000 merks.

A measure of the loss of the ancient authority once held by the chiefs may be seen from two grants made to Sir Lauchlan MacKinnon by the Privy Council. He was granted a licence to shoot game within a mile of his house and given a royal charter to run ferry boats on the Kyle of Lochalsh.[24] Sir Lauchlan's father would no doubt have laughed at the arrogance of a Privy Council requiring him to have permission to hunt on his own land or dictating what he did with his boats.

The council also now asked the chiefs to answer for the behaviour of their clansmen. Sir Lauchlan MacKinnon was put in the position of having to name the following members of his clan as being in rebellion and disobedient and for whom he would not answer; Donald reagh M've Tearligh, Eane McTarliche ve Coneill, Angus McConeill ve Neill, Donald McNeill gurme and John Roy McTarlighe.

The Edinburgh meeting ended with the usual formalities. Sir Lauchlan MacKinnon became surety for MacLean of Coll. MacLean of Duart and his younger brother, Lauchlan, were slow in producing sureties so were detained in Edinburgh Castle until they could be arraigned.[25] Before departing, the chiefs agreed to appear before the council on the 10th of July every year from then onward. Before leaving Edinburgh, it appears the chiefs had also agreed to meet in Glasgow, on the way home, to settle some private business. The next month, on the 24th of August, Sir Lauchlan MacKinnon; Sir Ruairi MacLeod; Donald, Captain of Clanranald; and MacLean of Coll all met in Glasgow and signed a bond of friendship.[26]

The chiefs' next appearance before the Privy Council did not take place on the 10th of July as agreed in 1616.

Instead, the 1617 meeting took place on the 27th of July--some 17 days later. The delay may not have been caused by the chiefs, but rather to accommodate the king who happened to be in Edinburgh at this time. The chiefs who attended were: Sir Lauchlan MacKinnon; Sir Rauiri MacLeod of Dunvegan; Donald Gorm of Sleat; Sir Donald, Captain of Clanranald; Hector MacLean of Lochbuie; Lauchlan MacLean of Coll; and Lauchlan MacLean, younger brother of Duart.

Sir Lauchlan MacKinnon presented his uncle Ewen as the hostage demanded by the *"Regulations of the chiefs,"* but it does not appear that Ewen had been held in Edinburgh. At this appearance the only business required of the chiefs seems to be to have been for them to agree to the abolition of the practice of Calp.

In spite of the insistence of the government and agreement by the chiefs in 1616 to halt the practise of Calp, it continued to be practised on Skye for several hundred years. After the appearance before the Privy Council, King James knighted Donald Gorm and some of the other chiefs *"with great solemnitie, in the palace of Holyrudhous."*

King James had not made the journey north from London to interview the island chiefs. He came to meet with the clergy in Edinburgh and to authorise a general assembly so that his five articles of faith could be accepted by the Scottish Kirk. When these were rejected, he returned to London, nourishing a distain for the Scottish Presbyterians, which only widened the growing gulf between King James and his subjects in Scotland.

Sir Lauchlan, who appears to have not been married at this time, was concerned with the disposition of the clan lands in the event that he should die before he fathered an heir. To ensure the estates remained intact and in MacKinnon possession, Sir Lauchlan named Neil MacKinnon, the 16-year-old son of his brother, John Og, as his heir presumptive.[27]

Although the Hebrides now remained quiet, the government continued to summon the island chiefs to Edinburgh. During their appearance in July of 1619, the chiefs requested the date for subsequent meetings be changed from July to February. This change was apparently made in 1621, but it was changed back to July because of the uncertainty of the weather conditions during the spring.

Sir Lauchlan MacKinnon, along with most of the other chiefs, excepting only Hector MacLean of Duart, made these appearances with a tolerable regularity. At the meeting of July 1619, one of the two sons of Tearlach Skeanach accompanied Sir Lauchlan MacKinnon and his uncle Ewen. When Sir Lauchlan appeared before the Privy Council two years later in 1621, the same nephew once again appeared with him.

On June 21, 1621, there is a notice of Neil MacKinnon's resignation of the lands he held from the Earl of Argyle in favour of his son Neil.[28] We cannot be sure of the identity of the individual in question, nor of the location of the land transferred. However, this record does show that as early as seventeenth century some MacKinnons still held lands and farms from chiefs other than their own. It was common during this period for tenant farmers in the Isles to move about in an effort to find farms at reasonable rent.

The common method of transferring ownership of any amount of land between individuals in the feudal system then practised in Scotland involved the legal resignation of the land to a feudal superior. In this instance Neil MacKinnon would have surrendered all of his charters for the lands in question to the Earl of Argyll as his feudal superior. The Campbell chief would then have issued new charters to the grantee, Neil younger.

End Notes
Chapter 18

1. *Collectanea de Rebus Albanicis*, Iona Club, Stevenson, Edinburgh 1847, 153.

2. 'Handfasted' was a traditional form of irregular marrage. If no children were born to the couple they were free to disolve the union after a year and a day.

3. It has been suggested that this ship was in the wine trade and that young MacNeil took the wine.

4. Roderick MacNeil was forfeit in 1610, probably for the help he gave to the MacLeods against the Lewis settlers. Sir Roderick MacKenzie of Kintail became the superior of Barra and its Isles. He granted them back to Roderick on a payment of 60 merks annually. In 1655 Sir George MacKenzie of Tarbit was served heir to the Barony of Barray. In 1700 MacNeil of Barra held his lands from MacDonald of Sleat on payment annually of £40 and a hawk, as well as men if they were required.

5. *NLS-MS* 2134, Vol 275, fol. 201, Dec. 18th 1612. "*Action Sir Dougall Campbell of Auchenbreck, Cessioner & Assignee to the inhabitants of the Isles of Myngala, Bargera, Phappa, Sandra & Vattersa, Agt. Hector MacLean of Duart, Dunslav McQuarrie of Ulva, Lauchlan McKinnon of Strathsworradale, Allan MacLean of Ardtornish, Lauchlan MacLean of Colla, and Lauchlan MacLean of Cleat, Allan Beisker MacLean of Auchalmayne, Neil Oig McLean of Kilmoree in Rum, for spoilations committed in April of 1610".*

6. Cameron, A., *The History and Traditiona of the Isle of Skye*, E. Forsyth, Inverness, 1871, 66.

7. MacLeod, R. C., *The Book of Dunvegan I*, Spalding Club, 1939, 52. See Appendix 20.

8. This part of the confused series of risings by the Clan Ian Mor were underaken with three goals: the first goal was to keep the island of Islay out of the hands of Sir Ranald MacDonald of Dunluce; the second goal was to preserve the clan lands from being taken by the Campbells; and

the third goal was to recover the lands they had lost earlier during the struggle.

9. See Gregory, *History of the Western Highlands & Isles*, William Tait, Edinburgh, 1834, 349, for details of Campbell intrigue in this instance.

10. This was the period of the greatest Campbell expansion with several recent land grants by the king making Argyll feudal superior of:

Iona   Feb 1607   formerly belonged to the Bishop of the Isles

Kintyre   May 1607   formerly belonged to MacDonalds of Dunnyveg

Locheil   July 1608 formerly belonged to MacLean of Duart

Ardnamurchan   June 1610 formerly belonged to MacDonald of Claranald

Islay   Jan 1613   used as collateral for a loan given by the Earl of Argyll to Angus MacDonald of Dunnyveg. Even though the loan had been repaid, Campbell continued to press his claim on Islay.

11. The orders were issued April 26, 1615. The Privy Council had certainly misjudged the ease with which it could deprive the MacDonalds of their ancestral lands.

12. Alastair mac Ranald of Keppoch had two sons, Ranald og and Donald Glas, both who seem to have been involved against the Campbells.

13. The MacLeans were led by Allan, the chief's brother. The Privy Council was concerned by the numbers of very high-ranking clansmen from all over the Hebrides who were rallying to the banners of Sir James MacDonald.

14. Campbell, A., *History of the Clan Campbell*, The Bath Press, Bath 2000, Vol. 2, 166.

15. Ibid 167.

16. MacPhail, *Highland Papers,* Vol. 3, T. & A. Constable, Edinburgh, 1920, 241. See Appendix 21.
This letter was likely written on MacLeod discovering that Colkitto, with about 3 score men, had hidden on his island of St. Kilda after the escape from Dunnyveg. The MacDonalds stayed on MacLeod's island for the month of April before sailing on to Ireland in early May.

17. The Privy Council was so concerned about the affairs in the Highlands and Islands, that Argyll's lieutenancy was extended over all of Scotland if he were in pursuit of fugitives.

18. The attacking force, led by MacDougall of MacDougall, and MacDougall of Raray, with the Campbells of Lochnell, Cawder and Barbrech/Lochawe, contained some 800 men. Part of this fleet pursued Colkitto who, with three galleys, was sailing to reconnoitre in the vicinity of West Tarbert but instead stumbled on the Campbell fleet off Gigha island. The bulk of the Campbell fleet continued on to Cara Island.

19. The names of Argyll's lieutenants give an indication of the makeup of his army: Captain Boswell; Robert Campbell, Captain of Dunoon; Colin Campbell of Kirkmicheal; Campbell of Ardkinglas; Lamont of Lamont; and MacLauchlan of that Ilk

20. Hector MacLean of Duart was called to account for his brother and other kinsmen's support for the MacDonalds. Allan MacLean and Hector Roy MacLean of Coll appeared before the Privy Council to submit and swear allegiance to the king. Both were released when sureties were found for them, and they were permitted to return home.

21. Two years later in July 1618, because Keppoch and his son were still at large, a commission of fire and sword was issued against them to McIntosh. When McIntosh attempted to execute his commission, Lord Gordon was so offended that he used his influence at court to have McIntosh's commission withdrawn. However, by this time Keppoch and his son, Donald Glas, had joined Sir James MacDonald and the other rebel leaders in Spain. Keppoch's eldest son, Ranald, stayed concealed in Lochaber and there was a commission given to Lord Gordon to find and execute him in 1621. But as Keppoch was a vassal of Huntly's, it is unlikely Lord Gordon's commission was too eagerly pursued. In 1620 Sir James MacDonald and Keppoch would be recalled to London. Sir James would be granted a pension of 1000 merks and Keppoch granted a pension of 200 merks. The king granted them both a remission for their crimes.

22. Gregory, *History of the Western Highlands & Isles*, William Tait, Edinburgh, 1836, 393-395 & Rev. MacKinnon, D. D., *Memoirs of Clan Fingon*, Lewis Hepworth, Tunbridge Wells, 1899, 27.

23. Stevenson, D. , *Alasdair MacColla and the Highland Problem in the 17th Century*, John Donald, Edinburgh, 1980, 47.

24. Sillar, F. C., &. Meyler, R. M., *Skye*, David Charles, Devon, 1973, 83. The charter gave Lauchlan permission to run the ferry from the year 1616 until 1629. The charter was renewed in 1629. We do not know the period for which the charter was renewed. It is likely, however, that it would have run for another fourteen or fifteen years.

25- MacLean of Duart was released on surety of £40,000 of his own money and 500 merks pledged by his father-in-law, Acheson of Gosford. Duart's brother, Lauchlan, was held until the next year, when he produced a bond for both himself and his son.

26. MacLeod, R. C., *The Book of Dunvegan I*, Spalding Club, 1939, 48. See Appendix 22.

27. MacKinnon, J., *The Mackinnons of Kyle and Other Connections*, Longformacus, 1981.

28. MacLeod, R. C., *The Book of Dunvegan I*, Spalding Club, 40.

Appendix 1

Measurement systems

MacFirbis noted that Airbertach of Lorn *"Inhabited 12 treba among the Norse Greagrwghe of the warrior called Mull, and Tiree and Cruibhinis"*

The unit of measurement, the treba given above is now thought to refer to the tirunga shown in the chart below. The area of a piece of land in either the Lowlands or the Highlands was determined by the maintenance it was capable of supplying its owner and was not a set of standard dimensions. Scotland has used a number of measuring systems. Each system was introduced by a resident race and used in conjunction with the other systems.

The Angles and Saxons in the South East of Scotland used the *Oxengate* and *Plowgate* measures. These became the standard measures in the South

1oxengate=13acres   2 oxengates=husbandland
2 husbandlands=20shillingland   4 husbandland=1 plowgate or about 104 acres

The East of Scotland used the Celtic *davoch* and the Saxon *oxengate* system
             1 davoch=4 plowgates which was the unit of a barony

In Lowland charters land area was also commonly expressed by its rental value.

Central Highlands and Islands used the Celtic *davoch* which was divided it into the Norse *merk* and *pennylands*:
                           1 davoch=10 merkland=20Pennyland

It has been determined by examination of ancient charters that the following common units were equivalent;

Gaelic	Rental	Norse	Norse	Celtic	Saxon
1 Tirunga	133s.4d	10 merks	20d land	1 davoch	4 Plowgates
1 Ceathramh	33s.4d	2½ merks	5d	¼ davoch	
1 Ochdamh	16s.8d	1¼ merks	2½d	⅛ davoch	1 Plowgate
1 Leothas	8s.4d	⅝ merks	1¼d		
1 Cota-ban	4s.2d				1 Husbandland
1 Dha Sgillin	2s.1d				1 Oxengate

From the above charts it may be seen that Airbertach of Lorn would have been a man of considerable stature, holding the equivalent of some 12 Lowland baronies.

Appendix 2

Some stories of Skye dating from about the Viking period

The last stand of the Norse proper on Skye is said to have been at Blar a Bhuailte *"field of the stricken."* Both sides, knowing the battle was to be decisive, fought with determination. At last the leader of the Norse was killed and they were forced to retreat to their ships for safety. One Norse warrior, named Arco Brannmhor, with a small party of men decided to stay on Skye. They made their home in the an old Columban monastery located on an island in a loch. One of the local chiefs, when he determined to be rid of the Norse, promised a warrior named MacSween that, in exchange for Arco's head, he would be given the land of Braes near Protree. MacSween, realizing that an attack on the fort would fail decided to resort to trickery. Disguised as a storyteller MacSween was rowed to Arco's fort in the middle of the loch. Telling stories until Arco fell asleep, MacSween then pulled a dirk from under his rags and stabbed Arco to death. MacSween, who escaped by boat with Arco's head rushed to the home of the chief who hired him. MacSween was duly given the Braes, which remained in his family for many generations.

Pirates and private raiding parties continued to plague the islands for many years. When a Norse longship appeared off the Coast of Kilmuir on Skye, the local chief recruited a young archer to defeat the raiders. On the promise of a much coveted horse, the archer took the challenge. The young warrior then taking a good position near the coast, waited for the raiders to land. Taking careful aim, the archer was able to shoot the pirate leaders as they jumped ashore. Not wanting to share the fate of their leaders, the survivors quickly put back to sea never to return.

In a story related by Col. Lachie Robertson, the village of Elgol on the Strathaird peninsula was the site of a famous sea battle between local people and the Viking crew of a ship called the Swan. The captain of the Swan was killed during the battle but the fate of the crew in unknown. The ship evidently mourned the loss of her master, however, as the name Elgol is a corruption of the Gaelic for weeping Swan. In another version of this tale, Vortigern sent a fleet of five ships under the command of a Captain named Alla, to explore the western Isles. Alla was not welcomed by the people of Skye. The Picts and Scots are said to have joined together in gathering their ships and intercepted him at the mouth of Loch Scavaig. A fierce battle was fought in which the foreign ships were driven off. The name of their captain is, however, enshrined in the first syllable of Elgol.

Appendix 3

The Murder of Gillibride MacKinnon

These two brothers made a considerable figure during the reigns of Robert II.and III. The prominence of their father, as well as their own affable behavior and pleasing manners, gained for them the friendship of John, First Lord of the Isles, in so much so, that it excited the jealousy of the courtiers, among whom the chief of MacKinnon, the master of the household, became a most inveterate enemy. In order to accomplish his revenge, or satiate his jealousy, he determined to cut the brothers off by taking their lives while they were hunting with Lord John. Having been warned of MacKinnon's designs, the brothers easily thwarted his plans.

Shortly afterward, MacDonald (Lord of the Isles) started on some expedition from his castle, Aros in Mull (would it sound better to say - from Castle Aros in Mull) to the mainland, intending to remain for a season at his castle of Ardtornish in Morvern. MacKinnon, having been unavoidably detained, was to follow after, but, meeting the two brothers, he renewed the quarrel between them. Both parties were well armed, and had their retainers. In the affray which took place, MacKinnon was killed while in the act of mounting into his galley, and his followers dispersed. Skene calls this "one of the most daring actions which has ever been recorded of any Highland chief." His version, however, is somewhat different from the above.

Not knowing how the Lord of the Isles would take the death of the master of his household, they resolved to apply heroic measures, and keep, by force, that friendship which they thought might now be forfeited. They now proceeded to follow up their act by one still more daring. Immediately they They immediately manned MacKinnon's galley with their own men, and started in pursuit of John, whom they overtook a short distance from Ardtornish. They captured his vessel and carried him prisoner to one of the Garvelloch Islands. Here he was detained until he solemnly promised them to remain their true friend. Not satisfied with this, they conveyed him to the island of Iona and placed him on the Black Stone, which was held sacred in those days and used to confirm binding agreements. There he vowed indemnity, not only for the death of MacKinnon, but also for the violence done his own person.

He also moreover, obligated himself to give his daughter, Margaret, in marriage to Lachlan and would use his influence with MacLeod of Lewis to obtain the hand of a daughter of that chief for his brother Hector. Still Lachlan was not satisfied, for he demanded of the captive chief: "I shall have your daughter," said he, "yet it is but meet you should give her a dowery." "Speak out and let me hear the price of your demands," said MacDonald. "Eniskir with its isles," replied Lachlan. This was promised him, as well as voluntarily appointing him lieutenant-general in war, and gave to him and his posterity the right hand of all the clans in battle, which was never once disputed with them.

Appendix 4

Treaty between MacDougall of Lorn & MacDonald of the Isles

Anno Domini m ccc quinquagesimo quarto in nativitatc Beate Marie Virginis apud Iwon scl:" facta fuit lice conventio et interposita inter nobles viros Johannem De Yle dominum Insularum ex una parte et Joannem de Larin dominum Ergadie ex altera super quibus defenderunt et finaliter concordarunt. Inprimis predictus Joannes de Larin concedit et quietum clamat cum fusto et baculo omne jus et clameum quod habuit vel habet seu habere poterit Joanni De Yle domino Insularum de omnibus terris castris et insulin cum pertinenciis suis inferius nominandis de quibus dictus Joannes De Yle incartatus per dominum David vcl dominum Robertum . . . patrem ejusdem Reges Scotie videlicet castra de Kerneburch et Hvstylburch cum omnibus insulis suis t juribus totam insulam') de Mule cum omnibus suis pertinenciis t castrum de Dunconill cum omnibus pertinenciis suis t insulis superiore parte' de Duray cum suis pertinenciis insulam de Tereyd cum omnibus pertinenciis suis t libertatibus exceptis terris infrascriptis videlicet insula de Colic cum omnibus suis pertinenciis t tribus unciatis tcrris de Tereyd que propinquiores sunt terre de Colic demptis terris liberis ecclesiarum de Durobwar t Glencowan cum omnibus suis pertinenciis quas terris t insulam cum omnibus suis justis pertinenciis t consuetudinibus aut exaccionibus quibuscunque idem Joannes De Yle dominus Insularum dat concedit t per presentes confirmat absque calumpnia vel repetitione seu clameo aliquo a predicto Joanne vel heredis suis in perpetuum predicto Joanni de Larin libere et pacifice' possidendas. Item ordinatum est quiscunque fuerit sent in predictis tribus unciatis ter-re de Tereyd ex parte' Johannis de Larin non faciet domesticaturam seu habitaculum in predicta insula sine licentia predicti Johannis De Yle. Item concordatum est inter predictos nobiles quod semper de etero ex nunc sint carnales fratres t compatres singuli alterius commodum respicientes liceat enim eidem Johanni de Larin componere seu fabricare octo naves que snit de numero xvi remorum vel xii remorum in sua debita forma t quantitate. Insuper ordinatum est inter predictos nobiles quod Joannes de Larin dabit Joanni De Yle tres obsides in manu sua dunce habuerit castrum de Kerneburch sibi deliberatum viz unum filium legitimum Lachlani filii Alexandri t alium filium Iegitimum Ywari M'Lulli et filium legitimum Johanni M'Molmari vel alterius boni parentela sua. Item Johannes De Yle obligat se quod nunquam impetrabit nec capiet literas donum vel infeodacionem a quoque rege vel custode regni Scocie super predictis terris per ipsum concessis eider]) Johanni de Larin. Item concordat est inter predictos quod ideal Johannes De Yle nunquam insurget ad guerram contra Johannem de Larin per se vel per alium vel alterum auxilium dabit cum quacunque persona vivente presente vel futuro excepta persona Regis Scocie simili modo idem Johannes de

Larin se obligat Johanni De Yle. Concordatum est quod Johannes De Yle nunquam dabit custodiam castri de Kerneburch ulli de nacione clan Fynwyne Item conventum est quod quiscunque fecerit vel perpetraverit homicidium ex premeditata nesquiscia inter predictos nobiles exilio ab utroquc specialiter deputtur. Item si quis a retinentia unius ad retinentia alterius propter malefacta sua procedere voluerit ab altero non admittatur nisi de suis transgressionibus justicie complementum voluerit exhibere. Et ad omnia ista t premissorum singula fideliter observanda tactis Dei evangeliis ac diversis aliis sanctontm reliquiis ct sanctuariis corporalia prestiterunt juramcnta. Parti vero hujus indenture remanenti penes Johannem de Larin sigillum Johannis De Yle est appensum parti vero remanenti penes Johannem De Yle sigillum Johannis de Larin est appensum. Datum die t loco t anno supradictis.

(1) John of Lorn quit claims to John of the Isles lands, islands and castles for which John of the Isles had charters from King David or King Robert, his father viz. Cairn na Bergh More and Cairn na Bergh Beg, the island of Mull, Dun Chonnuill, the islands of the upper part of Jura, and the island of Tiree, except the island of Coll, three unciates of land of Tiree nearest Coll (subtracting the free land of the churches of Duror and Glencoe) which island and lands John of the Isles grants to John of Lorn.

(2) Whoever is Lorn's steward in the Tiree: lands shall not make a dwelling there without leave from John of the Isles.

(3) They will act as brothers and John of Lorn will have the right to build eight vessels of I6 or 12 oars.

(4) John of Lorn will give three hostages to John of the Isles until the castle of Cairn na Burgh More is handed over.

(5) John of the Isles obliges himself to accept no letters, gift or feu from any king or guardian of Scotland over the said lands conceded to John of Lorn.

(6) They will not rise in war against each other with anyone but the King of Scotland.

(7) John of the Isles undertakes never to give custody of Cairn na Burgh More to any member of the clan Fynwyne (MacKinnon).

(8) Anyone doing murder will he exiled by both.

(9) Wrongdoers will not be allowed to transfer from the retinue of one party to the other unless willing to answer for his wrongdoings. 'Iwon sele', 8 September 1354.

Appendix 5

Documents and Commentaries Relating to Iona

Reg. Aven. 141, fol. 50v.
COMMISSION to the BISHOP OF DUNKELD
to provide an Abbot for the Monastery of Hy, 22nd March 1358-9
Gratis

Venerabili fratri Johanni Episcopo Dunkelden. salutem, etc. Attenta meditatione pensantes dispendia et incomoda que interdum incurrunt ex vacatione diutina ecclesie et monasteria gubernatoris presidio destituta reddimur mente vigiles et solertes ut eadem ecclesie et monasteria et presertim Romane ecclesie immediate subjecta ab incommodis hujusmodi preserventur nostreque diligentie studio de celeris ac utilis provisionis remedio succurratur eisdem : Cum itaque monasterium Sancte Columbe de Hy dicte Romane ecclesie immediate subjectum ordinis Sancti Benedicti Sodoren. diocesis per obitum quondam Petri Abbatis dicti monasterii qui extra Romanam curiam diem clausit extremum vacaverit et vacet ad presens licet per dilectum filium Fyningonum Bricii monachum qui falso se gerit pro abbate ipsius monasterii detineatur indebite occupatum : Nos cupientes eidem monasterio ne diuturne vacationis detrimenta sustineat de persona ydonea celeriter et utiliter provideri fraternitati tue de qua in hiis et aliis spccialcm in Domino fiduciam obtinemus per apostolica scripta mandamus quatenus si vocatis dicto Fyningono et aliis qui fuerint evocandi rectius inveneris ita esse de aliqua persona dicti ordinis ad hujusmodi regimen utili et ydonea super quo tuam conscientiam oneramus eidem monasterio auctoritate nostra provideas ac hujusmodi personam de qua ipsi monasterio providebis eidem monasterio preficias in Abbate curam et administrationem ipsius monasterii sibi in spiritualibus et temporalibus amoto exinde
dicto Fyningono plenarie committendo sibique faciendo a suis subditis reverentiam et obedientiam debitam exhiberi contradictores per censuram ecciesiasticam appellatione postposita compescendo et insuper eidem persone de qua dicto monasterio providebis munus benedictionis impendas vel per alium antistitem gratiam et communionem apostolice sedis habentem impendi facias : Volumus autem quod tu si impenderis seu idem antistes qui impendet munus predictum ab ea persona cui munus ipsum impensum fuerit recipias seu recipiat nostro et dicte ecclesie Romane nomine fidelitatis debite solitum juramentum juxta formam quam sub bulla nostra mittimus interclusam ac formam juramenti quod eadem persona prestabit nobis per ipsius persone patentes litteras ejusque sigillo signatas per proprium nuncium quam tocius destinari procures sell procuret. Datum Avinione xi Kalendas Aprilis anno septimo.

Commentary

Since the monastery of St. Columba of Hy, O.S.B., Sodor diocese, immediately subject to the Roman Church, has become void by the death, outwith the Roman Court, of Peter, late Abbot of said monastery and is void at present, although detained in unlawful occupation by Fyningonus, son of Brice, monk, who falsely bears himself as Abbot, we, desiring a fit person to be provided speedily and advantageously to the said monastery and reposing special faith in you, give you mandate by apostolic writings that if, having summoned the said Fyningonus and others who ought to be summoned, you find the foregoing to be true, you provide by our authority a fit person of said order to said monastery and set him over the rule and administration thereof in spiritualities and temporalities, removing Fyningonus, causing due obedience to the Abbot to be given by the subjects, and suppressing contradictors by ecclesiastical censure without appeal; and that you bestow blessing upon the Abbot whom you provide, or cause the same to be bestowed by some other priest in communion with the Apostolic See ; and that you, or the other priest whom you may depute, receive the Abbot's due and accustomed oath of fidelity according to the form which we send under our bull ; and cause the Abbot to send the form of oath by his letters patent under his seal, as soon as possible

Reg. Aven. 304, fol. 523.
CONFIRMATION of the Election of Fingon, Abbot of IIy,
21st October 1397

Rubric :—Fingonio Abbati monasterii de IIy Sodorensis diocesis electio et confirmacio de co ad dictum monasterium et munus benedictionis ei facte approbantur et al) ipso omnis infamie macula per cum certa de causa contracta abolatur.

x
x

1e camera. Jo. de Neapoli.   x

A. Dialect filio Fingonio Abbati monasterii de IIy ordinis Sancti Benedicti Sodorensis diocesis salntem etc. Gerentes ill votis ut status ecclesiarum et monasteriorum omnium et personarum cis presidentium salubriter dirigatur, Illa libenter concedimus que ad hec fore conspicimus oportuna : Exhibita siquidem nobis pro parte tua petitio continebat quod dudum quadraginta Lanni elapsi sunt vel circiter monasterium de Hy ordinis Sancti Bcnedicti Sodorensis diocesis tune per liberam resignationem quondam Petri ipsius monasterii Abbatis in manibus dilectorum filiorum conventus ejnsdem extra Romanam curiam sponte factam et per cosdem conventum ad eos dicti monasterii resignacionis recepcio de antiqua et approbata et hactenus pacifice observata consuetudine pertineat extra eandem curiam admissam vacans dicti conventus te monachum dicti monasterii ordinem ipsum expresse professum et in presbiteratus ordinem constitutum in eorum et dicti monasterii abbatem concorditer elegerunt tuque electioni hujusmodi illius tibi presentato decreto consenciens obtinuisti cam a bone memorie Wilelmo Episcopo Sodoren. auctoritate ordinaria confirmari, Et deinde per eundem Episcopum tibi munus benedictionis impendi canonice nisi apostolice reservaciones obstarent ac possessionem pacificam administrationis bonorum ipsius monasterii fuisti assecutus et monasterium ipsum extune registi prout regis de presenti : Cum autem sicut eadem pctitio subjngebat tu dubites monasterium ipsum tempore resignationis electionis et confirmation is hujusmodi fuisse dispositioni apostolice specialiter vel generaliter reservatum et propterea electionem et confirmationem hujusmodi viribus non subsistere pro parte tua nobis fuit humiliter supplicatum ut tibi ac too et predicti monasterii statui super premissis providere de benignitate apostolica dignaremur : Nos igitur attendentes grandium virtutum merita quiffs ut fidedignorum testimonio accepimus personam tuam altissimus insignivit ac volentes te meritorum ipsorum intuitu favore prosequi gratie specialis]hujusmodi supplicationibus inclinati omnem inhabilitatis et infamie maculam sive notam per te premissorum occasione contractam apostolica auctoritate penitus abolemus tibique concedimus quod electio et confirmacio de te facte ut prefertur et quecunque inde secuta a data presencium valeant et plenam roboris firmitatem obtineant perinde ac si tempore resignationis electionis et confirmationis predictarum prefatum monasterium dispositioni apostolice specialiter vel generaliter quomodolibet reservatum non extitisset et insuper hujusmodi muneris benedictionis impensionem et ea qie circa administrationem dicti monasterii medic) tempore alias tamen rite per te gesta stint eadem auctoritate ratificamus et eciam approbamus coiistitiitionibus apostolicis ac statutis et consuctudinibus monasterii et ordinis predictorum juramento confirmacione apostolica vel quacumque firmitate ilia roboratis contrariis non obstantibus quibuscumque : Nulli ergo etc. nostre abolicionis concessionis ratificacionis et approbacionis infringere etc. Datum Avinione xii Kal. Novembris anno quarto. Expedita iiii Idus Novembris anno quarto,

P. de Valle. Tradita parti ii Idus Novembris anno quarto, P. bouqueys [sic].

Commentary

To Fingon, Abbot of the monastery of Hy, Order of St. Benedict, Sodor diocese, greeting. A petition laid before us on your behalf contained that forty years ago or thereabout, on the voidance of the monastery of Hy, O.S.B., Sodor diocese, by the free resignation made by the late Abbot Peter in the hands of the convent, outwith the Roman court, and admitted by the said convent (to whom the reception of the resignation pertained by old, approved and hitherto peaceably observed custom), the convent unanimously elected you, monk of said monastery, professed of the Order and in priest's orders, to the abbacy of the said monastery; and you, consenting to the said election, obtained confirmation from William Bishop of Sodor of happy memory by ordinary authority : and that then you had yourself blessed by the said Bishop canonically (but for apostolic reservations), and obtained peaceable administration of the goods of the monastery and ruled from that time, as you do at present. But since (as the petition added) you fear that at the time of the foresaid resignation, election and confirmation the monastery was specially or generally reserved to apostolic disposition and that therefore the election and confirmation are not valid, it was petitioned on your behalf that we would take thought for you and the monastery. We therefore, and by apostolic authority, absolve you from all stain of inhability and infamy contracted by reason of the above, and grant that your election and confirmation and all the consequences be valid and binding from the date of these presents in all respects as if at the time of the foresaid resignation, election and confirmation the monastery had not been generally or specially reserved to apostolic disposition.

Reg. Aven. 319, fol. 711.
COMMISSION to hear complaints against FINGONUS, Abbot of Iona,
with authority to depose him, 26th August 1405

V. G. pro Domino Vicecancellario.x

Benedictus etc. Venerabilibus fratribus Glasguen. et Dunkelden. Episcopis salutem et apostolicam benedictionem. Nuper ad nostrum dilecto filio Johanne Goffredi priore claustrali monasterii Yensis ordinis Sancti Benedicti Sodorensis diocesis nobis refferente pervenit auditum quod dilectus filius Fingonus 1 Abbas dicti monasterii quamdam mulierem publice in concubinam multis temporibus tenuit et ex ea plures filios et filias procreavit ipsosque concubinamfilios et filias de bonis ejusdem monasterii enutrivit ac tres ex ipsis filiabus maritavit et magnam dotem de bonis predictis eis constituit atque dedit et tam propterea quam alias diversimode bona predicta dilapidavit et edificia predicti monasterii corrui permisit ac alias monasterium ipsum usque ad valorem quadringentarum marcharum argenti dampnificavit et dampnificabit fortius in futurum nisi super hoc eidem monasterio de salubri remedio suecuratur : Nos igitur nolentes sicut nec velle debemus premissa si veritate nitantur conniventibus oculis pertransire fraternitati vestre de qua in hiis et aliis specialem in Domino fiduciam obtinemus per apostolica scripta committimus et mandamus quatenus vocatis dicto Abbate et aliis qui fuerint evocandi super premissis omnibus et singulis auctoritate nostra inquiratis diligentius veritatem et si per inquisitionem hujusmodi prefatum abbatem reppereritis culpabilem in premissis vel aliquo eorumdem quod ad deposicionem ipsius sufficiat eundem abbatem ab administratione bonorum predicti monasterii auctoritate predicta deponatis prout de jure fuerit faciendum, contradictores per censuram ecclesiasticam appellatione postposita compescendo, non obstantibus tam felicis recordationis Bonifacii Pape viii. predecessoris nostri in quibus cavetur ne aliquos extra suam civitatem et diocesim nisi in certis exceptis casibus ac in illis ultra unam dietam a fine sue diocesis ad judicium evocetur, seu ne judices a sede apostolica deputati aliquos ultra unam dietam a fine dioces. eorumdem trahere presumant et de duabus dietis in Concilio Generali quam aliis constitutionibus apostolicis contrariis quibuseumque seu si eidem Abbati vel quibusvis aliis communiter vel divisim a sede apostolica sit indultum quod interdici suspendi vel excommunicari non possit per literas apostolicas non facientes plenam et expressam ac de verbo ad verbum de indulto hujusmodi mencionem. Datum Janue vii Kalendas Septembris pontificatus nostri anno undecimo. Expedita iiii Kalendas Octobris anno undecimo, H. de Spina.

Commentary

Lately the report has been brought to us by John Goffredi, claustral prior of the monastery of Iona, O.S.B., Sodor diocese, that Fingon, Abbot of said monastery, has for a long time maintained a certain woman publicly as his concubine, and has had several sons and daughters by her, and has nurtured the said concubine, sons and daughters out of the goods of the said monastery, and has married three of his daughters with a large dowry from the foresaid goods; and that he has moreover dilapidated the same in many other ways and has allowed the monastery buildings to become ruinous, and otherwise has damaged the monastery to the value of 500 marks of silver, and will damage it further in future unless remedy be found. We therefore, being unwilling to allow such things to go on if they be true, and reposing special faith in you, give you mandate by apostolic writings that, having summoned the said Abbot and all who ought to be summoned, you enquire diligently into all and sundry the foregoing, and if you find the said Abbot to be culpable in the same or any part thereof, that you depose him from the administration of the goods of the monastery (as ought of right to be done), repressing contradictors by apostolic censure without appeal; notwithstanding the constitutions of Pope Boniface viii forbidding anyone to be summoned in judgement outwith his city and diocese unless in certain excepted cases, and then not more than one day's journey from the border of their diocese and two days' journey in General Council; and notwithstanding whatsoever other apostolic constitutions in the contrary.

Reg. Suppliche 151, fol. 126 verso.
Martin v. Prothonotarius de Branc.
(In margin) Dispensatio.

Beatissime pater Cum monasterium de Hy-insula ordinis Sancti Benedicti Sodorensis diocesis per continuos guerrarum fremitus in partibus insulanis regno Scocie subiectis hactenus vigentes in edificiis et redditibus adeo collapsum destructum et depauperatum miserabiliter existit quod dicti monasterii monachi super eiusdem redditibus vivere et monasterium ipsum reparare ac hospitalitatem quam ipsos iuxta illarum consuetudinem parcium eciam invite exhibere oporteat tenere nullatenus valeant nisi per vestre sanctitatis clemenciam eorum necessitatibus misericorditer provideatur Supplicat ergo sanctitati vestre devotus eiusdem sanctitatis orator Fyngonius presbiter monachus expresse professus et prior claustralis dicti monasterii quatenus secum ut in dictorum gravaminum relevamen parrochialem ecclesiam aut parrochialis ecclesie perpetuam vicariam si sibi alias canonice conferatur licite de sui abbatis licencia recipere et libere retinere necnon super defectu natalium quem patitur de presbitero genitus et soluta ut huiusmodi parrochialem ecclesiam et perpetuam vicariam ac sui ordinis beneficia curata administrationes officia prioratus ac dignitates etiam abbatiales si sibi alias canonice conferantur seu ad ilia eligatur defectu predicto non obstante licite recipere et libere retinere valeat dignemini misericorditer dispensare Regulis statutis et consuetudinibus sue professionis ac constitutionibus et ordinacionibus apostolicis ceterisque in contrarium editis non obstantibus quibuscumque cum clausulis oportunis. Fiat ut petitur de consensu et dispensatione O.

Datum Rome apud Sanctumpetrum nonis Decembris anno quinto (5 Dec. 1421).

Commentary

WHEREAS [in the circumstances stated supra] the Monastery of Hy and the monks thereof are in great necessity, the presbyter Fyngonius, professed monk and prior claustral of the said monastery, prays that he may be permitted to hold a parish church or perpetual vicarage if such he can obtain, and that notwithstanding the defect of his birth as the son of a priest and an unmarried woman.

Granted, 5 Decr. 1421.

Reg. Later. 406. 1448-4. An. iii. Eug. iv. Fol. 112 v.)
*PAPAL MANDATE to the Bishop Of Ossero to inquire into certain matters
relating to the*
Monastery of St. Columba, in Iona, with powers. 8th Jan. 1443-4.

Eugenius etc. Venerabili Fratri Petro Episcopo Auserensi in romana curia
residenti salutem etc. Apostolice sedis circumspecta benignitas circa
concessionum gratias in quibus multorum voces frequenter exaudit, illam sibi
providentiam reservare intendit, ut ex illis eis proveniat commodum quod aliis
materia scandali seu gravaminis, ac etiam monasteriis nec non in eis sub regulari
habitu degentibus personis non immineat detrimentum et, si secus comperit fore
gestum, illud renuat et admittat, prout negotium revocat personarum, locorum
ac temporum qualitate pensata in altissimo conspicit salubriter expedire. Dudum
siquidem felicis recordationis Martino papa v. predecessori nostro pro parte
dilectorum filiorum Dominici abbatis et conventus monasterii sancti Columbe
insule de Hy ordinis sancti Benedicti Sodorensis diocesis exposito quod
nonnulli de nobili genere procreati abbates dicti monasterii qui illius regiminiet
administrationi in spiritualibus et temporalibus praefuerant pro tempore gressus
suos in semitis continentie non dirigentes, quasdam etiam de nobili genere
genitas mulieres ex quibus gradientes super terram procrearant, in concubinas
tenuerant ac proprie salutis immemores de bonis prefati monasterii tanquam de
hereditate propria concubinis partem assignarant et gradientibus ipsis de vite ac
victus necessariis provideant, bona eadem multipliciter dilapidando, quodque
nobiles ipsi prefatum monasterium intrantes, non devotionis sed bonorum illius
administrationis causa, communiter ordinem ipsum profitebantur in non
modicam divini cultus diminutionem grave prejudicium dicto monasterio ac
scandalum plurimorum ; idem predecessor per quasdam literas statuit et etiam
ordinavit quod ex tunc in antea perpetuis futuris temporibus nullus de nobili
genere procreatus cujuscumque etiam dignitatis, status, gradus, ordinis vel
conditionis foret, ex cuius receptione scandalum verisimiliter sequi posset,
auctoritate literarum apostolicarum cuiquam sub quavis etiam forma verborum
a sede predicta vel ejus auctoritate concessarum, tunc vel in antea
concedendarum, seu alias in dicto monasterio recipi deberet vel admitti,
decernens literas concessas vel concedendas praedictas et processus habitos pro
tempore per easdem cum provisionibus per illas seu earum vigore factis et
faciendis ac omnibus aliis inde secutis, etiam si ipsius et illorum totis tenoribus
ipsis literis de verbo ad verbum habenda esset mentio specialis, aut quicquid
alias a quoquam quavis auctoritate scienter vel ignoranter in contrarium
contingeret attemptari, irrita existere et inania nulliusque roboris vel momenti.
Et deinde per ipsum praedecessorem accepto quod dilectus filius Fyngonius
Fyngonii tunc acolitus dicte diocesis cupiebat in monasterio prefato una cum
abbate et conventu prefatis sub regulari habitu virtutum Domino famulari, dictus

predecessor dileetis filiis . . abbati monasterii de Dunfermelyn Sanctiandree
diocesis cius proprio nomine non expresso et Molcalmo MacDugaylbyg ac
Doncano Doncani canonicis ecclesie Lysmorensis per alias suas literas dedit in
mandatis, ut ipsi aut unus eorum eundem Fyngonium asserentem se de nobili
genere procreatum existere et in jure canonico aliquandiu studuisse ac dictum
Dominicum eundem Fyngonium quod ipse in illius abbatis prejudicium et
gravamen dictum monasterium nunquam monachus ingrederetur aut inibi
predictum ordinem profiteretur, induxisse corporale prestare iuramentum si
esset ydoneus et aliud canonicum non obstaret juramento predicto, ipsi
Fyngonio per eos primitus relaxato in dicto monasterio si in eo certus
monachorum numerus non habebatur et illud ex hoc nimium non gravaretur, vel
etiam si hujusmodi numerus forsan existeret et de ipso numero aliquis tunc
deesset ex tunc alioquin quantum aliquem de ipso numero deesse contingeret,
in monachum et in fratrem recipi sibique iuxta ipsius monasterii consuetudinem
regularem habitum exhiberi ac de communibus eiusdem monasterii proventibus
sicut uni ex aliis prefati monasterii monachis integre provideri ipsumque ibidem
sincera in Domino caritate tractari facerent, prout in eisdem literis plenius
continetur. Postmodum vero, sicut exhibita nuper nobis qui dicto predecessore
sicut Domino placuit sublato de medio divinafavente clementia ad apicem
summi apostolatus assumpti fuimus, pro parte dictorum abbatis et conventus
petitio continebat, Malcalmus et Doncanus predicti ad earundem posteriorum
literarum executionem perperam procedentes illarum pretextu ad instantiam
dicti Fyngonii prefatos abbatem et conventum per suas certi tenoris literas
monuerunt et mandarunt eisdem ut sub excommunicationis aliisque
ecclesiasticis sententiis, censuris et penis tunc expressis infra certum
peremptorium terminum etiam tunc expressum ipsum Fyngonium in eorum
monasterio iuxta dictarum posteriorum literarum formam in monachum atque
fratrem reciperent et admitterent ac ei regularem habitum exhiberent, eumque
inibi sincera in Domino caritate tractari facerent, quodque postmodum in
singulos ex abate et conventu predictis quia monitioni ,et mandato prefatis prout
nec tenebantur non. paruerant, extra excommunicationis et universas
suspensionis sententias promulgarunt licet de facto ac subsequenter prefatus
Fyngonius postquam de premissis ut apparebat dolens eisdem posterioribus
literis et rode secutis coram certis notario et testibus sponte et libere cesserat,
apostolicas ad venerabiles fratres nostros . . Valven. et . . Sodoren. episcopos
ac Doncanum predictum a nobis sub certa forma literas impetravit, quarum
pretextu ven. frater noster Joannes episcopus Sodoren. et dictus Doncanus etiam
postquam abbas et conventus prefati a nonnullis sufficientibus sibi ab eisdem
Joanne, Doncano et Fyngonio illatis gravaminibus ad sedem tandem
appellaverant, abbatem et conventum predictos sententias, censuras et penas
hujusmodi incurrisse mandarunt publice nuntiari ipsique Fyngonio regularem
habitum eiusdem ordinis per tres ex novitiis dicti monasterii eiusdem Fyngoni

fautores exhiberi fecerunt et procurarunt similiter de facto. Cum autem, sicut eadem petitio subjungebat, tam priores quam posteriores per ipsum Fyngonium impetrate litere predicte pro eo quod in illis de statuto et ordinatione ac super illis habitis literis prefatis et quod idem Fyngonius cuiusdam filii quondam Fyngonii ipsius monasterii abbatis de nobili genere procreati, qui quidem Fyngonius abbas vitam dissolutam duxit ac bona dicti monasterii concubinis et filiis ac filiabus suis distribuendo plurimum dissipavit ac dilapidavit natus foret in ipsis quoque posterioribus literis de cessione predicta mentio aliqua facta non fuit surreptionis vitio subiaceant et alias predictus Fyngonius Fyngonii pudicitie laxatis habenis cum dilecta in Christo filia Mariota Suignici muliere prefate Sodoren. diocesis tractaverit ut dilectam in Christo filiam Mor ipsius Mariote filiam in concubinam haberet ac cum effect pepigerit et se obligaverit quod eidem Mor quadraginta vacas dotalitias ad estimationem consuetam terrarum insularum illarum partium daret et persolveret ac ipsi concubine esculenta et poculenta necnon pannos competentes ministraret et eam ut concubinam honorifice tractaret, ipseque Fyngonius Fyngonii dictam Mor post priorum et ante posteriorum literarum predictarum impetrationes per aliquot annos in concubinam tenuerit ac tempore impetrationis posteriorum literarum hujusmodi excommunicatus fuerit cum nonnullisquoque fautoribus suis a dicto monasterio, quedam bona ad illud spectantia violenter asportaverit ac publicus fornicator lubricus periurus, scandalosus et pluribus aliis criminibus irretitus necnon abbati et conventui prefatis ac dilectis His patrono eiusdem monasterii et dominis temporalibus partium earundem propter ejus inhonestam vitam et conversationem plurimum exosus reputetur, pro parte eorundem abbatis et conventus asserentium quodsi forsan contingeret ipsum Fyngonium Fyngonii in dicto monasterio in monachum recipi et in fratrem dictusque patronus de hoc non contentus reliquias et ossa progenitorum suorum in ipso monasterio sepultorum necnon pretiosa ibidem erogata abinde verisimiliter extrahi et ad alia loca transferri faceret et procuraret ipseque patronusper suas patentes literas asseruit quod si prefatus Fyngonius Fyngonii, ut premittitur, in eodem monasterio recipietur, sua conscientia sibi non permittit tempore eiusdem Fyngonii Fyngonii prefatum monasterium augmentare sed potius minuere nobis fuit humiliter supplicatum ut super hiis oportune providere de benignitate apostolica dignaremur. Nos igitur qui de premissis certain noticiam non habemus ac literarum tenores nec non omnium et singularum premissarum status presentibus pro expressis habentes, huiusmodi nec non charissimi in Christo filii nostri Jacobi regis Scotie illustris ac patroni et dominorum predictorum, nec non dilectorum filiorum nobilium insularum illarum partium nobis super hoc humiliter supplicantium, supplicationibus inclinati, fraternitati tue per apostolica scripta mandamus quatenus auctoritate nostra si vocatis dicto Fyngonio Fyngonii et aliis qui fuerint evocandi per audientiam contradictarum romane curie infra trey dies tibi quod in dictis posterioribus per ipsum Fyngonium

Fyngonii impetratis literis nulla de statuto et ordinatione ac prioribus literis predictis mentio faeta fuerit aut quod ipse Fyngonius Fyngonii eisdem prioribus per eum impetratis literis rode secutis cesserit, ut prefcrtur, seu quod concubinam tenuerit etilli obligaverit vel quod tempore date posteriorum literarum earundem periurus publieus seu vinculo maioris excommunicationis innodatus fuerit aut quod prefato monasterio sancti Columbe scandalosus et minus utilis ac dicto patrono exosus seu alias quovis modo ad dictas per eum impetratas literas obtinendum inhabilis existat legitime constiterit abbatem et conventum predietos a sententiis censuris et penis prefatis absolvas in forma ecclesie consueta, iniunctis sibi pro modo culpe penitentia salutari et aliis que de jure fuerint injungenda, ac cum eis super irregularitate si quam sententiis et censuris huiusmodi vel earum aliqua forsan ligati missas et alia divina officia non tamen in contemptu clavium celebrando aut illis se immiscendo quomodolibet contraxerunt, dispenses absolvasque ab ipsis omnem inhabilitatis et infamie maculam sive notam per eos dicta actione contractam. Et nihilominus literas per dictum Fyngonium Fyngonii impetratas predictas et processus desuper habitos ac quecumque rode secuta revoces, casses et annulles nulliusque roboris vel momenti facere, necnon dictos abbatem et conventum ad receptionem eiusdem Fyngoni Fyngonii in monachum et in fratrem pretextu literarum per eum impetratarum huiusmodi seu alias deinceps non teneri decernas ac ipsum Fyngonum Fyngonii dictum habitum dimittere facias et compellas eique super premissis perpetuum silentium imponas et alia que circa premissa fuerint necessaria scu quomodolibct oportuna facias, statuas et ordines, contradictores quos literis [sic : quoere ` quoslibet '] super hiis per te habendis servatis processibus aggravarc curabis per censuram eeclesiasticam et alia juris remedia appcllatione postposita compescendo invocato ad hoc si opus fuerit auxilio brachii secularis. Non obstantibus pie memorie Bonifacii PP. VIII. etiam predecessoris nostri quibus cavetur ne quis extra suam civitatem vel diocesim nisi in certis exceptis casibus et in illis ultra unam dietam a fine sue diocesis ad iudieium evocetur, ac de duabus dietis in concilio generali editis et quibusvis aliis constitutionibus et ordinibu s apostolicis ceterisque contrariis quibuscumque.Aut si dicto Fyngonio Fyngonii vel quibusvis aliis communiter vel divisim ab eadem sit sede indultum quod extra vel ultra tertia loca ad judicium evocari aut quod interdici, suspendi vel excommunicari non possint per literas apostolicas non facientes plena et expressam ac de verbo ad verbum de indulto hujusmodi mentionem.

Datum Rome apud S. Petrum anno Incarnationis
Dominice millesimo quadringentesimo quadragesimo tertio,sexto idus Januarii anno tertiodecimo. An. xxxx. de Adria.

Commentary

By the end of the ninth century Iona had lost its ecclesiastical importance through the raids of the heathen Northmen, and their repeated massacres of the brethren. In Scotland its pre-eminence had passed to Dunkeld, and in Ireland to Kells. But the veneration in which the faithful held the little island remained unaffected, and Queen Margaret is said to have rebuilt the monastery, and placed monks there with a suitable endowment. Unfortunately no details have been preserved. Later, Reginald, Dominus de Inchegall, the son of Somerled, who succeeded his father in 1164, and died in 1208, founded there a Benedictine monastery, which he amply endowed, as well as a nunnery, of which his sister Bethoc was the first prioress. This foundation was confirmed by Pope Innocent III in 1203, and from the Bull of confirmation it appears that the abbot was then a certain Celestine--a name strangely regarded as synonymous with Gilleasbuig or Archibald--and that the possessions of the monastery were extensive.

The Bull sets them forth thus, viz.: Locum ipsum in quo prefatum Monasterium situm est, cum omnibus pertinentiis suis; Ecclesias de Insegal, de Mule de Coluansei de Cheldabsenaig, de Chelcenneg et de Ile; Insulas Hy Mule Coluansei Oruansei Canei et Calue. Terra de Magenburg, de Mangecheles de Herilnean de Sotesdal. Terras de Abberarde in Yle de Markarna et de Camusnanesre.

At this time, it will be remembered, the Isles belonged to Norway, and accordingly Iona was under the jurisdiction of the Archbishop of Trondhjem, and not subject to the Bishop of Sodor, a circumstance not without bearing on its subsequent history, and resulting probably in the abbot having greater practical independence of control than was altogether desirable. In the year 1499 John, Bishop of the Isles, was appointed Abbot of Hy, and the abbacy was thereafter held with the bishopric, the occupant of the see being thus Bishop of the Isles and perpetual Commendator of the monastery. A rental showing the extent of the bishop's possessions in his twofold character, circa 1561, is printed in the Collectanea de Rebus Albanicis, p. 1.

Somewhere about 1410, according to Hugh Macdonald, the Abbot of Hy was one of the clan Fynnon, known as the Green Abbot (vide ante, p. 32). He is said to have been a subtle and wicked councillor, and to have contrived a plot against Donald, Lord of the Isles. The next abbot whose name is recorded was John, probably his successor, who died about 1420, and was succeeded by Dominic, the son of Kenneth. For some time, it would seem, the abbacy of Iona had come to be regarded as a prize worth capturing by the lesser magnates of the Isles ; and accordingly Dominic, who seems to have desired to put things on a different footing, attempted to discourage the entrance into the monastery of well-born young men with worldly ambition. On representing to Martin v. that a number of abbots of noble race had kept as their concubines women, also of noble race, by whom they had had children, and had squandered the goods of the monastery upon the said concubines and children, he obtained from that pope an ordinance that no one of noble race from whom such scandal might be expected should be admitted into the monastery by virtue of papal letters. There was, however, a certain acolyte, to wit Fyngonius Fyngonii, or Mackinnon, a grandson of the Green Abbot, who seems to have had a mind for ecclesiastical preferment. Although of noble birth, and a student of canon law, he had the misfortune to be the son of an unmarried man and an unmarried woman. From this defect, however, he was dispensed in 1426, in order that he might receive a benefice (Papal Registers, vii. 461).

The abbot seems to have suspected his intentions, and had somehow induced him to swear that he would never enter the monastery or make his profession therein. But influence was brought to bear at Rome, and a mandate, dated 6 July 1426, was addressed to the Abbot of Dunfermline, and Malcolm MacDugal beg, and Duncan MacDuncan, canons of Lismore, to release him from his oath, and cause him to be received into the monastery. He next appears in 1433 as having held the perpetual vicarage of St. Fynnoga's of Coll, one of the churches belonging to Hy, for more than a year, without having been ordained a priest, for which he is accordingly deprived, and his benefice given to Lachlan M'Cormack. Meantime, according to the document now printed, he had been making things unpleasant for the abbot and convent, who had refused to receive him as a monk, and had been excommunicated in consequence.

With the help of three friendly monks he received the habit, notwithstanding that the abbot and convent had appealed to the Holy See, and proceeded to follow the example of his grandfather. In particular he took as his concubine a lady named M or, the daughter of Mariota MacSween, with her mother's full consent, and under an agreement to provide suitably for her ; and he also proceeded to lay violent hands on the goods of the said monastery, whereby great scandal had arisen, and even danger that the patron might remove the bones and relics of his progenitors who were buried there. All these things were finally brought under the notice of the Holy See, with the result that a remit to inquire into the whole matter, and to exercise all necessary discipline, was made by the mandate now printed.

With regard to the charges brought against the Green Abbot and his grandson a few words may be said. It must be kept in view that the clergy of the Celtic Church were, as a rule, married men. In the great controversy between them and Queen Margaret, their tonsure, their Easter, their ritual, their neglect of the Sabbath, and even some disregard of the forbidden degrees, were all vehemently assailed by her. But she made no attack on their marriage. This might be thought curious, if it be not remembered that married clergy were also common in England whence she came. The Roman Church had, no doubt, set its face against the marriage of priests ; but these marriages, though forbidden, were perfectly valid till long afterwards, as they are in the Eastern church until this day. Apart from monastic vows, the celibacy of the Roman clergy is due to a mere ecclesiastical rule or bylaw, which can be rescinded at any time, and from which a dispensation can be given on cause shown. And, as a matter of fact, the case of the Uniats shows how such an exemption exists on a wholesale scale when that is found desirable. In Scotland there was no public feeling against a married priest ; and though the lady who shared his somewhat meagre living is usually called evil names by papal scribes and the framers of ecclesiastical canons, it is doubtful if, in ordinary circumstances, either the spouses or the parishioners regarded the alliance as anything but verum matrimonium, or contrary to good morals, though no doubt, like other things, it was now forbidden by meddlesome ecclesiastics.

It is therefore curious every now and then to find lists of priests' bastards put forward as evidence of the corruption of the mediaeval Church. The industrious statisticians who thus labour in support of Lutheran or Calvinistic theology do not seem to realise that they are identifying themselves with the ultramontane view as to clerical celibacy, which was then as little in accordance with popular feeling as is nowadays the Royal Marriage Act of George.

In the Western Islands especially, where memories of the Celtic Church would naturally linger, more or less obscurely, long after the formal introduction of the Roman system, and the niceties of the new-fangled monasticism be regarded as of little account, it would in no way seem out of place for even an abbot to be married, or to pass on his office and its emoluments to his son.

Whatever may have been the outcome of the proceedings against Fyngonius Fyngonii, it is interesting that among the monuments in Iona, which have survived the insensate fury of the Reformers and the callous neglect of their successors, are two closely associated with his race.

They are (first) a magnificent cross, with the inscription :
" HAEC EST CRUX LACCLANI MEIC FINGONE ET EIUS FILII JOHANNIS ABB ATIS DE HY. FACTA ANNO DOMINI MCCCC LXXXIX";

and (second), an ornate tomb, in-scribed:
"JOIIANNES MACFINGON ABBAS DE Y. QUI OBIIT ANNO DNI MILLESIMO QUINGENTESIMO."

Appendix 6

Battle Chant of MacMhuririch, the Bard of the Isles

A Chlanna Cuinn, cuimhnichibh
Cruas an am na h-iorghaile:
Gu h-àirneach, gu h-arranta,
Gu h-athlamh, gu h-allanta
Gu beòdha, gu barramhail,
Gu brìoghmhor, gu buan-fheargach
Gu calma, gu curanta,
Gu cròdha, gu cath-bhuadhach,
Gu dùr is gu dàsannach,
Gu dian is gu deagh-fhulang,
[Gu h-èasgaidh, gu h-eaghnamhach,
Gu h-éidith, gu h-eireachdail,]
Gu fortail, gu furachail,
Gu frithir, gu forniata,
Gu gruamach, gu gràineamhail,
Gu gleusta, gu gaisgeamhail,
Gu h-ullamh, gu ioghaileach,
Gu h-olla-bhorb, gu h-àibheiseach,
Gu h-innill, gu h-inntinneach,
Gu h-iomdha, gu h-iomghonach,
Gu [laomsgar], gu làn-[ath] lamh,
Gu làidir, gu luath-bhuilleach,
Gu mearghanta, gu mór-chneadhach,
Gu meanmnach, gu mileanta,
Gu neimhneach, gu naimhdeamhail,
Gu niatach, gu neimh-eaglach
[Gu h-obann, gu hu-olla-ghnìomhach,
Gu h-oirdheirc, gu h-oirbheartach,]
Gu [prap] is gu priomh-ullamh,
Gu prosta gu [prionnsamhail],
Gu ruaimneach, gu ro-dhàna,
Gu ro-bhorb, gu rìoghamhail,
Gu sanntach, gu sèanamhail,
Gu socair, gu sàr-bhuailleach,
Gu teannta, gu [togarrach],

O Children of Conn, remember
Hardihood in time of battle:
Be watchful, daring,
Be dexterous, winning renown,
Be vigorous, pre-eminent,
Be strong, nursing your wrath,
Be stout, brave
Be valiant, triumphant
Be resolute and fierce
Be forceful and stand your ground,
Be nimble, valorous,
Be well-equipped, handsomely
accoutered,
Be dominant, watchful
Be fervid, pugnacious,
Be dour, inspiring fear,
Be ready for action, warrior-like,
Be prompt, warlike,
Be exceedingly fierce, recklessly
daring,
Be prepared, willing,
Be numerous, giving battle,
Be fiery, fully-ready,
Be strong, dealing swift blows,
Be spirited, inflicting great wounds,
Be stout-hearted, martial,
Be venomous, implacable,
Be warrior-like, fearless,
Be swift, performing great deeds,
Be glorious, nobly powerful,
Be rapid [in movement], very quick,
Be valiant, princely,
Be active, exceedingly bold,
Be ready, fresh and comely,
Be exceedingly fierce, king-like,

Gu talcmhor, gu traigh-èasgaidh,

Gu h-urlamh, gu h-ùr-mhaiseach
Do chosnadh [na] cath làthrach
Re bronnaibh bhar biodhbhadha.
A Chlanna Cuinn Cead-chathaich
[A] nois uair bhar n-aitheanta, [A
chuileanan confadhach],
A bhleithrichean bunanta,
A leómhannan làn-[ghasta], [A
onchonaibh iorghaileach], Chaoiribh
chròdha, churanta,

De Chlanna Cuinn Cèad-chathaich-

A Chlanna Cuinn, [cuimhnichibh
Cruas an am na h-iorgha

Be unhurried, striking excellent
blows,
Be compact [in your ranks], elated,
Be vigorous, nimble-footed In
winning the battle Against your
enemies.
O Children of Conn of the Hundred
Battles.
Now is the time for you to win
recognition,
O raging whelps, O sturdy heroes,
O most sprightly lions,
O battle-loving warriors,
O brave heroic firebrands,
The Children of Conn of the Hundred
Battles,
O Children of Conn, remember
Hardihood in time of battle.

Appendix 7

Relationship of Donald Dubh to some other Highland Chiefs

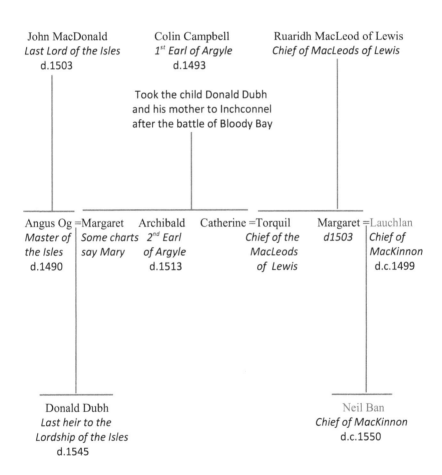

John MacDonald
Last Lord of the Isles
d.1503

Colin Campbell
1ˢᵗ Earl of Argyle
d.1493

Ruaridh MacLeod of Lewis
Chief of MacLeods of Lewis

Took the child Donald Dubh
and his mother to Inchconnel
after the battle of Bloody Bay

Angus Og =Margaret
Master of | *Some charts*
the Isles | *say Mary*
d.1490

Archibald
2ⁿᵈ Earl
of Argyle
d.1513

Catherine =Torquil
Chief of the
MacLeods
of Lewis

Margaret =Lauchlan
d1503 | *Chief of*
MacKinnon
d.c.1499

Donald Dubh
Last heir to the
Lordship of the Isles
d.1545

Neil Ban
Chief of MacKinnon
d.c.1550

Appendix 8

The Heirs to the Lordship of the Isles

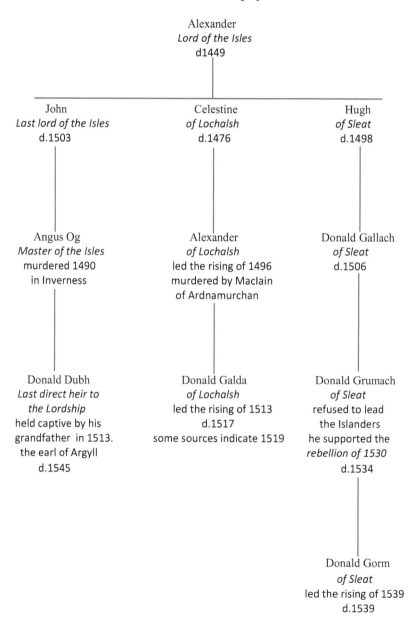

Alexander
Lord of the Isles
d1449

John	Celestine	Hugh
Last lord of the Isles	*of Lochalsh*	*of Sleat*
d.1503	d.1476	d.1498

Angus Og	Alexander	Donald Gallach
Master of the Isles	*of Lochalsh*	*of Sleat*
murdered 1490	led the rising of 1496	d.1506
in Inverness	murdered by MacIain	
	of Ardnamurchan	

Donald Dubh	Donald Galda	Donald Grumach
Last direct heir to	*of Lochalsh*	*of Sleat*
the Lordship	led the rising of 1513	refused to lead
held captive by his	d.1517	the Islanders
grandfather in 1513.	some sources indicate 1519	he supported the
the earl of Argyll		*rebellion of 1530*
d.1545		d.1534

Donald Gorm
of Sleat
led the rising of 1539
d.1539

Appendix 9

MacLeans Petition to the Lords in Council 1517

To Lauchlane Makclanis desiris of Dowfart. In the first anent the rmisssioun desiryt be him to his self kynnismen seruandis frendis and portakars that Makulane Gillonan Makmakele of Barry Nele Makynnon of Mesnes Dwnsleif Makcura of Ulway and Lauchlan McEwin of Ardgour for all crimes be past.

The lordis counsalis that my lord governour grant this remission and gif the samyn the said Mukclane gevand plegis sufficient sic a. the governour and counsale saII devise and mene be thair names for gude reule in tyme cumin

Anent the hundreth merk landis of the Ile of Tery and utheris land is in the Mule to the said soume desirit he Makclane for the inhringing of the Kingis malis in all placis within the Row, Ardnamurquban, exceptand samekiII as partenis to Makcane for quhilk he sall answer.

The lordis understandis that tbe Kingis Iandis may nocht be givin in heretage notycles for the gude service done be the said LauchInne McClane and to be done counsalis the governour to suffer the said Lauchlane to intromett and uptake the proffeitis pertenyng to the King ot' the said Ile of Tere to his awn *vtilte* induring my lord governouris administration with condition that the said Lauchlane answer and caus the Kingis servitouris to be answerit zerlie to the Kingi. grace and his sevitouris according to his Rentnle of the said boundis and gevand cautioull thorfor, .

Anent the service of the tennentis of the Kingis Grace desirit be the said Lauchlane the lords counsalis my lord governour grant to him the service of thai tennents of the Kingis quhilk his forbearis as he ha.d grantit to thame of hefoir of the King and to do him service in his just materis the Kingis grace my lord governour nnd the Erll of Ergile lieutenent exceppit,

Anent the gellerall acquittane desirit be the said Lauchlane of all malis fermes and dewiteis pertenyng to the King oure Souerane of Tere Mull Ylay and Germarry intromettit be the said Lauchlane, The lordis thinkis and counsalis the govermour to gif this discharge with condition that gif the said Lauchlane failzeis. hereftir to the Kingis grace or inbringing of his. malis. and answering thairintill occording to the kingis. rentale the samyn discharge to stand of name avale to him, As to the landis. of MIll and uthers landis that the said Lauchlane had of befoir of the Kingis grace now desirit in fewferm be him

The lordis counsalis my lord governour to lait thame stand in tak to the said Lauchlane as he had thamesem the Kingis landis may nocht be gevin in herelage the said Lauchlane fynd and cautioun for payment of the malis and dewities of the said landis,

As to the justifying of Donaldi. twa brethil' and forfactour aganis the said Donald the temporale lordis will shaw my lord governour thair mynde quhilkis temporle lordis that is to say Huntlie Levinax Drummond Ogelby Balwery and Kers referris to my lord goveruour quhat he thinkis. to be done ,with the saidis personis. And the remanent of my saidis lordis temporale that is to say Ergile Cassillis Erskin Borthnick Avend.ale Lees Kincavil Canpitan of the Caslel Comptrollair and Otterburn deliveris the saidis personis to be justifyt eftir thair demeritis.

The lordis counsalis my lord governour to admit any resignatioun of landis or officis maid in his handis be resignatioun personaJy maid be the possessouris. in favouris of the said Lauchlnne and to gif him infeftment thairof referrand the samin resignatioun and infeitment to my Lord gouvernouris plessour, as he claims

LACHLANE MAKLANE OF DOWARD
Wt
my hand on ye pen

Appendix 10

A Proposal For Uniting Scotland With England, Addressed To King Henry Viii. By John Elder, Clerke, A Reddshanke 1542 or 1543

To the most Noble, Vietorious, and Redoubted Prynce HENRY the Eight, by the grace of God, of England,
France, and Irland, Kynge, Defender of the Christen Faithe, and in erth next vnto God, of the Churche of England and Irland Supreme lied, JOHNE ELDAR, Clerk, a Reddshank, wisseth all wealth, all honour, and triumph-ant victory ouer all his enemies.

ALBEIT that fere, for laick of leirnyng and witt (moost high, excellent, and myghtie Prynce), oftentymes persuadid me to withdraw my pene, from writting vnto your noble Grace : Yeit, neuer the les, perceaving emonges other thinges, in what miserable estate the realme of Scotland is presently ill, for neld of a wise gouernour, syns the soden death of our noble Prynce Kynge James the Fyfte, your Majesties nephew, laite Kynge of the same, now after his decese, being reuled as it was in his tyme, be the advyse of the Cardinall, associatt with proud papisticall buschops, which euer allured our said noble Prynce in his dales, with their fals:, flatteringe, and jugglinge boxes, from the naturall inelinacion, and lone, which he ought vnto your Maiestie, his moost myghtie and naturall Vnc,le. Consideringe also what ease and quiettues, what wealth and ryches we shuide haue in Scotland in few yeares, yf now after our said noble Kynges decese, Prynce Edowarde, whom God preserue, your Maiesties naturall sonne and heare of the noble empyr of England, shuld, as he shall by the grace of God, marye our younge Queyne of Scotland; by reason whereof, the forsaid buschops, which be the Dewils convocacion, and the father of mischief, Dauid Beton ther cardinall, with Beelzebub's flesmongers, the abbotes and all ther adherentes, beinge quyte expulsed and drywyne away, boith the realmes of England and of Scotland may be joynede in one ; and so your noble Maiestie for to be superiour and kynge. Furthermore knowinge what trew faithfull hartes the moost part of the commons of Scotland, (yf they durst speke), beyound the watir of Forth, haue to your highnes, and wold hardy and glaidly so continew, yf the said pestiferous Cardinall, and his blynd ignoraunt buschops, with certane other wylde, fals, crafty bores, which haue drunkyne the Frence kynges wynes, and taistide of his cwps, plainge leger de mane (as they say) with boithe haundes, wer tyied vp in ropis and halters. Moreouer, heringe and seinge what lone and fauour the valiaunt Yrishe lordes of Scotland, other wayes callid the Reddshankes, (excepte the Erll of Argyll, whieh is ravisshide onelye from the opinioun of the rest, be the Cardinall and his bussehops, becaus he is novrisshed and brought vp in ther bosomes, and lyis vnder tller wynges), beris vnto your said Maiestie, of whois princely maguanimitie, Salomonicall wysdome, and sa-pienee, and heroicall humanitie and beneuolence, now syns the death of our said lord naturall aud Kynge, is euer ther comnumicacion, and euer tller reasonynge Sene they heire and vnderstand, how mercifully, how graciously, and how liberally your noble Grace bath vsed, orderide, and dealide with the lordes of Irland, ther ny hboures, which hale continewid so many yeares rebellis ; perdonying and forgyving theame ther offences aud trespasses; creating of them, some erlis, some lordes, and some barons; rewarding theame more like princis then erlis and lordis, with gold, siluer, and riches ; and sending theame home agane with gorgious indumentis, and rich apparell. Also, perceavinge what sedicion and variance, what dissension and insurreecions, what theifte and extortions, what dearth and misery, what, pryde and hypocrisy, what invye and haterat we shall baue in Scotland, so long as this miserable, wretched Cardinall and his husscheps reagnethe and reulithe emonge ws tller, without your Highnes, by the prouision of God, hunt and drywe theame shortly fourth of the same with fyre aud swerde : I can no les do, then offer this plotte of the realme of Scotland vnto your excellent Maiestie, wherein your Highnes shall perceaue and se, not onely the description of all the notable townes, castels, and abbeis ther set fourthe, and situat in ther propir places, as they stand in euery countle aud schyre, with the situaciou of all the principal) yles, marched with the same, callid Orknay and Schetlande, and of the Out-ysles, commonly namede the Sky and the Lewys: but also your noble Grace shall se the cost of the same, the dangers lying therby, with euery port, ryver, loigh, creke, and haven there, so truely drawyn and set fourthe as my poore witt and lernynge can vtter and discerne. Which plotte, I haue not made by relacion of others ; but in so moche (and pleas your Highnes) that I was borne in Caitnes, which is the northe part of the saide plotte, marched with the East *yles* of the same, callid Orknay ; educatt, and brought vp, not onely in the West yles of the same plotte, namede Sky and the Lewis, wher I haue bene often tymes with my friendis, in ther longe galleis, arrywing to dyvers and syndrle places in Scotland, wher they had a do : but also, beinge a scholer and a student in the southe partis of it, callid Sanctandrois, Abirdene, and Glasgw, for the space of XIIt^h yeares, wher I haue travailde, aswell by see as by the land, dyuers tymes ; by reason whereof, knowinge all the notable places ther euery wher, with ther lordis and masters names, and from thens vnto the said countreth wher I was borne, I am the bolder (pardon cravide) to offer the saide plotte vnto your excellent Maiestie;—wherein, becaus it bicommes not me, a wretche destitute of all good lernynge and eloquence, to interturbe your noble Grace with theis my rude, barbourous, and fessious lettres, in declaring of the forsaide plotte in this litle boke, I haue written the principal erlis and lordis names in Scotlande, annext to ther common habitacion and duellinge place in the same; with a brief declaration of all the ryvers, loighis, and havens tiler also, to the intent your noble Maiestie may perceaue, se, and reide the same ther, without any farther investigacion. And fforsomoche, and pleas your Grace, that I bane written the names of all the Yrische lordes of Scotland, commonly callit the Reddshanckes, and by historiographouris, Pictis ; joynede also to ther cuntreth and duellinge places, I will, be your Majesties pardon, writ somethinge of theame heir, whois names, bicause they be Yrishe, and soundis not well to be interprete in Englis, I will declair theame to your Grace in Latyne. Therfor, if it pleas your excellent Maiestie, Scotland, a part of your Highnes empyre of England, bifor the incummynge of Albanactus, Brutus secound some, was inhabitede, as we reide in auncient Yrische storeis, with gyauntes and Wylde people, without or-dour, ciuilitie, or maners, and spake none other language but Yrische, and was then called Eyrvn veagg, that is to say, little Irlaud ; and the people were callit Eyrynghe, that is to say, Irlande men. But after the incummynge of Albanactus, he reducynge theame to ordour and ciuilitie, they changed the forsaid name, Eyryn veagg, and callid it Albon, and their owne names also, and callid theame Albonyghe ; which too Yrische wordes, Albon, that is to say, Scotland, and Albonyghe, that is to say, Scottische men, be drywyne from Albanactus, our first gouernour and kynge. Which dirivacion (and like your Highnes) the papistical, curside spiritualitie of Scot-land, will not heir in no maner of wyse, nor confesse that euer such a kynge, namede Albanactus, reagnede ther. The which dirivacion, all the Yrische men of Scotland, which be the auncient stoke, can not, nor will not denye. For as Sanctus Columba, a Pict and a busshep, who in prechinge of Goddis worde syncerly in Eyrische, in followinge of the holy apostlis in godlie imitacion, doctryne, and pouertie, excellid then our proude Romische Cardinall, and his bussheps now adaies in Scotlande, writtethe in his monumentis of the same, we haue our names of Albanactus, and so haithe Scotlande also.* But our said bussheps (and pleas your Grace) drywith Scotland and theame selfes, from a certane lady, namede Scota, which (as they alledge) come out of Egipte, a maraculous hot cuntreth, to recreatt hir self emonges theame in the cold ayre of Scotland, which they can not afferme be no probable auncient author. Now, and pleas your excellent Maiestie, the said people which inhabitede Scotland afoir the incummyng of the said Albanactus, (as I haue said), beinge valiant, stronge, and couragious, although they wer savage and wilde, had strange names, as Morwhow .1. Mordachus ; Gillecallum .1. Malcolmus; Donyll .1. Donaldus, and so fourth. Then ther sonnis followinge theame in manheid and valiauntnes, callide theame selfes after this maner of wyse, leaving ther propir name vnexpresside, Makconyll .1. filius Donaldi ; Makgillecallum .1. filius Malcolmi, etc.:and so they haue contenewide vnto this daye, and neuer expressis ther propir names, but when they subscryue a lettir, as Donyll Mak Leode Lewis .1. Donaldus filius Ludouici de Levisia, etc ᵉ. The Yrische lordis names in the saide plotte be theis, Mak Eoyn whanyghe .1. filius Joannis bellicosi ;1- Mak-kye .1. filius Hugonis ; Mak Leode Lewis .1. filius Ludovici de Levisia ; Mak Leode ne Harr .1. filius Ludouici de Hartha insula; Mak Yllean .1. filius Kellani ; Mak Kymmy .1. filius Kymmeci ; Mak Kenny .1. filius Kennici ; Mak Tossigh .1. filius Tossei ; Mak Allan .1. filius Allani ; Mak Neill Varray .l. filius Nigelli de Barra insula :—for Mak in Eyrisehe signifieth a sonne Likwise your Majesties subiectis, the lordes of Inland veto this tyme, that your noble Grace haithe moost royally changede their names, and creatide theaane erlis and lordis, wer callide 0 Neill .1. nepos Nlgclli ; 0 Lien .1. nepos Bernardi ; 0 Conwhir .1. nepos Conradi ; a degre forthir of, then the Eyrische lordes in Scotland, bicans the sonnis of the forsaide Neill, Bren, and Conwhir, and so of the rest, chancede not to be so valiaunt in manhede aud chivalre at the begynning as ther ffathers, but ther nephiew. Therfor they wer callit O'Neill, O'Bren, O Conwhir ; omittinge also ther propir names, and pleas your Hignes, but when they subscryuede a lettir, as Ewwyn O'Neill .1. Eugenius nepos Nigelli ; for 0' in Eyrische signifiethe a nephew. Moreouer, wherfor they call ws in Scotland Reddshankes, and in your Graces dominion of England, roghe footide Scottis, Pleas it your Maiestie to vnderstande, that we of all people can tollerat, suftir, and away best with colde, for boithe sinner and wyntir, (excepte whene the froest is mooste vehemonte,) goynge alwaies 'hair leggide and bair footide, our delite and pleasure is not onely in hwntyngc of redd deir, wolfes, foxes, and graies, whereof we abounde, and haue greate plentie, but also in rynninge, leapinge, swymmynge, shootynge, and thrawinge of dartis : therfor, in so moche as we vse and delite so to go alwaies, the tendir delicat gentillmen of Scotland call ws Reddshankes. And agayne in wyntir, when the froest is mooste vehement (as I haue saide) which we can not suffir hair footide, so weill as snow, whiche can neuer hurt ws whene it cummes to our girdills, we go a hwntvnge, and after that we haue slayne redd deir, we flaye of the skyne, bey and bey, and settinge of our hair foote on the insyde thereof, for neide of cunnyge shoe-makers, by your Graces pardon, we play the swtters ; cornpasinge and mesuringe so moche therof, as shall retch vp to our ancklers, pryckynge the vpper part thereof, also with holis, that the water may repas when it entres, and stretchide vp with a strange thwange of the same, meitand aboue our saide ancklers, so, and pleas your noble Grace, we make our shoois : Therfor, we vsinge such maner of shoois, the roghe hairie syde outwart, in your Graces dominion of England, we be callit roghe footide Scottis ; which mailer of schoois (and pleas your Highnes) in Latyne be called perones, wherof the poet Virgill makis mencioun, sayinge, That the olde auncient Latyns in tyme of warrs vside snche maner of schoos. And althoughe a greate some of ws Reddshankes go after this maner in our countrethe, yeit neuer the les, and pleas your Grace, whene we come to the courte (the Kinges grace our great master being alyve) waitinge on our Lordes and maisters, who also, for velvettis and silkis be right well araide, we haue as good garmentis as some of our fellowis whiche gyve attendaunce in the court euery daye. And howbeit the babalonicall busscheps and the great courtyours of Scotland repute the forsoide Yrishe Lordes as wilde, rude, and barbarous people, brought vp (as they say) without lerninge and nourtour, yeit they passe theame a greate deale in faithe, honestie, in policy and witt, in good ordour and ciuilitie ; ffor wher the saide Yrische Lordes promises faithe they keipe it truely, be holdinge vp of ther formest fyngar, and so will they not, with ther sealis and subscripcions, the holy Euangel twichide. Therfor, and pleas your Highnes, like as the saide bussheps and ther adherentis repute ws rude and barbarous people, euen so do we esteme theame all, (as they be,) that is to say, ffals, flatteringe, fraudelent subtile, and covetous. Your noble Grace haithe many good hartis emonges the forsaide Yrische Lordes of Scotland, bicaus they vnderstand and heire how mercifully and how liberally (as I haue saide) your Highnes haith orderide the Lordes of Ireland. Therfor I have wrltten the said Yrische Lordes names of Scotlande in the said plotte, as Your Grace may perceaue and se ; wherfor I most humbly exhort your excellent Maiestie, of your royall humanitie and gentilnes, to accepte and pardon my good will therein ; and wher I haue failide in my Cosmographie, in drawing and settinge fourthe of the same, I shall not faille (willing God) in declaringe of all thinges therein contanide, to any to whom your Highnes shall pleas to apoint me so to do. What plotte, truely (and pleas your Grace), I haue drawene for that same porpas and intent, that yonr Royal Majestic shall not onely se and perceaue the similitude and ymage of the saide realme of Scotland in the same, which your Highnes haithe (all ambiguitie set apart) a thousand tymes bettir set fourthe, then my sclendir capacitie and Witt is able to expres and declair heir : but also, yf thar be any thing in the saide plotte concerninge the land, wherein your Maiestie doubtis, and woll haue the treuthe of the same schawene and notifiede to your excellent Grace, that I (yf your royall Maiestie pleas to accepte and allowe my good will therin) maye declair the same (as I haue said), so farr, by the helpe of God, as my know-ledge and vnderstandinge will vttir and serue ; wheron I shalbe alwayes, and pleas your noble Grace, redy with hart and hand to wait and gyre attendanee. For suerly (moost humbly besechinge your Highnes heir of pardon) yf my' dreade Soueraigne Lorde and Kinge, my liege Lorde, naturall and superiour, Kinge James the Fyfte, laitc Kinge of Scotlande, and your Majesties nephew, wer alyve, whom soden deathe (allace,) haithe ravissede from ws for euermore ; or yf he hade lefte ws a Prynce lawfully begotten of his body, to whom, after his decese, our joye and comforte, our hope and felicitie, shulde haue bene aflixt, I wolde in no manner of wise presume to sham and declair the privities of Scotlande to no Prynce Christen. Therefor, in so moche as our saide noble Prynce (whom the Hewingly Kinge, I praye God the Father, superior ouer all, mercifully receaue in his celestiall throne,) haithe lefte ws (the Lorde be thankede) as chaunce is, a Prynces, whom your excellent Maiestie moost godly desyres for to be mariede with noble Prynce Edwarde, your Graces lawfull be-gotten sonne and heare of the empyre of England; by reason wherof, hypocrisy and supersticioun abolissede, and the Frence Kinge cleane pluckt out of our hartis, England and Seotland, and the posteritie of boith, may hue for euer in peax, love, and emitie ; which godly porpas and desire beinge contrariede by a sortie of Papist preistis, according to their accustomed falshede and disceite, which allurede riot only our noble Prince in his daies from our Maiestie, whom his Grace vndoubtedly loude aboue all Pryncis mortall, in his hart; and hath provide so, yf the said traiterous had not bene allwaies roundinge in his Graces eyris, which, as often as his Highnes proposede a metinge with your Maiestie, seduced and blindide him with their boxis ; as often as he intendide to repair to your Graee, causide invasions and roddis ; and as often as he wolde speke of your Highnes, allectide him with armonie, fables, and songs : but also now, by ther presumption, intendeth to drounde all Scotland in blonde, I can no less do, by Goddis law, mannis law, and all humanitie, then invent, declair, expres, notifie, labour, and studie for that thing vnto your excellent Maiestle, (whom all honest stomakes in Scotland, presumpcion and arrogancy set asyde, shulde, with all ther tiaras, lone for our noble Pryncis sak) which myght bringe the forsaid traiterous preistis of Scotland, if it wer possible, to mischeif and vttir ruyne : ffor ther is no people, and pleas your Grace, in no region in Europe, so perturbed, so molestide, so vexide, and so vtterly opprest with bussheps, monckes, Rome-rykers, and preistis, and euer haue bene, a cardinal, a carlis-birde, a cornmon-cluner, and a hen-kyller, sometymes in France, now beinge ther capitane, as they which inhabite the realme of Scotland ; and so shall contenewe without your Highnes, (who haith moost juste caus and quarell, euery thinge considerit syns the reagne of your Maiesties nephew, vnto this daye, to invade theame) by the help and asslstance of God, hwnt, drywe, and smoyke the forsaide fals papisticall foxis, with all ther partakers, out of ther cavis, with bowis, billis, fyre, and swerde. At the which hwntyinge, wold God that I and euerye haire in my head (I meane faithfully, without any dissimulacion, I take God to recorde) wer a man with your noble Grace, havinge, as poetis feane, if it wer possible Hercules strength and fortitude to owerthraw and wressell with the saide Cardinall and his chaplans; Hectours manhede and chivalrie to fyght withe the fals, wylde, craftie boris, whiche have plaide bo peip withe bothe haundes ; and, finally, Achilles subtiltie and witt, to invent gyrnis and traps for the fals bussheps of Scotland, and all ther adherentis. I keipe your Highnes to longe with my barbourous and rude talke, wherfor, moost noble Prynce (pardon cravide) I will make an end, mooste humbly exhortinge your excellent Maiestie to pardon and accepte the foresaide plotte in gre, and not to regarde the rudenes therof, but rather the faithefulnes of me, your Majesties poore oratour ; and for so moch as I know myself vnmerite to do any bodely seruice condigne to so noble and excellent a Prynce ; yeit, at the least, I shall gyve unto your excellent Maiestie the thing which, as well the feble as the stronge may gyve, that is say, hartie prayers to Almyghtie God for the longe perseruacion of so mercifull, so faithefull, and so gentiil a Kinge, to the settinge fourthe of his wordes, to the comforte and joye of all thoise which loue your Highnes, and to the destruction and vttir ruyne of our high presumptuous Scottis Cardinall, his bussheps, and ther partakers, and death of all the pryde and popery. Amen.

Appendix 11

The letter from the Council of the Isles to the Earl of Lennox
July 28 1545

Quhairfor, voiit' Lordships sall considder we have bevne nuld enemys to the realme of Scotland, and qulien they had peasehe with ye kings hienis, thei hanged. bedit, presoned, and destroied many of our kyn, friendis, and forbearis. as testifies be our Master, th Erie of Ross, now the king's grace's subject, ye quhilk bath lyin in presoun afoir he was borne of his moder, and is iiot releiffit with their will, bot now laitlie be ye grace of God. In lykewise, the Lord Maclain's fader was cruellie murdressit, under traist, in his bed, in the town of Edinbruch, be Sir .John Campbell of Calder, brudir to th' Erll of Argyle. The capitane of Clanranald, this last zeir ago in his defens, slew the Lord Lovett, his son-in-law his three brethren, with xiii scoir of men; and many uther crewell slachtei, hurnying, and herschip that, bath beyn betwix us and the saidis Scottis, the quhilk war lang to wryte. Hector Maclane, lord of Dowart Johne Macallister, capitane of Clanranald Rorye Maclend of Lewis; Alexander Macleod of Dumbeggsne; Murdoch Maclane of Lochbuy Angus Maconnill; ALane Maclane of Turloske, brudir germane to the Lord Maclane; Archibald Maconnill, capitane of Clan Houston; Alexander Mackeyti of Ardnamurchane; Jbone Maclane of Coil; Gilliganan Macneill of Barray; Ewin Macinnon of Straguhordill .Jhone Macquarre of Ulway ; Jhona Maclane of Ardgour, Alexander Ranaldsoun of Glengarrie; Angus Ranaklsoun of Knwdort; Donald Maclane of Kengariloch.

Appendix 12

***From: Sir Donald Monro, Description of the Western Isles of Scotland
Called Hybrides, TD Morison, Glasgow, 1884***

MULL Twelfe myle northward from the iyle of Colnansay lyes the iyle of Mull, ane grate rough ile, noch the les it is fertile and fruitful. This ile contains in lenth from the northeist to the southweste twenty-four myles, and in breid from the eist southeist to west northwest uther twenty-four myles, with certain woodes, maney deire, and verey fair hunting games, with many grate mertines and cunnings for hunting, with a guid raid fornent Colmkill, callit Pollaisse. There is sevin paroche kirks within this iyle, and thre castles, to wit the castle of Doward, a strenthey place, bigged on a craige at the sea syde; the castle of Lochbowy, pertaining to M'Gillayne of Lochbowy; the castle of Arose, quhilk in former time pertinet to the Lord of the iyles, and now is bruked be M'Gillayne of Doward. In this ile there is twa guid fresche waters, ane of them are callit Ananva, and the water of Glenforsay, full of salmond, with uther waters that has salmond in them, but not in sic aboundance as the twa forsaid waters. This ile hath alsa salt water loches, to wit, Loch Ear, ane little small loche, with guid take of herringes: this loche layes in the southwest of the countrey. Then is Loch Fyne, quherin ther is a guid take of herrings. Northwest fra this loche, lyes Loch Seaforte, guid for the herring fishing. Lykwayes on the east pairt of the countrey layes ane loche, callit Lchepetit. Narrest this loche, in the southe southeist, layes Lochbowy, a fair braid loche, quherin there is grate take of herring and uther fishings. As als within this ile ther is twa freshe water loches; the ane is callit Loche Strathsenaban, with an ile in it, callit by the Erische Ellan Strathsenaban; the uther fresche water loche is callit Lochebaa, with an iyle therein. Thir iyles are baith strenthe and inhabit. This iyle pertains pairtly to M'Gillayne of Doward, pairtly to M'Gillayne of Lochbowy, pairtly to M'Kynnoun, and pairtly to the Clandonald of awld. This iyland layes but four myle from the firme land of Moriwarne.

COLMKILL. Narrest this, be twa myles of sea, layes the ile the Erische callit I-colm-kill, that is, Sanct Colm's ile, an faire mayne ile of twa myle lange and maire, and ane myle braid, fertill, and fruitfull of corne and store, and guid for fishing. Within this ile there is a monastery of mounckes, and ane uther of nuns, with a paroche kirke, and sundrie uther chapells, dotat of auld by the kings of Scotland, and be Clandonald of the iyles. This abbay forsaid was the cathedrall kirk of the bishops of the iyles, sen the tyme they were expulsed out of the ile of Man by the Englishmen, for within the ile of Man was ther cathedrall kirk and living of auld, as I have already said in the description of that ile. Within this ile of Colmkill, there is ane sanctuary also, or kirkzaird, callit in Erische Religoran, quhilk is a very fair kirkzaird, and weill biggit about with staine and lyme. Into this sanctuary ther is three tombes of staine, formit like little chapels, with ane braid gray marble or quhin staine in the gavill of ilk ane of the tombes. In the staine of the ane tombe there is wretten in Latin letters, Tumulus Regum Scotiæ, that is, The tombe ore grave of the Scotts Kinges. Within this tombe, according to our Scotts and Erische cronikels, ther layes fortey-eight crouned Scotts kings, through the quhilk this ile has been richlie dotat be the Scotts kings, as we have said. The tombe on the south syde forsaid hes this inscription, Tumulus Regum Hyberniæ, that is, The tombe of the Irland kinges; for we have in our auld Erische cronickells, that ther wes foure Irland kinges eirdit in the said tombe. Upon the north syde of our Scotts tombe, the inscriptione beares Tumulus Regum Norwegiæ, that is, The tombe of the kings of Norroway; in the quhilk tombe, as we find in our ancient Erische cronickells, ther layes eight kings of Norroway, and als we find, in our Erishe cronickells, that Coelus king of Norroway commandit his nobils to take his bodey and burey it in Colmkill, if it chancit him to die in the iles; bot he was so discomfitit, that ther remained not so maney of his armey as wald burey him ther; therefor he wes eirded in Kyle, after hc stroke ane field against the Scotts, and was vanquisht be them. Within this sanctuary also lyes the maist pairt of the Lords of the iles, with their lineage. Twa Clan Lynes with their lynage, M'Kynnon and M'Guare with their lynages, with sundrie uthers inhabitants of the hail iles, because this sanctuarey wes wont to be the sepulture of the best men of all the iles, and als of our kings, as we have said; becaus it was the maist honorable and ancient place that was in Scotland in thair dayes, as we reid.

SKY. North fra the ile Soa Urettill, be twa myle of sea, lyes the grate ile of Sky, tending from the south to the north to fortey twa myles, roughe and hard land; that is to say, from the south poynt of Sleitt to the north poynt of Trouternesse, and eight myle braid in some places, and in uther places twalve myles braid. In this ile there is twalve paroche kirkes, manurit and inhabit, fertill land, namelie for aitis, excelling aney uther, ground for grassing and pastoures, abounding in store, and of studds in it, maney woods, maney forrests, maney deire, fair hunting games, maney grate hills, principally Euilvelimi and Glannock. Within this ile ther is gud take of salmant upon five watters principally, to wit, the water of Sneisport, Sligachan, Straitswardill, Ranlagallan, and Kilmtyne, with seven or aught uther smallar watters, quherupon salmont are also slayne. In this ile there is ane freshe water loche, callit the loche of Glenmoire, quheron ther is abundance of salmont and kipper slane. Within this ile of Sky there is five castills; to wit, the castill of Dunbeggan, pertaining to M'Cloyd of Herray, ane starke strengthe, biggit upon ane craig; the castill of Dunnakyne, perteining to

Mackynnoun; the castill Dunringill, perteining to the said Mackynnoun; the castill of Camns in Sleit, perteining to Donald Gromsone; the castill of Dunskay, perteining to the said Donald Gromsone; and the castill of Donntwyline, perteining to Donald Gromesone lykeways. Within this ile ther is seven sundry countreys: to wit, Slaitt; perteining to Donald Gromsone; Straytsnardill, perteining to M'Kynnoun, quhilk lies next the Sleit; Menzenise, perteining to M'Cloyde of Herrays; Brachedill, perteining to the said M'Cloyde; Watterness, perteining to M'Cloyd of the Lewis; and Trontieness, perteining to Donald Gromesone. Into this isle ther is three principal salt water loches; to wit, Loch Sleigachan, Loch Downort, and Loch Sleippan. In thir three principal loches there is a guid take of herrings, for by thir three principal loches, there is thirteen salt water loches also within this ile, to wit, 1. Loche Skahanask, 2. Loche Emorte, 3. Loche Vrakdill, 4. Loche Kensale serloss, 5. Loche Dunbegan, 6. Loche Gorsarmis, 7. Loche Arnoffort, 8. Loche Snasporte, 9. Loche Portri, 10. Loche Ken, 11. Loch Nadalae, in Sleit. The uther twa loches my memorey is fayled of them; but in mony of them ther is guid tack of herrings sometymes, but nought so guid by far as in the three first loches. This iyle is callit by the Erishe Ellan Skyane, that is to say in Englishe the Wingitt ile, be reason it has maney wyngs and points lyand furth frae it, through the devyding of thir loches.

PABAY. At the shore of Sky foresaid, lyes ane iyle callit Pabay, neyre ane myle in lenthe, full of woodes, guid for fishing, and a main shelter for thieves and cut-throats. It perteins to M'Kynnoun.

SCALPAY. Fra this ile of Pabay, northwest be aught myle of sea, lyes ane ile callit Scalpay, foure myle lange, and als meikle in breid, ane faire hunting forrest, full of deire, with certain little woodis and small tounes, weill inhabit and manurit, with maney strenthey coves, guid for fishing. In heritage it perteines to M'Gillayne of Dowarde.

Auth note: (the MacKinnons did not obtain this island until about 1664)

Appendix 13

Burrowis contra Hielandmen
11th November 1586.

ANENT oure Soverane Lordis lettres rasit at the instance of t haill inhabitantis of THE Bunnowis OF THIS REALME, Mak, and mention That quhair it is nocht unknawne to his M jestie and Lordis of Secrete Counsale quhat greit proffite and commoditie hes redoundit to all esteatis of personis within this realme be the trade of fischeing in the north pairtis and.'. Iles of the samyn, Seeing thairby nocht only is his Hienes customis greitlie advancit besyde the furneissing his awin houssis and the houssis of all esteatis of personis within this realme be the said fischeing upoun ressonabill pryceis; bot also the idill men and vagaboundis quhilkis uthirwayis Wald be sus.tenit as idill belleis on the sweit of Whir menis browis, ar be thair awin wark and labour sufficientlie furnissit and uthirwayisbrocht to ane civile forme of leving to the greit ease and comoditie of the commounwelth of the cuntrey: Quhilkis being forsene be his Majesteis maist nobill progenitouris, King Jamesthe Fyft and thaireftir lie the Quene Dowerare Regent of this realme for the tyme, wer nocht onlie maist cairfull to bringthe said fischeing to practise, hot sum of thame be thair awin presens in the saidis pairtis did quhat in thame lay to repress all sic as maid hinderance thairto, sua that be interponing thair authoritie the saidis complenaris and thair predicessouris occuput the said trade of fischeing belie and without impediment, for payment of every last of fischeis to be had in the said Iles to the mister of the ground for ground leave anchorage and all tither asiamentis and deweteis iij iiij onelie; By and attoure his Majesteis ordinar custumes pait to his Hienes Custumar at ane frie port befoir thay receave thair cocquett, ac-cording to the kiwis and actis of Parliament : NOCIITTHELESS DONALD Gorme IN THE SKY; McCleud, Hereiss, thair; James McKonnell of Sklaittay; Doule McKanzie of Lochkames; Johne MeKynnaud of Lochslaban; Rory MeKalland of Lochgair; Hucheoun MWKgillespy of Trouternes; Duncane Raw-say of that ilk; John McKanzie of ; Rory M Kanzie of Lochgarlin; Kanycoch McKmurroquhyof Glansgaroy; Donald McKado, Bailie at the Logy; Allaster Neilsoan; Coline McKanzie of Kintale; Torquhill McCloyd of the Cogoych; Robert Munro of Foulis; Rory McCleud of the Lewis; McCleud, Heretour of the landis of Lochgair; Allaster McAllaster McKy; James McKinmoir; Neill Angussoun ; The Laird of Trouternes ; and certane utheris cuntreymen adjacent and duelling in thay pairtis, mynding appeirandlic to prejuge the haill cuntrey of this commoun benefite have of laic by accustumat forme rased greit exac-tiounis With of victuall and money upoun the saidis complcnaris,—I low beit be act of Parliament it is expressly statute and ordanit that all sic custumes and exactionis be dischargit and uocht rasit nor upliftit fra the personis quha traflickis in taking ofthe said fischis, undir the panes to be callit as oppressouris and punist thairfoir conforme to the lawis of this realrne except the payment of the fishchearis allanerlie and his Majesteis custumesas saidis : FOR the saidis persones hes laitlie be thair Bailleis and servandis of thair direc:tioun and command at thair awin handis compellit the saidis complenaris to pay for the ground leave of everie last xx and to thair Bailleis iiij with ane firlot of mein, ane porte galloun aill extending to thre gallounis aill, and iiij for the stance of ilk barren; and for the wair pullit be thameselffis quhairwith the samyn is coverit iiij for ilk last by and attoure ane barrell of aill and ane barrell of salt : AND albeit the saidis complenaris have biggit thair houssis with thair awin tymmer and cover the same with thair schip saillis for saulftie of thair geir fra the rayne thay compeil the saidis complenaris to pay aucht pundis even as thay had biggit the same upoun thair awin expenssis : AND siclike the saidis personis and thair Bailleis compellis the saidis complenaris to ansuer to thair courtis, and gif thay put thair nettis in his Majesteis watteris but thair license thay onlaw and poindis thair guidis at thair pleasure : Lyke as thay and thair freindis of thair command as said is and utheris broken men of the cuntrey, sornaris, resortis at all tyme to the saidis complenaris and nocht onlie consumis thair victuallis but steillis thair nettis, and sumtymes maisterfullie and perforce revis the same: AND albeit for hastie expeditious of thair voyage that' ar accustumat to buy small bottis of intentioun at thair depairting to sell thame agane ; Yit the saidis complenaris ar compellit be the saidis personis and thair foirsaidis to delyver the same to thame and receive quhat they pleiss, gif fer within the just avale and price thairof: AN n gif thay cast thair anchoris in the watter, thay ar constrainit to pay to thame in name of anchorage vj viij : BE THE QUHILK form of doing the saidis complenaris ar havelie hurte and ar nocht abill onywayis to traflique in thair lawfull besines and effearis in thay watteris as his Majesteis frie liegis ; to the Breit contempt of his Hines auctoritie and evill exempill to utheris to commit the lyke gif this remane unpunist.

[The cause being called and none of the Highlanders appearing, although regularly summoned, to answer to the charge, the Council ordained them to be denounced as rebels and put to the horn. On the same day, the Council directed a Proclamation to be issued against the exporting offish., particularly the herring of Lochbromn, until the home market were first supplied.]

Appendix 14

Contract By Which Archibald, Seventh Earl Of Argyle, Gives His Bond Of Maintenance To Lauchlan Mackinnon Of Strathordill, And Receives The Latter's Bond Of Manrent In Return, 1601

AT DONNONE the Aucht day of Januar the yeir of God I sax hundreth ane, yeiris:

It is appointit and aggreit betwixt ane noble and potent Lord ARCHIBALD ERLE OF ERGYLE, Lord Campbell and Lorn &c. Lord of the Regalitie of the samyne, Justice Generall of Scotland, on the ane pairt ; [and] LACHLANE MCKYNNONE OF STRATHORDILL on the tither pairt, as followis :

FORSAMEKLE as the bandis, freindschip and amitie that hes bein betwix the said noble Lord and his predicessouris and the forbearis of the said Lachlane, is notoriouslie knawin and manifest unto baith the saidis pairteis; And that' being willing to reiterat and renew the saidis bandis in thair awin persones and to interteinnie and continew in the samyne forme of doing of freindschip as thair predicessouris did:

THAIRFOIR the said noble Lord hes acceptit and be the tennour heirof acceptis the said Lachlane as his Lordschipis native and kyndlie freind, servand and dependar, promesing faythfullie eftir his micht power and habilitie to protect man tene and defend the said Lachlane his men tennentis and ser- vandis in thair bodeis, landis, heretages, stedingis, rowmes possessiounis and in all and sundrie thair honest, lesum and 'upricht actionis movit or to be movit, caussis, querrellis, de.. baittis and contraverseis as his Lordschip sail do to ony of his awin surname or to ony uther his native kyndlie freind and dependar:

FOR THE QUHILKIS CAUSSIS to be performeit and in effect acomplishit be the said noble Lord towardis the said Lachlane in maner above mentionat, the said Lachlane sall await and depend upone the said noble Lord and serve him be sea and land as his native and kyndlie maister, protectour and defendar and sail tak ane upricht trew and afauld pairt with his Lordschip in all and sindrie his honest lesum actiones in.. tentit or to be intentit, caussis, querrellis, debaittis and con.. traverseis but dissimilatioune as becummis ane onwaitter and dependar to do towards his Maister:—Nather sail lie witt the said noble Lord his hurt, dampnage, skaith or appeirand per. rell in bodie, fame, honour, guidis or geir, bot he sail impede, lett, hinder or stop the samyne at his utter powar, force, moyen, micht and ingyne :—And baith the saidis pairteis bindis and obleissis thame to observe keip and fulfill the pre-misses ilkane to utheris contrair all that leiff or die (oure Soverane Lord and his authoritie allanerlie exceptit) eftir the maist strait forme of band and obligatioun :—In wit-nes quhairof baith the saidis pairteis have subscrivit thir presentis with thair handis the said noble Lordis signet affixit heirto; day, yere, and place foirsaid, befoir thir witnessis Hectour McClayne of Doward, Johne Campbell of Caddaill, Dougale Campbell of Auchinbreck, Duncane Campbell of .Ormadill, Charlie McClayne Tutour of Ardgoure.

Sic subscribitur,   ARGYLL.

NOTE.—*The above woodcut is a facsimile of Mackinnon's signature in the Gaelic language and character. It reads Lachlan mise Mcfionguine, e. Lauchian I Mackinnon.*

Appendix 15

Another account of the battle of Coolin

Duncan, the eldest son of Christopher, was one of the largest and strongest men, in North Britain. He was equal in height and bulk of body with the then Laird of Glenmorriston, who competed for biggness anu might of body with the Earl of Moreton. Duncan could not enter in at the kirk door of Kintail, till he turned one side foremost. He was a stout, forward and bloody man, and delighted much in arms, an instance of which I shall mention, and is as follows. On a certain day, he and John Oig MacUnlay Dhui, another Kintail man, having gone to the Isle of Sky, to bring horses, in their return home, observed, at some distance, the MacDonalds and MacLeods, who had abruptly declared war against each other, ready to engage in battle, at a place called Culinn. Duncan and John would not, as they easily might have done, pass bye the armies but were both desirous of seeing the event of the engagement, and Duncan having enticed John to go, they drew, and resolved one of them should join either party. John Oig made choice of joining the MacLeods, being his mother's kindred, and Duncan, who joined the MacDonalds, had a sturdy, able fellow for a servant, who acted a notable piece of service thus,—There was a pass, over a rough burn or water, that was interjected between the parties, who were both striving who should be first there. This fellow outruns them all, and stood defending the pass against the MacLeods, until the MacDonalds came up, and by having thus obtained the advantage of the ground, and making a great slaughter, carried the victory. The MacLeods being routed, and Duncan having received thanks from the MacDonalds, waited no longer, but went in search of his comrade John Oig whom having found, they both went home with their two servants and horses without scar or wound.

Song written by Donald mac Iain mahic Sheanuis the Macdonald warrior 1601

Latha dhomb 's a'Chuith-lionn
chreagach;

,
Chuala mi phiob mhor 'ga
spreigeadh;

Nuallan a' chruidh laoigh 'ga
freagairt;

Bha beul-sios air luchd an
leadain;

Bha larach am brog 'san eabar;

'S iad Clann Dho-uill rinn an
leagadh

One day as I happened in rocky
Cullin

I heard the great war pipe a
strumming,

Lowing of milch kine responding,

Ill luck befell the men of (long
locks),

The imprints of their brogues in
the mire,

Clan Donald was responsible for
their whelming

Appendix 16

Relationship between the English & Scots Royal Families

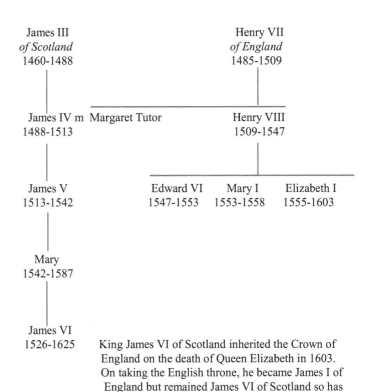

James III
of Scotland
1460-1488

Henry VII
of England
1485-1509

James IV m Margaret Tutor
1488-1513

Henry VIII
1509-1547

James V
1513-1542

Edward VI   Mary I   Elizabeth I
1547-1553   1553-1558   1555-1603

Mary
1542-1587

James VI
1526-1625   King James VI of Scotland inherited the Crown of
England on the death of Queen Elizabeth in 1603.
On taking the English throne, he became James I of
England but remained James VI of Scotland so has
been popularly designated James I & VI

Appendix 17

Bond By Nine Of The Principal Islesmen, Declaring Their Religion, And Binding Themselves For The Improvement Of The Isles Both In Religion And Obedience To The Civil Law, 1609

We and everie ane of us principal gentillmen Indwellaris within the West-and North Illis of Scotland, undersubscrivaris, Acknawlegeing and now be experience finding that the speciall cause of the grate miserie barbaritie and povertie unto the quhilk for the present our barrane cuntrie is subject, lies proceidit of the unnaturall deidlie feidis quhilkis Des bene foisterit amangis us in this last aige: In respect that thairby not onlie the feare of God and all religioun bot alsua the cair of keping ony dewytie and geving obedvence unto our Gracious Soverane the Kingis Majestie and his hienes lawis for the waist pairt wes decayit : And now seeing it hes plesit God in his mercie to remove thir unhappie distractionis with the causes of thame all frome amangis us; and undirstanding that the recoverie of the peace of our conscience, our prosperitie weill and quyetnes consistis in the acknawlegeing of our dewtie towardis our God and his trew worschip, and of our humble obedience to our dreid Soverane and his hienes lawis of this his Majesteis Kin dome : And also being persuadit of mercie and forgivenes of all our bipast offensses of his Majesteis accustomat clemencie: BINDIS and oblissis ourselffis be the fayth and treuth in our bodyis undir the pane of periurie and defamation for evir,—and forder under sic uther penalteis as it sail pleis his Majestie and his honnorable counsell to subject us unto at our nixt compeirance befoir thair Lordschippis : THAT as we presentlie profess the trew religioun publictlie taucht, preichit and proffessit within this realme of Scotland and imbraicit be his Majestie and his estaitis of this realme as the onlie and undoubtit treuth of God; Sua be his grace we sail continew in the proffessioun of the samyn without hypocracy to our lyveis end ; and sail dewtifullie serve his Majestie in maintenance of that treuth, libertie of the samyn and of all the lawis and privilegeis of ony pairt of his Hienes dominionis with our bodyis and goodis without excuiss or .weyring to our last breath: LYKE AS alsua we and everie ane of us protestis in the sicht of the everleving God that we acknawlege and reverence our Soverane Lord his sacred Majestic allanerlie Supreme Juge undir the eternall God in all causses and above all personis boith spiritual and temporal avowing our loyaltie and obedience to his Heynes onlie, conforme to his Majesteis most loveable act of Supremacie, quhilk we imbrace and subscryve unto with our hairtis; and forder undir the samyn aith and panes we faythfullie promeiss dewtifull obedience to the halsome lawis actis of Parliament and constitutions of this his Heynes Kingdome of Scotland, and to observe and kelp everie poynt and ordinance of the samyn as that' are observit be the rest of his Majesteis maist loyall subjectis of this realme; And to be answerable to his Majestic and to his Heynes counsale as we sal be requrit upoun our obedience thairto; and forder as sail be mair particularlie injoynit unto us for our weill and reformatioun of this our puir cuntrey be his Majestie and Counsale having consideratioun quhat it may heir and we ar able to performe; And also as mair speciallie we half aggreit unto, sett down and establissit as necessar lawis to be keipit amang is ourselffis in our particular Courtis haldin be his Majesteis Commissionar Andro Bischop of the Ells and subscryvit with all our handis in his presence : AND finalie we bind and. obleiss ourselffis under the aith and panes foirsaidis that in caiss ony of us and our fiiendis,dependaries or servandis upoun ony evill or turbulent motioun (as God forbid they doe) disobey ony of the foirsaidis Ordinanceis or be found remiss or negligent in observing of the speciall pointis of our obligatioun abone writtin and being convict thairof be the Juge ordinar of the cuntrey spirituall or temporall, That then and in that cais we sail afauldlie concur togidder conjunct-lie and severalie as we salbe imployit be his Hienes or the said Juge ordinar or Schirreff; and sail concur with the said Schirreff or Juge quhatsumevir having warrand of .his Majestie to persew, tak apprehend and present to justice the said disobedient rsone, intromet with his landis guidis and geir and dispone thairupoun as we sail haif Commissioun of his Majestie AND heirto we and everie ane of us faithfullie promitt, bind and obleiss us by our grite aithis as we sal be savit and condempnit upoun the grite day of the grite Juge of the world, to observe keip and fulfill the premisses; and for the mair securitie gif neid beis we ar content and consentis that thir present's be insert and registrat in his Hienes buikis of Secrete Counsale of this realme, and the samyn to haif the strenth of ane Act and Decrete of the Lordis thairof interponit heirto with executoriallis to be direct hereupoun in forme as effeiris; And to that effect makis and constitutes our Procuratouris conjunctlie and severalie in uberiori forma, promitten. de rato ; In witnes quhairof We half subscrwit thir presentis with our handis as followis (written be Johnne Henrysoun Notar Publict, Commissar of the Illis) at Icolmakill the xxiiij day of August the year of God VD, and nyne yeiris, befoir thir,

Witnesses, Johnne Hamiltoun of. Woodhall; Johnne 'Stewart of Ascock; Johnne Colquhoun younger of Camstrodane; Mathow Semple Servitour to Ito.. Bert Lord Semple; .Aulay McCauley of Stuck ; and Mr Malcolme. Colquhoun'.—

Sic Subscribitur Angus McConeill of. Dunivaig ; MeClane of, Dowart; Donald gorme of Slait; Mc Cloud; McKynnowne; McClane of Cole; Donald McDonald of Illintyrim; MaClane of Lochbowy; Maquirie.

Appendix 18

Two Statutes For Forwarding The Interests Of Religion And Promoting Morality And Education Among The Islanders; Agreed To By The Principal Men Of The Isles In A Court Held By Their Bishop At Icolmkill, Under A Special Commission From The King And Privy Council Of Scotland, 1609.

THE COURT of the South and North Illis of Scotland haldin at Icolmekill be ane Reverend fader in God, ANDRO BISCHOP OF THE ILLIS haveand speciall pouer and commissioun to that effect of his Majestie and Counsell the tuentie thrie day of August the yeir of God 1609 yeiris; the suitis callit and the Court lauchfullie affirmit be

THE QUHIlK DAY in presence of the said Reverend fader, the speciall Baronis and Gentilmen of the saidis Yllis undirwrittin Vizt. ANGUS McDONALD OF DUNNOVEG ; Hector McCleane of Dowart; Donald Gorme McDonald of Slait; Rorie McCloyd of Hareiss; Donald McAllane vceane of Ilanterame; Lauchlane McCleane of Coill; Lauchlane. McKynnoun of that ilk; Hector t M Cleane of Lochbowie; Lauchlane and Allane McCleanes brothers germane to the said Hector McClane of Dowart; Gillespie Mcquirie of Ullova; Donald Mcfie in Collonsaye: Togidder with the maist part of thair haill speciall freindis, dependaris and tennentis compeirand judiciallie :-

AND UNDERSTANDING and considering the grite ignorance unto the quhilk not onlie thay for the maist pairt thame selffis, bot alsua the haill commonalitie, inhahitantis of the Illandis hes bene and ar subject to, quhilk is the taus of the neglect of all dewtie to God and of his trew worship to the grite grouth of all kind of vice proceiding partly fra the laik of pastouris plantit and partly of the contempt of these quha ar alreadie plantit:—For remeid quhairof thay haif all aggreit in ane voce, Lyke as it is presentlie concludit and inactit, That the ministeris alswele plantit as to be plantit within the parochynnis of the saidis Illis, sal be reuerentlie obeyit ; thair stipendis dewtifullie payit thame; the rwynous kirkis with reasonable diligence repanit; the Sabothis solemplie kepit; adultereis, fornicationis, insest and sic uther vyle sklanderis seveirlie punist; marriageis contractit for certane yeiris simpliciter dischargeit and the committaris thairof repute and punist as fornicatouris; and that conforme to the loveable actis of parliament of this realme and disciplein of the reformeit Kirk; the quhilk the foirsaidis personis and everie ane of thame within thair awne boundis faithfullie promeiss to sie put to dew executioun.

THE QUHIlK DAY it being understand that the ignorance and incivilitie of the saidis his hes daylie incressit be the negligence of gaid educatioun and instructioun of the youth in the knowlege of God and good lettres : FOR remeid quhairof it is enactit that everie gentilman or yeaman within the saidis Ilandis or ony of thame having children maill or famell and being in goodis worth thriescoir ky, sall putt at the leist thair eldest sone or, having na childrene maill, thair eldest dochtir to the scuillis in the lawland and interteny and bring thame up thair quhill thay nlay be found able sufficientlie to speik, read and wryte Inglische.

Appendix 19

Ane Bond Betwix Mccloud And Donald Gorme 1609.
(Iona, August, 1609)

At Icolmekill the day of august the yeir of God Jai sax hundret and nyne zeiris It is appoyntit unedit concordit and finalie aggreit and endit betwix the ryt honorabill personis parteis underwrittin to wit donald gorme mcdonald of Sclait on the one part and Rorie Mccloyde of hareis on the other part.

In maner forme and effect as efter followis. That is to saye fforsamekle as the foirsaidis personis parteis aboue namit being certenelie perswadit of thair dreid souerane his Magestie's clemencie and mercye towardis thame and willing of yair reformatioun and thair leiving heirefter in peace as his hienes quyet modest and peceable subjectis. And yat be his Matie and lordis of his Hienes secreit counsales willis and directiounis comittit to ane reverend father andro bischope of the Iyles. And the saidis parteis consideding the godles and unhappie turnis done be other of thame yair freyndis serwandis tennentis dependaris and partakeris to utheris quhilkis frome yair hairtis ai and ilkame of thame now repentis Thairfoir the saidis donald gorme mcdonald and Rorie mccloyid parteis above rehersit takand ye burdein on thame ilkane of yame for yair awin kin freyndis tennentis dependaris and aleyis to haif remittit frilie dischargit and forgevin Lyke be the tennor heirof fra yair hartis ffreilie remittis dischargis and forgevis ilkane of thame utheris and yair foirsaidis ffor all and quhatsumevir slauchteris Murthowris hairschippis spuilzeis of guidis and raising of fyre comittit be ather of thame agains utheris yair freyndis seruandis tennentis and dependaris at on y tyme preceiding the dait heirof Renunceand all actioun instance and persute quhatsumeivir criminall or ciuile yat can or may be competent in ather of yair personis or yair foirsaidis aganis utheris for the samyn jure lite et causa for evir without prejudice to ather of ye saidis parteis to suit yair quhatsumiver landis alledgit pertening to ather of yame lyand within utheris boundis as law will. And for yair fardder securitie bindis and obleiss thame to bind the burdein on thame as said is Ilkane to mak subscribe and delyver Letteris of sleins to utheris for quhatsumevir slauchteris comittit be ather of thame on utheris freyndis serwandis and tennentis in deu and competent forme gif neid beis. Sua yat the saidis parteis and ilkane of yame be yair awin moyennis and diligence maye deill and travell with his Matie and counsale for his hienes remissioun for the samyn, And heirto layth the saidis parteis bindis and obleiss thame be the fayth and trewth in yair bodyis to observe keip and fulfill the premiss ilkane to utheris And nevir to cum in the contrair heirof derectlie nor Inderectlie Under the pane of periurie and defamatioun for euir, And farder faythfullie promittis bindis and obleiss thame to leif heirefter (be the grace of God) in Christiane societie and peace and Ilkane to assist and mantein utheris in yair honest and lesum effaires and busynes, And for the mair securitie gif neid be yai ar content and consentis yat yir presentis be insert and registrat in ye buikis of consale and sessioun and ye samin to haif ye strent of ane act and decreit of the Lordis yairof Interponit heirto with executoris to be derect heirupoun In forme as effeiris.

And to yat effect makis and constitutis yair procurators coniunctlie and severalie In priori forma promittentes de rato. In witnes quahirof bayth the saidis parteis hes subscruyit yir presentis with yair handis as followis writtin be jon henryson comissr of the Iyles daye zeir and place foirsaidis Befoir yir witness Lauchlane McKynnoun of Strathordell, Ewin McKynoun his fayer broyer Allane 0 Colgan minister of durneiss and ewin camron seruitor to the Laird of coll and ye said Jon henryson.

L McKynnoun	Donald Gorme
Ewin McKynawne Witness	off Sleat
Allane 0 colgan minister	Macleoid in str qr
of dowrnes wytnes.	

Appendix 20

Contract of Marriage Between John Moydert, Son of Clanronald And Moir, Daughter of Rory Macleod of Dunvegan, Dated Feb. 15th, 1613.

At Glasgow the ffytene day of Ffebruar the zeir of God ane thousand sex hundreth and threttein zeiris ; it is contractit and agreit betwix the honorabill personeis pairties underwrettin viz. Rorie MakCloyd of Hareiss for himself and takand ye burdene in and upone him for Mor MacCloyd his lauchfull dochtir on the ane pairt Donald MacAllaine Vichean of Ilandtirim for himself and takand the burdene in and upone him for Johne Moydert his lauchfull Sone on the uther pairt in maner following Forsameikle as ye said Johne and Moire with consent of their gudis parentis obleist thame God willing to perform the band of Matrimonie with utheris in presense of Chrysts Kirk with all dew solem Rities requisite at sic tyme as yair saidis parentis thinkis guid and befoir the compleiting of ye said marriage the said Donald MacAllane obleissis him dewly and lauchfullie to infeft ye said Johne his sone and Moire McCloyd his future spouse and the langest livar of thame twa and the airis to be procreat betwix thame and these failzieing the airis of the said Jon quhatsumevir in all and haill ye particular landis efter specefeit extending to twentie twa merkland being ane pairt of his twentie pund land in Arrasyle with ye pertinentis thairof halden be him of our Soverane Lord ye King, His Majestic, his undoubtit superiour of ye samen, lyand within ye Sheriffdome of Inverness. Be resignatioun thairof in ye handis of our said Soverane Lord or onie uyer persuin his superior of ye samen, having power to receave ye said resignatioun for heritabill infeftment to be maid gevin and grantit thairof to ye said future spousis and ye langest levar of thame twa and to yair airis foresaid The quilkis landis quhairintill yai ar to be infeft is namit efter yis maner viz, three pennie land of Daibuaith, half pennie land of Killibeg ane pennie land of Manuis ane pennie land of Ardnopeill thrie pennie land of Ardnasule Twa pennie land of Dinloes, Twa pennie land of Douchamdis, twa penny half penny land of Ardgasrie of Torbi ane pennie land of Larichuar threi pennie land of Sidoyie ane pennie half pennie land of, ane pennie land of Barridill, half pennie land of Laynloith Aylers extending in haill to ye foresaid twentie twa merkland of Attoure ye said Donald McAllane for himself and takand burdene on him for ye said Jon Moydert his sone and ye said Jon for himself obleissis thame and thair airis to ye said Rorie MacCloyd and to ye said Moir his dochter that quhatsumevir landis heritages tackis possessiones and annel rentis that it sail happin ye said Johne to congudis in ye time of ye said Moir to provyde ye same congudis quhatsumevir to him and ye said Moir in lyfe rent and to ye langist livar of yame twain conjunclie and to t hair airis as above writtin For the quhilkis premisses to be done and the marriage to be compleited the said Rorie McCloyd obleissis him his airis executeris and assignayis to randir and delyver to ye said Johne Moydert his airis executeris or assignayis in name of tochyr with ye said Moir nine score of gud and sufficient quick ky togyddir with othir twentie ky incais the said Johne sail desyre thaime and ane gaillay of twentie foure airis with her sailling and rowing gear gud and sufficient within ye spaice of ane zeir eftir ye compleition of ye said mariage but forder delay. And for securitie ye saidis pairteis consentis thir presentis be insert and registrat in ye buikis of counsale with letteris and executorialis of horning on ane simple charge of sax dayis, poynding and warding but prejudice of us be direct yairupone and to yat effect constitute yair procurators conjunctlie and severallie prommittentes de rato. In witness quhairof yir presentis writtin be Jon Craig notarie in Glasgow ye saidis pairtres hes subscryuit as followis at day zeir and place ffoirsaid. Befoir thir witnesses. L. McFiongh Lauchlane McKynone of Strath Ordill, Allane McAllane aperand of Moror, Jon Ronnald Persoun of Ellinfinne, Allain Mac Olgane, minister at Draur, Matthew Trunbill Baillie of Glasgow, Hew Camerone merchand Burges, etc., Thomas Donaldsone Servitour to ye said Donald McAllaine

L McFiongh McFiongh   MACLEOID

Allane McRanald witnes   JOHNE MACRONALD

Moir Maclaud   Donald Macallaine

Johne Person of Ellanfinne   Ita est Johannes Craig

Mathew Trumble witnes   notarius publicus de mandato

Allaine Mcolgaine witnes   dicti Donaldi Mcallaine de

H. Cameron witnes   Illandtyrie, scribere nescientis.

Thomas Donaldson manu   Ita est David Galfoir

mea propria scripsi.notarius et testis de mandato dicti Donald scribere nescienti manu propria scripsit

Note inserted in margin in original.

And in cais it happin yat the said twentie twa meirk land be evictit fra ye said Jon and Moir quhairby they may not bruik yir coniunct fee, yairof during yir lyfetime. In yat cais ye said Donald McAllaine obleissis him and his airis to infeft yaime in uyer twentie twa merk land of ye best of onie uyer landis he hes quhairby ye said Moir sal be suir of her coniunct fee yairof during her lyfetime.   This note is signed by principals and witnesses.

Appendix 21
Sir Rorie M`Leod of Harris to Lord Binning. letter 18th June 1615

My Lord,

My humble duty, after all reverence and service remembered. In the beginning of April I left Edinburgh and passed to Glasgow to visit my bairns, who are at schul there, where I remained the space of 15 days ; and thereafter I passed to Stirling, and, going into the town, I met my Lord Fleming coming out of the town, who had a led courser beside, and I riding on another courser, both the coursers " brailes " together ; and I was forced to leave and fall off my horse, where I broke two ribs in my side and lay for the space of 15 days in Perth, underthe cure of physic, and thereafter I retired to my own country. And in the meantime of my absence Coil Makgillespik and his company come to the north Isles and stopped the first night, at the Isle of Canis, and thereafter pushed directly to North Wyest, Donald Gorme his lands, where he was received, his men entertained and Makintoshes daughter, Donald Gormes wife, being for the time in that country, together with young Donald Gorme ; Mackenzie's good-brother send to the said Coill, being scant of viuerse,1 four horse load of meat in which there were two swine, one salted and one unsalted. And the said Coill and his company was persuaded, moved and requested by the said Donald Gorme's wife, and young Donald, and clan Neill Vaine, the special tenants of North Wyest, to pass to an Isle of mine called Zirta,2 a day and a night sailing from the rest of the North Isles, far out on the ocean sea ; and to that effect directed two of the tenants of North Wyest to be their guide and pilot there, for they were unknown themselves there, and coming to the Isle, they slew all the beastial of the Isle, both cows and horses and sheep, and took away all the spoil of the Isle ; only reserved the lives of the inhabitants thereof. And when all was done, they returned to North Wyest again, where they rendered their guides and piolits again, and gave to the inhabitants thereof all and whole the spoil of my Isle ; and before my coming to the Isles, the said Coill Makgillespik passed away south to Ila again. Now since I see Sir James has broken his word and come to Lochaber, and out of that come to Moran Knoddart, where he took perforce a young youth, the second son of Glengarry, on a horse, and keeps him still in custody, and the captain's son ; and thereafter come to Sleat, to Donald Gorme's bounds, where he got a big boat with oars, sails and tackle, and intercommuned at length with Donald Gorme there ; and a number of Donald Gorme's folk at Sleat, called clan Tarlich, is gone with him : And thereafter passed to the Isle of Egga, where he met Coill and his company, together with his base son, and a son of Sir James MakSorle of the Route : and they are in number, as I learn, twelve or thirteen score at the present time, and whether they go south or north, I cannot tell, at the writing hereof. It is my advice to your Lordship and council that your Lordship direct an ample command and charge, to all and sundry the superiors of the Isles, to convocate themselves in arms, with a full commission to everyone of us to pursue the said rebels, by sea and land, by fire and sword, in this form, in three several armies and companies : That is MacLean of Douart, and MacLean of Lochbuy, in a company and army ; Donald Gorme and the captain of clanranald in another army ; and I, the Laird of Coill, and Mackinnon, and my Lord of Kintails forces, in another company ; and let everyone of these armies endeavour themselves to his Majesty's service, and he that doeth best therein have the greatest honour and preferment, and reward of his Majesty and council. And because the said Sir James and his company have taken themselves to the sea in two barks, and sundry other boats, it were expedient that your lordship and council should send me a commission and power to embark any ship I can apprehend in these Isles, to the better pursuit of them in these Isles ; otherwise your lordship and council to furnish two or three ships, well provided, to these Isles, and direct one of them to me, that I and they may concur together in his Highness's service ; and I desir the Isles superiors to be divided in three factions, for this cause. Sir James and the rebels of the clan Donald are of kin, blood, and allied to Donald Gorme, and to the captain of clan Ronald ; and Sir James and his rebels are deadly enemies to the Mackenzie and his name, and they will never agree in a company and army ; and as for me, your lordship knows very well that I have given proof of my obedience and service to his Majesty and council already in taking and apprehending, and delivering my own name and blood, the rebels of the Laws, and in making these lands peaceable to his Majesty. Let the rest do the like service now to his Majesty. And it is very well known to his Majesty and nobility of Scotland that my house never rebelled, nor yet shall rebel ; but as it has been aye subject to his Majesty's will, so shall I continue, God villing, to my life's end ; and shall endeavour myself, with all possible force and power, to pursue these rebels, and all other rebels that shall rebel against his Highness's authority, yea, if it were my father, brother or son ; for, blessed be God and His Majesty, I have whereon to live his Majesty's peaceable subject, which I will not lose for my life and all the world ; and, if your lordship thinks it expedient, I care not suppose your lordship presents this letter to the council. I received my commission concerning Coill Makgillespik on Wednesday before I came home, and after that Coill was away at Isla. I request your lordship in humility and humbleness, to advertise me of all occurrent news. I end giving your lordship to God's most holy tuition.

Your Lordship's humble servitor at power,
Sir Rorie Makcleud.

Appendix 22

Bond Of Friendship Between Sir Rory Macleod, Donald Mcallane Of Clanranald, Lauchlane Mackynone Of Strathordell And Lauchlane Mcclane Of Coll, Dated Aug. 24th 1616.

Be it kend till all men be thir present letteris We Sir Rorie McCloid of Dunvegane Knicht, Donald MacAllane, Vickean of Ilantvrim capitane of Clanranald, Sir Lauchlane McKynnone of Strathordell Knyt and Lauchlane McClane of Coll Forsameikell as it hes plesit the Kings Majesty and His Hienes secreit counsale to ordane us to leve in mutuall societie and friendshyp wuth utheris as His Majesties subiectis aucht to do, and to yateffect ilkane of us ar becum actit bund and obleist as cautioners for uyis to conforme to ye actis of secreit counsall set down yairanent. And we, being maist willing to obey the samen haive agreeit and concludit amovnges our selis and be ye tenour heirof bindis and obleiss us ilk ane to utheris, and takand ye burdene on us for all our kin, freindis, aleyis, men, tennentis, servandis, and dependaris quhatsumevir ylka or onie of us may command ayer within our awin boundis and landis or outis ye samen during all ye dayes of our lyftimes to fortifie assist maintein and defend utheris in all and quhatsumevir actionis effairis and bussynes yat we or onie of us sal have to do at ony tyme heiref ter against all and quhatsumevir personeis trubilling or inquyeting our estatis (except His Maiestie and lawis of yis realm) And we nor nane of us nevir to cum in ye contraire of uyeris directlie nor indirectlie in tyme cuming. And giue we or onie of us at any tyme heireftir sal be fund to failze ayer be our selfis or be onie of our kin freindis alleyis men tennentis servandis and dependaris in onie point of ye promissis in yat cais we ye saidis Sir Rorie McCloyd of Dunvegane Knight, Donald McAlane Vichean of Ilandtirim, Sir Lauchlane McKynone of StrathOrdell Knicht and Lauchlane McClane of Coll be yir presentis bindis and obleissis us our airis executoris and assignayis to content and pay to ye Keiperis of yir band and performaris thairof ye soume of five thousand Merkis Scottis money immediatlie efter ye failzie presentlie agreit upone and monefeit betwix us renouncing all exceptioun actioun suspensioun or benefite of ye law the saimen kan or may be proponit or allegit in ye contrair And for Securitie we ar content yir presentis be registrat in ye buikis of Counsall with execution of Hornyng of six days poynding and warding but prejudice of us to be direct yairupone and to yat effect constitute our procuratores conjunctlie and severallie promittente de rato in witnes quhairof yir presentis wrettin be Jon Craig notar in Glasgow. We haive subscriut as followes at Glasgow be us ye saidis Sir Rorie Donald McAllane, Lauchlane McClayne the twentie fower daye of August ye zeir of God ane thousand six hundreth and sixtein zeiris Befoir yir witnessis to our subscribing viz Colline Caimpbell Baillie of Glasgow, Thomas Donaldsoun servitor and William McCloyd wyth John Collime Caimpbell younger sone to ye said Colline Caimpbell, Baillie S. R. MacLeoyd.

Be ye saidis Donald MacAllane Vichean and Lauchlane McClane with oure handis at ye pen led be ye notaris underwrytten at our command becaus we can nocht writ. Ita est Johannes Craig Notarius publicus de mandatis predictarum duarum personarum scribere nescientes.

Ita est Matheris Fischer Notarius Publicus de mandatis dictarum duarum personarum nescientes scribere.

Coline Campbell	witnes	W. McCloyd	witnes.
Thomas Donaldsone	witnes	Coline Campbell,	witnes.
Bernaird Gillespie	witnes	younger	

Genealogy of the Chiefs of MacKinnon

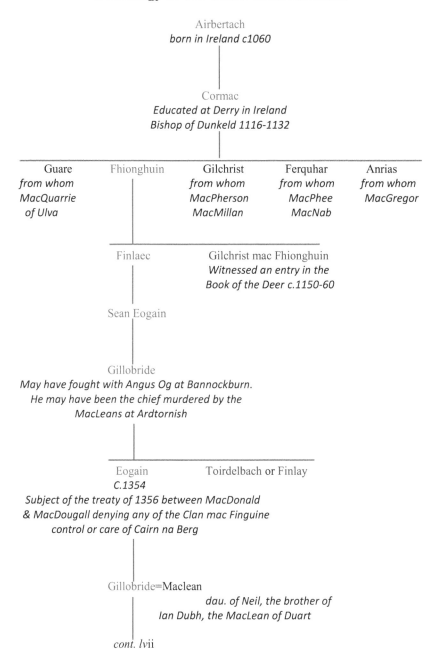

Airbertach
born in Ireland c1060

Cormac
Educated at Derry in Ireland
Bishop of Dunkeld 1116-1132

Guare	Fhionghuin	Gilchrist	Ferquhar	Anrias
from whom		*from whom*	*from whom*	*from whom*
MacQuarrie		*MacPherson*	*MacPhee*	*MacGregor*
of Ulva		*MacMillan*	*MacNab*	

Finlaec

Gilchrist mac Fhionghuin
Witnessed an entry in the
Book of the Deer c.1150-60

Sean Eogain

Gillobride
May have fought with Angus Og at Bannockburn.
He may have been the chief murdered by the
MacLeans at Ardtornish

Eogain   Toirdelbach or Finlay
C.1354
Subject of the treaty of 1356 between MacDonald
& MacDougall denying any of the Clan mac Finguine
control or care of Cairn na Berg

Gillobride=Maclean
dau. of Neil, the brother of
Ian Dubh, the MacLean of Duart

cont. lvii

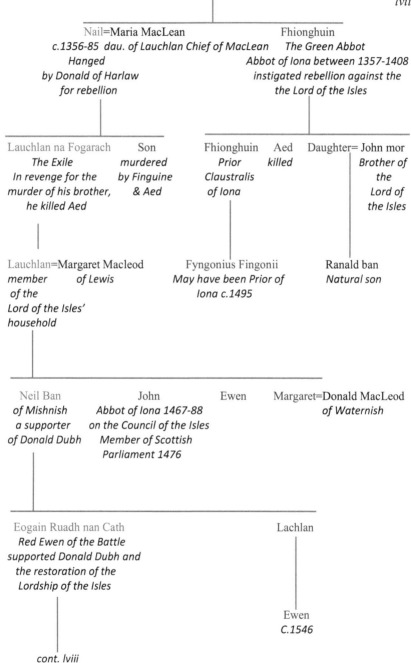

Nail=Maria MacLean
c.1356-85 dau. of Lauchlan Chief of MacLean
Hanged
by Donald of Harlaw
for rebellion

Fhionghuin
The Green Abbot
Abbot of Iona between 1357-1408
instigated rebellion against the
the Lord of the Isles

Lauchlan na Fogarach
The Exile
In revenge for the
murder of his brother,
he killed Aed

Son
murdered
by Finguine
& Aed

Fhionghuin
Prior
Claustralis
of Iona

Aed
killed

Daughter= John mor
Brother of
the
Lord of
the Isles

Lauchlan=Margaret Macleod
member   of Lewis
of the
Lord of the Isles'
household

Fyngonius Fingonii
May have been Prior of
Iona c.1495

Ranald ban
Natural son

Neil Ban
of Mishnish
a supporter
of Donald Dubh

John
Abbot of Iona 1467-88
on the Council of the Isles
Member of Scottish
Parliament 1476

Ewen

Margaret=Donald MacLeod
of Waternish

Eogain Ruadh nan Cath
Red Ewen of the Battle
supported Donald Dubh and
the restoration of the
Lordship of the Isles

Lachlan

Ewen
C.1546

cont. lviii

Lauchlan Dubh or Fynon
1557-98
Charged by the Bishop of the Isles with
molestations and impediments

Lauchlan Og=Janet Fraser	John	Eoghan	Finovola=John Maclean
1540-90 of Guishachan	*of Canna*	*dsp 1618*	*3rd son of the*
aided the MacLeans			*MacLean of Coll*
and the MacLeods			
against the MacDonalds			

Sir Lauchlan* =1. Mary MacLean 2. Mary MacDonald
1587-1634   2nd dau of Duart   Sister of MacDonald of Sleet
signed the statutes of Iona
Knighted by James IV in 1613
Charles I made him a Baron
in 1628

*Sir Lauchlan had five siblings
Lauchlan Og =Janet Fraser

Neil	Tearlach Skianach	John Og=MacDonald	Mary=MacLeod	Jane
	his descendants	*his descendants*	*of Talisker*	
	founded the	*founded the Kyle*		
	Corry family	*family*		

Lauchlan

A Select Bibliography

Alexander, D., T. Neighbor, R. Oram, "Glorious Victory?*," History Scotland,* Vol. 2, #2, Mar/Apr 2002.

Anderson, *Early Sources of Scottish History*, 2Vols.

Arbman, H., *Vikings*, Thames and Hudson, London, 1961.

Armit, I., *The Archaeology of Skye and the Western Isles,* Edinburgh University Press, 1996.

Bain, J.*, Dean of Limerick's Account of the Western Isles of Scotland,* 13 Vols., Edinburgh, 1898-1969.

Bannerman, "Senchus Fer N-Alban," *Celteca*, 4 Vols., Dublin Institute for Advanced Studies, 1966.

Brown, *History of the Highlands*, Fullarton, Edinburgh,1885, 4 Vols.

Byrne, K., *Colkitto*, House of Lochar, Isle of Colonsay, 1997.

Cameron, A., *History and Traditions of Skye*, E. Forsyth, Inverness, 1871.

Campbell, A., *History of Clan Campbell*, Edinburgh University Press, 2002, 4 Vols.

Campbell, A. " The Nearest Guard," *West Highland Notes & Queries*, Aug, 2007.

Cathcart, A., "Domhnal Dubh: The Restoration of an Ideal," *History Scotland*, Vol. 2, #5, Sept/Oct 2002, 13.

Clark, H., & B. Ambrosiani, *Towns in the Viking Age*, St. Martins, New York, 1991.

Craik, G.L., & C. MacFarlane, *Pictorial History of England*, 8 Vols., Charles Knight, London, 1837.

Dark, K., "Changing Places? 5th and 6th Century Culture in Britain and Ireland," *Minerva*, Vol. 13 #6, Nov/Dec 2002.

Douglas, A., *Weekly Scotsman*, 20 Sept. 1962.

Erskine, & Beveridge, *Coll and Tiree*, T. & A. Constable, Edinburgh, 1903.

Foote, P., & D. Wilson, *Viking Achievement*, Sedgwick & Jackson, London, 1990.

Grant, I. F., *The Lordship of the Isles*, Moray Press, Edinburgh, 1935.

Grant, I.F., *The MacLeods: The History of a Clan*, Holmes MacDougall, Edinburgh, 1959.

Grant, I. F., *Social & Economic Development of Scotland Before 1603*, Oliver and Boyd, Edinburgh, 1930.

Gregory, *Western Highlands & Isles*, William Tate, Edinburgh, 1836.

Gordon, *A Genealogical History of the Earldom of Sutherland*, A. Constable, Edinburgh, 1813.

Iona Club, *Collectanea de Rebus Albanicis*, Stevenson, Edinburgh, 1847.

Keltie, J., *History of the Scottish Highlands*, 2 Vol, A. Fullarton, Edinburgh, 1875.

Kirk, J., "Jacobean Church," *17th Century in the Highlands*, Inverness Field Club, John Eccles, 1986.

Laing, L., & J. Laing, *The Picts and the Scots*, Sutton, Wrens, Mid-Glamorgan, 1993.

Lamont, Rev. D., *Strath: In Isle of Skye*, Celtic Press, Glasgow, 1913.

Launay, O., *The Civilization of the Celts*, Ferne, Geneva, 1978.

MacCulloch, J. A., *Misty Isle of Skye*, Eneas MacKay, Sterling, 1946.

MacDonald, *Clan Donald*, MacDonald, Loanhead Midlothian, 1978.

MacDonald, A., "Treachery in the Remotest Territories of Scotland," *Canadian Journal of History*, Vol. 33, Aug. 1999.

MacDonald, R. A., *Kingdom of the Isles,* Tuckwell Press, East Lothian, 1997.

MacDugall, W., *Journeying in MacDougall Country*, Milo Printing, Maine, 1984.

MacKenzie, W. C., *The Highlands and Islands of Scotland*, Moray Press, Edinburgh, 1949.

MacKenzie, G. M., *The Origins and Early History of the MacMillians and Related Kindreds*, Highland Roots, Inverness, 2002.

MacKenzie, A., *Celtic Magazine*, Inverness, 1880.

MacKinnon, Rev. D. D., *Memoirs of Clan Fingon*, Lewis Hepworth, Tunbridge Wells, 1899.

MacKinnon, Rev. D. D., *Memoirs of Clan Fingon*, Lewis Hepworth, Tunbridge Wells, 1884.

MacKinnon, Rev. D., *The Chiefs and Chiefship of Clan MacKinnon*, Portree, 1931.

MacKinnon, Rev. D., *How to see Skye, A Guide*, Moray & Nairn, Elgin, 1937.

MacKinnon, Rev. D., *The MacLeods*, J. & G. Innes, Cupar Fife, 1950.

MacKinnon, Rev. D., *The MacLeods--The Genealogy of a Clan*, Clan MacLeod Society, 1969.

MacKinnon, Rev. D., *The MacLeods--The Genealogy of a Clan*, 4 Vols., Associated Clan Macleod Societies, Edinburgh, 1999.

MacKinnon, J., *The MacKinnons of Kyle and Other Connections*, Longformacus, 1981.

MacLean, J. P., *History of the Island of Mull*, MacLean, San Mateo, 1925.

MacLean, J. P., *History of the Clan MacLean*, Clarke & Co, Cincinnati, 1889.

MacLean-Bristol, N., *Warriors & Priests*, Tuckwell Press, East Lothian, 1995.

MacLean, Rev. S. A., *Celtic Review,* Vol. IV.

MacLeod, R. C., *The Book of Dunvegan*, 2Vols, Spalding Club, 1939.

MacNab, P. A., *The Isle of Mull*, David & Charles, Newton Abbot, 1970.

MacNab, P. A., *History of the Island of Mull*, Jobes & Sons, Ohio, 1923.

MacPhail, *Highland Papers*, Vol. 1, T. & A. Constable, Edinburgh, 1914.

MacQuarrie, A., "Kings Lords and Abbots," *Transactions of the Gaelic Society of Inverness*, LVIII, 1984.

MacQuarrie, A., & E. M. MacArthur, *Iona through the Ages*, Society of West Highland & Island Historical Research, Highland Printers, Inverness, 1992.

McWhannell, D., "Ship Service and Indigenous Sea Power in the West of Scotland," *West Highland Notes & Queries*, Society of West Highland and Island Historical Research, Breacachadh Castle, Coll, Aug. 2000.

M.S. 1307 #83, National Library of Scotland.

Monro, Sir Donald, *Descriptions of the Western Isles of Scotland*, University Press, Robert Maclehouse, Glasgow, 1884.

Monro, R. W. & A. MacQuarrie, *Clan MacQuarrie,* Bruce MacQuarrie, Auburn, 1996.

Munro, J. & R. W. Munro, *Acts of the Lords of the Isles,* Blackwood, Pillans & Wilson, Edinburgh, 1986.

Nicolson, A., *History of Skye*, Glasgow, Alex MacLaren & Sons, 1930.

Nicolson, A., *Nicolson's Guide to the Isle of Skye*, Glasow, (nd)

Origines Parochiales Scotiae, 2 Vols. W. H. Lizars, St James Sq., Edinburgh.

RCAHMS, *The Outer Hebrides, Skye and the Small Isles,* HMSO, Edinburgh, 1928.

RCAHMS, *Argyll, Vol 1 Kintyre*, HMSO, Glasgow, 1971.

RCAHMS, *Argyll, Vol 2 Lorn*, HMSO, Edinburgh, 1975.

RCAHMS *Argyll, Vol. 3, Mull, Tiree, Coll, and Northern Argyll*, Edinburgh, 1980.

RCAHMS, *Argyll, Vol 4, Iona*, HMSO, Edinburgh, 1982.

RCAHMS, *Argyll, Vol 5, Islay, Jura,, Colonsay & Oronsay*, HMSO, 1984.

Ritchie, A., *Viking Scotland*, B.T. Batsford/Historic Scotland, London, 1993.

Rixson, D., *The West Highland Galley*, Birlinn, Edinburgh, 1989.

Sadler, J., " The Reid Harlaw," *History Scotland*, Vol. 2, #4, July/Aug 2002.

Sawyer, P. H., *Kings and Vikings*, Routledge, London, 1989.

Skene, W. F., *Celtic Scotland*, 3 Vols., David Douglas, Edinburgh, 1886.

Sprat, A., *The Scots Lords and the Spanish Armada* 1585 to 1597, 2000.

Steer, & Bannerman, *Late Mediaeval Monumental Sculpture in the West Highlands*, RCAHMS, HMSO Press, Edinburgh, 1977.

Stevenson, D., *Alasdair MacColla and the Highland Problem in the 17th Century*, John Donald, Edinburgh, 1980.

Swire, Otta, *Skye The Island and its Legends*, Blackie & Son, Glasgow, 1961.

Swire, Otta F., *The Inner Hebrides and their Legends,* Collins, Glasgow, 1964.

Sillar, F. C. &. R. M. Meyler *Skye*, David Charles, Devon, 1973.

Scott, Sir W., *The Lord of the Isles*. James Ballantyne, 1815.

Williams, R., *Lords of the Isles*, Hogarth Press, London, 1984.

Young, A., *Robert Bruce's Rivals: The Comyns 1212-1314*, Tuckwell Press, East Linton, 1997.